Mathew 16-19,

TO BE LIKE JESUS

ELLEN G. WHITE

Daily Devotionals

REVIEW AND HERALD® PUBLISHING ASSOCIATION
HAGERSTOWN, MD 21740

Bible texts credited to ARV are from *The Holy Bible,* edited by the American Revision Committee, Thomas Nelson and Sons, 1901.

Bible texts credited to MLB are from *The Modern Language Bible: The New Berkeley Version in Modern English.* Copyright © 1945, 1959, 1969, 1970, 1987, Hendrickson Publishers, Inc. Used by permission.

Texts credited to NKJV are from the New King James Version. Copyright © 1979, 1980, 1982 by Thomas Nelson, Inc. Used by permission. All rights reserved.

Scripture quotations marked NLT are taken from the *Holy Bible,* New Living Translation, copyright © 1996. Used by permission of Tyndale House Publishers, Inc., Wheaton, Illinois 60189. All rights reserved.

Bible texts credited to NRSV are from the New Revised Standard Version of the Bible, copyright © 1989 by the Division of Christian Education of the National Council of the Churches of Christ in the U.S.A. Used by permission.

Bible texts credited to RV are from *The Holy Bible,* Revised Version, Oxford University Press, 1911.

This book was
Copyedited by James Cavil and Delma Miller
Cover designed by Leumas Design/Willie Duke
Cover photo by Getty Images
Typeset: 11/12.5 Bembo

PRINTED IN U.S.A.

08 07 06 05 04   5 4 3 2 1

R&H Cataloging Service
White, Ellen Gould Harmon, 1827-1915.
   To be like Jesus.

   1. Devotional calendar—Seventh-day Adventists.

                242.2

ISBN 0-8280-1835-9

To order additional copies of *To Be Like Jesus,* or other books by Ellen G. White, call 1-800-765-6955.

Visit us at www.reviewandherald.com for information on other Review and Herald® products.

Monthly Topics

JANUARY
Communing With God

FEBRUARY
The Blessings of Obedience

MARCH
Investing Time and Other Talents

APRIL
Exploring God's Word

MAY
The Day That God Made Holy

JUNE
Doing the King's Business

JULY
Practicing the End-time Lifestyle

AUGUST
Relating to the Natural World

SEPTEMBER
Sharing the Good News

OCTOBER
Enjoying Good Health

NOVEMBER
Worshiping at Home

DECEMBER
Repenting, Then Growing

Foreword

TO BE LIKE JESUS—this is the goal set forth by John the Beloved: "Whoever says, 'I abide in him,' ought to walk just as he walked" (1 John 2:6, NRSV). And Peter declared: "Christ also suffered for us, leaving us an example, that ye should follow his steps" (1 Peter 2:21).

In support of this challenging objective, Ellen White wrote: "Talk as Christ talked. Work as Christ worked. We must look to Christ and live. Catching sight of His loveliness, we long to practice the virtues and righteousness of Christ."[1]

The present volume, prepared in the offices of the Ellen G. White Estate, is designed to help readers fix their eyes on Jesus, noting how He lived, studying His attitudes and practices, and encouraging them to follow His example. How important was prayer in His life? How did He relate to inspired writings? How did He use time and other God-given talents? What was His attitude toward the natural world, toward the moral law, toward healthful living? The daily readings are grouped around these and other practical topics month by month, helping to make clear that salvation involves much more than simply saying, "I believe." It means loving Jesus, obeying Him, and seeking to be like Him.

The devotional readings have been selected from a wide range of Ellen White articles, books, and letters, written over a span of many decades. To confine them to a single page, repetitive or less-pertinent portions of the original message have been omitted, but these omissions, indicated by marks of ellipsis, have in no way distorted or changed the meaning of the original passage.

Most of the texts used at the beginning of the daily readings are quoted from the New King James Version of the Bible, but a few have been taken from the New Revised Standard Version because in these texts gender-inclusive language sets forth more precisely the meaning of the Bible writer. For the same reason, without making any change in Mrs. White's thought this book uses inclusive language where it is clear that Ellen White meant to include both males and females in a passage.

During a difficult experience in her 70-year ministry Ellen White wrote: "Jesus is my precious Savior. I want to copy the Pattern. How exact in principle and upright in conduct was He! He gave no place to Satan when He was tempted. How wide awake He had to be to discern the tempter's wiles. Oh, if we would only walk and work as Jesus worked, how strict would be all our transactions with believers and unbelievers;

how tender, how charitable, how meek and lowly of heart would we become, because we have learned of Him. How dimly we reflect the great glory of our Lord! . . . We need to behold Him more steadfastly, that we may be changed into His image."[2]

It is our hope and prayer that this book of devotional messages may help every reader reach the goal set forth in the words of this old familiar hymn:

> "Be like Jesus, this my song,
> In the home and in the throng;
> Be like Jesus all day long!
> I would be like Jesus."

The Trustees of
The Ellen G. White® Estate
Silver Spring, Maryland

[1] *The Upward Look,* p. 344.
[2] *Manuscript Releases,* vol. 7, p. 146.

JANUARY

❧

Communing With God

Jesus, Our Pattern,
Depended on Prayer

Who, in the days of His flesh, when He had offered up prayers
and supplications, with vehement cries and tears to Him who was able to save
Him from death, and was heard because of His godly fear. Hebrews 5:7, NKJV.

EVENING IS DRAWING on as Jesus calls to His side three of His disciples, Peter, James, and John, and leads them across the fields, and far up a rugged path, to a lonely mountainside. . . .

The light of the setting sun still lingers on the mountaintop, and gilds with its fading glory the path they are traveling. But soon the light dies out from hill as well as valley, the sun disappears behind the western horizon, and the solitary travelers are wrapped in the darkness of night. . . .

Presently Christ tells them that they are now to go no farther. Stepping a little aside from them, the Man of Sorrows pours out His supplications with strong crying and tears. He prays for strength to endure the test in behalf of humanity. He must Himself gain a fresh hold on Omnipotence, for only thus can He contemplate the future. And He pours out His heart longings for His disciples, that in the hour of the power of darkness their faith may not fail. . . .

At first the disciples unite their prayers with His in sincere devotion; but after a time they are overcome with weariness, and, even while trying to retain their interest in the scene, they fall asleep. Jesus has told them of His sufferings; He has taken them with Him that they might unite with Him in prayer; even now He is praying for them. The Savior has seen the gloom of His disciples, and has longed to lighten their grief by an assurance that their faith has not been in vain. . . . Now the burden of His prayer is that they may be given a manifestation of the glory He had with the Father before the world was, that His kingdom may be revealed to human eyes, and that His disciples may be strengthened to behold it. He pleads that they may witness a manifestation of His divinity that will comfort them in the hour of His supreme agony with the knowledge that He is of a surety the Son of God and that His shameful death is a part of the plan of redemption.

His prayer is heard. While He is bowed in lowliness upon the stony ground, suddenly the heavens open, the golden gates of the City of God are thrown wide, and holy radiance descends upon the mount, enshrouding the Savior's form. Divinity from within flashes through humanity, and meets the glory coming from above. Arising from His prostrate position, Christ stands in godlike majesty. The soul agony is gone. His countenance now shines "as the sun," and His garments are "white as the light."—*The Desire of Ages,* pp. 419-421.

Christ's Example Gives Power to Resist Temptation

It came to pass that Jesus also was baptized; and while He prayed, the heaven was opened. And the Holy Spirit descended in bodily form like a dove upon Him, and a voice came from heaven which said, "You are My beloved Son; in You I am well pleased." Luke 3:21, 22, NKJV.

CHRIST'S PROFESSED FOLLOWERS may be strong in the Lord if they avail themselves of the provisions made for them through the merits of Jesus. God has not closed the heavens against the humble prayers of repenting, humble, believing souls. The humble, simple, earnest, persevering prayer of the faithful one will now penetrate heaven, as surely as did the prayer of Christ [when He was baptized]. Heaven opened to His prayer, and this shows us that we may be reconciled to God, and that communication is established between God and us through the righteousness of our Lord and Savior. Christ took upon Him humanity, and yet He was in close, intimate relationship with God. He linked humanity with His divine nature, making it possible for us also to become partakers of the divine nature, and thus escape the corruption that is in the world through lust.

Christ is our example in all things. In response to His prayer to His Father, heaven was opened, and the Spirit descended like a dove and abode upon Him. The Holy Spirit of God is to communicate with men and women and to abide in the hearts of the obedient and faithful. Light and strength will come to those who earnestly seek it in order that they may have wisdom to resist Satan, and to overcome in times of temptation. We are to overcome even as Christ overcame.

Jesus opened His public mission with fervent prayer, and His example makes manifest the fact that prayer is necessary in order to lead a successful Christian life. He was constantly in communion with His Father, and His life presents to us a perfect pattern which we are to imitate. . . .

We are dependent upon God for success in living the Christian life, and Christ's example opens before us the path by which we may come to a never-failing source of strength, from which we may draw grace and power to resist the enemy and to come off victorious.—*Signs of the Times,* July 24, 1893.

Approaching God
With Reverence

*He said to them, "When you pray, say: Our Father in heaven,
hallowed be Your name. Your kingdom come." Luke 11:2, NKJV.*

TO HALLOW THE NAME of the Lord requires that the words in which
we speak of the Supreme Being be uttered with reverence. "Holy and rev-
erend is his name" (Ps. 111:9). We are never in any manner to treat lightly
the titles or appellations of the Deity. In prayer we enter the audience
chamber of the Most High; and we should come before Him with holy
awe. The angels veil their faces in His presence. The cherubim and the
bright and holy seraphim approach His throne with solemn reverence.
How much more should we, finite, sinful beings, come in a reverent manner before the Lord, our Maker!

But to hallow the name of the Lord means much more than this. We
may, like the Jews in Christ's day, manifest the greatest outward reverence
for God, and yet profane His name continually. "The name of the Lord"
is "merciful and gracious, longsuffering, and abundant in goodness and
truth . . . forgiving iniquity and transgression and sin" (Ex. 34:5-7). Of the
church of Christ it is written, "This is the name wherewith she shall be
called, The Lord our Righteousness" (Jer. 33:16). This name is put upon
every follower of Christ. It is the heritage of the child of God. The family
are called after the Father. The prophet Jeremiah, in the time of Israel's
sore distress and tribulation, prayed, "We are called by thy name; leave us
not" (Jer. 14:9).

This name is hallowed by the angels of heaven, by the inhabitants of
unfallen worlds. When you pray, "Hallowed be thy name," you ask that it
may be hallowed in this world, hallowed in you. God has acknowledged
you before men and angels as His child; pray that you may do no dishonor
to the "worthy name by the which ye are called" (James 2:7). God sends
you into the world as His representative. In every act of life you are to make
manifest the name of God. This petition calls upon you to possess His character. You cannot hallow His name, you cannot represent Him to the
world, unless in life and character you represent the very life and character
of God. This you can do only through the acceptance of the grace and righteousness of Christ.—*Thoughts From the Mount of Blessing,* pp. 106, 107.

Pray for Daily Bread

Give us this day our daily bread. Matthew 6:11, NKJV.

LIKE [A] CHILD, you shall receive day by day what is required for the day's need. Every day you are to pray, "Give us this day our daily bread." Be not dismayed if you have not sufficient for tomorrow. You have the assurance of His promise, "So shalt thou dwell in the land, and verily thou shalt be fed." David says, "I have been young, and now am old; yet have I not seen the righteous forsaken, nor his seed begging bread" (Ps. 37:3, 25). . . .

He who lightened the cares and anxieties of His widowed mother and helped her to provide for the household at Nazareth sympathizes with every mother in her struggle to provide her children food. He who had compassion on the multitude because they "fainted, and were scattered abroad" (Matt. 9:36) still has compassion on the suffering poor. His hand is stretched out toward them in blessing; and in the very prayer which He gave His disciples, He teaches us to remember the poor. . . .

The prayer for daily bread includes not only food to sustain the body, but that spiritual bread which will nourish the soul unto life everlasting. Jesus bids us, "Labour not for the meat which perisheth, but for that meat which endureth unto everlasting life" (John 6:27). He says, "I am the living bread which came down from heaven: if any man eat of this bread, he shall live for ever" (verse 51). Our Savior is the Bread of Life, and it is by beholding His love, by receiving it into the soul, that we feed upon the bread which came down from heaven.

We receive Christ through His Word, and the Holy Spirit is given to open the Word of God to our understanding and bring home its truths to our hearts. We are to pray day by day that as we read His Word, God will send His Spirit to reveal to us the truth that will strengthen our souls for the day's need.

In teaching us to ask every day for what we need—both temporal and spiritual blessings—God has a purpose to accomplish for our good. He would have us realize our dependence upon His constant care, for He is seeking to draw us into communion with Himself. In this communion with Christ, through prayer and the study of the great and precious truths of His Word, we shall as hungry souls be fed; as those that thirst, we shall be refreshed at the fountain of life.—*Thoughts From the Mount of Blessing,* pp. 111-113.

Have a Forgiving Spirit

*If you forgive others their trespasses, your heavenly Father will also
forgive you; but if you do not forgive others, neither will your
Father forgive your trespasses. Matthew 6:14, 15, NRSV.*

OUR SAVIOR TAUGHT His disciples to pray: "Forgive us our debts, as we forgive our debtors." A great blessing is here asked upon conditions. We ourselves state these conditions. We ask that the mercy of God toward us may be measured by the mercy which we extend to others. Christ declares that this is the rule by which the Lord will deal with us. "If ye forgive men their trespasses, your heavenly Father will also forgive you: but if ye forgive not men their trespasses, neither will your Father forgive your trespasses." Wonderful terms! but how little are they understood or heeded.

One of the most common sins, and one that is attended with most pernicious results, is the indulgence of an unforgiving spirit. How many will cherish animosity or revenge and then bow before God and ask to be forgiven as they forgive. Surely they can have no true sense of the import of this prayer or they would not dare to take it upon their lips. We are dependent upon the pardoning mercy of God every day and every hour; how then can we cherish bitterness and malice toward our fellow sinners! If, in all their daily relations, Christians would carry out the principles of this prayer, what a blessed change would be wrought in the church and in the world! This would be the most convincing testimony that could be given to the reality of Bible religion. . . .

We are admonished by the apostle: "Let love be without dissimulation. Abhor that which is evil; cleave to that which is good. Be kindly affectioned one to another with brotherly love; in honour preferring one another." Paul would have us distinguish between the pure, unselfish love which is prompted by the spirit of Christ, and the unmeaning, deceitful pretense with which the world abounds. This base counterfeit has misled many souls. It would blot out the distinction between right and wrong, by agreeing with the transgressors instead of faithfully showing them their errors. Such a course never springs from real friendship. The spirit by which it is prompted dwells only in the carnal heart.

While Christians will be ever kind, compassionate, and forgiving, they can feel no harmony with sin. They will abhor evil and cling to that which is good, at the sacrifice of association or friendship with the ungodly. The spirit of Christ will lead us to hate sin, while we are willing to make any sacrifice to save the sinner.—*Testimonies for the Church,* vol. 5, pp. 170, 171.

Have a Heart
Filled With Gratitude

Then Moses and the children of Israel sang this song to the Lord, and spoke, saying: "I will sing to the Lord, for He has triumphed gloriously! The horse and its rider He has thrown into the sea! The Lord is my strength and song, and He has become my salvation. He is my God, and I will praise Him; my father's God, and I will exalt Him." Exodus 15:1, 2, NKJV.

LIKE THE VOICE of the great deep, rose from the vast hosts of Israel that sublime ascription. It was taken up by the women of Israel, Miriam, the sister of Moses, leading the way, as they went forth with timbrel and dance. Far over desert and sea rang the joyous refrain, and the mountains re-echoed the words of their praise. . . .

This song and the great deliverance which it commemorates made an impression never to be effaced from the memory of the Hebrew people. From age to age it was echoed by the prophets and singers of Israel, testifying that Jehovah is the strength and deliverance of those who trust in Him. That song does not belong to the Jewish people alone. It points forward to the destruction of all the foes of righteousness and the final victory of the Israel of God. The prophet of Patmos beholds the white-robed multitude that have "gotten the victory," standing on the "sea of glass mingled with fire," having "the harps of God. And they sing the song of Moses the servant of God, and the song of the Lamb" (Rev. 15:2, 3). . . .

Such was the spirit that pervaded Israel's song of deliverance, and it is the spirit that should dwell in the hearts of all who love and fear God. In freeing our souls from the bondage of sin, God has wrought for us a deliverance greater than that of the Hebrews at the Red Sea. Like the Hebrew host, we should praise the Lord with heart and soul and voice for His "wonderful works to the children of men." Those who dwell upon God's great mercies, and are not unmindful of His lesser gifts, will put on the girdle of gladness and make melody in their hearts to the Lord. The daily blessings that we receive from the hand of God, and above all else the death of Jesus to bring happiness and heaven within our reach, should be a theme for constant gratitude. What compassion, what matchless love, has God shown to us, lost sinners, in connecting us with Himself, to be to Him a peculiar treasure!—*Patriarchs and Prophets*, pp. 288, 289.

Pray in Jesus' Name

My little children, these things I write to you, that you
may not sin. And if anyone sins, we have an Advocate with
the Father, Jesus Christ the righteous. 1 John 2:1, NKJV.

WE HAVE AN advocate at the throne of God, which is encircled by the bow of promise, and we are invited to present our petitions in the name of Christ before the Father. Jesus says: Ask what ye will in My name, and it shall be done unto you. In presenting My name, you bear witness that you belong to Me, that you are My sons and daughters, and the Father will treat you as His own, and love you as He loveth Me.

Your faith in Me will lead you to exercise close, filial affection toward Me and the Father. I am the golden chain by which your heart and soul are bound in love and obedience to My Father. Express to My Father the fact that My name is dear to you, that you respect and love Me, and you may ask what you will. He will pardon your transgressions, and adopt you into His royal family—make you a child of God, a joint heir with His only-begotten Son.

Through faith in My name He will impart to you the sanctification and holiness which will fit you for His work in a world of sin, and qualify you for an immortal inheritance in His kingdom. The Father has thrown open, not only all heaven, but all His heart, to those who manifest faith in the sacrifice of Christ, and who through faith in the love of God return unto their loyalty. Those who believe in Christ as the sin-bearer, the propitiation for their sins, the intercessor in their behalf, may through the riches of the grace of God lay claim to the treasures of heaven. . . .

The prayer of the contrite heart unlocks the treasure-house of supplies, and lays hold of omnipotent power. This kind of prayer enables the suppliant to understand what it means to lay hold of the strength of God, and to make peace with Him. This kind of prayer causes us to have an influence over those with whom we associate. . . . It is our privilege and duty to bring the efficacy of the name of Christ into our petitions, and use the very arguments that Christ has used in our behalf. Our prayers will then be in complete harmony with the will of God.—*Signs of the Times,* June 18, 1896.

Our Prayers
Will Be Answered

For then you will have your delight in the Almighty, and lift up your face to God. You will make your prayer to Him, He will hear you, and you will pay your vows. Job 22:26, 27, NKJV.

IN HIS PRAYER for His disciples Christ said: "I sanctify myself, that they also might be sanctified through the truth. Neither pray I for these alone, but for them also which shall believe on me through their word." In His prayer Christ includes all those who shall hear the words of life and salvation through the messengers whom He sends. . . .

Can we by faith comprehend the fact that we are beloved by the Father even as the Son is beloved? Could we indeed lay hold of this and act up to it, we would indeed have the grace of Christ, the golden oil of heaven, poured into our poor, thirsty, parched souls. Our light would no longer be fitful and flickering, but would shine brightly amid the moral darkness that like a funeral pall is enveloping the world. We should by faith hear the prevailing intercession that Christ continually presents in our behalf, as He says: "Father, I will that they also, whom thou hast given me, be with me where I am; that they may behold my glory, which thou hast given me; for thou lovedst me before the foundation of the world." . . .

Our Redeemer encourages us to present continual supplications. He makes to us most decided promises that we shall not plead in vain. He says: "Ask, and it shall be given you; seek, and ye shall find; knock, and it shall be opened unto you. For every one that asketh receiveth; and he that seeketh findeth; and to him that knocketh it shall be opened."

He then presents the picture of a child asking bread of its father, and shows how much more willing God is to grant our requests than parents are to grant their child's petition. . . .

Our precious Savior is ours today. In Him our hopes of eternal life are centered. He is the One who presents our petitions to the Father, and communicates to us the blessing for which we asked.—*Signs of the Times,* June 18, 1896.

Not Only Pray, but Ask and Work!

Then the king said to me, "What do you request?" So I prayed to the God of heaven. And I said to the king, "If it pleases the king, . . . I ask that you send me to Judah, to the city of my fathers' tombs, that I may rebuild it." Nehemiah 2:4, 5, NKJV.

WHILE NEHEMIAH implored the help of God, he did not fold his own hands, feeling that he had no more care or responsibility in the bringing about of his purpose to restore Jerusalem. With admirable prudence and forethought he proceeded to make all the arrangements necessary to ensure the success of the enterprise. . . .

The example of this holy man should be a lesson to all the people of God, that they are not only to pray in faith, but to work with diligence and fidelity. How many difficulties we encounter, how often we hinder the working of Providence in our behalf, because prudence, forethought, and painstaking are regarded as having little to do with religion! This is a grave mistake. It is our duty to cultivate and to exercise every power that will render us more efficient workers for God. Careful consideration and well-matured plans are as essential to the success of sacred enterprises today as in the time of Nehemiah. . . .

Men and women of prayer should be men and women of action. Those who are ready and willing will find ways and means of working. Nehemiah did not depend upon uncertainties. The means which he lacked he solicited from those who were able to bestow.

The Lord still moves upon the hearts of kings and rulers in behalf of His people. Those who are laboring for Him are to avail themselves of the help that He prompts men and women to give for the advancement of His cause. The agents through whom these gifts come may open ways by which the light of truth shall be given to many benighted lands. These people may have no sympathy with God's work, no faith in Christ, no acquaintance with His Word; but their gifts are not on this account to be refused.

The Lord has placed His goods in the hands of unbelievers as well as believers; all may return to Him His own for the doing of the work that must be done for a fallen world. As long as we are in this world, as long as the Spirit of God strives with human hearts, so long are we to receive favors as well as to impart them.—*Southern Watchman, Mar. 15, 1904.*

Pray in Submission
to God's Will

Watch therefore, and pray always that you may be counted worthy to escape all these things that will come to pass, and to stand before the Son of Man. Luke 21:36, NKJV.

PRAY OFTEN TO your heavenly Father. The oftener you engage in prayer, the closer your soul will be drawn into a sacred nearness to God. The Holy Spirit will make intercession for the sincere petitioner with groanings which cannot be uttered, and the heart will be softened and subdued by the love of God. The clouds and shadows which Satan casts about the soul will be dispelled by the bright beams of the Sun of Righteousness, and the chambers of mind and heart will be illuminated by the light of Heaven.

But be not discouraged if your prayers do not seem to obtain an immediate answer. The Lord sees that prayer is often mixed with earthliness. People pray for that which will gratify their selfish desires, and the Lord does not fulfill their requests in the way which they expect. He takes them through tests and trials, He brings them through humiliations, until they see more clearly what their necessities are. He does not give to His children those things which will gratify a debased appetite, and which will prove an injury to human agents, and make them a dishonor to God. He does not give men and women that which will gratify their ambition, and work simply for self-exaltation. When we come to God, we must be submissive and contrite of heart, subordinating everything to His sacred will.

In the garden of Gethsemane, Christ prayed to His Father, saying, "O my Father, if it be possible, let this cup pass from me." The cup which He prayed should be removed from Him, that looked so bitter to His soul, was the cup of separation from God in consequence of the sin of the world. He who was perfectly innocent and unblamable became as one guilty before God, in order that the guilty might be pardoned and stand as innocent before God. When He was assured that the world could be saved in no other way than through the sacrifice of Himself, He said, "Nevertheless not what I will, but what thou wilt." The spirit of submission that Christ manifested in offering up His prayer before God is the spirit that is acceptable to God. Let the soul feel its need, its helplessness, its nothingness, let all its energies be called forth in an earnest desire for help, and help will come.—*Review and Herald,* Nov. 19, 1895.

To Avoid Darkness,
Stay Close to God

Praying always with all prayer and supplication in the Spirit, being watchful to this end with all perseverance and supplication for all the saints. Ephesians 6:18, NKJV.

SOME ARE NOT naturally devotional, and therefore should encourage and cultivate a habit of close examination of their own lives and motives, and should especially cherish a love for religious exercises and for secret prayer. They are often heard talking of doubts and unbelief, and dwelling upon the wonderful struggles they have had with infidel feelings. They dwell upon discouraging influences as so affecting their faith, hope, and courage in the truth and in the ultimate success of the work and cause in which they are engaged, as to make it a special virtue to be found on the side of the doubting.

At times they seem to really enjoy hovering about the infidel's position and strengthening their unbelief with every circumstance they can gather as an excuse for their darkness. To such we would say: You would better come down at once and leave the walls of Zion until you become converted. . . .

But what is the reason of these doubts, this darkness and unbelief? I answer: These men and women are not right with God. They are not dealing honestly and truly with their own souls. They have neglected to cultivate personal piety. They have not separated themselves from all selfishness and from sin and sinners. They have failed to study the self-denying, self-sacrificing life of our Lord and have failed to imitate His example of purity, devotion, and self-sacrifice.

The sin which easily besets has been strengthened by indulgence. By their own negligence and sin they have separated themselves from the company of the divine Teacher. . . .

We are engaged in an exalted, sacred work. Those who profess to be called to teach the truth to those who sit in darkness should not be bodies of unbelief and darkness themselves. They should live near to God, where they can be all light in the Lord. The reason why they are not so is that they are not obeying the Word of God themselves; therefore doubts and discouragements are expressed, when only words of faith and holy cheer should be heard.—*Testimonies for the Church*, vol. 2, pp. 513-516.

Pray to Reflect
Christ's Unfathomable Love

He who did not spare His own Son, but delivered Him up for us all,
how shall He not with Him also freely give us all things? Romans 8:32, NKJV.

WHO CAN MEASURE the love Christ felt for a lost world as He hung upon the cross, suffering for the sins of the guilty? This love was immeasurable, infinite.

Christ has shown that His love was stronger than death. He was accomplishing humanity's salvation; and although He had the most fearful conflict with the powers of darkness, yet, amid it all, His love grew stronger and stronger. . . . The price was paid to purchase the redemption of men and women, when, in the last soul struggle, the blessed words were uttered which seemed to resound through creation: "It is finished." . . .

The length, the breadth, the height, the depth, of such amazing love we cannot fathom. The contemplation of the matchless depths of a Savior's love should fill the mind, touch and melt the soul, refine and elevate the affections, and completely transform the whole character. . . .

Some have limited views of the atonement. They think that Christ suffered only a small portion of the penalty of the law of God; they suppose that, while the wrath of God was felt by His dear Son, He had, through all His painful sufferings, the evidence of His Father's love and acceptance; that the portals of the tomb before Him were illuminated with bright hope, and that He had the abiding evidence of His future glory. Here is a great mistake. Christ's keenest anguish was a sense of His Father's displeasure. His mental agony because of this was of such intensity that many can have but faint conception of it. . . .

Here is love that no language can express. It passes knowledge. Great is the mystery of godliness. Our souls should be enlivened, elevated, and enraptured with the theme of the love of the Father and the Son to humanity. The followers of Christ should here learn to reflect in some degree that mysterious love preparatory to joining all the redeemed in ascribing "blessing, and honour, and glory, and power, . . . unto him that sitteth upon the throne, and unto the Lamb for ever and ever."—*Testimonies for the Church,* vol. 2, pp. 212-215.

Gain Spiritual
Strength Through Prayer

Now in the morning, having risen a long while before daylight, He went
out and departed to a solitary place; and there He prayed. Mark 1:35, NKJV.

BECAUSE THE LIFE of Jesus was a life of constant trust, sustained by continual communion, His service for heaven was without failure or faltering. Daily beset by temptation, constantly opposed by the leaders of the people, Christ knew that He must strengthen His humanity by prayer. In order to be a blessing to people, He must commune with God, from Him obtaining energy, perseverance, steadfastness.

The Savior loved the solitude of the mountain in which to hold communion with His Father. Through the day He labored earnestly to save men, women, and children from destruction. He healed the sick, comforted the mourning, called the dead to life, and brought hope and cheer to the despairing. After His work for the day was finished, He went forth, evening after evening, away from the confusion of the city, and bowed in prayer to His Father. Frequently He continued His petitions through the entire night; but He came from these seasons of communion invigorated and refreshed, braced for duty and for trial.

Are the ministers of Christ tempted and fiercely buffeted by Satan? So also was He who knew no sin. In the hour of distress He turned to His Father. Himself a source of blessing and strength, He could heal the sick and raise the dead; He could command the tempest, and it would obey Him; yet He prayed, often with strong crying and tears. He prayed for His disciples and for Himself, thus identifying Himself with human beings. He was a mighty petitioner. As the Prince of life, He had power with God, and prevailed. . . .

Those who teach and preach the most effectively are those who wait humbly upon God, and watch hungrily for His guidance and His grace. Watch, pray, work—this is the Christian's watchword. The life of a true Christian is a life of constant prayer. He knows that the light and strength of one day is not sufficient for the trials and conflicts of the next. Satan is continually changing his temptations. Every day we shall be placed in different circumstances; and in the untried scenes that await us we shall be surrounded by fresh dangers, and constantly assailed by new and unexpected temptations. It is only through the strength and grace gained from heaven that we can hope to meet the temptations and perform the duties before us.—*Gospel Workers,* pp. 255-258.

Plead for
Wisdom and Power

As the deer pants for the water brooks, so pants my soul for You, O God.
My soul thirsts for God, for the living God. Psalm 42:1, 2, NKJV.

THOSE WHO AT Pentecost were endued with power from on high were not thereby freed from further temptation and trial. As they witnessed for truth and righteousness they were repeatedly assailed by the enemy of all truth, who sought to rob them of their Christian experience. They were compelled to strive with all their God-given powers to reach the measure of the stature of men and women in Christ Jesus. Daily they prayed for fresh supplies of grace, that they might reach higher and still higher toward perfection.

Under the Holy Spirit's working even the weakest, by exercising faith in God, learned to improve their entrusted powers and to become sanctified, refined, and ennobled. As in humility they submitted to the molding influence of the Holy Spirit, they received of the fullness of the Godhead and were fashioned in the likeness of the divine.

The lapse of time has wrought no change in Christ's parting promise to send the Holy Spirit as His representative. It is not because of any restriction on the part of God that the riches of His grace do not flow earthward to humanity. If the fulfillment of the promise is not seen as it might be, it is because the promise is not appreciated as it should be. If all were willing, all would be filled with the Spirit. Wherever the need of the Holy Spirit is a matter little thought of, there is seen spiritual drought, spiritual darkness, spiritual declension and death. Whenever minor matters occupy the attention, the divine power which is necessary for the growth and prosperity of the church, and which would bring all other blessings in its train, is lacking, though offered in infinite plenitude. . . .

Companies of Christian workers should gather to ask for special help, for heavenly wisdom, that they may know how to plan and execute wisely. Especially should they pray that God will baptize His chosen ambassadors in mission fields with a rich measure of His Spirit. The presence of the Spirit with God's workers will give the proclamation of truth a power that not all the honor or glory of the world could give.—*The Acts of the Apostles,* pp. 49-51.

Pray Silently, Continually

Let the hearts of those rejoice who seek the Lord! Seek the Lord and
His strength; seek His face evermore! 1 Chronicles 16:10, 11, NKJV.

PRAYER IS NOT understood as it should be. Our prayers are not to in-form God of something He does not know. The Lord is acquainted with the secrets of every soul. Our prayers need not be long and loud. God reads the hidden thoughts. We may pray in secret, and He who sees in secret will hear, and will reward us openly.

The prayers that are offered to God to tell Him of all our wretched-ness, when we do not feel wretched at all, are the prayers of hypocrisy. It is the contrite prayer that the Lord regards. "For thus saith the high and lofty One that inhabiteth eternity, whose name is Holy; I dwell in the high and holy place, with him also that is of a contrite and humble spirit, to re-vive the spirit of the humble, and to revive the heart of the contrite ones."

Prayer is not intended to work any change in God; it brings us into harmony with God. It does not take the place of duty. Prayer offered ever so often and ever so earnestly will never be accepted by God in the place of our tithe. Prayer will not pay our debts to God. . . .

The strength acquired in prayer to God will prepare us for our daily duties. The temptations to which we are daily exposed make prayer a ne-cessity. In order that we may be kept by the power of God through faith, the desires of the mind should be continually ascending in silent prayer.

When we are surrounded by influences calculated to lead us away from God, our petitions for help and strength must be unwearied. Unless this is so, we shall never be successful in breaking down pride and over-coming the power of temptation to sinful indulgences which keep us from the Savior. The light of truth, sanctifying the life, will discover to the re-ceiver the sinful passions of the heart which are striving for the mastery, and which make it necessary . . . to stretch every nerve and exert all the powers to resist Satan that he or she may conquer through the merits of Christ.—*Messages to Young People*, pp. 247, 248.

Take Your Children
to Jesus in Prayer

*Then little children were brought to Him that He might put His hands
on them and pray, but the disciples rebuked them. Matthew 19:13, NKJV.*

IN THE DAYS of Christ mothers brought their children to Him, that He
might lay His hands upon them in blessing. By this act they showed their
faith in Jesus and the intense anxiety of their hearts for the present and future welfare of the little ones committed to their care. But the disciples could
not see the need of interrupting the Master just for the sake of noticing the
children, and as they were sending these mothers away Jesus rebuked the disciples and commanded the crowd to make way for these faithful mothers
with their little children. Said He, "Suffer little children, and forbid them
not, to come unto me: for of such is the kingdom of heaven."

As the mothers passed along the dusty road and drew near the Savior,
He saw the unbidden tear and the quivering lip, as they offered a silent
prayer in behalf of the children. He heard the words of rebuke from the
disciples, and promptly countermanded the order. His great heart of love
was open to receive the children. One after another, He took them in His
arms and blessed them, while one little child lay fast asleep, reclining
against His bosom. Jesus spoke words of encouragement to the mothers in
reference to their work, and oh, what a relief was thus brought to their
minds! With what joy they dwelt upon the goodness and mercy of Jesus,
as they looked back to that memorable occasion! His gracious words had
removed the burden from their hearts and inspired them with fresh hope
and courage. All sense of weariness was gone.

This is an encouraging lesson to mothers for all time. After they have
done the best they can do for the good of their children, they may bring
them to Jesus. Even the babes in their mothers' arms are precious in His
sight. And as the mother's heart yearns for the help she knows she cannot
give, the grace she cannot bestow, and she casts herself and children into the
merciful arms of Christ, He will receive and bless them, He will give peace,
hope, and happiness to mother and children.—*Good Health,* January 1880.

A Prayer
That Includes Us

Then Jesus said, "Father, forgive them, for they do not know what they do."
And they divided His garments and cast lots. Luke 23:34, NKJV.

A GREAT MULTITUDE followed the Savior to Calvary, many mocking and deriding; but some were weeping and recounting His praise. Those whom He had healed of various infirmities, and those whom He had raised from the dead, declared His marvelous works with earnest voice, and demanded to know what Jesus had done that He should be treated as a malefactor. . . .

Jesus made no murmur of complaint; His face remained pale and serene, but great drops of sweat stood upon His brow. There was no pitying hand to wipe the death-dew from His face, nor words of sympathy and unchanging fidelity to stay His human heart. He was treading the winepress all alone; and of all the people there was none with Him. While the soldiers were doing their fearful work, and He was enduring the most acute agony, Jesus prayed for His enemies—"Father, forgive them; for they know not what they do."

His mind was borne from His own suffering to the crime of His persecutors, and the terrible but just retribution that would be theirs. He pitied them in their ignorance and guilt. No curses were called down upon the soldiers who were handling Him so roughly, no vengeance was invoked upon the priests and rulers who were the cause of all His suffering, and were then gloating over the accomplishment of their purpose, but only a plea for their forgiveness—"for they know not what they do."

Had they known that they were putting to exquisite torture One who had come to save the sinful race from eternal ruin, they would have been seized with horror and remorse. But their ignorance did not remove their guilt; for it was their privilege to know and accept Jesus as their Savior. They rejected all evidence, and not only sinned against Heaven in crucifying the King of Glory, but against the commonest feelings of humanity in putting to a torturous death an innocent man. Jesus was earning the right to become the Advocate for humanity in the Father's presence. That prayer of Christ for His enemies embraced the world, taking in every sinner who should live, until the end of time.—*The Spirit of Prophecy*, vol. 3, pp. 152-154.

In Sincere Pursuit of
Truth We Commune With God

The eyes of your understanding being enlightened; that you may know
what is the hope of His calling, what are the riches of the glory of
His inheritance in the saints. Ephesians 1:18, NKJV.

IN A KNOWLEDGE of God all true knowledge and real development have their source. Wherever we turn, in the physical, the mental, or the spiritual realm; in whatever we behold, apart from the blight of sin, this knowledge is revealed. Whatever line of investigation we pursue, with a sincere purpose to arrive at truth, we are brought in touch with the unseen, mighty Intelligence that is working in and through all. The mind of humanity is brought into communion with the mind of God, the finite with the Infinite. The effect of such communion on body and mind and soul is beyond estimate.

In this communion is found the highest education. It is God's own method of development. "Acquaint now thyself with him" (Job 22:21) is His message to humankind. The method outlined in these words was the method followed in the education of the father of our race. When in the glory of sinless manhood Adam stood in holy Eden, it was thus that God instructed him. . . .

When Adam came from the Creator's hand, he bore, in his physical, mental, and spiritual nature, a likeness to his Maker. "God created man in his own image" (Gen. 1:27), and it was His purpose that the longer human beings lived the more fully they should reveal this image—the more fully reflect the glory of the Creator. All the faculties were capable of development; their capacity and vigor were continually to increase. Vast was the scope offered for their exercise, glorious the field opened to their research. . . . Face-to-face, heart-to-heart communion with his Maker was his high privilege. Had he remained loyal to God, all this would have been his forever. . . .

But by disobedience this was forfeited. Through sin the divine likeness was marred, and well-nigh obliterated. Man's physical powers were weakened, his mental capacity was lessened, his spiritual vision dimmed. He had become subject to death. Yet the race was not left without hope. By infinite love and mercy the plan of salvation had been devised, and a life of probation was granted. To restore in the human family the image of their Maker, to bring them back to the perfection in which they were created, to promote the development of body, mind, and soul, that the divine purpose in their creation might be realized—this was to be the work of redemption. This is the object of education, the great object of life.—*Education*, pp. 14-16.

Prayer Closely
Related to Reformation

*If My people who are called by My name will humble themselves, and pray
and seek My face, and turn from their wicked ways, then I will hear from
heaven, and will forgive their sin and heal their land. 2 Chronicles 7:14, NKJV.*

IN THE PROPHETIC prayer offered at the dedication of the Temple
whose services Hezekiah and his associates were now restoring, Solomon
had prayed, "When thy people Israel be smitten down before the enemy,
because they have sinned against thee, and shall turn again to thee, and
confess thy name, and pray, and make supplication unto thee in this house:
then hear thou in heaven, and forgive the sin of thy people Israel" (1 Kings
8:33, 34).

The seal of divine approval had been placed upon this prayer; for at its
close fire had come down from heaven to consume the burnt offering and
the sacrifices, and the glory of the Lord had filled the Temple. (See
2 Chron. 7:1.) And by night the Lord had appeared to Solomon to tell him
that his prayer had been heard, and that mercy would be shown those who
should worship there. . . .

For many years the Passover had not been observed as a national festival. The division of the kingdom after the close of Solomon's reign had
made this seem impracticable. But the terrible judgments befalling the ten
tribes were awakening in the hearts of some a desire for better things; and
the stirring messages of the prophets were having their effect. . . . The
impenitent turned lightly aside; nevertheless some, eager to seek God
for a clearer knowledge of His will, "humbled themselves, and came
to Jerusalem" (2 Chron. 30:10, 11).—*Prophets and Kings,* pp. 335-337.

For stricken Israel there was but one remedy—a turning away from the
sins that had brought upon them the chastening hand of the Almighty, and
a turning to the Lord with full purpose of heart. To them had been given
the assurance, "If I shut up heaven that there be no rain, or if I command
the locusts to devour the land, or if I send pestilence among my people; if
my people, which are called by my name, shall humble themselves, and
pray, and seek my face, and turn from their wicked ways; then will I hear
from heaven, and will forgive their sin, and will heal their land" (2 Chron.
7:13, 14). It was to bring to pass this blessed result that God continued to
withhold from them the dew and the rain until a decided reformation
should take place.—*Ibid.,* p. 128.

Prayers Enlist
the Help of Angels

For he who sows to his flesh will of the flesh reap corruption, but he who sows
to the Spirit will of the Spirit reap everlasting life. Galatians 6:8, NKJV.

YOUNG MEN AND WOMEN, you are accountable to God for the light that He has given you. This light and these warnings, if not heeded, will rise up in the judgment against you. Your dangers have been plainly stated; you have been cautioned and guarded on every side, hedged in with warnings. In the house of God you have listened to the most solemn, heart-searching truths presented by the servants of God in demonstration of the Spirit. What weight do these solemn appeals have upon your hearts? What influence do they have upon your characters? You will be held responsible for every one of these appeals and warnings. They will rise up in the judgment to condemn those who pursue a life of vanity, levity, and pride. . . .

After this light has been given, after your dangers have been plainly presented before you, the responsibility becomes yours. The manner in which you treat the light that God gives you will turn the scale for happiness or woe. You are shaping your destinies for yourselves. You all have an influence for good or for evil on the minds and characters of others. And just the influence which you exert is written in the book of records in heaven. An angel is attending you and taking record of your words and actions. When you rise in the morning, do you feel your helplessness and your need of strength from God? And do you humbly, heartily make known your wants to your heavenly Father? If so, angels mark your prayers, and if these prayers have not gone forth out of feigned lips, when you are in danger of unconsciously doing wrong and exerting an influence which will lead others to do wrong, your guardian angel will be by your side, prompting you to a better course, choosing your words for you, and influencing your actions. . . .

Immortal glory and eternal life is the reward that our Redeemer offers to those who will be obedient to Him. He has made it possible for them to perfect Christian character through His name and to overcome on their own account as He overcame in their behalf. He has given them an example in His own life, showing them how they may overcome. "The wages of sin is death; but the gift of God is eternal life through Jesus Christ our Lord."—*Testimonies for the Church,* vol. 3, pp. 363-365.

By Prayer, Prepare
for Convocations

Draw near to God and He will draw near to you. Cleanse your hands,
you sinners; and purify your hearts, you double-minded. . . . Humble yourselves
in the sight of the Lord, and He will lift you up. James 4:8-10, NKJV.

HERE IS A WORK for families to engage in before coming up to our holy convocations. Let the preparation for eating and dressing be a secondary matter, but let deep heart-searching commence at home. Pray three times a day, and, like Jacob, be importunate. At home is the place to find Jesus; then take Him with you to the meeting, and how precious will be the hours you spend there. But how can you expect to feel the presence of the Lord and see His power displayed when the individual work of preparation for that time is neglected?

For your soul's sake, for Christ's sake, and for the sake of others, work at home. Pray as you are not accustomed to pray. Let the heart break before God. Set your house in order. Prepare your children for the occasion. Teach them that it is not of so much consequence that they appear with fine clothes as that they appear before God with clean hands and pure hearts. Remove every obstacle that may have been in their way—all differences that may have existed among themselves or between you and them. By so doing you will invite the Lord's presence into your homes, and holy angels will attend you as you go up to the meeting, and their light and presence will press back the darkness of evil angels. . . .

Oh, how much is lost by neglecting this important work! You may be pleased with the preaching, you may become animated and revived, but the converting, reforming power of God will not be felt in the heart, and the work will not be so deep, thorough, and lasting as it should be. Let pride be crucified and the soul be clad with the priceless robe of Christ's righteousness, and what a meeting will you enjoy. It will be to your soul even as the gate of heaven.

The same work of humiliation and heart-searching should also go on in the church, so that all differences and alienations among the members may be laid aside before appearing before the Lord. . . . Set about this work in earnest . . . ; for if you come up to the meeting with your doubts, your murmurings, your disputings, you bring evil angels into the camp and carry darkness wherever you go.—*Testimonies for the Church, vol. 5, pp. 164, 165.*

Look to
Jesus in Prayer

And as Moses lifted up the serpent in the wilderness,
even so must the Son of Man be lifted up. John 3:14, NKJV.

THROUGHOUT THE CAMP of Israel there were the suffering and the dying who had been wounded by the deadly sting of the serpent. But Jesus Christ spoke from the pillar of cloud, and gave directions whereby the people might be healed. The promise was made that whosoever looked upon the brazen serpent should live; and to those who looked the promise was verified. But if anyone said: "What good will it do to look? I shall certainly die under the serpent's deadly sting"; if they continued to talk of their deadly wound, and declared that their case was hopeless, and would not perform the simple act of obedience, they would die. But everyone who looked lived. . . .

Our attention is now called to the Great Physician. "Behold the Lamb of God, which taketh away the sin of the world." Just as long as we look at our sins, and talk of and deplore our wretched condition, our wounds and putrefying sores will remain. It is when we take our eyes from ourselves, and fasten them upon the uplifted Savior, that our souls find hope and peace. The Lord speaks to us through His Word, bidding us "look and live." "He that hath received his testimony hath set to his seal that God is true. For he whom God hath sent speaketh the words of God: for God giveth not the Spirit by measure unto him. The Father loveth the Son, and hath given all things into his hand. He that believeth on the Son hath everlasting life."

There is every reason why we should be encouraged to hope for the salvation of our souls. In Jesus Christ every provision for our salvation has been made. No matter what may have been our sins and shortcomings, there is a fountain open in the house of David for all sin and uncleanness. "Come now, and let us reason together, saith the Lord; though your sins be as scarlet, they shall be as white as snow; though they be red like crimson, they shall be as wool." This is the word of the Lord. Shall we accept it? Shall we believe on Him?—*Signs of the Times,* Apr. 2, 1894.

Prayers of a Godly
Woman Answered

For this child I prayed, and the Lord has granted me
my petition which I asked of Him. 1 Samuel 1:27, NKJV.

ELKANAH, A LEVITE of Mount Ephraim, was a man of wealth and influence, and one who loved and feared the Lord. His wife, Hannah, was a woman of fervent piety. Gentle and unassuming, her character was marked with deep earnestness and a lofty faith.

The blessing so earnestly sought by every Hebrew was denied this godly pair; their home was not gladdened by the voice of childhood; and the desire to perpetuate his name led the husband—as it had led many others—to contract a second marriage. But this step, prompted by a lack of faith in God, did not bring happiness. Sons and daughters were added to the household; but the joy and beauty of God's sacred institution had been marred and the peace of the family was broken. Peninnah, the new wife, was jealous and narrow-minded, and she bore herself with pride and insolence. To Hannah, hope seemed crushed and life a weary burden; yet she met the trial with uncomplaining meekness. . . .

The burden which she could share with no earthly friend she cast upon God. Earnestly she pleaded that He would take away her reproach and grant her the precious gift of a son to nurture and train for Him. And she made a solemn vow that if her request were granted, she would dedicate her child to God, even from its birth. . . .

Hannah's prayer was granted; she received the gift for which she had so earnestly entreated. As she looked upon the child, she called him Samuel—"asked of God." As soon as the little one was old enough to be separated from his mother, she fulfilled her vow. . . . From Shiloh, Hannah quietly returned to her home at Ramah, leaving the child Samuel to be trained for service in the house of God, under the instruction of the high priest. From the earliest dawn of intellect she had taught her son to love and reverence God and to regard himself as the Lord's. By every familiar object surrounding him she had sought to lead his thoughts up to the Creator. When separated from her child, the faithful mother's solicitude did not cease. Every day he was the subject of her prayers. . . . She did not ask for her son worldly greatness, but she earnestly pleaded that he might attain that greatness which Heaven values—that he might honor God and bless his fellow human beings.—*Patriarchs and Prophets*, pp. 569-572.

What It Means to
Pray in Christ's Name

And whatever you ask in My name, that I will do, that the Father may be glorified in the Son. If you ask anything in My name, I will do it. John 14:13, 14, NKJV.

THE LORD IS DISAPPOINTED when His people place a low estimate upon themselves. He desires His chosen heritage to value themselves according to the price He has placed upon them. God wanted them, else He would not have sent His Son on such an expensive errand to redeem them. He has a use for them, and He is well pleased when they make the very highest demands upon Him, that they may glorify His name. They may expect large things if they have faith in His promises.

But to pray in Christ's name means much. It means that we are to accept His character, manifest His spirit, and work His works. The Savior's promise is given on condition. "If ye love me," He says, "keep my commandments." He saves men and women, not in sin, but from sin; and those who love Him will show their love by obedience.

All true obedience comes from the heart. It was heart-work with Christ. And if we consent, He will so identify Himself with our thoughts and aims, so blend our hearts and minds into conformity to His will, that when obeying Him we shall be but carrying out our own impulses. The will, refined and sanctified, will find its highest delight in doing His service. When we know God as it is our privilege to know Him, our life will be a life of continual obedience. Through an appreciation of the character of Christ, through communion with God, sin will become hateful to us. . . .

We cannot depend for counsel upon humanity. The Lord will teach us our duty just as willingly as He will teach somebody else. If we come to Him in faith, He will speak His mysteries to us personally. Our hearts will often burn within us as One draws nigh to commune with us as He did with Enoch. Those who decide to do nothing in any line that will displease God will know, after presenting their case before Him, just what course to pursue. And they will receive not only wisdom, but strength. Power for obedience, for service, will be imparted to them, as Christ has promised.—*Review and Herald,* July 14, 1910.

Spiritual Growth
Through Prayer

Ask, and it will be given to you; seek, and you will find; knock, and it will
be opened to you. For everyone who asks receives, and he who seeks finds,
and to him who knocks it will be opened. Matthew 7:7, 8, NKJV.

MINISTERS [AND ALL] WHO would labor effectively for the salvation
of souls must be both Bible students and men and women of prayer. It is
a sin for those who attempt to teach the Word to others to be themselves
neglectful of its study. All who feel the worth of souls will flee to the
stronghold of truth, where they may be furnished with wisdom, knowledge, strength, and divine power to work the works of God. They should
not rest without the holy unction from on high. Too much is at stake for
them to dare to be careless in regard to their spiritual advancement. . . .

Ministers of Christ [and others] whom God has made the depositaries
of His law, you have an unpopular truth. You must bear this truth to the
world. Warnings must be given . . . to prepare for the great day of God.
You must reach those whose hearts are calloused by sin and love of the
world. Continual and fervent prayer, and earnestness in well-doing, will
bring you into communion with God; your mind and heart will imbibe a
sense of eternal things, and the heavenly unction, which springs from connection with God, will be poured upon you. It will render your testimony
powerful to convict and convert. Your light will not be uncertain, but
your path will be luminous with heavenly brightness. God is all-powerful,
and Heaven is full of light. You have only to use the means God has placed
in your power to obtain the divine blessing.

Be instant in prayer. You are a savor of life unto life, or of death unto
death. You occupy a fearfully responsible position. I entreat you to redeem
the time. Come very near to God in supplication, and you will be like a
tree planted by the river of waters, whose leaf is always green, and whose
fruit appears in due season. . . . Only go to God, and take Him at His
word, and let your works be sustained by living faith in His promises. God
does not require from you eloquent prayers and logical reasoning; but only
a humble, contrite heart, ready and willing to learn of Him.—*Review and
Herald,* Aug. 8, 1878.

Walking With
God Through Prayer

Enoch walked with God three hundred years, and begot sons and daughters. . . . And Enoch walked with God; and he was not, for God took him. Genesis 5:22-24, NKJV.

WHILE ENGAGED IN our daily work, we should lift the soul to heaven in prayer. These silent petitions rise like incense before the throne of grace; and the enemy is baffled. The Christian whose heart is thus stayed upon God cannot be overcome. No evil arts can destroy his or her peace. All the promises of God's Word, all the power of divine grace, all the resources of Jehovah, are pledged to secure his or her deliverance. It was thus that Enoch walked with God. And God was with him, a present help in every time of need.

Prayer is the breath of the soul. It is the secret of spiritual power. No other means of grace can be substituted and the health of the soul be preserved. Prayer brings the heart into immediate contact with the Wellspring of life, and strengthens the sinew and muscle of the religious experience. Neglect the exercise of prayer, or engage in prayer spasmodically, now and then, as seems convenient, and you lose your hold on God. The spiritual faculties lose their vitality, the religious experience lacks health and vigor. . . .

It is a wonderful thing that we can pray effectually, that unworthy, erring mortals possess the power of offering their requests to God. What higher power can human beings desire than this—to be linked with the infinite God? Feeble, sinful human beings have the privilege of speaking to their Maker. We may utter words that reach the throne of the Monarch of the universe. We may speak with Jesus as we walk by the way, and He says, I am at thy right hand.

We may commune with God in our hearts; we may walk in companionship with Christ. When engaged in our daily labor, we may breathe out our heart's desire, inaudible to any human ear; but that word cannot die away into silence, nor can it be lost. Nothing can drown the soul's desire. It rises above the din of the street, above the noise of machinery. It is God to whom we are speaking, and our prayer is heard.—*Messages to Young People,* pp. 249, 250.

Prayer an Effective Weapon Against Satan

Resist the devil and he will flee from you. Draw near to God and He will draw near to you. James 4:7, 8, NKJV.

SATAN IS CONSTANTLY at work, but few have any idea of his activity and subtlety. The people of God must be prepared to withstand the wily foe. It is this resistance that Satan dreads. He knows better than we do the limit of his power and how easily he can be overcome if we resist and face him.

Through divine strength the weakest saint is more than a match for him and all his angels, and if brought to the test [the weakest saint] would be able to prove . . . superior power. Therefore Satan's step is noiseless, his movements stealthy, and his batteries masked. He does not venture to show himself openly, lest he arouse the Christian's dormant energies and send him or her to God in prayer.

The enemy is preparing for his last campaign against the church. He has so concealed himself from view that many can hardly believe that he exists, much less can they be convinced of his amazing activity and power. . . . Boasting of their independence they will, under his specious, bewitching influence, obey the worst impulses of the human heart and yet believe that God is leading them. Could their eyes be opened to distinguish their captain, they would see that they are not serving God, but the enemy of all righteousness. They would see that their boasted independence is one of the heaviest fetters Satan can rivet on unbalanced minds.

Human beings are Satan's captives and are naturally inclined to follow his suggestions and do his bidding. They have in themselves no power to oppose effectual resistance to evil. It is only as Christ abides in them by living faith, influencing their desires and strengthening them with strength from above, that they may venture to face so terrible a foe. Every other means of defense is utterly vain. It is only through Christ that Satan's power is limited. This is a momentous truth that all should understand. Satan is busy every moment, going to and fro, walking up and down in the earth, seeking whom he may devour. But the earnest prayer of faith will baffle his strongest efforts. Then take "the shield of faith," brethren and sisters, "wherewith ye shall be able to quench all the fiery darts of the wicked."—*Testimonies for the Church,* vol. 5, pp. 293, 294.

Transformed by Communion With God

But we all, with unveiled face, beholding as in a mirror the glory of the Lord, are being transformed into the same image from glory to glory, just as by the Spirit of the Lord. 2 Corinthians 3:18, NKJV.

DURING THAT LONG time spent in communion with God, the face of Moses had reflected the glory of the divine Presence; unknown to himself his face shone with a dazzling light when he descended from the mountain. Such a light illumined the countenance of Stephen when brought before his judges; "and all that sat in the council, looking stedfastly on him, saw his face as it had been the face of an angel" (Acts 6:15).

Aaron as well as the people shrank away from Moses, and "they were afraid to come nigh him." Seeing their confusion and terror, but ignorant of the cause, he urged them to come near. He held out to them the pledge of God's reconciliation, and assured them of His restored favor. They perceived in his voice nothing but love and entreaty, and at last one ventured to approach him. Too awed to speak, he silently pointed to the countenance of Moses, and then toward heaven. The great leader understood his meaning. In their conscious guilt, feeling themselves still under the divine displeasure, they could not endure the heavenly light, which, had they been obedient to God, would have filled them with joy. . . .

By this brightness God designed to impress upon Israel the sacred, exalted character of His law, and the glory of the gospel revealed through Christ. While Moses was in the mount, God presented to him, not only the tables of the law, but also the plan of salvation. He saw that the sacrifice of Christ was prefigured by all the types and symbols of the Jewish age; and it was the heavenly light streaming from Calvary, no less than the glory of the law of God, that shed such a radiance upon the face of Moses. That divine illumination symbolized the glory of the dispensation of which Moses was the visible mediator, a representative of the one true Intercessor.

The glory reflected in the countenance of Moses illustrates the blessings to be received by God's commandment-keeping people through the mediation of Christ. It testifies that the closer our communion with God, and the clearer our knowledge of His requirements, the more fully shall we be conformed to the divine image, and the more readily do we become partakers of the divine nature.—*Patriarchs and Prophets*, pp. 329, 330.

Pray Earnestly for
Christian Character

*Until all of us come to the unity of the faith and of the knowledge of the Son of God,
to maturity, to the measure of the full stature of Christ. Ephesians 4:13, NRSV.*

WE CAN NEVER SEE our Lord in peace, unless our souls are spotless. We must bear the perfect image of Christ. Every thought must be brought into subjection to the will of Christ. As expressed by the great apostle, we must come into "the measure of the stature of the fulness of Christ." We shall never attain to this condition without earnest effort. We must strive daily against outward evil and inward sin if we would reach the perfection of Christian character.

Those who engage in this work will see so much to correct in themselves, and will devote so much time to prayer and to comparing their characters with God's great standard, the divine law, that they will have no time to comment and gossip over the faults or dissect the characters of others. A sense of our own imperfections should lead us to humility and earnest solicitude lest we fail of everlasting life. The words of inspiration should come home to every soul: "Examine yourselves, whether ye be in the faith; prove your own selves. Know ye not your own selves, how that Jesus Christ is in you, except ye be reprobates?"

If the professed people of God would divest themselves of their self-complacency and their false ideas of what constitutes a Christian, many who now think they are in the path to heaven would find themselves in the way of perdition. Many proudhearted professors [of religion] would tremble like an aspen leaf in the tempest could their eyes be opened to see what spiritual life really is. Would that those now reposing in false security could be aroused to see the contradiction between their profession of faith and their everyday demeanor.

To be living Christians, we must have a vital connection with Christ. . . . When the affections are sanctified, our obligations to God are made primary, everything else secondary. To have a steady and ever-growing love for God, and a clear perception of His character and attributes, we must keep the eye of faith fixed constantly on Him. Christ is the life of the soul. We must be in Him and He in us, else we are sapless branches.—*Review and Herald,* May 30, 1882.

Pray in
Humbleness of Heart

*Likewise the Spirit also helps in our weaknesses. For we do not know what
we should pray for as we ought, but the Spirit Himself makes intercession
for us with groanings which cannot be uttered. Romans 8:26, NKJV.*

PRAYER IS ACCEPTABLE to God only when offered in humility and
contrition and in the name of Christ. He who hears and answers prayer
knows those who pray in humbleness of heart. The true Christians ask for
nothing except in the name of Christ, and they expect nothing except
through His mediation. They desire that Christ shall have the glory of presenting their prayers to the Father, and they are willing to receive the blessing from God through Christ.

The Spirit of God has much to do with acceptable prayer. He softens
the heart; He enlightens the mind, enabling it to discern its own wants; He
quickens our desires, causing us to hunger and thirst after righteousness;
He intercedes in behalf of the sincere suppliant. . . .

Human beings must draw nigh to God, realizing that they must have
the help that God alone can give. It is the glory of God to be known as
the hearer of prayer because the human suppliant believes that He will hear
and answer. . . .

The prayer of faith is the key that unlocks the treasury of heaven. As
we commit our souls to God, let us remember that He holds Himself responsible to hear and answer our supplications. He invites us to come to
Him, and He bestows on us His best and choicest gifts—gifts that will
supply our great need. He loves to help us. Let us trust in His wisdom and
His power. Oh, what faith we should have! Oh, what peace and comfort
we should enjoy! Open your heart to the Spirit of God. Then the Lord
will work through you and bless your labors.—*Manuscript Releases,* vol. 8,
pp. 195, 196.

Shall we not humble ourselves before God in behalf of those who apparently have little spiritual life? Shall we not have appointed seasons of
prayer for them? Shall we not pray every day for those who seem to be
dead in trespasses and sins? As we plead with God to break the hearts of
stone, our own hearts will become more sensitive. We shall be quicker to
see our own sin.—*Ibid.,* p. 197.

Prayer Helps
Guide to Truth

If anyone wants to do His will, he shall know concerning the doctrine, whether it is from God or whether I speak on My own authority. John 7:17, NKJV.

BEFORE JESUS WENT forth to His final conflict with the powers of darkness, He lifted up His eyes to heaven and prayed for His disciples. . . .

The burden of Jesus' request was that those who believed on Him might be kept from the evil of the world, and sanctified through the truth. He does not leave us to vague surmising as to what the truth is, but adds, "Thy word is truth." The Word of God is the means by which our sanctification is to be accomplished.

It is of the greatest importance, then, that we acquaint ourselves with the sacred instruction of the Bible. It is as necessary for us to understand the words of life as it was for the early disciples to be informed concerning the plan of salvation. We shall be inexcusable if, through our own negligence, we are ignorant of the claims of God's Word. God has given us His Word, the revelation of His will, and has promised the Holy Spirit to them that ask Him, to guide them into all truth; and every soul who honestly desires to do the will of God shall know of the doctrine. . . .

Since the time when the Son of God breasted the haughty prejudices and unbelief of humankind, there has been no change in the attitude of the world toward the religion of Jesus. The servants of Christ must meet the same spirit of opposition and reproach, and must go "without the camp, bearing his reproach." . . .

His [Jesus'] teaching was plain, clear, and comprehensive. The practical truths He uttered had a convincing power, and arrested the attention of the people. Multitudes lingered at His side, marveling at His wisdom. His manner corresponded with the great truths He proclaimed. There was no apology, no hesitancy, not the shadow of a doubt or uncertainty that it might be other than He declared. He spoke of the earthly and the heavenly, of the human and the divine, with positive authority; and the people "were astonished at his doctrine: for his word was with power." . . .

It is a matter of the highest importance and interest to us that we understand what the truth is, and our petitions should go forth with the intense earnestness that we may be guided into all truth.—*Review and Herald*, Feb. 7, 1888.

FEBRUARY

❧

The Blessings of Obedience

Obey God,
Just as Jesus Did

This is the love of God, that we keep His commandments.
And His commandments are not burdensome. 1 John 5:3, NKJV.

THE ONLY-BEGOTTEN SON of the infinite God has, by His words and in His practical example, left us a plain pattern which we are to copy. By His words He has educated us to obey God, and by His own practice He has showed us how we can obey God. This is the very work He wants every person to do, to obey God intelligently, and by precept and example teach others what they must do in order to be obedient children of God.

Jesus has helped the whole world to an intelligent knowledge of His divine mission and work. He came to represent the character of the Father to our world; and as we study the life, the words, and works of Christ, we are helped in every way in the education of obedience to God; and as we copy the example He has given us, we are living epistles known and read of all men. We are the living human agencies to represent to the world the character of Christ. Not only did Christ show us how we may become obedient children, but He showed us in His own life and character just how to do those things which are right and acceptable with God, so there is no reason why we should not do those things which are pleasing in His sight.

We are ever to be thankful that Jesus has proved to us by actual life that we can keep the commandments of God, contradicting Satan's falsehood that we cannot keep them. The great Teacher came to our world to stand at the head of humanity, to thus elevate and sanctify humanity by His holy obedience to all the requirements of God, showing it is possible to obey all the commandments of God. He has demonstrated that a lifelong obedience is possible. Thus He gives people to the world, as the Father gave the Son, to exemplify in their life the life of Christ.

Christ redeemed Adam's disgraceful failure and fall, and was conqueror, thus testifying to all the unfallen worlds and to fallen humanity that through the divine power granted to Him of heaven human beings can keep the commandments of God. Jesus, the Son of God, humbled Himself for us, endured temptation for us, overcame in our behalf, to show us how we may overcome; by the closest ties He bound up His interest with humanity, and gave positive assurance that we shall not be tempted above that we are able; for with the temptation He will make a way of escape.—*Signs of the Times,* Apr. 17, 1893.

Everything Lost
by Disobedience

For God knows that in the day you eat of it your eyes will be opened,
and you will be like God, knowing good and evil. Genesis 3:5, NKJV.

WHEN EVE SAW "that the tree was good for food, and that it was pleasant to the eyes, and a tree to be desired to make one wise, she took of the fruit thereof, and did eat." It was grateful to the taste, and, as she ate, she seemed to feel a vivifying power, and imagined herself entering upon a higher state of existence. Having herself transgressed, she became a tempter to her husband, "and he did eat" (Gen. 3:6).

"Your eyes shall be opened," the enemy had said; "ye shall be as gods, knowing good and evil" (Gen. 3:5). Their eyes were indeed opened; but how sad the opening! The knowledge of evil, the curse of sin, was all that the transgressors gained. There was nothing poisonous in the fruit itself, and the sin was not merely in yielding to appetite. It was distrust of God's goodness, disbelief of His word, and rejection of His authority that made our first parents transgressors, and that brought into the world a knowledge of evil. It was this that opened the door to every species of falsehood and error.

Man and woman lost all because they chose to listen to the deceiver rather than to Him who is Truth, who alone has understanding. By the mingling of evil with good, their minds had become confused, their mental and spiritual powers benumbed. No longer could they appreciate the good that God had so freely bestowed.

Adam and Eve had chosen the knowledge of evil, and if they ever regained the position they had lost they must regain it under the unfavorable conditions they had brought upon themselves. No longer were they to dwell in Eden, for in its perfection it could not teach them the lessons which it was now essential for them to learn. In unutterable sadness they bade farewell to their beautiful surroundings and went forth to dwell upon the earth, where rested the curse of sin. . . .

Although the earth was blighted with the curse, nature was still to be humanity's lesson book. It could not now represent goodness only; for evil was everywhere present, marring earth and sea and air with its defiling touch. Where once was written only the character of God, the knowledge of good, was now written also the character of Satan, the knowledge of evil. From nature, which now revealed the knowledge of good and evil, humankind was continually to receive warning as to the results of sin.— *Education*, pp. 25, 26.

41

The Promise
of Redemption

I will put enmity between you and the woman, and between your seed and her Seed;
He shall bruise your head, and you shall bruise His heel. Genesis 3:15, NKJV.

IN DROOPING FLOWER and falling leaf Adam and his companion witnessed the first signs of decay. Vividly was brought to their minds the stern
fact that every living thing must die. Even the air, upon which their life
depended, bore the seeds of death.

Continually they were reminded also of their lost dominion. Among
the lower creatures Adam had stood as king, and so long as he remained
loyal to God, all nature acknowledged his rule; but when he transgressed,
this dominion was forfeited. The spirit of rebellion, to which he himself
had given entrance, extended throughout the animal creation. Thus not
only the life of humans, but the nature of the beasts, the trees of the forest, the grass of the field, the very air they breathed, all told the sad lesson
of the knowledge of evil.

But mortals were not abandoned to the results of the evil they had
chosen. In the sentence pronounced upon Satan was given an intimation
of redemption. "I will put enmity between thee and the woman," God
said, "and between thy seed and her seed; it shall bruise thy head, and thou
shalt bruise his heel" (Gen. 3:15). This sentence, spoken in the hearing of
our first parents, was to them a promise. Before they heard of the thorn
and the thistle, of the toil and sorrow that must be their portion, or of the
dust to which they must return, they listened to words that could not fail
of giving them hope. All that had been lost by yielding to Satan could be
regained through Christ.

This intimation also nature repeats to us. Though marred by sin, it
speaks not only of creation but of redemption. Though the earth bears testimony to the curse in the evident signs of decay, it is still rich and beautiful in the tokens of life-giving power. The trees cast off their leaves, only
to be robed with fresher verdure; the flowers die, to spring forth in new
beauty; and in every manifestation of creative power is held out the assurance that we may be created anew in "righteousness and holiness of truth"
(Eph. 4:24, margin). Thus the very objects and operations of nature that
bring so vividly to mind our great loss become to us the messengers of hope.

As far as evil extends, the voice of our Father is heard, bidding His
children see in its results the nature of sin, warning them to forsake the evil,
and inviting them to receive the good.—*Education*, pp. 26, 27.

God's Word the Supreme Authority

Then Samuel said: "Has the Lord as great delight in burnt offerings and sacrifices, as in obeying the voice of the Lord? Behold, to obey is better than sacrifice, and to heed than the fat of rams." 1 Samuel 15:22, NKJV.

THE WORD OF THE LORD is to be obeyed without question; it is to be the supreme authority in our life. Saul departed from the express commandment of the Lord, and sought to quiet the compunctions of conscience by persuading himself that the Lord would accept his sacrifice and overlook his disobedience. When Samuel, the prophet, came to meet him, Saul acted as though he regarded himself as a righteous man, and exclaimed, "Blessed be thou of the Lord; I have performed the commandment of the Lord."

But the unmistakable tokens of his disobedience were so manifest that his assertion of obedience was of little weight. "And Samuel said, What meaneth then this bleating of the sheep in mine ears, and the lowing of the oxen which I hear? And Saul said, They have brought them from the Amalekites: for the people spared the best of the sheep and of the oxen, to sacrifice unto the Lord thy God." "And Samuel said, Hath the Lord as great delight in burnt offerings and sacrifices, as in obeying the voice of the Lord? Behold, to obey is better than sacrifice, and to hearken than the fat of rams. For rebellion is as the sin of witchcraft, and stubbornness is as iniquity and idolatry. Because thou hast rejected the word of the Lord, he hath also rejected thee from being king." . . .

The Word of God is to be of supreme authority. The Lord says, "My covenant will I not break, nor alter the thing that is gone out of my lips." God could not change one tittle of His law without ceasing to be supreme. People cannot bend the law of God to suit their ideas, and, failing to bring it into harmony with themselves, they break its commands and violate its precepts. All too late the world will learn that they cannot judge the Word of God, but that the Word of God will judge them. Would that everyone would consider how foolish and how wicked it is to contend with God! Would that they would cease to oppose their will against the will of the Infinite! Those who oppose God will yet learn that in so doing they have forsaken the only path that leads to holiness, happiness, and heaven.—*Signs of the Times,* Jan. 9, 1896.

Jesus Showed
That We Can Obey

Now he who keeps His commandments abides in Him, and He in him. And by this we know that He abides in us, by the Spirit whom He has given us. 1 John 3:24, NKJV.

"HE THAT HATH my commandments, and keepeth them, he it is that loveth me: and he that loveth me shall be loved of my Father, and I will love him, and will manifest myself to him" (John 14:21).

"He that hath my commandments" means a person that hath light upon what constitutes the commandments of God, and will not disobey His commandments, although it might seem an advantage to do so. . . . If it were not possible for us to keep the commandments of God, we should all be lost. But under the Abrahamic covenant, the covenant of grace, every provision for salvation has been made. "By grace ye are saved." "But as many as received him, to them gave he power to become the sons of God." . . .

There are but two classes in our world, the obedient and the disobedient, the holy and the unholy. When our transgressions were laid upon Jesus, He was numbered among the unholy on the sinner's account. He became our substitute, our surety, before the Father and all the heavenly angels. By imputing the sins of the world to Jesus, He became the sinner in our stead, and the curse due to our sins came upon Him. It becomes us to contemplate Christ's life of humiliation and His agonizing death; for He was treated as the sinner deserves to be treated. He came to our world, clothing His divinity with humanity, to bear the test and proving of God. By His example of perfect obedience in His human nature, He teaches us that we may be obedient.

And the apostle writes, "Grace and peace be multiplied unto you through the knowledge of God, and of Jesus our Lord, according as his divine power hath given unto us all things that pertain unto life and godliness, through the knowledge of him that hath called us to glory and virtue: whereby are given unto us exceeding great and precious promises; that by these ye might be partakers of the divine nature, having escaped the corruption that is in the world through lust." It is here plainly revealed that all who believe in Jesus Christ become partakers of the divine nature. Let divinity and humanity cooperate, and fallen human beings may be more than conquerors through Christ Jesus.—*Signs of the Times,* Apr. 24, 1893.

Obey From Principle

*Therefore, brothers and sisters, be all the more eager to confirm your
call and election, for if you do this, you will never stumble. 2 Peter 1:10, NRSV.*

ETERNAL LIFE IS worth your all, and Jesus has said, "Whosoever he be of
you that forsaketh not all that he hath, he cannot be my disciple" (Luke
14:33). He who does nothing, but waits to be compelled by some supernatural agency, will wait on in lethargy and darkness. God has given His
Word. God speaks in unmistakable language to your soul. Is not the word
of His mouth sufficient to show you your duty, and to urge its fulfillment?

Those who humbly and prayerfully search the Scriptures, to know and
to do God's will, will not be in doubt of their obligations to God. For "if
any man will do his will, he shall know of the doctrine" (John 7:17). If you
would know the mystery of godliness, you must follow the plain word of
truth—feeling or no feeling, emotion or no emotion. Obedience must be
rendered from a sense of principle, and the right must be pursued under all
circumstances. This is the character that is elected of God unto salvation.

The test of a genuine Christian is given in the Word of God. Says
Jesus, "If ye love me, keep my commandments" (John 14:15). "He that
hath my commandments, and keepeth them, he it is that loveth me: and
he that loveth me shall be loved of my Father, and I will love him, and will
manifest myself to him. . . . If a man love me, he will keep my words: and
my Father will love him, and we will come unto him, and make our abode
with him. He that loveth me not keepeth not my sayings: and the word
which ye hear is not mine, but the Father's which sent me" (verses 21-24).

Here are the conditions upon which every soul will be elected to eternal life. Your obedience to God's commandments will prove your right to
an inheritance with the saints in light. God has elected a certain excellence
of character; and everyone who, through the grace of Christ, shall reach
the standard of His requirement will have an abundant entrance into the
kingdom of glory.—*Christian Education*, pp. 117, 118.

Israel Pledges to Obey God's Commandments

Then he took the Book of the Covenant and read in the hearing of the people. And they said, "All that the Lord has said we will do, and be obedient." Exodus 24:7, NKJV.

PREPARATION WAS NOW made for the ratification of the covenant, according to God's directions. [Exodus 24:4-8 quoted.]

Here the people received the conditions of the covenant. They made a solemn covenant with God, typifying the covenant made between God and every believer in Jesus Christ. The conditions were plainly laid before the people. They were not left to misunderstand them. When they were requested to decide whether they would agree to all the conditions given, they unanimously consented to obey every obligation. They had already consented to obey God's commandments. The principles of the law were now particularized, that they might know how much was involved in covenanting to obey the law; and they accepted the specifically defined particulars of the law.

If the Israelites had obeyed God's requirements, they would have been practical Christians. They would have been happy; for they would have been keeping God's ways, and not following the inclinations of their own natural hearts. Moses did not leave them to misconstrue the words of the Lord or to misapply His requirements. He wrote all the words of the Lord in a book, that they might be referred to afterward. In the mount he had written them as Christ Himself dictated them.

Bravely did the Israelites speak the words promising obedience to the Lord, after hearing His covenant read in the audience of the people. They said, "All that the Lord hath said will we do, and be obedient" (Ex. 24:7). Then the people were set apart and sealed to God. A sacrifice was offered to the Lord. A portion of the blood of the sacrifice was sprinkled upon the altar. This signified that the people had consecrated themselves—body, mind, and soul—to God. A portion was sprinkled upon the people. This signified that through the sprinkled blood of Christ, God graciously accepted them as His special treasure. Thus the Israelites entered into a solemn covenant with God.—*Manuscript Releases*, vol. 1, pp. 114, 115.

Christ's Perfect Obedience Can Be Ours

For as by one man's disobedience many were made sinners, so also by one Man's obedience many will be made righteous. Romans 5:19, NKJV.

[SCRIPTURE TELLS] THE STORY so important for every human being to know. On the one hand is presented the disobedience of Adam, with its consequences; on the other, the obedience of Christ. The Garden of Eden was disgraced by Adam's disobedience; but as by that one transgression many were made sinners, so by the obedience of One, many are made righteous.

The world has been honored with the presence of one Man who was wholly and entirely obedient—One who not only believed and taught the claims of God's law, but who *lived* the law. His whole life was a representation of its holy principles. His obedience was manifested in the awful agony He endured in the Garden of Gethsemane; and through His suffering He has brought pardon to the disobedient.

When Christ gave to His disciples the conditions of salvation, He said, "If any man will come after me, let him deny himself, and take up his cross, and follow me." Self-denial and crosses lie directly in the path of every soul who will follow Jesus. Our advance heavenward will be opposed at every step; for Satan will come in many ways to mislead, to deceive, and to clothe sin with the appearance of good. . . .

I would urge you . . . carefully to consider the self-denial and self-sacrifice that Christ has endured in your behalf, that you, if you choose, may have that happiness and peace in this life which He alone can give, and an eternity of bliss by and by. Then will you not become missionaries for Christ? Are you not willing to deny self for His sake? to consider how you can do Him service who has done such service for you in redeeming your soul from the power of sin and Satan? When upon earth, Christ said of Himself, "I am among you as he that serveth." He did not strive to obtain the highest place; for He was meek and lowly in heart. He invites you to learn of Him, to wear His yoke—the yoke of obedience to every precept of Jehovah.—*Youth's Instructor*, Apr. 1, 1897.

Obedience Through Grace

For by grace you have been saved through faith,
and that not of yourselves; it is the gift of God. Ephesians 2:8, NKJV.

GOD DESIRES US TO reach the standard of perfection made possible for us by the gift of Christ. He calls upon us to make our choice on the right side, to connect with heavenly agencies, to adopt principles that will restore in us the divine image. In His written Word and in the great book of nature He has revealed the principles of life. It is our work to obtain a knowledge of these principles, and by obedience to cooperate with Him in restoring health to the body as well as to the soul.

Human beings need to learn that the blessings of obedience, in their fullness, can be theirs only as they receive the grace of Christ. It is His grace that gives men and women power to obey the laws of God. It is this that enables them to break the bondage of evil habit. This is the only power that can make them and keep them steadfast in the right path. . . .

When the gospel is received in its purity and power, it is a cure for the maladies that originated in sin. The Sun of Righteousness arises, "with healing in his wings" (Mal. 4:2). Not all that this world bestows can heal a broken heart, or impart peace of mind, or remove care, or banish disease. Fame, genius, talent—all are powerless to gladden the sorrowful heart or to restore the wasted life. The life of God in the soul is humanity's only hope.

The love which Christ diffuses through the whole being is a vitalizing power. Every vital part—the brain, the heart, the nerves—it touches with healing. . . . It implants in the soul joy that nothing earthly can destroy—joy in the Holy Spirit—health-giving, life-giving joy. . . .

Although for ages sin has been strengthening its hold on the human race, although through falsehood and artifice Satan has cast the black shadow of his interpretation upon the Word of God, and has caused men and women to doubt His goodness; yet the Father's mercy and love have not ceased to flow earthward in rich currents. If human beings would open the windows of the soul heavenward, in appreciation of the divine gifts, a flood of healing virtue would pour in.—*The Ministry of Healing*, pp. 114-116.

Christ, the Model of True Obedience

*Do you not know that to whom you present yourselves
slaves to obey, you are that one's slaves whom you obey, whether of
sin to death, or of obedience to righteousness? Romans 6:16, NKJV.*

ADAM DID NOT STOP to calculate the result of his disobedience. . . .
With the aftersight we are privileged to have, we can see what it means to
disobey God's commandments. Adam yielded to temptation, and as we
have the matter of sin and its consequences laid so distinctly before us, we
can read from cause to effect and see the greatness of the act is not that
which constitutes sin; but the disobedience of God's expressed will, which
is a virtual denial of God, refusing the laws of His government.

The happiness of men and women is in their obedience to the laws of
God. In their obedience to God's law they are surrounded as with a hedge
and kept from the evil. They cannot be happy and depart from God's specified requirements, and set up a standard of their own, which they decide
they can safely follow. Then there would be a variety of standards to suit
the different minds, and the government [would be] taken out of the
Lord's hands and human beings [would] grasp the reins of government.
The law of self is erected, the will of humankind is made supreme, and
when the high and holy will of God is presented to be obeyed, respected,
and honored the human will wants its own way to do its own promptings,
and there is a controversy between the human agent and the divine.

The fall of our first parents broke the golden chain of implicit obedience of the human will to the divine. Obedience has no longer been
deemed an absolute necessity. The human agents follow their own imaginations, which the Lord said of the inhabitants of the old world were evil
and that continually. The Lord Jesus declares, "I have kept my Father's
commandments." How? As a man. Lo, I come to do Thy will, O God. To
the accusations of the Jews He stood forth in His pure, virtuous, holy character and challenged them, "Which of you convinceth me of sin?" . . .

The only-begotten Son of the infinite God has, by His words, His practical example, left us a plain pattern which we are to copy. By His words
He has educated us to obey God, and by His own practice He has showed
us how we can obey God.—*Manuscript Releases,* vol. 6, pp. 337-339.

Happiness Guarded by God's Law

For what the law could not do in that it was weak through the flesh,
God did by sending His own Son in the likeness of sinful flesh, on
account of sin: He condemned sin in the flesh. Romans 8:3, NKJV.

THE HAPPINESS OF human beings must always be guarded by the law of God. In obedience only can they find true happiness. The law is the hedge which God has placed about His vineyard. By it those who obey are protected from evil. In transgression Adam became a law to himself. By disobedience he was brought under bondage. Thus a discordant element, born of selfishness, entered human beings. Their will and God's will no longer harmonized. Adam had united with the disloyal forces, and self-will took the field.

By Christ the true standard is presented. He made it possible for humankind to be once more united with God. He came to take the sentence of death for the transgressor. Not one precept of the law could be altered to meet men and women in their fallen condition; therefore Christ gave His life in their behalf, to suffer in their stead the penalty of disobedience. This was the only way in which humanity could be saved, the only way in which it could be demonstrated that it is possible for them to keep the law. Christ came to this earth and stood where Adam stood, overcoming where Adam failed to overcome. He is made unto us wisdom and righteousness and sanctification and redemption. . . .

Before the foundation of the world, Christ pledged His word that He would give His life as a ransom if men and women turned from their allegiance to God. He revealed His love by humbling Himself, stooping from heaven to work among fallen, disorderly, lawless human beings. Of themselves they could not possibly cope with the enemy. Christ offers Himself and all He has, His glory, His character, to the service of those who return to their loyalty and keep the law of God. This is their only hope. Christ says definitely, I came not to destroy the law. It is a transcript of God's character, and I came to carry out its every specification. I came to vindicate it by living it in human nature, giving an example of perfect obedience.—*Signs of the Times,* June 13, 1900.

Obedience to Be Rewarded

*Children, obey your parents in all things, for
this is well pleasing to the Lord. Colossians 3:20, NKJV.*

CHILDREN WHO DISHONOR and disobey their parents, and disregard their advice and instructions, can have no part in the earth made new. The purified new earth will be no place for the rebellious, the disobedient, the ungrateful, son or daughter. Unless such learn obedience and submission here, they will never learn it; the peace of the ransomed will not be marred by disobedient, unruly, unsubmissive children. No commandment breaker can inherit the kingdom of heaven. . . .

The young are required in whatsoever they do, in word or deed, to do all in the name of the Lord Jesus, giving thanks to God and the Father by Him. I saw that but few of the youth understand what it is to be Christians, to be Christlike. They will have to learn the truths of God's Word before they can conform their lives to the pattern. There is not one young person in twenty who has experienced in his or her life that separation from the world which the Lord requires of all who would become members of His family, children of the heavenly King. "Wherefore come out from among them, and be ye separate, saith the Lord, and touch not the unclean thing; and I will receive you, and will be a Father unto you, and ye shall be my sons and daughters, saith the Lord Almighty."

What a promise is here made upon condition of obedience! Do you have to cut loose from friends and relatives in deciding to obey the elevated truths of God's Word? Take courage, God has made provision for you, His arms are open to receive you. Come out from among them and be separate, and touch not the unclean, and He will receive you. He promises to be a Father unto you. Oh, what a relationship is this! higher and holier than any earthly tie. If you make the sacrifice, if you have to forsake father, mother, sisters, brothers, wife, and children for Christ's sake, you will not be friendless. God adopts you into His family; you become members of the royal household, sons and daughters of the King who rules in the heaven of heavens. Can you desire a more exalted position than is here promised? Is not this enough?—*Testimonies for the Church,* vol. 1, pp. 497-510.

Commandment-keeping Families Glorify Christ

Train children in the right way, and when
old, they will not stray. Proverbs 22:6, NRSV.

CHILDREN MUST BE taught that they are a part of the home firm. They are fed, and clothed, and loved, and cared for; and they must respond to these many mercies by bringing all the happiness possible into the family of which they are members. Thus they become children of God, missionaries in the home circle.

If parents neglect the education of their children, they deprive them of that which is necessary for the development of a symmetrical, all-sided character, which will be of the greatest blessing to them all through their life. If children are allowed to have their own way, they receive the idea that they must be waited upon, cared for, indulged, and amused. They think that their wishes and their will must be gratified. Educated in this way, they carry through all their religious experience the deficiencies of their home training.

God would have our families symbols of the family in heaven. Let parents and children bear this in mind every day, relating themselves to one another as members of the family of God. Then their lives will be of such a character as to give to the world an object lesson of what families who love God and keep His commandments may be. Christ will be glorified; His peace and grace and love will pervade the family circle like a precious perfume. A beautiful offering, in the lives of children of Christian missionaries, will be made to God. This will make the heart of Jesus glad, and will be regarded by Him as the most precious offering He can receive.

May the Lord Jesus Christ be an object of worship in every family. If parents give their children the proper education, they themselves will be made happy by seeing the fruit of their careful training in the Christlike character of their children. They are doing God the highest service by presenting to the world well-ordered, well-disciplined families, who not only fear the Lord, but honor and glorify Him by their influence upon other families; and they will receive their reward.—*Review and Herald,* Nov. 17, 1896.

Obedience Brings Peace and Happiness

And being found in appearance as a man, He humbled Himself and became obedient to the point of death, even the death of the cross. Philippians 2:8, NKJV.

BEFORE US IS HELD out the wonderful possibility of being like Christ—obedient to all the principles of the law of God. But of ourselves we are utterly powerless to attain to this condition. All that is good in human beings comes to them through Christ. The holiness that God's Word declares we must have before we can be saved is the result of the working of divine grace as we bow in submission to the discipline and restraining influence of the Spirit of truth.

Humanity's obedience can be made perfect only by the incense of Christ's righteousness, which fills with divine fragrance every act of true obedience. The part of the Christian is to persevere in overcoming every fault. Constantly he or she is to pray to the Savior to heal the disorders of their diseased souls. They have not the wisdom and strength without which mortals cannot overcome. These belong to the Lord, and He bestows them on those who in humiliation and contrition seek Him for help. . . .

The reason that many who once knew and loved the Savior are now in darkness, wandering far from Him, is because in self-confidence and self-sufficiency they have followed their own inclinations. They walked not in the way of the Lord—the only way of peace and happiness. By disobedience they cut themselves off from receiving His blessings, when by obedience they might have gone forward in His strength.

The abundant evidence given by God that He desires the salvation of all will be the condemnation of those who refuse the gift of heaven. At the last great day, when all will be rewarded or punished according to their obedience or disobedience, the cross of Calvary will appear plainly before those standing before the Judge of all the earth to receive sentence for eternity. They are made capable of comprehending something of the love that God has expressed for fallen human beings. They see how greatly He has been dishonored by those who have continued in transgression, choosing sides with Satan, and showing contempt for the law of Jehovah. They see that obedience to this law would have brought them life and health, prosperity and eternal good.—*Review and Herald,* Mar. 15, 1906.

Joy in Loving Obedience

*You were perfect in your ways from the day you were created,
till iniquity was found in you. . . . You became filled with
violence within, and you sinned. Ezekiel 28:15, 16, NKJV.*

SO LONG AS ALL created beings acknowledged the allegiance of love, there was perfect harmony throughout the universe of God. It was the joy of the heavenly host to fulfill the purpose of their Creator. They delighted in reflecting His glory and showing forth His praise. And while love to God was supreme, love for one another was confiding and unselfish. There was no note of discord to mar the celestial harmonies. But a change came over this happy state.

There was one who perverted the freedom that God had granted to His creatures. Sin originated with him who, next to Christ, had been most honored of God and was highest in power and glory among the inhabitants of heaven. Lucifer, "son of the morning," was first of the covering cherubs, holy and undefiled. He stood in the presence of the great Creator, and the ceaseless beams of glory enshrouding the eternal God rested upon him. . . .

Little by little Lucifer came to indulge the desire for self-exaltation. . . . Though all his glory was from God, this mighty angel came to regard it as pertaining to himself. Not content with his position, though honored above the heavenly host, he ventured to covet homage due alone to the Creator. Instead of seeking to make God supreme in the affections and allegiance of all created beings, it was his endeavor to secure their service and loyalty to himself. And coveting the glory with which the infinite Father had invested His Son, this prince of angels aspired to power that was the prerogative of Christ alone.—*Patriarchs and Prophets*, p. 35.

The law of love being the foundation of the government of God, the happiness of all intelligent beings depends upon their perfect accord with its great principles of righteousness. God desires from all His creatures the service of love—service that springs from an appreciation of His character. He takes no pleasure in a forced obedience; and to all He grants freedom of will, that they may render Him voluntary service.—*Ibid.*, p. 34.

Jesus Gives
Power to Obey

For we do not have a High Priest who cannot sympathize with our
weaknesses, but was in all points tempted as we are, yet without sin.
Let us therefore come boldly to the throne of grace, that we may obtain
mercy and find grace to help in time of need. Hebrews 4:15, 16, NKJV.

SATAN REPRESENTS GOD'S law of love as a law of selfishness. He declares that it is impossible for us to obey its precepts. The fall of our first parents, with all the woe that has resulted, he charges upon the Creator, leading men and women to look upon God as the author of sin, and suffering, and death. Jesus was to unveil this deception. As one of us He was to give an example of obedience. For this He took upon Himself our nature, and passed through our experiences. "In all things it behoved him to be made like unto his brethren" (Heb. 2:17).

If we had to bear anything which Jesus did not endure, then upon this point Satan would represent the power of God as insufficient for us. Therefore Jesus was "in all points tempted like as we are" (Heb. 4:15). He endured every trial to which we are subject. And He exercised in His own behalf no power that is not freely offered to us. As man, He met temptation, and overcame in the strength given Him from God. He says, "I delight to do thy will, O my God: yea, thy law is within my heart" (Ps. 40:8).

As He went about doing good, and healing all who were afflicted by Satan, He made plain to human beings the character of God's law and the nature of His service. His life testifies that it is possible for us also to obey the law of God.

By His humanity, Christ touched humanity; by His divinity, He lays hold upon the throne of God. As the Son of man, He gave us an example of obedience; as the Son of God, He gives us power to obey. . . .

Christ was treated as we deserve, that we might be treated as He deserves. He was condemned for our sins, in which He had no share, that we might be justified by His righteousness, in which we had no share. He suffered the death which was ours, that we might receive the life which was His. "With his stripes we are healed."—*The Desire of Ages*, pp. 24, 25.

Abraham's Great Example of Obedience

In your seed all the nations of the earth shall be blessed, because you have obeyed My voice. Genesis 22:18, NKJV.

ON MOUNT MORIAH, God again renewed His covenant, confirming with a solemn oath the blessing to Abraham and to his seed through all coming generations: "By myself have I sworn, saith Jehovah, for because thou hast done this thing, and hast not withheld thy son, thine only son, that in blessing I will bless thee, and in multiplying I will multiply thy seed as the stars of the heaven, and as the sand which is upon the sea shore." . . .

Abraham's great act of faith stands like a pillar of light, illuminating the pathway of God's servants in all succeeding ages. Abraham did not seek to excuse himself from doing the will of God. During that three days' journey he had sufficient time to reason, and to doubt God, if he was disposed to doubt. . . . Abraham was human; his passions and attachments were like ours; but he did not stop to question how the promise could be fulfilled if Isaac should be slain. He did not stay to reason with his aching heart. He knew that God is just and righteous in all His requirements, and he obeyed the command to the very letter. . . .

It was to impress Abraham's mind with the reality of the gospel, as well as to test his faith, that God commanded him to slay his son. The agony which he endured during the dark days of that fearful trial was permitted that he might understand from his own experience something of the greatness of the sacrifice made by the infinite God for humanity's redemption. No other test could have caused Abraham such torture of soul as did the offering of his son. . . . What stronger proof can be given of the infinite compassion and love of God? "He that spared not his own Son, but delivered him up for us all, how shall he not with him also freely give us all things?" (Rom. 8:32).—*Patriarchs and Prophets,* pp. 153, 154.

God's Law
Important for All Time

Now therefore, if you will indeed obey My voice and keep My covenant, then you shall be a special treasure to Me above all people; for all the earth is Mine. And you shall be to Me a kingdom of priests and a holy nation. Exodus 19:5, 6, NKJV.

THIS COVENANT [Exodus 19:1-6] is a revelation of God's goodness. The people had not sought for it. They were not reaching out their hands after God; but He Himself graciously extended His almighty arm, inviting them to link their arm with His, that He might be their defense. He voluntarily chose as His heritage a nation that had just come from Egyptian slavery, a people who must be educated and trained at every step. What an expression of omnipotent goodness and love! . . .

Over and over again, the Lord permitted His people to be brought into strait places, that in their deliverance, He might reveal His mercy and His goodness. If they now chose to disbelieve Him, they must doubt the evidence of their own eyes. They had had unmistakable proof that He was a living God, "merciful and gracious, longsuffering, and abundant in goodness and truth" (Ex. 34:6). He had honored Israel in the sight of all the heavenly intelligences. He brought them unto Himself—into covenant relation and communion with Him.

The children of Israel had been three months on their journey from Egypt, and were now camped before Mount Sinai, where in awful grandeur, the Lord spoke His law. He did not manifest Himself in grand buildings made with human hands, the structures of human device. He revealed His glory in a high mountain, a temple of His own creation. The top of Mount Sinai rose above all others, in a range of mountains in the barren desert. This mountain God chose as the place where He would make Himself known to His people.

He appeared to them in awful grandeur, and spoke in audible voice. He there revealed Himself to His people, as He never has at any other time, thereby showing the importance of the law for all ages. God is particular today that we keep His commandments.—*Manuscript Releases,* vol. 1, pp. 105, 106.

Disobedience
# Indicates Rebellion

Whoever breaks one of the least of these commandments, and teaches others to
do the same, will be called least in the kingdom of heaven; but whoever does them and
teaches them will be called great in the kingdom of heaven. Matthew 5:19, NRSV.

ANY PERSON WHO willfully breaks one commandment does not, in spirit and truth, keep any of them. "Whosoever shall keep the whole law, and yet offend in one point, he is guilty of all" (James 2:10).

It is not the greatness of the act of disobedience that constitutes sin, but the fact of variance from God's expressed will in the least particular; for this shows that there is yet communion between the soul and sin. The heart is divided in its service. There is a virtual denial of God, a rebellion against the laws of His government.

Were men and women free to depart from the Lord's requirements and to set up a standard of duty for themselves, there would be a variety of standards to suit different minds and the government would be taken out of the Lord's hands. The will of human beings would be made supreme, and the high and holy will of God—His purpose of love toward His creatures—would be dishonored, disrespected.

Whenever created beings choose their own way, they place themselves in controversy with God. They will have no place in the kingdom of heaven, for they are at war with the very principles of heaven. In disregarding the will of God, they are placing themselves on the side of Satan, the enemy of God and humanity. Not by one word, not by many words, but by every word that God has spoken, shall we live. We cannot disregard one word, however trifling it may seem to us, and be safe. There is not a commandment of the law that is not for the good and happiness of men and women, both in this life and in the life to come. In obedience to God's law, His children are surrounded as with a hedge and kept from the evil. Those who break down this divinely erected barrier at one point have destroyed its power to protect them; for they have opened a way by which the enemy can enter to waste and ruin.

By venturing to disregard the will of God upon one point, our first parents opened the floodgates of woe upon the world. And every individual who follows their example will reap a similar result. The love of God underlies every precept of His law, and those who depart from the commandment are working their own unhappiness and ruin.—*Thoughts From the Mount of Blessing*, pp. 51, 52.

Obedience Results in Happiness

Happy are those who do not follow the advice of the wicked . . . ; but their delight is in the law of the Lord, and on his law they meditate day and night. Psalm 1:1, 2, NRSV.

IT IS ESSENTIAL that every subject of the kingdom of God should be obedient to the law of Jehovah, in order that His infinite glory may have a perfect establishment. The professed followers of Christ are tested in this life to see whether or not they will be obedient to God. Obedience will result in happiness, and will insure the reward of eternal life.

Failure on the part of Adam on one point resulted in terrible consequences, and sin has grown to such vast proportions that it cannot be measured. But in the midst of rebellion and apostasy, in the midst of those who were disloyal, impenitent, and obstinate, God looks down upon those who love Him and keep His commandments, and says, "I love them that love me," and will cause them to inherit substance. "I will render vengeance to mine enemies, and will reward them that hate me."

Christ lived in accordance with the principles of God's moral government, and fulfilled the specifications of the law of God. He represented the beneficence of the law in His human life. The fact that the law is holy, just, and good is to be testified before all nations, tongues, and peoples, to worlds unfallen, to angels, seraphim, and cherubim. The principles of the law of God were wrought out in the character of Jesus Christ, and he who cooperates with Christ, becoming a partaker of the divine nature, will develop the divine character, and become an illustration of the divine law. Christ in the heart will bring the whole person, soul, body, and spirit, into captivity to the obedience of righteousness. Christ's true followers will be in conformity to the mind and will and character of God, and the far-reaching principles of the law will be demonstrated in humanity. . . .

Satan had declared that God knew nothing of self-denial, of mercy and love, but that He was stern, exacting, and unforgiving. Satan never tested the forgiving love of God; for he never exercised genuine repentance. His representations of God were incorrect; he was a false witness, an accuser of Christ, and an accuser of all those who throw off the satanic yoke, and come back to render willing allegiance to the God of heaven.—*Review and Herald,* Mar. 9, 1897.

Even Nature Obeys
Divine Commands

*And the men marveled, saying, "Who can this be, that even
the winds and the sea obey Him?" Matthew 8:27, NKJV.*

THE SAVIOR WAS wearied from His long and arduous labors, and being
now for a time relieved from the claims of the multitude, He stretched
Himself upon the hard plank of the fishermen's boat and fell asleep. Soon
after, the weather, which had been calm and pleasant, changed. The clouds
gathered darkly over the sky, and a furious storm, such as frequently visited
those parts, burst upon the sea. The sun had set, and the blackness of night
settled down upon the water. The angry waves dashed against the ship,
threatening every moment to engulf it. First tossed upon the crest of a
mountain billow, and then as suddenly plunged into the trough of the sea,
the ship was the plaything of the storm. . . . The strong and courageous
fishermen . . . knew not what to do in so terrible a gale. . . . The waves
break over them, and each one threatens them with destruction. . . .

"Master, carest thou not that we perish?" . . . This despairing cry
arouses Jesus from His refreshing sleep. . . . In His divine majesty He stands
in the humble vessel of the fishermen, amid the raging of the tempest, the
waves breaking over the bows, and the vivid lightning playing about His
calm and fearless countenance. He lifts His hand, so often employed in
deeds of mercy, and says to the angry sea, "Peace, be still." The storm
ceases, the heaving billows sink to rest. The clouds roll away, and the stars
shine forth; the boat sits motionless upon a quiet sea. Then, turning to His
disciples, Jesus rebukes them, saying, "Why are ye so fearful? how is it that
ye have no faith?"

A sudden hush crept over the disciples. Not a word was spoken; even
impulsive Peter did not attempt to express the reverential awe that filled
his heart. The boats that had set out to accompany Jesus had been in the
same peril with that of the disciples. Fear and finally despair had seized
their occupants; but the command of Jesus brought quiet where but a moment before all was tumult. All fear was allayed, for the danger was over.
The fury of the storm had driven the boats into close proximity, and all on
board beheld the miracle of Jesus. In the hush that followed the stilling of
the tempest, they whispered among themselves, "What manner of man is
this, that even the wind and the sea obey him?" Never was this impressive
scene forgotten by those who witnessed it.—*The Spirit of Prophecy,* vol. 2,
pp. 307-309.

Obey God, the Supreme Authority

Then Peter and the other apostles answered and said,
"We ought to obey God rather than men." Acts 5:29, NKJV.

THE PRINCIPLE FOR which the disciples stood so fearlessly when, in answer to the command not to speak any more in the name of Jesus, they declared, "Whether it be right in the sight of God to hearken unto you more than unto God, judge ye," is the same that the adherents of the gospel struggled to maintain in the days of the Reformation. When in 1529 the German princes assembled at the Diet of Spires, there was presented the emperor's decree restricting religious liberty, and prohibiting all further dissemination of the reformed doctrines. It seemed that the hope of the world was about to be crushed out. Would the princes accept the decree? Should the light of the gospel be shut out from the multitudes still in darkness? Mighty issues for the world were at stake. Those who had accepted the reformed faith met together, and their unanimous decision was, "Let us reject this decree. In matters of conscience the majority has no power" (Merle d'Aubigné, *History of the Reformation,* book 13, chap. 5).

This principle we in our day are firmly to maintain. The banner of truth and religious liberty held aloft by the founders of the gospel church and by God's witnesses during the centuries that have passed since then, has, in this last conflict, been committed to our hands. The responsibility for this great gift rests with those whom God has blessed with a knowledge of His Word. We are to receive this Word as supreme authority. We are to recognize human government as an ordinance of divine appointment, and teach obedience to it as a sacred duty, within its legitimate sphere. But when its claims conflict with the claims of God, we must obey God rather than human beings. God's Word must be recognized as above all human legislation. A "Thus saith the Lord" is not to be set aside for a "Thus saith the church" or a "Thus saith the state." The crown of Christ is to be lifted above the diadems of earthly potentates. . . .

We are not to say or do anything that would unnecessarily close up our way. We are to go forward in Christ's name, advocating the truths committed to us. If we are forbidden by others to do this work, then we may say, as did the apostles, . . . "We cannot but speak the things which we have seen and heard" (Acts 4:20).—*The Acts of the Apostles,* pp. 68, 69.

Make Obedience Attractive

Behold, I set before you today a blessing and a curse: the blessing, if you
obey the commandments of the Lord your God which I command you today;
and the curse, if you do not obey the commandments of the Lord your God, but turn
aside from the way which I command you today. Deuteronomy 11:26-28, NKJV.

MEN AND WOMEN are not to presume to put aside God's great moral standard and erect a standard according to their own finite judgment. It is because they are measuring themselves among themselves and living according to their own standard that iniquity abounds, and the love of many waxes cold. Contempt is shown to the law of God, and because of this many presume to transgress, and even those who have had the light of truth are wavering in their allegiance to the law of God. Will the current of evil that is setting so strongly toward perdition sweep them away? Or will they, with courage and fidelity, stem the tide and maintain loyalty to God amid the prevailing evil? . . .

Those who profess to serve God are to do the work of relieving the oppressed. They are to bear the fruit of the good tree. Those who are truly Christ's will not bring oppression in the home or in the church. Parents who are following the Lord will diligently teach their children the statutes and commandments of God; but they will not do it in such a way that the service of God will become repulsive to their children. Where parents love God with all their hearts, the truth as it is in Jesus will be practiced and taught in the home. . . .

We are closely to examine ourselves. . . . We should plead with God for spiritual eyesight, that we may discern our mistakes and understand our defection of character. If we have been critical and condemnatory, full of faultfinding, talking doubt and darkness, we have a work of repentance and reformation to do. We are to walk in the light, speaking words that will bring peace and happiness. Jesus is to abide in the soul. And where He is, instead of gloom, murmuring, and repining, there will be fragrance of character.—*Review and Herald,* June 12, 1894.

God's Law Is Perfect

The law of the Lord is perfect, converting the soul; the testimony of the Lord is sure,
making wise the simple; the statutes of the Lord are right, rejoicing the heart; the
commandment of the Lord is pure, enlightening the eyes. Psalm 19:7, 8, NKJV.

THE VERY SAME JESUS, who, veiled in the cloudy pillar, led the Hebrew hosts, is our leader. He who gave wise and righteous and good laws to Israel has spoken to us as verily as to them. Our prosperity and happiness depend upon our unwavering obedience to the law of God. Finite wisdom could not improve one precept of that holy law. Not one of those ten precepts can be broken without disloyalty to the God of heaven. To keep every jot and tittle of the law is essential for our own happiness, and for the happiness of all connected with us. "Great peace have they which love thy law: and nothing shall offend them." Yet finite creatures will present to the people this holy, just, and good law as a yoke of bondage—a yoke which they cannot bear! It is the transgressor that can see no beauty in the law of God.

The whole world will be judged by this law. It reaches even to the intents and purposes of the heart, and demands purity in the most secret thoughts, desires, and dispositions. It requires us to love God supremely, and our neighbor as ourselves. Without the exercise of this love, the highest profession of faith is mere hypocrisy. God claims, from every soul of the human family, perfect obedience to His law. "Whosoever shall keep the whole law, and yet offend in one point, he is guilty of all."

The least deviation from that law, by neglect, or willful transgression, is sin, and every sin exposes the sinner to the wrath of God. The unrenewed heart will hate the restrictions of the law of God, and will strive to throw off its holy claims. Our eternal welfare depends upon a proper understanding of the law of God, a deep conviction of its holy character, and a ready obedience to its requirements. Men and women must be convicted of sin before they will feel their need of Christ. . . . Those who trample under their feet the law of God have rejected the only means to define to the transgressor what sin is. They are doing the work of the great deceiver.—*Signs of the Times,* Mar. 3, 1881.

Jesus, the Perfect Pattern of Obedience

Then He went down with them and came to Nazareth, and was subject
to them, but His mother kept all these things in her heart. Luke 2:51, NKJV.

WHEN CHRIST WAS twelve years old, He went with His parents to Jerusalem to attend the feast of the Passover, and on their return He was lost in the multitude. After Joseph and Mary had searched for Him for three days, they found Him in the court of the Temple, "sitting in the midst of the doctors, both hearing them, and asking them questions. And all that heard him were astonished at his understanding and answers." He asked His questions with a grace that charmed these learned men. He was a perfect pattern for all youth. Ever He manifested deference and respect for age. The religion of Jesus will never lead any child to be rude and uncourteous.

When Joseph and Mary found Jesus, they were amazed, "and his mother said unto him, Son, why hast thou thus dealt with us? behold, thy father and I have sought thee sorrowing. And he said unto them, How is it that ye sought me?" Pointing heavenward, He continued, "Wist ye not that I must be about my Father's business?" As He spoke these words, divinity flashed through humanity. The light and glory of heaven illuminated His countenance. . . .

Christ did not enter upon His public ministry for eighteen years after this, but He was constantly ministering to others, improving every opportunity offered Him. Even in His childhood He spoke words of comfort and tenderness to young and old. His mother could not but mark His words, His spirit, His willing obedience to all her requirements.

It is not correct to say, as many writers have said, that Christ was like all children. He was not like all children. Many children are misguided and mismanaged. . . . Jesus was instructed in accordance with the sacred character of His mission. His inclination to right was a constant gratification to His parents. The questions He asked them led them to study most earnestly the great elements of truth. His soul-stirring words about nature and the God of nature opened and enlightened their minds.—*Youth's Instructor,* Sept. 8, 1898.

Our Obedience Enables God to Fulfill Promises

Today you have proclaimed the Lord to be your God, and that you will walk in His ways and keep His statutes, His commandments, and His judgments, and that you will obey His voice. Deuteronomy 26:17, NKJV.

LET US BE LOYAL and true to every precept of the law of God. The Lord declares that if we will obey the principles of His law, these principles will be our life. . . .

The precepts of God's law were not the production of any human mind, nor were they enacted by Moses. They were framed by the One infinite in wisdom, even Him who is King of kings and Lord of lords, and by Him were proclaimed from Sinai amidst scenes of awful grandeur. On obedience to these precepts depended Israel's prosperity.

"Thou shalt therefore keep and do them with all thine heart, and with all thy soul." God did not give His commandments to us for us to obey when we pleased, and to disregard at our pleasure. They are the laws of His kingdom, and are to be obeyed by His subjects. If His people would obey His law with the whole heart, decided witness would be borne to the world that those whom He has avouched to be His people, His peculiar treasure, do indeed honor Him in all they do. Loyalty to God, unquestioning obedience to His law, would make His people a wonder in the world, because He would be able to fulfill His rich and abundant promises to them, and make them a praise in the earth. They would be a holy people unto Him.

"Now therefore," God declares, "if ye will obey my voice indeed, and keep my covenant, then ye shall be a peculiar treasure unto me above all people: for all the earth is mine: and ye shall be unto me a kingdom of priests, and a holy nation." How wonderful the largeness of God's promises! And they are given to all who will hearken to His Word, believing His declarations, and obeying His commands. Obedience to His law is the condition of future and eternal happiness.—*Southern Watchman*, Feb. 16, 1904.

Obedience Has Immediate and Eternal Rewards

Therefore you shall lay up these words of mine in your heart and in your soul, and bind them as a sign on your hand, and they shall be as frontlets between your eyes. Deuteronomy 11:18, NKJV.

THESE WORDS [Deuteronomy 11:13-28 and 7:6-11] should be as distinctly stamped upon every soul as though written with a pen of iron. Obedience brings its reward, disobedience its retribution.

God has given His people positive instruction, and has laid upon them positive restrictions, that they may obtain a perfect experience in His service, and be qualified to stand before the heavenly universe and before the fallen world as overcomers. They are to overcome by the blood of the Lamb and the word of their testimony. Those who fall short of making the preparation essential will be numbered with the unthankful and the unholy.

The Lord brings His people by ways they know not, that He may test and prove them. This world is our place of proving. Here we decide our eternal destiny. God humbles His people that His will may be wrought out through them. Thus He dealt with the children of Israel as He led them through the wilderness. He told them what their fate would have been had He not laid a restraining hand upon that which would have hurt them. . . .

God blesses the work of human hands that they may return to Him His portion. They are to devote their means to His service, that His vineyard may not remain a barren waste. They are to study what the Lord would do were He in their place. They are to take all difficult matters to Him in prayer. They are to reveal an unselfish interest in the building up of His work in all parts of the world. . . .

Let us remember that we are laborers together with God. We are not wise enough to work by ourselves. God has made us His stewards, to prove us and to try us, even as He proved and tried ancient Israel. He will not have His army composed of undisciplined, unsanctified, erratic soldiers, who would misrepresent His order and purity.—*Review and Herald,* Oct. 8, 1901.

Genuine Sanctification Involves Obedience

For your obedience has become known to all. Therefore I am glad on your behalf; but I want you to be wise in what is good, and simple concerning evil. Romans 16:19, NKJV.

ADAM AND EVE dared to transgress the Lord's requirements, and the terrible result of their sin should be a warning to us not to follow their example of disobedience. Christ prayed for His disciples in these words: "Sanctify them through thy truth: thy word is truth" (John 17:17). There is no genuine sanctification except through obedience to the truth. Those who love God with all the heart will love all His commandments also. The sanctified heart is in harmony with the precepts of God's law; for they are holy, just, and good.

God's character has not changed. He is the same jealous God today as when He gave His law upon Sinai and wrote it with His own finger on the tables of stone. Those who trample upon God's holy law may say, "I am sanctified"; but to be indeed sanctified, and to claim sanctification, are two different things.

The New Testament has not changed the law of God. The sacredness of the Sabbath of the fourth commandment is as firmly established as the throne of Jehovah. John writes: "Whosoever committeth sin transgresseth also the law: for sin is the transgression of the law. And ye know that he was manifested to take away our sins; and in him is no sin. Whosoever abideth in him sinneth not: whosoever sinneth [transgresseth the law] hath not seen him, neither known him" (1 John 3:4-6).

We are authorized to hold in the same estimation as did the beloved disciple those who claim to abide in Christ, to be sanctified, while living in transgression of God's law. He met with just such a class as we have to meet. He said, "Little children, let no man deceive you: he that doeth righteousness is righteous, even as he is righteous. He that committeth sin is of the devil; for the devil sinneth from the beginning" (verses 7, 8). Here the apostle speaks in plain terms, as he deemed the subject demanded.

The epistles of John breathe a spirit of love. But when he comes in contact with that class who break the law of God and yet claim that they are living without sin, he does not hesitate to warn them of their fearful deception. [First John 1:6-10 quoted.]—*The Sanctified Life,* pp. 67-69.

MARCH

❧

Investing Time and Other Talents

Time to Study Revelation

Blessed is the one who reads aloud the words of the prophecy, and blessed are those who hear and who keep what is written in it; for the time is near. Revelation 1:3, NRSV.

AS WE NEAR THE close of this world's history, the prophecies relating to the last days especially demand our study. The last book of the New Testament is full of truth that we need to understand. Satan has blinded the minds of many, so that they have been glad of any excuse for not making the Revelation their study. . . .

There should be a closer and more diligent study of this book [Revelation], a more earnest presentation of the truths it contains, truths which concern all who are living in these last days. All who are preparing to meet their Lord should make this book the subject of earnest study and prayer. It is just what its name signifies—a revelation of the most important events that are to take place in the last days of this earth's history. John, because of his faithful trust in the Word of God and the testimony of Christ, was banished to the Isle of Patmos. But his banishment did not separate him from Christ. The Lord visited His faithful servant in his banishment, and gave him instruction regarding what was to come upon the world.

This instruction is of the greatest importance to us; for we are living in the last days of this earth's history. Soon we shall enter upon the fulfillment of the events which Christ showed John were to take place. As the messengers of the Lord present these solemn truths, they must realize that they are handling subjects of eternal interest, and they should seek for the baptism of the Holy Spirit, that they may speak, not their own words, but the words given them by God. . . .

The perils of the last days are upon us, and in our work we are to warn the people of the danger they are in. Let not the solemn scenes that prophecy has revealed are soon to take place be left untouched. We are God's messengers, and we have no time to lose. Those who would be coworkers with our Lord Jesus Christ will show a deep interest in the truths found in this book. With pen and voice they will strive to make plain the wonderful things that Christ came from heaven to reveal.—*Signs of the Times,* July 4, 1906.

Depend on Our
Divine Advocate

*Therefore rejoice, O heavens, and you who dwell in them! Woe to the inhabitants
of the earth and the sea! For the devil has come down to you, having great wrath,
because he knows that he has a short time. Revelation 12:12, NKJV.*

THOSE WHO KEEP the commandments of God and the faith of Jesus will feel the ire of the dragon and his hosts. Satan numbers the world as his subjects; he has gained control of the apostate churches. But here is a little company that are resisting his supremacy. If he could blot them from the earth, his triumph would be complete. As he influenced the heathen nations to destroy Israel, so in the near future he will stir up the wicked powers of earth to destroy the people of God. All will be required to render obedience to human edicts in violation of the divine law. Those who will be true to God and to duty will be menaced, denounced, and proscribed. They will be betrayed "both by parents, and brethren, and kinsfolks, and friends."

Their only hope is in the mercy of God; their only defense will be prayer. As Joshua was pleading before the Angel, so the remnant church, with brokenness of heart and earnest faith, will plead for pardon and deliverance through Jesus their Advocate. They are fully conscious of the sinfulness of their lives, they see their weakness and unworthiness; and as they look upon themselves, they are ready to despair.

The tempter stands by to accuse them, as he stood by to resist Joshua. He points to their filthy garments, their defective characters. He presents their weakness and folly, their sins of ingratitude, their unlikeness to Christ, which has dishonored their Redeemer. He endeavors to affright the soul with the thought that their case is hopeless, that the stain of their defilement will never be washed away. He hopes so to destroy their faith that they will yield to his temptations, turn from their allegiance to God, and receive the mark of the beast. . . .

While the followers of Christ have sinned, they have not given themselves to the control of evil. They have put away their sins, and have sought the Lord in humility and contrition, and the divine Advocate pleads in their behalf. He who has been most abused by their ingratitude, who knows their sin, and also their repentance, declares, "The Lord rebuke thee, O Satan. I gave My life for these souls. They are graven upon the palms of My hands."—*Review and Herald,* Jan. 9, 1908.

A Message
for Our Time

For we have become partakers of Christ if we hold the beginning of our confidence steadfast to the end. Hebrews 3:14, NKJV.

"AND THE ANGEL which I saw stand upon the sea and upon the earth lifted up his hand to heaven, and sware by him that liveth for ever and ever, who created heaven, and the things that therein are, and the earth, and the things that therein are, and the sea, and the things which are therein, that there should be time no longer" (Rev. 10:5, 6). This message announces the end of the prophetic periods. The disappointment of those who expected to see our Lord in 1844 was indeed bitter to those who had so ardently looked for His appearing. It was in the Lord's order that this disappointment should come, and that hearts should be revealed.

Not one cloud has fallen upon the church that God has not prepared for; not one opposing force has risen to counterwork the work of God but He has foreseen. . . . All His purposes will be fulfilled and established. His law is linked with His throne, and satanic agencies combined with human agencies cannot destroy it. Truth is inspired and guarded by God; it will live, and will succeed, although it may appear at times to be overshadowed.

The gospel of Christ is the law exemplified in character. The deceptions practiced against it, every device for vindicating falsehood, every error forged by satanic agencies, will eventually be eternally broken, and the triumph of truth will be like the appearing of the sun at noonday. The Sun of Righteousness shall shine forth with healing in His wings, and the whole earth shall be filled with His glory. . . .

Old controversies will be revived, and new theories will be continually arising. But God's people, who in their belief and fulfillment of prophecy have acted a part in the proclamation of the first, second, and third angels' messages, know where they stand. They have an experience that is more precious than fine gold. They are to stand firm as a rock, holding the beginning of their confidence steadfast unto the end.—*Selected Messages,* book 2, pp. 108, 109.

Work Faithfully, Using Time Wisely

I must work the works of Him who sent Me while it is day;
the night is coming when no one can work. John 9:4, NKJV.

CHRIST HAS GIVEN to all human beings their work, and we are to acknowledge the wisdom of the plan He has made for us by a hearty cooperation with Him. It is in a life of service only that true happiness is found. Those who live useless, selfish lives are miserable. They are dissatisfied with themselves and with everyone else.

True, unselfish, consecrated workers gladly use their highest gifts in the lowliest service. They realize that true service means to see and to perform the duties that God points out.

There are many who are not satisfied with the work that God has given them. They are not satisfied to serve Him pleasantly in the place that He has marked out for them, or to do uncomplainingly the work that He has placed in their hands.

It is right for us to be dissatisfied with the way in which we perform duty, but we are not to be dissatisfied with the duty itself [simply] because we would rather do something else. In His providence God places before human beings service that will be as medicine to their diseased minds. Thus He seeks to lead them to put aside the selfish preferences which, if cherished, would disqualify them for the work He has for them. If they accept and perform this service, their minds will be cured. But if they refuse it, they will be left at strife with themselves and with others.

The Lord disciplines His workers, so that they will be prepared to fill the places appointed them. He desires to mold their minds in accordance with His will. For this purpose He brings to them test and trial. Some He places where relaxed discipline and overindulgence will not become their snare, where they are taught to appreciate the value of time, and to make the best and wisest use of it.—*Manuscript Releases,* vol. 8, pp. 422, 423.

Submit to God's Training Process

Beware lest you also fall from your own steadfastness . . . ; but grow in the grace
and knowledge of our Lord and Savior Jesus Christ. 2 Peter 3:17, 18, NKJV.

THERE ARE SOME who desire to be a ruling power, and who need the sanctification of submission. God brings about a change in their lives, and perhaps places before them duties that they would not choose. If they are willing to be guided by Him, He will give them grace and strength to perform the objectionable duties in a spirit of submission and helpfulness. They are being qualified to fill places where their disciplined abilities will make them of the greatest service.

God trains some by bringing to them disappointment and apparent failure. It is His purpose that they shall learn to master difficulty. He inspires them with a determination to make every apparent failure prove a success.

Often men and women pray and weep because of the perplexities and obstacles that confront them. But if they will hold the beginning of their confidence steadfast unto the end, He will make their way clear. Success will come to them as they struggle against apparently insurmountable difficulties; and with success will come the greatest joy.

Many are ignorant of how to work for God, not because they need to be ignorant, but because they are not willing to submit to His training process. Moab is spoken of as a failure because, the Word declares, he "hath been at ease from his youth, . . . and hath not been emptied from vessel to vessel, . . . therefore his taste remained in him, and his scent is not changed" (Jer. 48:11). . . .

The Christian is to be prepared for the doing of a work that reveals kindness, forbearance, longsuffering, gentleness, patience. The cultivation of these precious gifts is to come into the discipline-life of Christians, that when called to service by the Master, they may be ready to exercise the energies of heart and mind in helping and blessing those who are ready to die [those who need salvation].—*Manuscript Releases,* vol. 8, pp. 423, 424.

Improving
Opportunities for Service

Whereas you do not know what will happen tomorrow. For what is your life? It is even a vapor that appears for a little time and then vanishes away. James 4:14, NKJV.

THERE IS NO RELIGION in the enthronement of self. God asks us to be *true* to Him, to trade upon the talents He has given us, that we may gain others. His will must be made our will in all things. Any departure from this standard degrades our moral nature. It may result in lifting us up, in enriching us, and in seating us beside princes; but in the eyes of God we are unclean and unholy. We have sold our birthright for selfish interest and gain, and in the books of heaven it is written of us, Weighed in the balances of the sanctuary, and found wanting.

But if we regard our talents as the Lord's gifts, and use them in His service by showing compassion and love toward our fellow beings, we are channels through which God's blessings flow to the world; and at the last great day we shall be greeted with the words "Well done, good and faithful servant; thou hast been faithful over a few things, I will make thee ruler over many things; enter thou into the joy of thy Lord."

Time, laden with precious, golden opportunities for serving the Lord, is fast passing into eternity. . . . Are you improving these opportunities as they pass? You cannot afford to slight them; for you must stand before the judgment seat of God, to answer for the deeds done in the body. Do your words cheer and encourage those who come to you for help and comfort? Does your influence strengthen those with whom you associate? Are your possessions faithfully given to the Lord?

Consecrate yourself today to the Lord's service. . . . Cast your care upon the Lord, and on no account allow the things of the world to separate you from Him. Consecrate all you have and are to Him. This is but "your reasonable service." Do not delay; for there is peril in a moment's delay. A few more years at the longest will be yours to work for the Master, and then the voice which you cannot refuse to answer will be heard, saying, "Give an account of thy stewardship."—*Signs of the Times,* Jan. 21, 1897.

Regularity and Promptness Are Religious Duties

To this end I also labor, striving according to His working which works in me mightily. Colossians 1:29, NKJV.

GOD HAS ENTRUSTED His sacred work to human beings, and He asks that they shall do it carefully. . . . They press too many things into their life, postpone until tomorrow that which demands their attention today, and much time is lost in painfully picking up the lost stitches. Men and women can reach a higher degree of usefulness than to carry with them through life an unsettled state of mind. They can improve the defective traits of their character contracted in their younger years. Like Paul, they can labor to reach a much higher degree of perfection.

The work of God must not be done by fits and starts. It will not be placed on vantage ground by following a sudden impulse. On the contrary, it is positively necessary to follow the good work patiently, day by day, progressing in our ways and methods. One should get up at a regular hour. If during the day the work is neglected, and the following night is spent in making up for lost time, the morrow and following day will show, as a result, a wearied brain and a general fatigue which constitute positive violations of the law of life and health.

There should be regular hours for rising, for family worship, for meals, and for work. And it is a religious duty . . . to maintain this by precept . . . by a firm example. Many squander the most precious hours of the morning hoping that they can terminate the work thus neglected during the hours which should be devoted to sleep. Godliness, health, success, everything suffers from this lack of true religious system. . . .

Some workers need to give up the slow methods of work which prevail, and to learn to be prompt. Promptness is necessary, as well as diligence. If we wish to accomplish the work according to the will of God, it must be done in an expeditious manner, but not without thought and care.—*Manuscript Releases,* vol. 8, pp. 326, 327.

Every Hour Is Valuable

How long will you slumber, O sluggard?
When will you rise from your sleep? Proverbs 6:9, NKJV.
Go to the ant. . . . Consider her ways and be wise. Verse 6, NKJV.

GOD HAS NO USE for lazy men or women in His cause; He wants thoughtful, kind, affectionate, earnest workers. Active exertion will do our preachers good. Indolence is proof of depravity. Every faculty of the mind, every bone in the body, every muscle of the limbs, shows that God designed our faculties to be used, not to remain inactive. . . . Those who will unnecessarily take the hours of daylight for sleep have no sense of the value of precious, golden moments. . . .

Persons who have not acquired habits of close industry and economy of time should have set rules to prompt them to regularity and dispatch. George Washington [the first United States president] was enabled to perform a great amount of business because he was thorough in preserving order and regularity. Every paper had its date and its place, and no time was lost in looking up what had been mislaid.

Men and women of God must be diligent in study, earnest in the acquirement of knowledge, never wasting an hour. Through persevering exertion they may rise to almost any degree of eminence as Christians, as people of power and influence. But many will never attain superior rank in the pulpit or in business, because of their unfixedness of purpose, and the laxness of habits contracted in their youth. Careless inattention is seen in everything they undertake. A sudden impulse now and then is not sufficient to accomplish a reformation in these ease-loving, indolent ones; this is a work which requires patient continuance in well-doing. Persons of business can be truly successful only by having regular hours for rising, for prayer, for meals, and for retiring. If order and regularity are essential in worldly business, how much more so in the work of God!

The bright morning hours are wasted by many in bed. These precious hours, once lost, are gone never to return; they are lost for time and for eternity. Only one hour lost each day, and what a waste of time in the course of a year! Let slumberers think of this, and pause to consider how they will give an account to God for lost opportunities.—*Gospel Workers,* pp. 277, 278.

Buried Talents
Should Be Used

Walk in wisdom toward those who are outside, redeeming the time.
Let your speech always be with grace, seasoned with salt, that you may
know how you ought to answer each one. Colossians 4:5, 6, NKJV.

SEEK CONVERSION OF body, soul, and spirit. Unfold your napkin, and begin to trade with your Lord's goods. In so doing, you will gain other talents. Every soul entrusted with talents is to use them to benefit others. Who in the great day of final reckoning will say, "I was afraid, and went and hid thy talent in the earth: lo, there thou hast that is thine"? To such the Lord will say, "Thou wicked and slothful servant . . . : thou oughtest therefore to have put my money to the exchangers, and then at my coming I should have received mine own with usury."

The Lord is still calling those who are apparently blind to their deficiencies, the self-complacent ones, who plan and devise how they can best serve themselves. God help the spiritually blind to see that there is a world to be saved. The truth is to be made manifest to those who know it not, and this work calls for the self-denying grace of Christ.

Thousands who are now of no use in God's cause should be digging up their buried talents, and putting them out to the exchangers. Those who think that they will surely reach heaven while they follow their own ways and imaginations might better break the seal, and reexamine their title to the treasures of heaven. The men and women who feel at ease in Zion might better become anxious about themselves, and inquire: What am I doing in the Lord's vineyard? Why am I not yoked up with Christ, a laborer together with God? Why am I not learning in Christ's school His meekness and lowliness of heart? Why have I no burdens to bear in the service of Christ? Why am I not a decided Christian, employing all my powers in laboring for the salvation of the souls who are perishing around me? Saith not the Word, "We are labourers together with God: ye are God's husbandry, ye are God's building"? Shall I not with God's help build a character for time and eternity, and promote godliness in myself and in others through the sanctification of the truth?—*Review and Herald*, Aug. 21, 1900.

How to "Redeem" Time

See then that you walk circumspectly, not as fools but as wise, redeeming the time, because the days are evil. Ephesians 5:15, 16, NKJV.

THE VALUE OF TIME is beyond computation. Christ regarded every moment as precious, and it is thus that we should regard it. Life is too short to be trifled away. We have but a few days of probation in which to prepare for eternity. We have no time to waste, no time to devote to selfish pleasure, no time for the indulgence of sin. It is now that we are to form characters for the future, immortal life. It is now that we are to prepare for the searching judgment.

The human family have scarcely begun to live when they begin to die, and the world's incessant labor ends in nothingness unless a true knowledge in regard to eternal life is gained. The people who appreciate time as their working day will fit themselves for a mansion and for a life that is immortal. It is well that they were born.

We are admonished to redeem the time. But time squandered can never be recovered. We cannot call back even one moment. The only way in which we can redeem our time is by making the most of that which remains, by being coworkers with God in His great plan of redemption. In those who do this, a transformation of character takes place. They become sons and daughters of God, members of the royal family, children of the heavenly King. They are fitted to be companions of the angels.

Now is our time to labor for the salvation of others. There are some who think that if they give money to the cause of Christ, this is all they are required to do; the precious time in which they might do personal service for Him passes unimproved. But it is the privilege and duty of all who have health and strength to render to God active service. All are to labor in winning souls to Christ. Donations of money cannot take the place of this. . . .

The opportunity that is now ours to speak to some needy soul the word of life may never offer again. God may say to that one, "This night thy soul shall be required of thee," and through our neglect he or she may not be ready (Luke 12:20). In the great judgment day, how shall we render our account to God?—*Christ's Object Lessons*, pp. 342, 343.

Use Even One
Talent Wisely

"I was afraid, and went and hid your talent in the ground. Look, there you have
what is yours." But his lord answered and said to him, "You wicked and lazy servant.
. . . You ought to have deposited my money with the bankers, and at my coming
I would have received back my own with interest." Matthew 25:25-27, NKJV.

NONE SHOULD MOURN that they have not larger talents. When they use to the glory of God the talents He has given them, they will improve. It is no time now to bemoan our position in life, and excuse our neglect to improve our abilities because we have not another's ability and position, saying, Oh, if I had his or her gift and ability, I might invest a large capital for my Master. If such persons use their one talent wisely and well, that is all the Master requires of them.

Look into our churches. There are only a few real workers in them. The majority are irresponsible men and women. They feel no burden for souls. They manifest no hungering and thirsting for righteousness. They never lift when the work goes hard. These are the ones who have but one talent, and hide that one in a napkin, and bury it in the world; that is, they use all the influence they have in their temporal matters. In seeking the things of this life, they lose the future, eternal life, the far more exceeding and eternal weight of glory. What can be said and done to arouse this class of church members to feel their accountability to God? Must the mass of professed Christian commandment keepers hear the fearful words "Cast ye the unprofitable servant into outer darkness; there shall be weeping and gnashing of teeth"?

Every man and woman and child should be a worker for God. Where there is now one who feels the burden of souls there should be one hundred. What can we do to arouse the people to improve what influence and means they already have to the glory of the Master? Let those who have one talent use that well, and in so doing they will find it doubled. God will accept "according to that a man hath, and not according to that he hath not."—*Review and Herald,* Mar. 14, 1878.

Use Abilities and
Means for God's Glory

*To all those who have, more will be given, and they will have
an abundance; but from those who have nothing, even what
they have will be taken away. Matthew 25:29, NRSV.*

THERE ALWAYS HAS BEEN, and there always will be, diversity of gifts. It is not the great gifts alone that God requires and accepts, but He calls for the smaller talents, and will accept them if men and women will use them to His glory. Have we not become servants of the Master by His grace? It is not, then, our own property that is entrusted to us, but the Lord's talents. The capital is His, and we are responsible for its use or its abuse.

I hope efforts will be made in every church to arouse those who are doing nothing. May God make these realize that He will require of them the one talent with improvement; and if they neglect to gain other talents besides the one, they will meet with the loss of that one talent and their own souls also. We hope to see a change in our churches.

The Householder is preparing to return and call His stewards to account for the talents He has entrusted to them. God pity the do-nothings then! Those who hear the welcome applaudit "Well done, good and faithful servant" will have well done in the improvement of their abilities and means to the glory of God. Who will come up to the help of the Lord, to the help of the Lord against the mighty?

Satan is active, persevering, a faithful general in his work, leading on his armies. He has his faithful sentinels everywhere. What are the servants of Jesus Christ doing? Have they the armor on? Are they vigilant and faithful to meet and resist the strong forces of the enemy? Or are they asleep, expecting another to do their work? . . .

Let all awake; for the time is at hand when it will be said, "He which is filthy, let him be filthy still; and he that is righteous, let him be righteous still; and he that is holy, let him be holy still." Just now is the time to seek purity and holiness of character, and obtain white robes, that we may be prepared for a seat at the marriage supper of the Lamb.—*Review and Herald,* Mar. 14, 1878.

A Time for
Vigilant Work

And do this, knowing the time, that now it is high time to awake out of sleep;
for now our salvation is nearer than when we first believed. Romans 13:11, NKJV.

THERE IS ANOTHER class who meet with loss because they are indolent, and spend their powers in pleasing themselves, in using their tongues, and letting their muscles rust with inaction. They waste their opportunities by inaction, and do not glorify God. They might do much if they would put their time and physical strength to use by acquiring means with which to place their children in favorable positions to acquire knowledge; but they would rather let them grow up in ignorance than to exercise their own God-given ability to do something whereby their children might be blessed with a good education. Such men and women are being weighed in the balances of the heavenly sanctuary and found wanting.

There is something for everyone to do in this world of ours. The Lord is coming, and our waiting is to be not a time of idle expectation, but of vigilant work. We are not to spend our time wholly in prayerful meditation, neither are we to drive and hurry and work as if this were required in order that we should gain heaven, while neglecting to devote time to the cultivation of personal piety. There must be a combination of meditation and diligent work. As God has expressed it in His Word, we are to be "not slothful in business; fervent in spirit; serving the Lord." Worldly activities are not to crowd out the service of the Lord. The soul needs the riches of the grace of God, and the body needs physical exercise, in order to accomplish the work that must be done for the promulgation of the gospel of Christ.

Those who cultivate a spirit of idleness commit sin against God every day; for they do not put to use the power God has given them with which to bless themselves, and to be a blessing to their families. Parents should teach their children that the Lord means them to be diligent workers, not idlers in His vineyard. They must make a diligent use of their time, if they are to be useful working agents, acting their part in the vineyard of the Lord. They are to be faithful stewards, improving every entrusted gift of power that has been bestowed upon them.—*Home Missionary,* October 1894.

Both Money and Active Service Needed

Speak to the children of Israel, that they bring Me an offering. From everyone who gives it willingly with his heart you shall take My offering. Exodus 25:2, NKJV.

I HAVE HEARD men and women who have been engaged in the work in the publishing houses and sanitarium complain of having to work over hours. If they cannot stop work after eight hours' labor, they become dissatisfied. But these very ones, when they enter business for their own private benefit, will work on fully ten hours as they do in America and often extend their labor to twelve hours. They make no complaint, because it is in their own personal interest. It makes every difference whether the time is to be employed to their own special advantage or for the service of God or their neighbor. . . .

Willing service in saving the means that is so limited is more satisfactory than hoarding means. With the right motive in view, such time would be reckoned as devoted to the service of God. This definite work for God in building, in planting, in reaping harvest, or any line of work, will cost considerable thought and labor. But it pays. God will multiply the resources; He will help in producing the means.

Many are already working in this line, and have always done so. The devotion of time to God in any line of work is a most important consideration. Some can use the pen to write a letter to some far-off friend. By consecrated personal labor we may in many ways do personal service for God.

Some think that if they give a portion of their money to the cause of God, this is all they are required to do, and the precious time given them of God, in which they could do hours of personal service for Him, passes by unimproved. It is the privilege and duty of all who have health and strength to render to God active service. The giving of donations in money cannot take the place of this. Those who have no money can substitute personal labor, and even money can be made in various ways in this work.

Everyone may be a laborer together with God. The hours which have been usually spent in recreation that has not rested or refreshed either body or soul may be spent in seeking to help some poor soul who is in need of help, in visiting the poor, the sick, and the suffering. Our time is God's, and as Christians, we must use it to the glory of God.—*Manuscript Releases, vol. 6, pp. 79, 80.*

Work for Low Wages
Rather Than Be Idle

But he answered one of them and said, "Friend, I am doing you no wrong.
Did you not agree with me for a denarius? Take what is yours and go your way.
I wish to give to this last man the same as to you." Matthew 20:13, 14, NKJV.

GOD HAS GRACIOUSLY entrusted us with twenty-four hours in each day and night. This is a precious treasure by which much good can be accomplished. How are we using God's golden opportunities? We must, as Christians, set the Lord always before us, if we would not lose precious hours in uselessness, and have nothing to show for our time.

Time is money. If people refuse to work because they cannot obtain the highest wages, they are pronounced idlers. Far better would it be for them to work, even if they receive much less than they suppose their labors are worth.

Time is a talent committed to our trust that may be shamefully misused. Every child of God, man, woman, youth or child, should consider and appreciate the value of the moments of time. If they do this, they will keep themselves employed, even if they do not receive as high wages as they have been able to command. They should show their appreciation of diligence, and work, receiving what wages they can get. The idea of a poor person with a family refusing to work for moderate wages, because it is not showing, as he or she supposes, sufficient dignity for their trade, is folly that is not to be encouraged.

How little thought has been bestowed upon this subject. How much greater prosperity might have attended the missionary enterprises if this talent of time had been thoughtfully considered and faithfully used. We are each one answerable to God for the time that has been wantonly thrown away, and for the use of which we must give an account to God. This is a stewardship that has been but little appreciated; many think it not sin to waste hours and days in doing nothing to benefit themselves or to bless others.—*Manuscript Releases,* vol. 6, pp. 80, 81.

Every Spiritual Gift Is Important

There are diversities of gifts, but the same Spirit. And there are differences of administrations, but the same Lord. 1 Corinthians 12:4, 5.

STUDY THIS SCRIPTURE carefully. God has not given to everyone the same line of work. It is His plan that there shall be unity in diversity. When His plan is studied and followed, there will be far less friction in the working of the cause.

"There are many members in the body, and all the members have not the same office, but each one is essential to the perfection of the work." "The body is not one member, but many. If the foot shall say, Because I am not the hand, I am not of the body; is it therefore not of the body? And if the ear shall say, Because I am not the eye, I am not of the body; is it therefore not of the body? If the whole body were an eye, where were the hearing? If the whole were hearing, where were the smelling? But now hath God set the members every one of them in the body, as it hath pleased him. And if they were all one member, where were the body?"

"Now ye are the body of Christ, and members in particular. And God hath set some in the church, first apostles, secondarily prophets, thirdly teachers, after that miracles, then gifts of healing, helps, governments, diversities of tongues."

The Lord desires His church to respect every gift that He has bestowed on the different members. Let us beware of allowing our minds to become fixed on ourselves, thinking that other people cannot be serving the Lord unless they are working on the same lines as those on which we are working.

Never is a worker to say, "I do not want to work with such a one, because he does not see things as I do. I wish to work with someone who will agree with all I say, and follow out all my ideas." The one the worker thus refuses to connect with may have truths to present that have not yet been presented. Because of the worker's refusal to accept the help provided by the Lord, the work is made one-sided.—*Pacific Union Recorder,* Dec. 29, 1904.

Be Satisfied
With Humble Work

Having then gifts differing according to the grace that is given to us, let us use them:
if prophecy, let us prophesy in proportion to our faith. Romans 12:6, NKJV.

BOTH WOMEN AND MEN may accomplish a good work for God, if they will first learn the precious, all-important lesson of meekness in the school of Christ. They will be able to benefit humanity by presenting to them the all-sufficiency of Jesus. When all the members of the church realize their own individual responsibility, when they humbly take up the work which presents itself before them, the work will go on to success. God has given to all human beings their work according to their several abilities.

It will not be an easy task to work for the Master in this age. But how much perplexity might be saved, if workers continually relied upon God, and duly considered the directions that God has given. He says, "Having then gifts differing according to the grace that is given to us, whether prophecy, let us prophesy according to the proportion of faith; or ministry, let us wait on our ministering: or he that teacheth, on teaching; or he that exhorteth, on exhortation: he that giveth, let him do it with simplicity; he that ruleth, with diligence; he that sheweth mercy, with cheerfulness" (Rom. 12:6-8).

This is a subject that demands close, critical study. Many mistakes are made because people do not heed this instruction. Many who are entrusted with some humble line of work to do for the Master soon become dissatisfied, and think that they should be teachers and leaders. They want to leave their humble ministering, which is just as important in its place as the larger responsibilities. Those who are set to do visiting soon come to think that anyone can do that work, that anyone can speak words of sympathy and encouragement, and lead others in a humble, quiet way to a correct understanding of the Scriptures. But it is a work that demands much grace, much patience, and an ever-increasing stock of wisdom.—*Manuscript Releases,* vol. 11, pp. 278, 279.

Every Person Has a Gift and Is Accountable

Whatever your hand finds to do, do it with your might; for there is no work or device or knowledge or wisdom in the grave where you are going. Ecclesiastes 9:10, NKJV.

THE PARABLE OF the talents should be a matter of the most careful and prayerful study; for it has a personal and individual application to every man, woman, and child possessed of the powers of reason. Your obligation and responsibility are in proportion to the talents God has bestowed upon you. There is not a follower of Christ but has some peculiar gift for the use of which he or she is accountable to God.

Many have excused themselves from rendering their gift to the service of Christ, because others were possessed of superior endowments and advantages. The opinion has prevailed that only those who are especially talented are required to sanctify their abilities to the service of God. It has come to be understood that talents are given only to a certain favored class, to the exclusion of others who, of course, are not called upon to share in the toils or rewards.

But it is not so represented in the parable. When the master of the house called his servants, he gave to every man *his* work. The whole family of God are included in the responsibility of using their Lord's goods. Every individual, from the lowliest and most obscure to the greatest and most exalted, is a moral agent endowed with abilities for which they are accountable to God. To a greater or less degree, all are placed in charge of the talents of their Lord. The spiritual, mental, and physical ability, the influence, station, possessions, affections, sympathies, all are precious talents to be used in the cause of the Master for the salvation of souls for whom Christ died. . . .

God requires everyone to be a worker in His vineyard. You are to take up the work that has been placed in your charge, and to do it faithfully. "Whatsoever thy hand findeth to do, do it with thy might; for there is no work, nor device, nor knowledge, nor wisdom, in the grave, whither thou goest."—*Review and Herald,* May 1, 1888.

Small Talents Have
Value and Can Increase

The words of the wise are like goads, and the words of scholars are like well-driven nails, given by one Shepherd. Ecclesiastes 12:11, NKJV.

LET BUSINESS MEN or women do business in a way that will glorify their Master because of their fidelity. Let them carry their religion into everything that is done and reveal to others the Spirit of Christ. Let the mechanic be a diligent and faithful representative of Him who toiled in the lowly walks of life in the cities of Judea. Let everyone who names the name of Christ so work, that others by seeing their good works may be led to glorify their Creator and Redeemer. "Whatsoever ye do, do it heartily, as to the Lord." Let the upbuilding of the kingdom of Christ be your constant thought, and let every effort be directed toward this one end.

Those who have been blessed with superior talents should not depreciate the value of the services of those who are less gifted than themselves. The smallest trust is a trust from God. The one talent, through diligent use with the blessing of God, will be doubled, and the two used in the service of Christ will be increased to four; and thus the humblest instrument may grow in power and usefulness. The earnest purpose, the self-denying efforts, are all seen, appreciated, and accepted by the God of heaven. "Take heed that ye despise not one of these little ones." God alone can estimate the worth of their service, and see the far-reaching influence of those who work for the glory of their Maker.

We are to make the very best use of our opportunities, and to study to show ourselves approved unto God. God will accept our best efforts; but let no one imagine He will be pleased with ignorance and inability when, with proper improvement of privileges bestowed, a better service might be supplied. We are not to despise the day of small things; but by a diligent care and perseverance, we are to make the small opportunities and talents minister to our advancement in divine life, and hasten us on to a more intelligent and better service.—*Review and Herald,* May 1, 1888.

Work Faithfully
Where You Are

*So then, each of us will be accountable to God. Let us therefore
no longer pass judgment on one another. Romans 14:12, 13, NRSV.*

WHEN WE HAVE done all that we can do, we are to count ourselves unprofitable servants. There is no room for pride in our efforts; for we are
dependent every moment upon the grace of God, and we have nothing
that we did not receive. Says Jesus, "Without me ye can do nothing."

We are responsible only for the talents which God has bestowed upon
us. The Lord does not reprove the servants who have doubled their talents, who have done according to their ability. Those who thus prove
their fidelity can be commended and rewarded; but those who loiter in
the vineyard, those who do nothing, or do negligently the work of the
Lord, make manifest their real interest in the work to which they have
been called, by their works. . . . The talent given to them for the glory of
God and the salvation of souls has been unappreciated and abused. The
good it might have done is left unaccomplished, and the Lord cannot receive His own with usury.

Let none mourn that they have not larger talents to use for the Master.
While you are dissatisfied and complaining, you are losing precious time
and wasting valuable opportunities. Thank God for the ability you have,
and pray that you may be enabled to meet the responsibilities that have
been placed upon you. If you desire greater usefulness, go to work and acquire what you mourn for. Go to work with steady patience, and do your
very best, irrespective of what others are doing. "Every one of us shall give
account of himself to God." Let not your thought or your words be "O
that I had a larger work! O that I were in this or that position!"

Do your duty where you are. Make the best investments possible
with your entrusted gift in the very place where your work will count
the most before God. Put away all murmuring and strife. Labor not for
the supremacy. Be not envious of the talents of others; for that will not
increase your ability to do a good or a great work. Use your gift in
meekness, in humility, in trusting faith, and wait till the day of reckoning, and you will have no cause for grief or shame.—*Review and Herald,*
May 1, 1888.

Working With Jesus
to Save the Lost

Behold, I am coming quickly, and My reward is with Me, to give to every one according to his work. Revelation 22:12, NKJV.

THE LORD JESUS will scrutinize every talent, and expect interest in proportion to the amount of capital entrusted. By His own humiliation and agony, Christ has paid the purchase money for our salvation, and He has a right to our services. The very name of servant implies the doing of work, the bearing of responsibility. All our capabilities, all our opportunities, have been entrusted to us for wise improvement, that Christ may receive His own with usury.

The heavenly Master ascended on high, and led captivity captive, and gave gifts unto men and women—divine treasures of truth to be presented to all the world. What use are we individually making of these gifts, the talents in our hands? Are we like the unwise and unfaithful servant, burying these talents in the world, where they will bring no returns to God? It behooves all with careful fidelity to improve the talents entrusted to them; for talents will increase as they are used for the good of humanity and the glory of God.

Every soul should seek first the kingdom of God and His righteousness. We are not to use up all the strength of brain, bone, and muscle in worldly business interests; for if we do, we imperil our spiritual interests, and we shall lose an eternity of bliss. The whole unfallen universe is interested in the great work which Jesus came to our world to accomplish, even the salvation of our souls. And shall not mortals on earth cooperate with our Redeemer, who has ascended into heaven to make intercession for us? Shall we show no special zeal, no devoted interest, in the work that was devised in heaven to be carried forward in the world for the good of men and women? Shall we who have been bought with the precious blood of Christ refuse to do the work left in our hands—refuse to cooperate with the heavenly agencies in the work of saving the fallen? Shall we not go even to the ends of the earth to let the light of truth given to us of heaven shine forth to our fellow human beings?—*Review and Herald*, Jan. 24, 1893.

One Talent, Used Faithfully, Will Gain Other Talents

The kingdom of heaven is like a man traveling to a far country, who called his own servants and delivered his goods to them. And to one he gave five talents, to another two, and to another one, to each according to his own ability; and immediately he went on a journey. Matthew 25:14, 15, NKJV.

LET NOT THE WORK that needs to be done wait for the ordination of ministers. If there are not ministers to take up the work, let men and women of intelligence, with no thought of how they can accumulate the most property, establish themselves in these cities and towns, and lift up the standard of the cross, using the knowledge they have gained in winning souls to the truth.

The knowledge of the truth is altogether too precious to be hoarded up, and bound about, and hid in the earth. Even the one talent entrusted by the Master is to be faithfully employed to gain other talents also. Where are the men and women who have been refreshed with rich streams of blessing from the throne of God? Let them ask themselves what they have done to communicate this light to those who have not had like advantages. How will those who have neglected to use their talents stand in the judgment, when every motive will be brought under scrutiny? The heavenly Master has committed to every one of His servants talents. "And unto one he gave five talents, to another two, and to another one; to every man according to his several ability."

God has not given talents to merely a chosen few, but to everyone He has committed some peculiar gift to be used in His service. Many to whom the Lord has given precious talents have refused to employ them for the advancement of the kingdom of God; nevertheless, they are under obligation to God for their use of His gifts. Everyone, whether serving God or pleasing self, is a possessor of some trust, whose proper use will bring glory to God and whose perverted use will rob the Giver. That possessors of talents do not acknowledge God's claims upon them does not make their guilt the less. If they choose to stand under the black banner of the prince of darkness through this life, they will stand unconfessed by Christ in the day of final accounts.—*Signs of the Times,* Jan. 23, 1893.

Faithful Users of Talents
Will Hear "Well Done"

*The one who had received the five talents went off at once and traded
with them, and made five more talents. In the same way, the one who had
the two talents made two more talents. Matthew 25:16, 17, NRSV.*

"GOD SO LOVED the world, that he gave his only begotten Son, that
whosoever believeth in him should not perish, but have everlasting life."
The ransom money has been paid for every son and daughter of Adam, and
[the fact] that those who have been ransomed by the precious blood of
Christ refuse allegiance to Him will not shield them from the retribution
that will come upon them in the last day. They will have to answer for
their neglect to use their entrusted talents for the Master. They will have
to answer for their reproaches against their Maker and Redeemer, and for
their robbery of God in withholding their talents from His service, and
burying their Lord's goods in the earth.

The human family is composed of responsible moral agents, and from
the highest and most gifted to the lowest and most obscure, all are invested
with the goods of heaven. Time is an entrusted gift of God, and is to be
diligently employed in the service of Christ. Influence is a gift of God, and
is to be exerted for the forwarding of the highest, noblest purposes. Christ
died on Calvary's cross that all our influence might be used to lift Him up
before a perishing world. Those who behold the Majesty of heaven dying
on the cross for their transgressions will value their influence only as it
draws men and women to Christ, and they will use it for this purpose only.
Intellect is an entrusted talent. Sympathy and affection are talents to be sacredly guarded and improved, that we may render service to Him whose
purchased possession we are.

All that we are or can be belongs to God. Education, discipline, and
skill in every line should be used for Him. . . . Whether the amount entrusted is large or small, the Lord requires that His householders do their
best. It is not the amount entrusted or the improvement made that brings
to men and women the approbation of heaven, but it is the faithfulness,
the loyalty to God, the loving service rendered, that brings the divine
benediction "Well done, good and faithful servant; thou hast been faithful
over a few things, I will make thee ruler over many things; enter thou into
the joy of thy Lord." This reward of joy does not wait until our entrance
into the City of God, but the faithful servant has a foretaste of it even in
this life.—*Signs of the Times,* Jan. 23, 1893.

Use Well the Talent of Speech

You are fairer than the sons of men; grace is poured upon Your lips;
therefore God has blessed You forever. Psalm 45:2, NKJV.

BY DILIGENT EFFORT all may acquire the power to read intelligibly, and to speak in a full, clear, round tone, in a distinct and impressive manner. By doing this we may greatly increase our efficiency as workers for Christ.

Every Christian is called to make known to others the unsearchable riches of Christ; therefore all should seek for perfection in speech. They should present the Word of God in a way that will commend it to the hearers. God does not design that His human channels shall be uncouth. It is not His will that human beings shall belittle or degrade the heavenly current that flows through Him to the world.

We should look to Jesus, the perfect pattern; we should pray for the aid of the Holy Spirit, and in His strength we should seek to train every organ for perfect work.

Especially is this true of those who are called to public service. Every minister and every teacher should bear in mind that they are giving to the people a message that involves eternal interests. The truth spoken will judge them in the great day of final reckoning. And with some souls the manner of the one delivering the message will determine its reception or rejection. Then let the Word be so spoken that it will appeal to the understanding and impress the heart. Slowly, distinctly, and solemnly should it be spoken, yet with all the earnestness which its importance demands.

The right culture and use of the power of speech has to do with every line of Christian work; it enters into the home life, and into all our relations with one another. We should accustom ourselves to speak in pleasant tones, to use pure and correct language, and words that are kind and courteous. Sweet, kind words are as dew and gentle showers to the soul. The Scripture says of Christ that grace was poured into His lips that He might "know how to speak a word in season to him that is weary" (Isa. 50:4).—*Christ's Object Lessons*, pp. 335, 336.

Reveal Jesus' Love
Through Speech

*The Lord God has given Me the tongue of the learned, that I should know
how to speak a word in season to him who is weary. Isaiah 50:4, NKJV.*

ALL AROUND US are afflicted souls. Here and there, everywhere, we
may find them. Let us search out these suffering ones and speak a word in
season to comfort their hearts. Let us ever be channels through which shall
flow the refreshing waters of compassion.

In all our associations it should be remembered that in the experience
of others there are chapters sealed from mortal sight. On the pages of memory are sad histories that are sacredly guarded from curious eyes. There stand
registered long, hard battles with trying circumstances, perhaps troubles in
the home life, that day by day weaken courage, confidence, and faith.
Those who are fighting the battle of life at great odds may be strengthened
and encouraged by little attentions that cost only a loving effort. To such
the strong, helpful grasp of the hand by a true friend is worth more than
gold or silver. Words of kindness are as welcome as the smile of angels.

There are multitudes struggling with poverty, compelled to labor hard
for small wages, and able to secure but the barest necessities of life. Toil
and deprivation, with no hope of better things, make their burden very
heavy. When pain and sickness are added, the burden is almost insupport-
able. Careworn and oppressed, they know not where to turn for relief.
Sympathize with them in their trials, their heartaches, and disappoint-
ments. This will open the way for you to help them. Speak to them of
God's promises, pray with and for them, inspire them with hope. . . .

Be coworkers with Him. While distrust and alienation are pervading
the world, Christ's disciples are to reveal the spirit that reigns in heaven.
Speak as He would speak, act as He would act. Constantly reveal the
sweetness of His character. Reveal that wealth of love which underlies all
His teachings and all His dealings with humanity. The humblest workers,
in cooperation with Christ, may touch chords whose vibrations shall ring
to the ends of the earth and make melody throughout eternal ages.—*The
Ministry of Healing,* pp. 158, 159.

Use Responsibly the Gifts of Speech and Influence

Meanwhile praying also for us, that God would open to us a door for the word, to speak the mystery of Christ, for which I am also in chains, that I may make it manifest, as I ought to speak. Colossians 4:3, 4, NKJV.

GOD HAS NOT given talents capriciously. He who knows all things, who is acquainted with each one, has given to every person his or her work. Those to whom He has entrusted much are not to boast, for what they possess is not their own; it is lent them on trial; and the greater the endowment, the greater the returns required. Day by day God is testing men and women, to see whether they will acknowledge Him as the giver of all that they have. He watches to see whether they will prove themselves worthy of eternal riches. The use they make of their precious endowments decides their destiny for eternity.

Of all the gifts that God has bestowed upon His children, none is capable of being a greater blessing than the gift of speech. With the tongue we convince and persuade; with it we offer prayer and praise to God; and with it we tell others of the Redeemer's love. God would have us consecrate this gift to His service, speaking only such words as will help those around us. And if Christ rules in our hearts, our words will reveal the purity, beauty, and fragrance of a character molded and fashioned by Him. But if we are under the guidance of the enemy of all good, our words will echo his sentiments. Watch well your words. Consecrate your gift of speech to the Lord's service; for He will one day require it at your hands.

Every one of us exerts an influence on those with whom we come in contact. This influence we have from God, and we are responsible for the way it is used. God designs that it shall tell on the side of right; but it rests with each one of us to decide whether our influence shall be pure and elevating, or whether it shall act as a poisonous malaria. Those who are partakers of the divine nature exert an influence that is Christlike. Holy angels attend them on their way, and all with whom they come in contact are helped and blessed. But those who do not receive Christ as their personal Savior cannot influence others for good. . . . Such lose all hope of eternal life themselves, and by their example lead others astray. Guard well your influence; it is "your reasonable service" to place it on the Lord's side.—*Signs of the Times, Jan. 21, 1897.*

Speak Winsomely
of the Savior

Let no corrupt communication proceed out of your mouth, but what is good for
necessary edification, that it may impart grace to the hearers. Ephesians 4:29, NKJV.

AS FOLLOWERS OF Christ we should make our words such as to be a
help and an encouragement to one another in the Christian life. Far more
than we do, we need to speak of the precious chapters in our experience.
We should speak of the mercy and loving-kindness of God, of the matchless depths of the Savior's love. Our words should be words of praise and
thanksgiving. If the mind and heart are full of the love of God, this will be
revealed in the conversation.

It will not be a difficult matter to impart that which enters into our
spiritual life. Great thoughts, noble aspirations, clear perceptions of truth,
unselfish purposes, yearnings for piety and holiness, will bear fruit in words
that reveal the character of the heart treasure. When Christ is thus revealed
in our speech, it will have power in winning souls to Him.

We should speak of Christ to those who know Him not. We should
do as Christ did. Wherever He was, in the synagogue, by the wayside, in
the boat thrust out a little from the land, at the Pharisee's feast or the table
of the publican, He spoke to men and women of the things pertaining to
the higher life. The things of nature, the events of daily life, were bound
up by Him with the words of truth. The hearts of His hearers were drawn
to Him; for He had healed their sick, had comforted their sorrowing ones,
and had taken their children in His arms and blessed them. When He
opened His lips to speak, their attention was riveted upon Him, and every
word was to some soul a savor of life unto life.

So it should be with us. Wherever we are, we should watch for opportunities of speaking to others of the Savior. If we follow Christ's example in doing good, hearts will open to us as they did to Him. Not abruptly,
but with tact born of divine love, we can tell them of Him who is the
"chiefest among ten thousand" and the One "altogether lovely" (Cant.
5:10, 16). This is the very highest work in which we can employ the talent of speech. It was given to us that we might present Christ as the sin-
pardoning Savior.—*Christ's Object Lessons,* pp. 338, 339.

Influence—A Power for Good or Evil

Do not grieve the Holy Spirit of God, by whom you were sealed for the day of redemption. . . . Be kind to one another, tenderhearted, forgiving one another, even as God in Christ forgave you. Ephesians 4:30-32, NKJV.

THE LIFE OF CHRIST was an ever-widening, shoreless influence, an influence that bound Him to God and to the whole human family. Through Christ, God has invested men and women with an influence that makes it impossible for them to live for themselves. Individually we are connected with other human beings, a part of God's great whole, and we stand under mutual obligations. No one can be independent of their fellow beings; for the well-being of each affects others. It is God's purpose that each person shall feel necessary to others' welfare, and seek to promote their happiness.

Every soul is surrounded by an atmosphere of its own—an atmosphere, it may be, charged with the life-giving power of faith, courage, and hope, and sweet with the fragrance of love. Or it may be heavy and chill with the gloom of discontent and selfishness, or poisonous with the deadly taint of cherished sin. By the atmosphere surrounding us, every person with whom we come in contact is consciously or unconsciously affected.

This is a responsibility from which we cannot free ourselves. Our words, our acts, our dress, our deportment, even the expression of the countenance, has an influence. Upon the impression thus made there hang results for good or evil which no one can measure. Every impulse thus imparted is seed sown which will produce its harvest. It is a link in the long chain of human events, extending we know not whither.

If by our example we aid others in the development of good principles, we give them power to do good. In their turn they exert the same influence upon others, and they upon still others. Thus by our unconscious influence thousands may be blessed.

Throw a pebble into the lake, and a wave is formed, and another and another; and as they increase, the circle widens, until it reaches the very shore. So with our influence. Beyond our knowledge or control it tells upon others in blessing or in cursing.—*Christ's Object Lessons*, pp. 339, 340.

God's Grace Essential
to Right Use of Influence

Whoever is faithful in a very little is faithful also in much; and whoever is dishonest in a very little is dishonest also in much. Luke 16:10, NRSV.

CHARACTER IS POWER. The silent witness of a true, unselfish, godly life carries an almost irresistible influence. By revealing in our own life the character of Christ we cooperate with Him in the work of saving souls. It is only by revealing in our life His character that we can cooperate with Him. And the wider the sphere of our influence, the more good we may do. When those who profess to serve God follow Christ's example, practicing the principles of the law in their daily life; when every act bears witness that they love God supremely and their neighbor as themselves, then will the church have power to move the world.

But never should it be forgotten that influence is no less a power for evil. To lose one's own soul is a terrible thing; but to cause the loss of other souls is still more terrible. That our influence should be a savor of death unto death is a fearful thought; yet this is possible. Many who profess to gather with Christ are scattering from Him. This is why the church is so weak. Many indulge freely in criticism and accusing. By giving expression to suspicion, jealousy, and discontent, they yield themselves as instruments to Satan. Before they realize what they are doing, the adversary has through them accomplished his purpose. The impression of evil has been made, the shadow has been cast, the arrows of Satan have found their mark. Distrust, unbelief, and downright infidelity have fastened upon those who otherwise might have accepted Christ.

Meanwhile the workers for Satan look complacently upon those whom they have driven to skepticism, and who are now hardened against reproof and entreaty. They flatter themselves that in comparison with these souls they are virtuous and righteous. They do not realize that these sad wrecks of character are the work of their own unbridled tongues and rebellious hearts. It is through their influence that these tempted ones have fallen.

So frivolity, selfish indulgence, and careless indifference on the part of professed Christians are turning away many souls from the path of life. Many there are who will fear to meet at the bar of God the results of their influence. It is only through the grace of God that we can make a right use of this endowment.—*Christ's Object Lessons*, pp. 340, 341.

Our Service Should
Meet Heaven's Approval

If you have not been faithful with what belongs to another, who will give
you what is your own? No slave can serve two masters; for a slave will either
hate the one and love the other, or be devoted to the one and despise the other.
You cannot serve God and wealth. Luke 16:12, 13, NRSV.

THERE ARE MANY who profess to be Christians who are not united with Christ. Their daily life, their spirit, testifies that Christ is not formed within, the hope of glory. They cannot be depended upon, they cannot be trusted. They are anxious to reduce their service to the minimum of effort, and at the same time exact the highest of wages. The name "servant" applies to every person; for we are all servants, and it will be well for us to see what mold we are taking on. Is it the mold of unfaithfulness, or of fidelity?

Is it the disposition generally among servants to do as much as possible? Is it not rather the prevalent fashion to slide through the work as quickly, as easily, as possible, and obtain the wages at as little cost to themselves as they can? The object is not to be as thorough as possible, but to get the remuneration. Those who profess to be the servants of Christ should not forget the injunction of the apostle Paul, "Servants, obey in all things your masters according to the flesh; not with eye-service, as menpleasers; but in singleness of heart, fearing God: and whatsoever ye do, do it heartily, as to the Lord, and not unto men; knowing that of the Lord ye shall receive the reward of the inheritance: for ye serve the Lord Christ."

Those who enter the work as "eye-servants" will find that their work cannot bear the inspection of mortals or of angels. The thing essential for successful work is a knowledge of Christ; for this knowledge will give sound principles of right, [and] impart a noble, unselfish spirit, like that of our Savior whom we profess to serve. Faithfulness, economy, care-taking, thoroughness, should characterize all our work, wherever we may be, whether in the kitchen, in the workshop, in the office of publication, in the sanitarium, in the college, or wherever we are stationed in the vineyard of the Lord. "He that is faithful in that which is least is faithful also in much: and he that is unjust in the least is unjust also in much."—*Review and Herald,* Sept. 22, 1891.

Using God's Gifts as He Wills

Do not be conformed to this world, but be transformed by the renewing of your mind, that you may prove what is that good and acceptable and perfect will of God. Romans 12:2, NKJV.

MANY, INSTEAD OF consecrating their means to God's service, look upon their money as their own, and say that they have a right to use it as they please. Like the inhabitants of the Noachian world, they use God's gifts in their own service. Even some who profess to know and love the Lord do this. God has revealed His will to them. He has called upon them to surrender all that they have to Him; but the love of the world has perverted their will, and hardened their hearts. They refuse to obey Him to whom they owe all that they have. Regardless of His call, they clasp their treasures in their arms, forgetting that the Giver has any claim upon them. Thus the blessings given by God are turned into a curse, because a wrong use is made of them.

Christ understood the danger of the love of money; for He said, "How hard is it for them that trust in riches to enter into the kingdom of God!" . . . Today He calls upon us to give close attention to our eternal interests. He would have us subordinate every earthly interest to His service. "For what shall it profit a man," He asks, "if he shall gain the whole world, and lose his own soul?"

God's right to our service is measured by the infinite sacrifice He has made for our salvation. "Behold, what manner of love the Father hath bestowed upon us, that we should be called the sons of God." For our sake Christ lived a life of sorrow and privation. He was pure and holy, yet on Him was laid the iniquity of us all. . . . With a touch of His hand He healed the sick; yet He suffered grievous bodily pain. He cast out demons with a word, and delivered those bound by Satan's temptations; yet temptations such as have never beset anyone assailed Him. He raised the dead by His power; yet He suffered the agony of a most terrible death.

All this Christ suffered for us. What are we giving Him in return? He, the Majesty of heaven, submitted patiently to scorn and insult. . . . Should we look upon any sacrifice as too great? Should we hesitate to render to God our reasonable service?—*Signs of the Times,* Jan. 21, 1897.

APRIL

❧

Exploring God's Word

No True Wisdom
Apart From God

*Happy are those who find wisdom, and those
who get understanding. Proverbs 3:13, NRSV.*

TRUE WISDOM IS a treasure as lasting as eternity. Many of the world's
so-called wise men and women are wise only in their own estimation.
Content with the acquisition of worldly wisdom, they never enter the garden of God, to become acquainted with the treasures of knowledge contained in His holy Word. Supposing themselves to be wise, they are
ignorant concerning the wisdom which all must have who gain eternal life.
They cherish a contempt for the Book of God, which, if studied and
obeyed, would make them truly wise.

The Bible is to them an impenetrable mystery. The grand, deep truths
of the Old and New Testaments are obscure to them, because spiritual
things are not spiritually discerned. They need to learn that the fear of the
Lord is the beginning of wisdom, and that without this wisdom, their
learning is of little worth.

Those who are striving for an education in the sciences, but who have
not learned the lesson that the fear of God is the beginning of wisdom, are
working helplessly and hopelessly, questioning the reality of everything.
They may acquire an education in the sciences, but unless they gain a
knowledge of the Bible and a knowledge of God, they are without true
wisdom. Unlearned persons, if they know God and Jesus Christ, have a
more enduring wisdom than have the most learned who despise the instruction of God.—*The Seventh-day Adventist Bible Commentary,* Ellen G.
White Comments, vol. 3, p. 1156.

True wisdom is infinitely above the comprehension of the worldly
wise. The hidden wisdom, which is Christ formed within, the hope of
glory, is a wisdom high as heaven. The deep principles of godliness are
sublime and eternal. A Christian experience alone can help us to understand this problem, and obtain the treasures of knowledge which have been
hidden in the counsels of God, but are now made known to all who have
a vital connection with Christ.—*Review and Herald,* July 18, 1899.

The Rewards
of Bible Study

If, after they have escaped the pollutions of the world through the knowledge
of the Lord and Savior Jesus Christ, they are again entangled in them and
overcome, the latter end is worse for them than the beginning. 2 Peter 2:20, NKJV.

GREAT LIGHT WAS given to the Reformers, but many of them received the sophistry of error through misinterpretation of the Scriptures. These errors have come down through the centuries, but although they be hoary with age, yet they have not behind them a "Thus saith the Lord." For the Lord has said, I will not "alter the thing that is gone out of my lips." In His great mercy the Lord has permitted still greater light to shine in these last days. To us He has sent His message, revealing His law and showing us what is truth.

In Christ is the fountain of all knowledge. In Him our hopes of eternal life are centered. He is the greatest teacher the world has ever known, and if we desire to enlarge the minds of the children and youth, and win them, if possible, to a love of the Bible, we should fasten their minds upon the plain and simple truth, digging out that which has been buried beneath the rubbish of tradition, and letting the jewels shine forth. Encourage them to search into these subjects, and the effort put forth will be an invaluable discipline.

The unfolding of God, as represented in Jesus Christ, furnishes a theme that is grand to contemplate, and that will, if studied, sharpen the mind, and elevate and ennoble the faculties. As the human agents learn these lessons in the school of Christ, trying to become as Christ was, meek and lowly of heart, they will learn the most useful of all lessons—that intellect is supreme only as it is sanctified by a living connection with God. . . .

The greatest wisdom, and most essential, is the knowledge of God. Self sinks into insignificance as it contemplates God and Jesus Christ whom He hath sent. The Bible must be made the foundation for all study. Individually we must learn from this lesson book, which God has given us, the condition of the salvation of our souls; for it is the only book that tells us what we must do in order to be saved. Not only this, but from it strength may be received for the intellect.—*Fundamentals of Christian Education,* pp. 450, 451.

The Spirit Must Illuminate the Word

We have received, not the spirit of the world, but the Spirit
who is from God, that we might know the things that have been
freely given to us by God. 1 Corinthians 2:12, NKJV.

GOD INTENDS THAT, even in this life, truth shall be ever unfolding to His people. There is only one way in which this knowledge can be obtained. We can attain to an understanding of God's Word only through the illumination of that Spirit by which the Word was given. "The things of God knoweth no man, but the Spirit of God"; "for the Spirit searcheth all things, yea, the deep things of God." And the Savior's promise to His followers was: "When he, the Spirit of truth, is come, he will guide you into all truth. . . . For he shall receive of mine, and shall shew it unto you."

God desires human beings to exercise their reasoning powers; and the study of the Bible will strengthen and elevate the mind as no other study can do. It is the best mental as well as spiritual exercise for the mind. Yet we are to beware of deifying reason, which is subject to the weakness and infirmity of humanity. If we would not have the Scriptures clouded to our understanding, so that the plainest truths shall not be comprehended, we must have the simplicity and faith of a little child, ready to learn, and beseeching the aid of the Holy Spirit. A sense of the power and wisdom of God, and of our inability to comprehend His greatness, should inspire us with humility, and we should open His Word, as we would enter His presence, with holy awe. When we come to the Bible, reason must acknowledge an authority superior to itself, and heart and intellect must bow to the great I AM.

We shall advance in true spiritual knowledge only as we realize our own littleness and our entire dependence upon God; but all who come to the Bible with a teachable and prayerful spirit, to study its utterances as the Word of God, will receive divine enlightenment. There are many things apparently difficult or obscure which God will make plain and simple to those who thus seek an understanding of them. . . .

There are mines of truth yet to be discovered by the earnest seeker. Christ represented the truth as treasure hid in a field. It does not lie right upon the surface; we must dig for it. But our success in finding it does not depend so much on our intellectual ability as on our humility of heart and the faith which will lay hold upon divine aid.—*Testimonies for the Church,* vol. 5, pp. 703, 704.

Seek God
for Wisdom

*From where then does wisdom come? And where
is the place of understanding? Job 28:20, NKJV.*

YOU WILL HAVE to wrestle with difficulties, carry burdens, give advice, plan and execute, constantly looking to God for help. Pray and labor, labor and pray; as pupils in the school of Christ, learn of Jesus.

The Lord has given us the promise "If any of you lack wisdom, let him ask of God, that giveth to all men liberally, and upbraideth not; and it shall be given him" (James 1:5). It is in the order of God that those who bear responsibilities should often meet together to counsel with one another, and to pray earnestly for that wisdom which He alone can impart. Talk less; much precious time is lost in talk that brings no light. Let church leaders unite in fasting and prayer for the wisdom that God has promised to supply liberally. Make known your troubles to God. Tell Him, as did Moses, "I cannot lead this people unless Thy presence shall go with me." And then ask still more; pray with Moses, "Shew me thy glory" (Ex. 33:18). What is this glory? The character of God. This is what He proclaimed to Moses.

Let the soul in living faith fasten upon God. Let the tongue speak His praise. When you associate together, let the mind be reverently turned to the contemplation of eternal realities. Thus you will be helping one another to be spiritually minded. When your will is in harmony with the divine will, you will be in harmony with one another; you will have Christ by your side as a counselor.

Enoch walked with God. So may every laborer for Christ. You may say with the psalmist, "I have set the Lord always before me: because he is at my right hand, I shall not be moved" (Ps. 16:8). While you feel that you have no sufficiency of yourself, your sufficiency will be in Jesus. If you expect all your counsel and wisdom to come from other people, mortal and finite like yourselves, you will receive only human help. If you go to God for help and wisdom, He will never disappoint your faith.—*Gospel Workers,* pp. 417, 418.

Reach for the Highest Standard of Personhood

Do not let the wise boast in their wisdom, do not let the mighty boast in their might, do not let the wealthy boast in their wealth. Jeremiah 9:23, NRSV.

GOD IS THE SOURCE of all wisdom. He is infinitely wise and just and good. [Apart from Christ,] the wisest people that ever lived cannot comprehend Him. They may profess to be wise; they may glory in their attainments; but mere intellectual knowledge, aside from the great truths that center in Christ, is as nothingness. . . .

If men and women could see for a moment beyond the [range of] finite vision, if they could catch a glimpse of the Eternal, every mouth would be stopped in its boasting. People living in this little atom of a world are finite; God has unnumbered worlds that are obedient to His laws and are conducted with reference to His glory. When human beings have gone as far in scientific research as their limited powers will permit, there is still an infinity beyond what they can apprehend.

Before humans can be truly wise, they must realize their dependence upon God, and be filled with His wisdom. God is the source of intellectual as well as spiritual power. The greatest people who have reached what the world regards as wonderful heights in science are not to be compared with the beloved John or the great apostle Paul. It is when intellectual and moral power are combined that the greatest standard of personhood is reached. Those who do this, God will accept as workers together with Him in the training of minds.

To know oneself is a great knowledge. The teachers who rightly estimate themselves will let God mold and discipline their minds. And they will acknowledge the source of their power. For "what hast thou that thou didst not receive? now if thou didst receive it, why dost thou glory, as if thou hadst not received it?" (1 Cor. 4:7). Self-knowledge leads to humility and to trust in God, but it does not take the place of efforts for self-improvement. Those who realize their own deficiencies will spare no pains to reach the highest possible standard of physical, mental, and moral excellence.—*Special Testimonies on Education,* pp. 49, 50.

Prepare Now
for Immortal Life

*That the God of our Lord Jesus Christ, the Father of glory, may give to you
the spirit of wisdom and revelation in the knowledge of Him, the eyes of
your understanding being enlightened. Ephesians 1:17, 18, NKJV.*

THE BEST WAY to prevent the growth of evil is to preoccupy the soil. The
greatest care and watchfulness is needed in cultivating the mind and sowing
therein the precious seeds of Bible truth. The Lord, in His great mercy, has
revealed to us in the Scriptures the rules of holy living. He tells us the sins
to shun; He explains to us the plan of salvation, and points out the way to
heaven. He has inspired holy men to record, for our benefit, instruction concerning the dangers that beset our path, and how to escape them. Those who
obey His injunction to search the Scriptures will not be ignorant of these
things. Amid the perils of the last days, members of the church should understand the reasons of their hope and faith—reasons which are not difficult
of comprehension. There is enough to occupy the mind, if we would grow
in grace and in the knowledge of our Lord Jesus Christ. . . .

If the Bible were studied as it should be, we would become strong in
intellect. The subjects treated upon in the Word of God, the dignified simplicity of its utterance, the noble themes which it presents to the mind, develop faculties in us which cannot otherwise be developed. . . .

God would have us avail ourselves of every means of cultivating and
strengthening our intellectual powers. We were created for a higher, nobler existence than the life that now is. This time is one of preparation for
the future, immortal life. Where can be found grander themes for contemplation, a more interesting subject for thought, than the sublime truths unfolded in the Bible? These truths will do a mighty work for us, if we will
but follow what they teach. . . .

If the Bible were read more, if its truths were better understood, we
should be a far more enlightened and intelligent people. Energy is imparted to the soul by searching its pages. Angels from the world of light
stand by the side of the earnest seeker after truth, to impress and illuminate the mind. All who are dark of understanding may find light
through an acquaintance with the Scriptures.—*Christian Temperance and
Bible Hygiene*, pp. 125, 126.

To Grow,
Study the Word

All scripture is inspired by God and is useful for teaching, for reproof, for correction, and for training in righteousness, so that everyone who belongs to God may be proficient, equipped for every good work. 2 Timothy 3:16, 17, NRSV.

THE TEACHER OF the truth should advance in knowledge, growing in grace and in Christian experience, cultivating habits and practices which will do honor to God and to His Word. He or she should show others how to make a practical application of the Word. Every advance we make in sanctified ability, in varied studies, will help us to understand the Word of God; and the study of the Scriptures helps us in the study of the other branches essential in education.

After the first acquaintance with the Bible, the interest of earnest seekers grows rapidly. The discipline gained by a regular study of the Word of God enables them to see a freshness and beauty in truth that they never before discerned. Reference to texts, when speaking, becomes natural and easy to a Bible student.

Above everything else, it is essential for the teachers of the Word of God to seek most earnestly to possess themselves of the internal evidence of the Scriptures. Those who would be blessed with this evidence must search the Scriptures for themselves. As they learn the lessons given by Christ, and compare scripture with scripture, to see whether they themselves bear its credentials, they will obtain a knowledge of God's Word, and the truth will write itself on their souls.

The truth is the truth. It is not to be wrapped up in beautiful adornings, that the outside appearance may be admired. The teacher is to make the truth clear and forcible to the understanding and to the conscience. The Word is a two-edged sword that cuts both ways. It does not tread as with soft, slippered feet.

There are many cases where people who have defended Christianity against skeptics have afterward lost their own souls in the mazes of skepticism. They caught the malaria, and died spiritually. They had strong arguments for the truth, and much outside evidence, but they did not have an abiding faith in Christ. Oh, there are thousands upon thousands of professed Christians who never study the Bible! Study the sacred Word prayerfully, for your own soul's benefit. When you hear the word of living preachers, if they have a living connection with God, you will find that the Spirit and the word agree.—*Review and Herald,* Apr. 20, 1897.

Learn the Truth, Then Live It

Your word I have hidden in my heart, that I might not sin against You. Psalm 119:11, NKJV.

STUDY THE WORD, which God in His wisdom and love and goodness has made so plain and simple. The sixth chapter of John tells us what is meant by a study of the Word. The principles revealed in the Scriptures are to be brought home to the soul. We are to eat the Word of God; that is, we are not to depart from its precepts. We are to bring its truths into our daily lives, grasping the mysteries of godliness.

Pray to God. Commune with Him. Prove the very mind of God, as those who are striving for eternal life, and who must have a knowledge of His will. You can reveal the truth only as you know it in Christ. You are to receive and assimilate His words; they are to become part of yourselves. This is what is meant by eating the flesh and drinking the blood of the Son of God. You are to live by every word that proceedeth out of the mouth of God; that is, what God has revealed. Not all has been revealed; we could not bear such a revelation. But God has revealed all that is necessary for our salvation. We are not to leave His Word for the suppositions of human beings.

Obtain an experimental knowledge of God by wearing the yoke of Christ. He gives wisdom to the meek and lowly, enabling them to judge of what is truth, bringing to light the why and wherefore, pointing out the result of certain actions. The Holy Spirit teaches the students of the Scriptures to judge all things by the standard of righteousness and truth and justice. The divine revelation supplies them with the knowledge that they need. . . .

Make the Bible the man of your counsel. Your acquaintance with it will grow rapidly if you keep your mind free from the rubbish of the world. The more the Bible is studied, the deeper will be your knowledge of God. The truths of His Word will be written in your soul, making an ineffaceable impression. . . .

Not only will the students themselves be benefited by a study of the Word of God. Their study is life and salvation to all with whom they associate. They will feel a sacred responsibility to impart the knowledge that they receive. Their lives will reveal the help and strength that they receive from communion with the Word. . . . Of such ones the Lord Jesus can indeed say, "Ye are laborers together with God."—*Counsels on Health*, pp. 370-372.

To Find the Word
Interesting, Receive the Spirit

Let my cry come before You, O Lord; give me
understanding according to Your word. Psalm 119:169, NKJV.

THE BIBLE HAS been placed in the background, while the sayings of great men and women, so-called, have been taken in its stead. May the Lord forgive us the slight we have put upon His Word. Though inestimable treasures are in the Bible, and it is like a mine full of precious ore, it is not valued, it is not searched, and its riches are not discovered.

Mercy and truth and love are valuable beyond our power to calculate; we cannot have too great a supply of these treasures, and it is in the Word of God [that] we find out how we may become possessors of these heavenly riches, and yet why is it that the Word of God is uninteresting to many professed Christians? Is it because the Word of God is not spirit and is not life? Has Jesus put upon us an uninteresting task, when He commands us to "search the scriptures"? Jesus says, "The words that I speak unto you, they are spirit, and they are life." But spiritual things are spiritually discerned, and the reason of your lack of interest is that you lack the Spirit of God.

When the heart is brought into harmony with the Word, a new life will spring up within you, a new light will shine upon every line of the Word, and it will become the voice of God to your soul. In this way you will take celestial observations, and know whither you are going, and be able to make the most of your privileges today.

We should ask the Lord to open our understanding, that we may comprehend divine truth. If we humble our hearts before God, empty them of vanity and pride and selfishness, through the grace abundantly bestowed upon us; if we sincerely desire and unwaveringly believe, the bright beams of the Sun of righteousness will shine into our minds, and illuminate our darkened understanding. Jesus is the light that lighteth every man that cometh into the world. He is the light of the world, and He bids us come unto Him and learn of Him. . . . He had come to seek and to save that which was lost, and He could not permit Himself to be turned from His one object. He allowed nothing to divert Him. This work He has given into our hands. Shall we do it?—*Review and Herald,* Nov. 24, 1891.

Treasures of Truth
Are for Those Who Dig

If you seek her as silver, and search for her as for hidden treasures; then you will understand the fear of the Lord, and find the knowledge of God. Proverbs 2:4, 5, NKJV.

LET NONE THINK that there is no more knowledge for them to gain. The depth of human intellect may be measured; the works of human authors may be mastered; but the highest, deepest, broadest flight of the imagination cannot find out God. There is infinity beyond all that we can comprehend. We have seen only the glimmering of divine glory and of the infinitude of knowledge and wisdom; we have, as it were, been working on the surface of the mine, when rich, golden ore is beneath the surface, to reward the one who will dig for it. The shaft must be sunk deeper and yet deeper in the mine, and the result will be glorious treasure. Through a correct faith, divine knowledge will become human knowledge.

No one can search the Scriptures in the spirit of Christ without being rewarded. When men and women are willing to be instructed as a little child, when they submit wholly to Christ, they will find the truth in His Word. If people would be obedient, they would understand the plan of God's government. The heavenly world would open its treasures of grace and glory for exploration. Human beings would be altogether different from what they are now; for by exploring the mines of truth, they would be ennobled. The mystery of redemption, the incarnation of Christ, His atoning sacrifice, would not be, as they are now, vague in our minds. They would be, not only better understood, but altogether more highly appreciated. . . .

The value of this treasure is above gold or silver. The riches of earth's mines cannot compare with it. "The depth saith, It is not in me: and the sea saith, It is not with me. It cannot be gotten for gold, neither shall silver be weighed for the price thereof. It cannot be valued with the gold of Ophir, with the precious onyx, or the sapphire. The gold and the crystal cannot equal it: and the exchange of it shall not be for jewels of fine gold. No mention shall be made of coral, or of pearls: for the price of wisdom is above rubies."—*Signs of the Times,* Sept. 12, 1906.

Ever Search
for More Light

*I set my heart to seek and search out by wisdom concerning
all that is done under heaven. Ecclesiastes 1:13, NKJV.*

WHATEVER MAY BE humanity's intellectual advancement, let no one
for a moment think that there is no need of thorough and continuous
searching of the Scriptures for greater light. As a people we are called individually to be students of prophecy. We must watch with earnestness
that we may discern any ray of light which God shall present to us. We are
to catch the first gleamings of truth; and through prayerful study clearer
light may be obtained, which can be brought before others.

When God's people are at ease and satisfied with their present enlightenment, we may be sure that He will not favor them. It is His will that
they should be ever moving forward to receive the increased and ever-
increasing light which is shining for them. The present attitude of the
church is not pleasing to God. There has come in a self-confidence that has
led them to feel no necessity for more truth and greater light. We are living at a time when Satan is at work on the right hand and on the left, before and behind us; and yet as a people we are asleep. God wills that a voice
shall be heard arousing His people to action.

Instead of opening the soul to receive rays of light from heaven, some
have been working in an opposite direction. Both through the press and
from the pulpit have been presented views in regard to the inspiration of
the Bible which have not the sanction of the Spirit or the Word of God.
Certain it is that no human being or set of human beings should undertake
to advance theories upon a subject of so great importance, without a plain
"Thus saith the Lord" to sustain them.

And when people, compassed with human infirmities, affected in a
greater or less degree by surrounding influences, and having hereditary and
cultivated tendencies which are far from making them wise or heavenly-
minded, undertake to arraign the Word of God, and to pass judgment
upon what is divine and what is human, they are working without the
counsel of God. The Lord will not prosper such a work. The effect will be
disastrous, both upon the one engaged in it and upon those who accept it
as a work from God.—*Testimonies for the Church,* vol. 5, pp. 708, 709.

Examine
Diligently Every Belief

*I applied my heart to know, to search and seek out wisdom
and the reason of things, to know the wickedness of folly,
even of foolishness and madness. Ecclesiastes 7:25, NKJV.*

I HAVE BEEN SHOWN that many who profess to have a knowledge of present truth know not what they believe. They do not understand the evidences of their faith. They have no just appreciation of the work for the present time. When the time of trial shall come, there are people now preaching to others who will find, upon examining the positions they hold, that there are many things for which they can give no satisfactory reason. Until thus tested they knew not their great ignorance.

And there are many in the church who take it for granted that they understand what they believe; but, until controversy arises, they do not know their own weakness. When separated from those of like faith and compelled to stand singly and alone to explain their belief, they will be surprised to see how confused are their ideas of what they had accepted as truth. Certain it is that there has been among us a departure from the living God and a turning to mortals, putting human in place of divine wisdom.

God will arouse His people; if other means fail, heresies will come in among them, which will sift them, separating the chaff from the wheat. The Lord calls upon all who believe His Word to awake out of sleep. Precious light has come, appropriate for this time. It is Bible truth, showing the perils that are right upon us. This light should lead us to a diligent study of the Scriptures and a most critical examination of the positions which we hold. God would have all the bearings and positions of truth thoroughly and perseveringly searched, with prayer and fasting. Believers are not to rest in suppositions and ill-defined ideas of what constitutes truth. Their faith must be firmly founded upon the Word of God so that when the testing time shall come and they are brought before councils to answer for their faith they may be able to give a reason for the hope that is in them, with meekness and fear. . . .

With those who have educated themselves as debaters there is great danger that they will not handle the Word of God with fairness. In meeting an opponent it should be our earnest effort to present subjects in such a manner as to awaken conviction in their mind, instead of seeking merely to give confidence to the believer.—*Testimonies for the Church,* vol. 5, pp. 707, 708.

Bible Study
Strengthens the Intellect

Every word of God is pure; He is a shield to those who
put their trust in Him. Do not add to His words, lest He reprove
you, and you be found a liar. Proverbs 30:5, 6, NKJV.

THE BURDEN NOW is to convince souls of the truth. This can best be done by personal efforts, by bringing the truth into their houses, praying with them, and opening to them the Scriptures.

Those who do this work should be just as careful not to become stereotyped in their plans of labor as should the minister who labors in the desk. They should be constantly learning. They should have a conscientious zeal to obtain the highest qualifications, to become able in the Scriptures. . . . They should cultivate habits of careful study and mental activity, giving themselves to prayer and to a diligent study of the Scriptures. Many are guilty of shortcomings on this point. The claims of God upon them are not small. But they are content with the limited understanding they have of the Scriptures, and do not seek to improve both mind and manners.

Every argument in prophetic history, every practical lesson given by Christ, should be carefully studied that they may be wanting in nothing. The mind gains strength, breadth, and acuteness by activity. It must be made to work, or it will grow weak. It must be trained to think, to think habitually, or it will in a great measure lose its power to think. Let the mind wrestle with the difficult problems in the Word of God, and the intellect will be thoroughly awakened to bring forth, not inferior discourses, but those that will be fresh and edifying; and these will be presented in the fervor of an active mind.

The servants of Christ must meet the highest standard. They are educators, and they should be thoroughly versed in the Scriptures. . . . The study of the Bible taxes the mind of the worker, strengthens the memory, and sharpens the intellect more than the study of all the subjects which philosophy embraces. The Bible contains the only truth that purifies the soul, and is the best book for intellectual culture. The dignified simplicity with which it handles important doctrines is just what every youth and every worker for Christ needs to teach him or her how to present the mysteries of salvation to those who are in darkness.—*Review and Herald,* Dec. 8, 1885.

Search the Word
Objectively and Personally

Lead me in Your truth and teach me, for You are the God of my salvation; on You I wait all the day. Psalm 25:5, NKJV.

IT IS DANGEROUS for us to make flesh our arm. We should lean upon the arm of infinite power. God has been revealing this to us for years. We must have living faith in our hearts, and reach out for larger knowledge and more advanced light.

Do not trust to the wisdom of any person, or to the investigations of any person. Go to the Scriptures for yourselves, search the inspired Word with humble hearts, lay aside your preconceived opinions; for you will obtain no benefit unless you come as children to the Word of God. You should say, "If God has anything for me, I want it. If God has given evidence from His Word to this or that person that a certain thing is truth, He will give it to me. I can find that evidence if I search the Scriptures with constant prayer, and I can know that I do know what is truth."

You need not preach the truth as the product of another person's mind; you must make it your own. When the woman of Samaria was convinced that Jesus was the Messiah, she hastened to tell her neighbors and townsmen. She said, "Come, see a man, which told me all things that ever I did: is not this the Christ? Then they went out of the city, and came unto him. . . . And many of the Samaritans of that city believed on him for the saying of the woman, which testified, He told me all that ever I did. . . . And many more believed because of his own word: and said unto the woman, Now we believe, not because of thy saying: for we have heard him ourselves, and know that this is indeed the Christ."

We must sink the shaft deep in the mine of truth. You may question matters with yourselves and with one another, if you only do it in the right spirit; but too often self is large, and as soon as investigation begins, an unchristian spirit is manifested. This is just what Satan delights in, but we should come with a humble heart to know for ourselves what is truth. The time is coming when we shall be separated and scattered, and each one of us will have to stand without the privilege of communion with those of like precious faith; and how can you stand unless God is by your side, and you know that He is leading and guiding you? Whenever we come to investigate Bible truth, the Master of assemblies is with us. The Lord does not leave the ship one moment to be steered by ignorant pilots. We may receive our orders from the Captain of our salvation.—*Review and Herald,* Mar. 25, 1890.

Preparing for Trying Times

That we should no longer be children, tossed to and fro and carried about with every wind of doctrine, . . . but, speaking the truth in love, may grow up in all things into Him who is the head—Christ. Ephesians 4:14, 15, NKJV.

THE LORD CALLS upon all His people to improve the ability He has given them. The mental powers should be developed to the utmost; they should be strengthened and ennobled by dwelling upon spiritual truths. If the mind is allowed to run almost entirely upon trifling things and the common business of everyday life, it will, in accordance with one of its unvarying laws, become weak and frivolous, and deficient in spiritual power.

Times that will try our souls are just before us, and those who are weak in the faith will not stand the test of those days of peril. The great truths of revelation are to be carefully studied, for we shall all want an intelligent knowledge of the Word of God. By Bible study and daily communion with Jesus we shall gain clear, well-defined views of individual responsibility and strength to stand in the day of trial and temptation. He whose life is united to Christ by hidden links will be kept by the power of God through faith unto salvation.

More thought should be given to the things of God, and less to temporal matters. The world-loving professors, if they will exercise their minds in that direction, may become as familiar with the Word of God as they now are with worldly business. "Search the scriptures," said Christ; "for in them ye think ye have eternal life; and they are they which testify of me."

The Christian is required to be diligent in searching the Scriptures, to read over and over again the truths of God's Word. Willful ignorance on this subject endangers the Christian life and character. It blinds the understanding and corrupts the noblest powers. It is this that brings confusion into our lives. Our people need to understand the oracles of God; they need to have a systematic knowledge of the principles of revealed truth, which will fit them for what is coming upon the earth and prevent them from being carried about by every wind of doctrine.—*Testimonies for the Church*, vol. 5, pp. 272, 273.

Do Not Merely Read the Scriptures, but Search

You search the Scriptures, for in them you think you have eternal life; and these are they which testify of Me. John 5:39, NKJV.

WE ARE THANKFUL that we have a sure word of prophecy, so that none of us need be deceived. We know that there are heresies and fables in our world at the present time, and we want to know what is truth. It becomes us to search carefully for ourselves that we may gain this knowledge. We cannot do this with a mere reading of the Scriptures, but we must compare scripture with scripture.

We must search the Scriptures for ourselves, so that we shall not be led astray; and while many may be led astray because there are all kinds of doctrines in our world, there is one truth. Many may come to you and tell you that they have the truth, but it is your privilege to search the Scriptures for yourself. "To the law and to the testimony: if they speak not according to this word, it is because there is no light in them." We must be acquainted with the Scriptures ourselves, that we may understand the true reason of the hope that is within us.

The apostle tells us that we are to give to everyone that asks us a reason of the hope that is within us, with meekness and fear. "The entrance of thy words giveth light; it giveth understanding unto the simple." It is not enough to merely read, but the Word of God must enter into our hearts and our understanding, in order that we may be established in the blessed truth. If we should neglect to search the Scriptures for ourselves, that we may know what is truth, then if we are led astray we are accountable for it. We must search the Scriptures carefully, so that we will know every condition that the Lord has given us; and if we have minds of limited capacity, by diligently searching the Word of God we may become mighty in the Scriptures, and may explain them to others.

Every church that shall be raised up . . . should be educated in regard to this truth. "The harvest truly is great, but the labourers are few." The teachers that shall present the truth cannot stand by you to see that you do not embrace the errors that are flooding our land; but if you are established in the Scriptures, you will feel the responsibility and will search the Scriptures for yourselves, so that you may be a help to others.—*Review and Herald,* Apr. 3, 1888.

Hear Christ's Voice Through the Word

Jesus answered and said to them, "You are mistaken, not knowing the Scriptures nor the power of God." Matthew 22:29, NKJV.

THE VOICE OF GOD is speaking to us through His Word, and there are many voices that we will hear; but Christ has said we should beware of them who will say, Here is Christ or there is Christ. Then how shall we know that they have not the truth, unless we bring everything to the Scriptures? Christ has warned us to beware of false prophets who will come to us in His name, saying that they are Christ.

Now, if you should take the position that it is not important for you to understand the Scriptures for yourselves, you will be in danger of being led away with these doctrines. Christ has said that there will be a company who in the day of retributive judgment will say, "Lord, Lord, have we not prophesied in thy name? and in thy name have cast out devils? and in thy name done many wonderful works?" But Christ will say, "Depart from me, ye that work iniquity."

Now, we want to understand what sin is; that it is the transgression of God's law. This is the only definition given in the Scriptures. Therefore we see that those who claim to be led of God, and go right away from Him and His law, do not search the Scriptures. But the Lord will lead His people; for He says that His sheep will follow if they hear His voice, but a stranger will they not follow. Then it becomes us to thoroughly understand the Scriptures. And we will not have to inquire whether others have the truth; for it will be seen in their characters.

The time is coming when Satan will work miracles right in your sight, claiming that he is Christ; and if your feet are not firmly established upon the truth of God, then you will be led away from your foundation. The only safety for you is to search for the truth as for hid treasures. Dig for the truth as you would for treasures in the earth, and present the Word of God, the Bible, before your heavenly Father, and say, Enlighten me; teach me what is truth. And when His Holy Spirit shall come into your hearts, to impress the truth into your souls, you will not let it go easily.—*Review and Herald,* Apr. 3, 1888.

Earnest Study
Produces True Conversion

Ezra had prepared his heart to seek the Law of the Lord, and to do it, and to teach statutes and ordinances in Israel. Ezra 7:10, NKJV.

BORN OF THE SONS of Aaron, Ezra, in addition to his priestly training, had acquired a familiarity with the writings of the magicians, the astrologers, and the so-called wise men of the Medo-Persian realm. But he was not satisfied with his spiritual condition. He longed to be in full harmony with God: he longed for wisdom to carry out God's will. And so he "prepared his heart to seek the law of the Lord, and to do it."

This led him to apply himself diligently to a study of the history of God's people, as given in the writings of Old Testament prophets and kings. He was impressed by the Spirit of God to search the historical and poetical books of the Bible, to learn why the Lord had permitted Jerusalem to be destroyed, and His people to be carried captive into a heathen land.

Ezra gave special study to the experiences of God's chosen people, from the time the promise was made to Abraham, to the deliverance from Egyptian bondage and the exodus. He studied the instruction given them at the foot of Mount Sinai, and throughout the long period of the wilderness-wandering. As he learned more and still more concerning God's dealings with His children, and began to realize how sacred was the law given at Sinai, Ezra's heart was stirred as never before. He experienced a new and thorough conversion, and determined to master the records of Old Testament history, that he might use this knowledge, not for selfish purposes, but to bring blessing and light to his people. Some of the prophecies were about to be fulfilled; he would search diligently for the light that had been obscured.

Ezra took pains with his studies. He endeavored to gain a heart-preparation for the work he believed was appointed him. He sought God earnestly, that he might be a workman of whom his Lord would not be ashamed. He searched out the words that had been written concerning the duties of God's denominated people; and he found the solemn pledge made by the Israelites, that they would obey the words of the Lord; and the pledge that God, in return, had made, promising them His blessing as a reward of obedience.—*Review and Herald*, Jan. 30, 1908.

God's Word the Standard of Judgment

God will bring every work into judgment, including every secret thing, whether it is good or whether it is evil. Ecclesiastes 12:14, NKJV.

THE BIBLE IS an unerring guide for the human race in every phase of life. In it the conditions of eternal life are plainly stated. The distinction between right and wrong is clearly defined, and sin is shown in its most revolting character, clothed with the robes of death. If this guide is studied and obeyed, it is to us as the pillar of cloud, which led the children of Israel through the wilderness; but if it is ignored and disobeyed, it will witness against us in the day of judgment. God will judge all by His Word; according as they have fulfilled or disregarded its requirements, they will stand or fall. . . .

"All things whatsoever ye would that men should do to you," said Christ, "do ye even so to them; for this is the law and the prophets." These words are of the highest importance, and should be our rule of life. But do we carry out this divine principle? Do we, when brought into contact with our fellow beings, deal with them just as we would desire them to deal with us in similar circumstances?

God tests men and women by their daily life. But many who make high professions of service to Him cannot bear this test. In their eagerness for gain they use false weights and deceitful balances. The Bible is not made their rule of life, and therefore they do not see the necessity of strict integrity and faithfulness. Anxious to amass wealth, they allow scheming dishonesty to come into their work. The world watches their conduct, and is not slow to measure their Christian worth by their business dealings. . . .

The Bible always tells the same story. With it sin is always sin, whether committed by the possessor of millions or by the beggar in the streets. Better a life of deepest poverty crowned with God's blessings, than all the world's treasure without it. We may be very rich; but unless we have the consciousness that God honors us, we are poor indeed.—*Signs of the Times,* Dec. 24, 1896.

Scripture's Grand Themes Expand the Mind

He shall write for himself a copy of this law in a book. . . . And it shall be with him, and he shall read it all the days of his life, that he may learn to fear the Lord his God and be careful to observe all the words of this law and these statutes. Deuteronomy 17:18, 19, NKJV.

LIGHT READING FASCINATES the mind, and makes the reading of God's Word uninteresting. The Bible requires thought and prayerful research. It is not enough to skim over the surface. While some passages are too plain to be misunderstood, others demand careful and patient study. Like the precious metal concealed in the hills and mountains, its gems of truth are to be searched out, and stored in the mind for future use.

And when you search the Scriptures with an earnest desire to learn the truth, God will breathe His Spirit into your heart, and impress your mind with the light of His Word. The Bible is its own interpreter, one passage explaining another. By comparing scriptures referring to the same subject, you will see harmony and beauty of which you have never dreamed. There is no other book whose perusal strengthens and enlarges, elevates and ennobles, the mind as does the perusal of this Book of books.

The injunction of the Word of God is "Work out your own salvation with fear and trembling. For it is God which worketh in you both to will and to do of his good pleasure." God and the human being are to cooperate. All are to work out that which God works in. Students of the Word of God are to use the knowledge they have gained. They are to improve the opportunities that are thrown in their way. With a settled conviction of duty, they are to use their knowledge and influence in any channel, to the end that they may gain more by their use. . . .

Study the life of Christ in this respect. Follow Him from the manger to Calvary, and act as He acted. The great principles which He maintained, you are to maintain. Your standard is to be the character of Him who was pure, holy, and undefiled.—*Youth's Instructor,* June 30, 1898.

Exciting Experiences
Await Bible Students

And He opened their understanding, that they might
comprehend the Scriptures. Luke 24:45, NKJV.

OPEN THE BIBLE to our youth, draw their attention to its hidden treasures, teach them to search for its jewels of truth, and they will gain a
strength of intellect such as the study of all that philosophy embraces could
not impart. The grand subjects upon which the Bible treats, the dignified
simplicity of its inspired utterances, the elevated themes which it presents
to the mind, the light, sharp and clear, from the throne of God, enlightening the understanding, will develop the powers of the mind to an extent
that can scarcely be comprehended, and never fully explained.

The Bible presents a boundless field for the imagination, as much
higher and more ennobling in character than the superficial creations of the
unsanctified intellect as the heavens are higher than the earth. The inspired
history of our race is placed in the hands of every individual. All may now
begin their research. They may become acquainted with our first parents
as they stood in Eden, in holy innocency, enjoying communion with God
and sinless angels. They may trace the introduction of sin, and its results
upon the race, and follow, step by step, down the track of sacred history,
as it records the disobedience and impenitence of the human race and the
just retribution for sin.

The readers may hold converse with patriarchs and prophets; they may
move through the most inspiring scenes; they may behold Christ, who was
Monarch in heaven, equal with God, coming down to humanity, and
working out the plan of redemption, breaking off from mortals the chains
wherewith Satan had bound them, and making it possible for them to regain their godlike humanity. Christ taking upon Himself humanity, and
preserving the level of a man for thirty years, and then making His soul an
offering for sin, that the human family might not be left to perish, is a subject for the deepest thought and the most concentrated study. . . .

People may have enjoyed the training of the schools, and may have
made themselves acquainted with the great writers on theology, yet truth
will open to the mind, and impress it with new and striking power, as the
Word of God is searched and pondered with an earnest, prayerful desire to
understand it.—*Review and Herald,* Jan. 11, 1881.

The Holy Spirit
Illuminates the Word

These were more fair-minded than those in Thessalonica, in
that they received the word with all readiness, and searched the Scriptures
daily to find out whether these things were so. Acts 17:11, NKJV.

"SEARCH THE SCRIPTURES," Christ declared, "for in them ye think ye have eternal life: and they are they which testify of me." Those who dig beneath the surface discover the hidden gems of truth. The Holy Spirit is present with the earnest searcher. Its illumination shines upon the Word, stamping the truth upon the mind with a new, fresh importance. The searcher is filled with a sense of peace and joy never before felt. The preciousness of truth is realized as never before. A new, heavenly light shines upon the Word, illuminating it as though every letter were tinged with gold. God Himself has spoken to the mind and heart, making the Word spirit and life.

True searchers of the Word lift their hearts to God, imploring the aid of the Spirit. And they soon discover that which carries them above all the fictitious statements of the would-be teacher, whose weak, tottering theories are not sustained by the Word of the living God. These theories were invented by those who had not learned the first great lesson, that God's Spirit and life are in His Word. If they had received in the heart the eternal element contained in the Word of God, they would see how tame and expressionless are all efforts to get something new to create a sensation. They need to learn the very first principles of the Word of God; they would then have the Word of life for the people, who will soon distinguish the chaff from the wheat, for Jesus left His promise with His disciples. . . .

"Peace I leave with you, my peace I give unto you: not as the world giveth, give I unto you. Let not your heart be troubled, neither let it be afraid" (John 14:27). These words are not half comprehended by individuals, by families, or by church members, to whom and through whom, as His family, God would represent pure, unadulterated truth, which, if received and properly digested, brings eternal life.—*Manuscript Releases,* vol. 21, pp. 131, 132.

Accept the Bible as
the Foundation of All Faith

Whatever things were written before were written for our learning, that we through the patience and comfort of the Scriptures might have hope. Romans 15:4, NKJV.

THE TEACHERS OF Israel were not sowing the seed of the Word of God. Christ's work as a teacher of truth was in marked contrast to that of the rabbis of His time. They dwelt upon traditions, upon human theories and speculations. Often that which mortals had taught and written about the Word, they put in place of the Word itself. Their teaching had no power to quicken the soul.

The subject of Christ's teaching and preaching was the Word of God. He met questioners with a plain "It is written." "What saith the Scriptures?" "How readest thou?" At every opportunity, when an interest was awakened by either friend or foe, He sowed the seed of the Word. He who is the Way, the Truth, and the Life, Himself the living Word, points to the Scriptures, saying, "They are they which testify of me" (John 5:39). And "beginning at Moses and all the prophets," He opened to His disciples "in all the scriptures the things concerning himself" (Luke 24:27).

Christ's servants are to do the same work. In our day, as of old, the vital truths of God's Word are set aside for human theories and speculations. Many professed ministers of the gospel do not accept the whole Bible as the inspired Word. One wise person rejects one portion; another questions another part. They set up their judgment as superior to the Word; and the Scripture which they do teach rests upon their own authority. Its divine authenticity is destroyed. Thus the seeds of infidelity are sown broadcast; for the people become confused and know not what to believe. There are many beliefs that the mind has no right to entertain.

In the days of Christ the rabbis put a forced, mystical construction upon many portions of Scripture. Because the plain teaching of God's Word condemned their practices, they tried to destroy its force. The same thing is done today. The Word of God is made to appear mysterious and obscure in order to excuse transgression of His law. Christ rebuked these practices in His day. He taught that the Word of God was to be understood by all. He pointed to the Scriptures as of unquestionable authority, and we should do the same. The Bible is to be presented as the word of the infinite God, as the end of all controversy and the foundation of all faith.—*Christ's Object Lessons*, pp. 38-40.

Have Fellowship With Jesus Through the Word.

Let us run with endurance the race that is set before us, looking unto Jesus, the author and finisher of our faith. Hebrews 12:1, 2, NKJV.

NO MAN, WOMAN, or youth can attain to Christian perfection and neglect the study of the Word of God. By carefully and closely searching His Word we shall obey the injunction of Christ, "Search the scriptures; for in them ye think ye have eternal life: and they are they which testify of me." This search enables the student to closely observe the divine Model, for they testify of Christ. The Pattern must be inspected often and closely in order to imitate it.

As human beings become acquainted with the history of the Redeemer, they discover in themselves defects of character; their unlikeness to Christ is so great that they see they cannot be followers without a very great change in their lives. Still they study, with a desire to be like their great Exemplar; they catch the looks, the spirit, of their beloved Master; by beholding they become changed. "Looking unto Jesus the author and finisher of our faith." It is not in looking away from Him, and in losing sight of Him, that we imitate the life of Jesus; but in dwelling upon and talking of Him, and seeking to refine the taste and elevate the character; seeking to approach through earnest, persevering effort, through faith and love, the perfect Pattern.

The attention being fixed upon Christ, His image, pure and spotless, becomes enshrined in the heart as "the chief among ten thousand and the one altogether lovely." Even unconsciously we imitate that with which we are familiar. By having a knowledge of Christ, His words, His habits, His lessons of instruction, and by borrowing the virtues of the character which we have so closely studied, we become imbued with the spirit of the Master which we have so much admired. . . .

The Word of God, spoken to the heart, has an animating power, and those who will frame any excuse for neglecting to become acquainted with it will neglect the claims of God in many respects. The character will be deformed, the words and acts a reproach to the truth.—*Review and Herald,* Nov. 28, 1878.

Enjoy the Rich
Banquet Found in the Word

The anointing which you have received from Him abides in you,
and you do not need that anyone teach you; but as the same anointing
teaches you concerning all things, and is true, and is not a lie, and just
as it has taught you, you will abide in Him. 1 John 2:27, NKJV.

LET US BELIEVE the Word. He who thus eats the bread of heaven is nourished every day, and will know what these words mean, "Need not that any man teach you" (1 John 2:27). We have lessons pure from the lips of Him who owns us, who has bought us with the price of His own blood.

The precious Word of God is a solid foundation upon which to build. When people come to you with their supposed suppositions, tell them that the Great Teacher has left you His Word, which is of incalculable value, that He has sent a Comforter in His own name, even the Holy Ghost. "He shall teach you all things, and bring all things to your remembrance, whatsoever I have said unto you." "I am the living bread which came down from heaven: if any man eat of this bread, he shall live for ever: and the bread that I will give is my flesh, which I will give for the life of the world."

Here is presented before us a rich banquet, of which all who believe in Christ as a personal Savior may eat. He is the tree of life to all who continue to feed on Him.

I am instructed to ask those who profess to receive Christ as their personal Savior, Why do you pass by the words of the Great Teacher, and send your letters to human beings for words of comfort? Why do you rely upon human help when you have the large, full, grand promises, "He that eateth my flesh, and drinketh my blood, dwelleth in me, and I in him. . . . This is that bread which came down from heaven: not as your fathers did eat manna, and are dead: he that eateth of this bread shall live for ever"? They may die, yet the life of Christ in them is eternal, and they will be raised up at the last day. "It is the spirit that quickeneth; the flesh profiteth nothing: the words that I speak unto you, they are spirit, and they are life." . . .

I am instructed by the Word of God that His promises are for me and for every child of God. The banquet is spread before us; we are invited to eat the Word of God, which will strengthen spiritual muscle and sinew.— *Manuscript Releases,* vol. 21, pp. 132, 133.

True Higher Education Found in the Word of God

*Get wisdom! Get understanding! Do not forget, nor turn away
from the words of my mouth. Proverbs 4:5, NKJV.*

THERE IS NO TIME now to fill the mind with false ideas of what is called
higher education. There can be no higher education than that which
comes from the Author of truth. The Word of God is to be our study. We
are to educate our children in the truths found therein. It is an inexhaustible treasure; but men and women fail to find this treasure because
they do not search until it is within their possession. In this Word is found
wisdom, unquestionable and inexhaustible wisdom, that did not originate
in the finite mind, but in the infinite mind.

When men and women are willing to be instructed as little children,
when they submit wholly to God, they will find in the Scriptures the science of education. When teachers and students enter Christ's school, to
learn from Him, they will talk intelligently of higher education, because
they will understand that it is that knowledge which enables people to understand the essence of science.

Those who would seek successfully for the hidden treasure must rise
to higher pursuits than the things of this world. Their affections and all
their capabilities must be consecrated to this search. Men and women of
piety and talent catch views of eternal realities, but often they fail to understand, because the things that are seen eclipse the glory of the unseen.
By many human wisdom is thought to be higher than the wisdom of the
divine Teacher, and God's lesson book is looked upon as old-fashioned, so
much so indeed as to be thought tame and stale. But by those who have
been vivified by the Holy Spirit it is not so regarded. They see the priceless treasure, and would sell all to buy the field that contains it. . . .

Those who make the Word of God their study, who dig for the treasures of truth, will appreciate the weighty principles taught, and will digest
them. As a result, they will be imbued with the Spirit of Christ; and by beholding, they will become changed into His likeness. They will teach like
disciples who have been sitting at the feet of Jesus, who have accustomed
themselves to learn of Him, that they might know Him whom to know
aright is life eternal.—*Review and Herald,* July 3, 1900.

To Understand God's Word Better, Be Obedient

The mind of one who has understanding seeks knowledge, but the mouths of fools feed on folly. Proverbs 15:14, NRSV.

NO ONE CAN search the Old and New Testaments in the Spirit of Christ without being rewarded. "Come unto me, all ye that labour and are heavy laden," the Savior says, "and I will give you rest. Take my yoke [of obedience] upon you, and learn of me; for I am meek and lowly in heart: and ye shall find rest unto your souls. For my yoke is easy, and my burden is light." The Great Teacher's invitation is before you. Will you willingly respond to it? You cannot draw near, placing yourself as a learner at the feet of Christ, without having your mind enlightened, and your heart quickened with a pure, holy admiration. You will then say, "Blessed is he that cometh in the name of the Lord."

Disobedience has closed the door to a vast amount of knowledge that might have been gained from the Word of God. Understanding means obedience to God's commandments. Had men and women been obedient, they would have understood the plan of God's government. The heavenly world would have opened its chambers of grace and glory for exploration. Human beings would have been altogether different from what they are now, in form, in speech, in song; for by exploring the mines of truth, they would have been ennobled. The mystery of redemption, the incarnation of Christ, His atoning sacrifice, would not be, as they are now, vague in our minds. They would have been not only better understood, but altogether more highly appreciated.

In eternity we shall learn that which, if we had received the enlightenment that it was possible for us to obtain here, would have opened our understanding. The themes of redemption will employ the hearts and minds and tongues of the redeemed through the everlasting ages. They will understand the truths that Christ longed to open to His disciples, but which they did not have faith to grasp. Forever and forever, new views of the perfection and glory of Christ will appear.—*Review and Herald,* July 3, 1900.

The Bible Reveals
the Way to Christ

Love one another fervently with a pure heart, . . . because "all flesh is as grass,
and all the glory of man as the flower of the grass. The grass withers, and its flower
falls away, but the word of the Lord endures forever." 1 Peter 1:22-25, NKJV.

THE BLESSED BIBLE gives us a knowledge of the great plan of salvation, and shows us how every individual may have eternal life. Who is the author of the Book? Jesus Christ. He is the True Witness, and He says to His own, "I give unto them eternal life; and they shall never perish, neither shall any man pluck them out of my hand." The Bible is to show us the way to Christ, and in Christ eternal life is revealed. Jesus said to the Jews and to those who pressed about Him in great multitudes, "Search the scriptures." The Jews had the Word in the Old Testament, but they had so mingled it with human opinions, that its truths were mystified, and the will of God to human beings was covered up. The religious teachers of the people are following their example in this age.

Though the Jews had the Scriptures which testified of Christ, they were not able to discern Christ in the Scriptures; and although we have the Old and the New Testament, people today wrest the Scriptures to evade their truths; and in their interpretations of the Scriptures, they teach, as did the Pharisees, the maxims and traditions of humanity for the commandments of God. In Christ's day the religious leaders had so long presented human ideas before the people, that the teaching of Christ was in every way opposed to their theories and practice.

His sermon on the mount virtually contradicted the doctrines of the self-righteous scribes and Pharisees. They had so misrepresented God that He was looked upon as a stern judge, incapable of compassion, mercy, and love. They presented to the people endless maxims and traditions as proceeding from God, when they had no "Thus saith the Lord" for their authority. Though they professed to know and to worship the true and living God, they wholly misrepresented Him; and the character of God, as represented by His Son, was as an original subject, a new gift to the world. Christ made every effort so to sweep away the misrepresentations of Satan, that the confidence of people in the love of God might be restored.— *Fundamentals of Christian Education*, pp. 308, 309.

Search the Scriptures, and Be Obedient

Anyone who resolves to do the will of God will know whether the teaching is from God or whether I am speaking on my own. John 7:17, NRSV.

THOSE WHO HUMBLY and prayerfully search the Scriptures, to know and to do God's will, will not be in doubt of their obligations to God. For "if any man will do his will, he shall know of the doctrine." If you would know the mystery of godliness, you must follow the plain word of truth— feeling or no feeling, emotion or no emotion. Obedience must be rendered from a sense of principle, and the right must be pursued under all circumstances. This is the character that is elected of God unto salvation.

The test of a genuine Christian is given in the Word of God. Says Jesus, "If ye love me, keep my commandments." . . . Here are the conditions upon which every soul will be elected to eternal life. Your obedience to God's commandments will prove your right to an inheritance with the saints in light. God has elected a certain excellence of character; and everyone who, through the grace of Christ, shall reach the standard of His requirement will have an abundant entrance into the kingdom of glory. All who would reach this standard of character will have to employ the means that God has provided to this end.

If you would inherit the rest that remaineth for the children of God, you must become a colaborer with God. You are elected to wear the yoke of Christ—to bear His burden, to lift His cross. You are to be diligent "to make your calling and election sure."

Search the Scriptures, and you will see that not a son or a daughter of Adam is elected to be saved in disobedience to God's law. The world makes void the law of God; but Christians are chosen to sanctification through obedience to the truth. They are elected to bear the cross, if they would wear the crown.

The Bible is the only rule of faith and doctrine. . . . Only Bible truth and Bible religion will stand the test of the judgment. We are not to pervert the Word of God to suit our convenience and worldly interest, but to honestly inquire, "What wilt thou have me to do?"—*Review and Herald,* July 17, 1888.

True Learners Accept
the Scriptures as God's Voice

If you abide in My word, you are My disciples indeed. And you shall know the truth, and the truth shall make you free. John 8:31, 32, NKJV.

THE YOUNG MEN and women who make the Bible their guide need not mistake the path of duty and of safety. That Book will teach them to preserve their integrity of character, to be truthful, to practice no deception. It will teach them that they must never transgress God's law in order to accomplish a desired object, even though to obey involves a sacrifice. It will teach them that the blessing of heaven will not rest upon them if they depart from the path of rightdoing; that although some may appear to prosper in disobedience, they will surely reap the fruit of their sowing.

Those only who read the Scriptures as the voice of God speaking to them are true learners. They tremble at the voice of God, for to them it is a living reality. They open their understanding to divine instruction and pray for grace, that they may obtain a preparation for service. As the heavenly torch is placed in their hands, the seekers for truth see their own frailty, their infirmity, the hopelessness of looking to themselves for righteousness. They see that there is in them nothing that can recommend them to God. They pray for the Holy Spirit, the representative of Christ, to be their constant guide, to lead them into all truth. They repeat the promise "The Comforter, which is the Holy Ghost, whom the Father will send in my name, he shall teach you all things" (John 14:26). . . .

Diligent Bible students will constantly increase in knowledge and discernment. Their intellect will grasp elevated subjects and lay hold of the truth of eternal realities. Their motives of action will be right. They will use their talents of influence to help others to understand more perfectly their God-given responsibilities. Their hearts will be a wellspring of joy as they see success attend their efforts to impart to others the blessings they have received.—*Counsels to Parents, Teachers, and Students*, pp. 449-451.

MAY

❧

The Day That God Made Holy

God's People to
Keep the Sabbath

*And on the seventh day God ended His work which He had done, and He
rested on the seventh day from all His work which He had done. Genesis 2:2, NKJV.*

GOD SANCTIFIED AND blessed the day in which He had rested from
all His wondrous work. And this Sabbath, sanctified of God, was to be kept
for a perpetual covenant. It was a memorial that was to stand from age to
age, till the close of earth's history.

God brought the Hebrews out of their Egyptian bondage, and commanded them to observe His Sabbath, and keep the law given in Eden.
Every week He worked a miracle to establish in their minds the fact that
in the beginning of the world He had instituted the Sabbath. . . .

In the third month they came to the desert of Sinai, and there the law
was spoken from the mount in awful grandeur. During their stay in Egypt,
Israel had so long heard and seen idolatry practiced that to a large degree
they had lost their knowledge of God and of His law, and their sense of
the importance and sacredness of the Sabbath; the law was given a second
time to call these things to their remembrance. In God's statutes was defined practical religion for all mankind. Before Israel was placed the true
standard of righteousness.

"And the Lord spake unto Moses, saying, Speak thou also unto the
children of Israel, saying, Verily my sabbaths ye shall keep." Some, who
have been anxious to make of none effect the law of God, have quoted
this word "sabbaths," interpreting it to mean the annual sabbaths of the
Jews. But they do not connect this positive requirement with that which
follows: "For it is a sign between me and you throughout your generations; that ye may know that I am the Lord that doth sanctify you. Ye
shall keep the sabbath therefore; for it is holy unto you: every one that
defileth it shall surely be put to death: for whosoever doeth any work
therein, that soul shall be cut off from among his people. Six days may
work be done; but in the seventh is the sabbath of rest, holy to the Lord:
whosoever doeth any work in the sabbath day, he shall surely be put to
death. Wherefore the children of Israel shall keep the sabbath, to observe
the sabbath throughout their generations, for a perpetual covenant. It is a
sign between me and the children of Israel for ever: for in six days the
Lord made heaven and earth, and on the seventh day he rested, and was
refreshed."—*Review and Herald,* Aug. 30, 1898.

The Sabbath
Intended for All Humankind

You made known to them Your holy Sabbath, and commanded them precepts, statutes and laws, by the hand of Moses Your servant. Nehemiah 9:14, NKJV.

THERE ARE THOSE who hold that the Sabbath was given only for the Jews; but God has never said this. He committed the Sabbath to His people Israel as a sacred trust; but the very fact that the desert of Sinai, and not Palestine, was the place selected by Him in which to proclaim His law reveals that He intended it for all humankind. The law of ten commandments is as old as Creation. Therefore the Sabbath institution has no special relation to the Jews, any more than to all other created beings. God has made the observance of the Sabbath obligatory upon all men and women.

"The sabbath," it is plainly stated, "was made for man." Let everyone, therefore, who is in danger of being deceived on this point give heed to the Word of God rather than the assertions of human beings.

In Eden, God said to Adam concerning the tree of knowledge, "In the day that thou eatest thereof thou shalt surely die." "And the serpent said unto the woman, Ye shall not surely die: for God doth know that in the day ye eat thereof, then your eyes shall be opened, and ye shall be as gods, knowing good and evil." Adam listened to the voice of Satan speaking through his wife; he believed another voice than that which spoke the law in Eden.

Every human being has been placed on trial, as were Adam and Eve in Eden. As the tree of knowledge was placed in the midst of the garden of Eden, so the Sabbath command is placed in the midst of the Decalogue. In regard to the fruit of the tree of knowledge, the restriction was made, "Ye shall not eat of it, . . . lest ye die." Of the Sabbath, God said, Ye shall not defile it, but keep it holy. "Remember the sabbath day, to keep it holy." As the tree of knowledge was the test of Adam's obedience, so the fourth command is the test that God has given to prove the loyalty of all His people. The experience of Adam is to be a warning to us so long as time shall last. It warns us not to receive any assurance from the mouth of mortals or of angels that will detract one jot or tittle from the sacred law of Jehovah.—*Review and Herald,* Aug. 30, 1898.

A Day Pointing to God's Power and Love

Then God blessed the seventh day and sanctified it, because in it He rested from all His work which God had created and made. Genesis 2:3, NKJV.

GOD LOOKED WITH satisfaction upon the work of His hands. All was perfect, worthy of its divine Author, and He rested, not as one weary, but as well pleased with the fruits of His wisdom and goodness and the manifestations of His glory.

After resting upon the seventh day, God sanctified it, or set it apart, as a day of rest for humankind. Following the example of the Creator, dwellers on earth were to rest upon this sacred day, that as they should look upon the heavens and the earth, they might reflect upon God's great work of creation; and that as they should behold the evidences of God's wisdom and goodness, their hearts might be filled with love and reverence for their Maker.

In Eden, God set up the memorial of His work of creation, in placing His blessing upon the seventh day. The Sabbath was committed to Adam, the father and representative of the whole human family. Its observance was to be an act of grateful acknowledgment, on the part of all who should dwell upon the earth, that God was their Creator and their rightful Sovereign; that they were the work of His hands and the subjects of His authority. Thus the institution was wholly commemorative, and given to the entire human race. There was nothing in it shadowy or of restricted application to any people. . . .

God designs that the Sabbath shall direct the minds of all people to the contemplation of His created works. Nature speaks to their senses, declaring that there is a living God, the Creator, the Supreme Ruler of all. "The heavens declare the glory of God; and the firmament sheweth his handiwork. Day unto day uttereth speech, and night unto night sheweth knowledge" (Ps. 19:1, 2). The beauty that clothes the earth is a token of God's love. We may behold it in the everlasting hills, in the lofty trees, in the opening buds and the delicate flowers. All speak to us of God. The Sabbath, ever pointing to Him who made them all, bids men and women open the great book of nature and trace therein the wisdom, the power, and the love of the Creator.—*Patriarchs and Prophets,* pp. 47, 48.

Six Days for Us,
Only One for God

Remember the Sabbath day, to keep it holy. Six days you shall labor and do all your work, but the seventh day is the Sabbath of the Lord your God. . . . Therefore the Lord blessed the Sabbath day and hallowed it. Exodus 20:8-11, NKJV.

AT THE VERY beginning of the fourth precept, God said, *"Remember,"* knowing that men and women, in the multitude of their cares and perplexities, would be tempted to excuse themselves from meeting the full requirements of the law or, in the press of worldly business, would forget its sacred importance. "Six days shalt thou labour, and do all thy work," the usual business of life, for worldly profit or pleasure. These words are very explicit; there can be no mistake.

Brother K, how dare you venture to transgress a commandment so solemn and important? Has the Lord made an exception by which you are absolved from the law He has given to the world? Are your transgressions omitted from the book of record? Has He agreed to excuse your disobedience when the nations come before Him for judgment? Do not for a moment deceive yourself with the thought that your sin will not bring its merited punishment. Your transgressions will be visited with the rod, because you have had the light, yet have walked directly contrary to it. "That servant, which knew his lord's will, and prepared not himself, neither did according to his will, shall be beaten with many stripes."

God has given us six days in which to do our own work and carry on the usual business of life; but He claims one day, which He has set apart and sanctified. He gives it to us as a day in which we may rest from labor and devote ourselves to worship and the improvement of our spiritual condition. What a flagrant outrage it is for us to steal the one sanctified day of Jehovah and appropriate it to our own selfish purposes!

It is the grossest presumption for mortal beings to venture upon a compromise with the Almighty in order to secure their own petty, temporal interests. It is as ruthless a violation of the law to occasionally use the Sabbath for secular business as to entirely reject it; for it is making the Lord's commandments a matter of convenience.—*Testimonies for the Church,* vol. 4, p. 249.

The Sabbath Turns
Minds to the Creator

*If you turn away your foot from the Sabbath, from doing your pleasure on My
holy day, and call the Sabbath a delight, the holy day of the Lord honorable,
. . . then you shall delight yourself in the Lord. Isaiah 58:13, 14, NKJV.*

MANY PROFESSING CHRISTIANS of today are closing their hearts and
minds to the Sun of Righteousness, whose bright beams would chase away
the darkness and mist that exist there. They refuse the light, and make
God's requirements and will of secondary importance. In place of the rest
day given them by Jehovah, they accept a counterfeit sabbath; they worship an idol, and transgress God's holy law in trampling upon the Sabbath
which He has instituted and blessed.

The object of the Sabbath was that all humanity might be benefited.
After God had made the world in six days, He rested, and blessed and sanctified the day upon which He rested from all His work which He had created and made. He set apart that special day for human beings to rest from
their labor, that as they should look upon the earth beneath, and the heavens above, the tangible proofs of God's infinite wisdom, their hearts might
be filled with love and reverence for their Maker.

Had the human family always kept the day which God has blessed and
sanctified, there would never have been an infidel in our world; for the
Sabbath was given as a memorial of the Creator's work; it was given that,
upon that day in a special sense, people might draw their minds away from
the things of earth to the contemplation of God and His mighty power. . . .

The heathen in their blindness bow down to idols of wood and stone.
"These be our gods," they say. But in the fourth commandment we have
the proof that our God is the true and living God. In it is the seal of His
authority: ". . . For in six days the Lord made heaven and earth, the sea,
and all that in them is, and rested the seventh day: wherefore the Lord
blessed the sabbath day and hallowed it." In the heavens that declare the
glory of their Maker—the sun, shining in its strength, giving life and
beauty to all created things; the moon, and the stars, the works of His
hands—we see the superiority of the God we worship. He is the God that
"made the earth and the heavens."—*Bible Echo,* Oct. 12, 1896.

On Day Six,
Prepare for the Sabbath

This is what the Lord has said: "Tomorrow is a Sabbath rest, a holy Sabbath to the Lord. Bake what you will bake today, and boil what you will boil; and lay up for yourselves all that remains, to be kept until morning." Exodus 16:23, NKJV.

ON THE SIXTH DAY, it was found that a double quantity [of manna] had been deposited, and the people gathered two omers for every person. When the rulers saw what they were doing, they hastened to acquaint Moses of this apparent violation of his directions; but his answer was "This is that which the Lord hath said, To-morrow is the rest of the holy sabbath unto the Lord: bake that which ye will bake to-day, and seethe that ye will seethe; and that which remaineth over lay up for you to be kept until the morning." They did so, and found that it remained unchanged. And Moses said, "Eat that to-day; for today is a sabbath unto the Lord: today ye shall not find it in the field. Six days ye shall gather it; but on the seventh day, which is the sabbath, in it there shall be none."

The Lord is no less particular now in regard to His Sabbath than when He gave the foregoing special directions to the children of Israel. He required them to bake that which they would bake, and seethe (that is, boil) that which they would seethe, on the sixth day, preparatory to the rest of the Sabbath. Those who neglect to make suitable preparation on the sixth day for the Sabbath violate the fourth commandment, and are transgressors of God's law. In His instructions to the Israelites, God forbade baking and boiling upon the Sabbath. That prohibition should be regarded by all Sabbathkeepers as a solemn injunction from Jehovah to them. The Lord would guard His people from indulging in gluttony upon the Sabbath, which He has set apart for sacred meditation and worship. . . .

God manifested His great care and love for His people in sending them bread from heaven. "Man did eat angels' food"; that is, food provided for them by the angels. . . . After they were abundantly supplied with food, they were ashamed of their unbelief and murmurings, and promised to trust the Lord for the future.—*Signs of the Times,* Apr. 15, 1880.

Threefold Miracle
Reveals Sabbath Sacredness

*And the children of Israel ate manna forty years, until they
came to an inhabited land; they ate manna until they came to
the border of the land of Canaan. Exodus 16:35, NKJV.*

EVERY WEEK DURING their long sojourn in the wilderness the Israelites
witnessed a threefold miracle, designed to impress their minds with the sacredness of the Sabbath: a double quantity of manna fell on the sixth day,
none on the seventh, and the portion needed for the Sabbath was preserved sweet and pure, when if any were kept over at any other time it became unfit for use.

In the circumstances connected with the giving of the manna, we have
conclusive evidence that the Sabbath was not instituted, as many claim,
when the law was given at Sinai. Before the Israelites came to Sinai they
understood the Sabbath to be obligatory upon them. In being obliged to
gather every Friday a double portion of manna in preparation for the
Sabbath, when none would fall, the sacred nature of the day of rest was
continually impressed upon them. And when some of the people went out
on the Sabbath to gather manna, the Lord asked, "How long *refuse* ye to
keep my commandments and my laws?"

"The children of Israel did eat manna forty years, until they came to
a land inhabited; they did eat manna, until they came unto the borders of
the land of Canaan." For forty years they were daily reminded by this
miraculous provision, of God's unfailing care and tender love. In the
words of the psalmist, God gave them "of the corn of heaven. Man did
eat angels' food" (Ps. 78:24, 25)—that is, food provided for them by the
angels. Sustained by "the corn of heaven," they were daily taught that,
having God's promise, they were as secure from want as if surrounded by
fields of waving grain on the fertile plains of Canaan.—*Patriarchs and
Prophets,* pp. 296, 297.

Satan's Attack
Against God's Memorial

*In vain they worship Me, teaching as doctrines
the commandments of men. Matthew 15:9, NKJV.*

THE ENEMY HAS worked in the religious world to deceive people into the belief that the law of God can be set aside. He has had long years of experience in this work, for he began with our first parents, using his powers to cause them to distrust God. If he could interpose himself between their souls and God, he knew that he would succeed. The prospect of becoming gods, knowing good and evil, was pleasing to Adam and Eve, and they yielded to the temptation.

In receiving a knowledge of good and evil, human beings feel that they are gaining much; but they do not understand the purposes of Satan. They do not understand that they are taken in his snare when they tamper with the law of God. The enemy knows that if the church can be controlled by political enactments, if it can be led to unite with the world, it virtually acknowledges him as its head. Then the authority of human-made commandments will work to oppose the rule of the government of heaven. Under the leadership of Satan there are those who will dispense with the righteous, holy enactments of God concerning the Sabbath, the observance of which is to be a sign between God and His people forever.

Satan's plan has taken with the religious world. He has created an order of things entirely his own, making void the law of God. Through his deceptive working he has gained in the professedly Christian world that which he thought to gain in heaven—an abrogation of the laws of Jehovah. Through the Roman power he has worked to remove God's memorial, and has erected a memorial of his own to sever God from His people. Today the Protestant world is estranged from God by its acceptance of a spurious sabbath. Not one iota of sacred authority can they find for doing this; yet, full of zeal, they assert that the Lord's memorial given at creation should be ignored, despised, trampled upon, and the first day of the week take its place.

No deeper wound could be inflicted on God than to ignore His holy day, and place in its stead a spurious sabbath that bears no mark of sanctity. God gave the Sabbath to the world to be set apart for His name's glory. He says: "It is a sign between me and you throughout your generations; that ye may know that I am the Lord that doth sanctify you. . . . Israel shall keep the sabbath, to observe the sabbath throughout their generations, for a perpetual covenant."—*Signs of the Times,* Nov. 22, 1899.

Sabbath Truth
Supported by the Word

Therefore the children of Israel shall keep the Sabbath, to observe the Sabbath throughout their generations as a perpetual covenant. Exodus 31:16, NKJV.

THE DAYS IN which we live are times that call for constant vigilance, times in which God's people should be awake to do a great work in presenting the light on the Sabbath question. They should arouse, and warn the inhabitants of the world that Christ is soon coming the second time with power and great glory. . . .

This is a time for the Lord's servants to work with undiminished zeal to carry the third angel's message to all parts of the world. The work of this message is spreading far and near; yet we should not feel satisfied, but hasten to carry to thousands more the truth regarding the perpetuity of the law of Jehovah. From all our institutions of learning, from our publishing houses, from our sanitariums, the message is to be proclaimed. The people of God everywhere are to be aroused to cooperate in the great, grand work represented by the first, second, and third angels' messages. This last warning to the inhabitants of the earth is to make everyone see the importance God attaches to His holy law. So plainly is the truth to be presented, that no transgressor, hearing it, shall fail to discern the importance of obedience to the Sabbath commandment. . . .

I am instructed to say to our people, Gather together from the Scriptures the proofs that God has sanctified the Sabbath, and let the words of the Lord be read before the congregations, showing that all who turn aside from a plain "Thus saith the Lord" will be condemned. The Sabbath has been the test of the loyalty of God's people in all ages. "It is a sign between me and the children of Israel for ever," the Lord declares.

In giving the Word of God to the people, there is nothing to be argued. The Word of the Lord is given for the observance of the seventh day; let this Word be given to the people, and not the words of human beings. In so doing you throw the burden of responsibility upon those who reject it; and the arguments of opposers are arguments against the specifications of the Word. While you exalt a "Thus saith the Lord," the controversy is not with the worker, but with God.—*Review and Herald,* Mar. 26, 1908.

The Sign of God's Authority

*Those from among you shall build the old waste places; you shall raise
up the foundations of many generations; and you shall be called the
Repairer of the Breach, the Restorer of Streets to Dwell In. Isaiah 58:12, NKJV.*

THE SABBATH IS a golden clasp that unites God and His people. But the Sabbath command has been broken. God's holy day has been desecrated. The Sabbath has been torn from its place by the man of sin, and a common working day has been exalted in its stead. A breach has been made in the law, and this breach is to be repaired. The true Sabbath is to be exalted to its rightful position as God's rest day.

In the fifty-eighth chapter of Isaiah is outlined the work which God's people are to do. They are to magnify the law and make it honorable, to build up the old waste places, and to raise up the foundations of many generations. To those who do this work God says: "Thou shalt be called, The repairer of the breach, The restorer of paths to dwell in. If thou turn away thy foot from the sabbath, from doing thy pleasure on my holy day; and call the sabbath a delight, the holy of the Lord, honourable; and shalt honour him, not doing thine own ways, nor finding thine own pleasure, nor speaking thine own words: then shalt thou delight thyself in the Lord; and I will cause thee to ride upon the high places of the earth, and feed thee with the heritage of Jacob thy father: for the mouth of the Lord hath spoken it" (verses 12-14).

The Sabbath question is to be the issue in the great final conflict in which all the world will act a part. Men and women have honored Satan's principles above the principles that rule in the heavens. They have accepted the spurious sabbath, which Satan has exalted as the sign of his authority. But God has set His seal upon His royal requirement. Each sabbath institution [both true and false] bears the name of its author, an ineffaceable mark that shows the authority of each. It is our work to lead the people to understand this. We are to show them that it is of vital consequence whether they bear the mark of God's kingdom or the mark of the kingdom of rebellion, for they acknowledge themselves subjects of the kingdom whose mark they bear. God has called us to uplift the standard of His downtrodden Sabbath. How important, then, that our example in Sabbathkeeping should be right.—*Testimonies for the Church,* vol. 6, pp. 351-353.

The Spurious Sabbath
a False Signpost

Speak also to the children of Israel, saying: "Surely My Sabbaths you shall keep, for it is a sign between Me and you throughout your generations, that you may know that I am the Lord who sanctifies you." Exodus 31:13, NKJV.

THE LORD HAS clearly defined the road to the City of God; but the great apostate has changed the signpost, setting up a false one—a spurious sabbath. He says: "I will work at cross-purposes with God. I will empower my delegate, the man of sin, to take down God's memorial, the seventh-day Sabbath. Thus will I show the world that the day sanctified and blessed by God has been changed. That day shall not live in the minds of the people. I will obliterate the memory of it. I will place in its stead a day bearing not the credentials of heaven, a day that cannot be a sign between God and His people.

"I will lead the people who accept this day to place upon it the sanctity that God placed upon the seventh day. Through my vicegerent I will exalt myself. The first day shall be extolled, and the Protestant world shall receive this spurious sabbath as genuine. Through the nonobservance of the Sabbath God instituted, I will bring His law into contempt. The words 'a sign between me and you throughout your generations' I will make to serve on the side of my sabbath. Thus the world will become mine. I will be ruler of the earth, prince of the world. I will so control the minds under my power that God's Sabbath shall be an object of contempt." . . .

The man of sin has instituted a false sabbath, and the professed Christian world has adopted this child of the papacy, refusing to obey God. Thus Satan leads men and women in a direction opposite to the city of refuge; and by the multitudes who follow him, it is demonstrated that Adam and Eve are not the only ones who have accepted the words of the wily foe.

The enemy of all good has turned the signpost round, so that it points to the path of disobedience as the path of happiness.—*The Seventh-day Adventist Bible Commentary,* Ellen G. White Comments, vol. 4, pp. 1171, 1172.

Do Good
on the Sabbath

"For the Son of Man is Lord even of the Sabbath." . . .
"It is lawful to do good on the Sabbath." Matthew 12:8-12, NKJV.

JESUS HAD LESSONS which He desired to give to His disciples, that when He was no longer with them, they might not be misled by the wily misrepresentations of the priests and rulers in regard to the correct observance of the Sabbath. He would remove from the Sabbath the traditions and exactions with which the priests and rulers had burdened it.

In passing through a field of grain on the Sabbath day, He and His disciples, being hungry, began to pluck the heads of grain and to eat. "But when the Pharisees saw it, they said unto him, Behold, thy disciples do that which is not lawful to do upon the sabbath day." To answer their accusation, He referred them to the action of David and others, saying: "Have ye not read what David did, when he was an hungred, and they that were with him; how he entered into the house of God, and did eat the shewbread, which was not lawful for him to eat, neither for them which were with him, but only for the priests? Or have ye not read in the law, how that on the sabbath days the priests in the temple profane the sabbath, and are blameless? But I say unto you, That in this place is one greater than the temple."

If excessive hunger excused David from violating even the holiness of the sanctuary, and made his act guiltless, how much more excusable was the simple act of the disciples in plucking grain and eating it upon the Sabbath day! Jesus would teach His disciples and His enemies that the service of God was first of all; and if fatigue and hunger attended the work, it was right to satisfy the wants of humanity even upon the Sabbath day. . . .

Works of mercy and of necessity are no transgression of the law. God does not condemn these things. The act of mercy and necessity in passing through a grainfield, of plucking the heads of wheat, of rubbing them in their hands, and of eating to satisfy their hunger, He declared to be in accordance with the law which He Himself had proclaimed from Sinai. Thus He declared Himself guiltless before scribes, rulers, and priests, before the heavenly universe, before fallen angels and fallen men.—*Review and Herald,* Aug. 3, 1897.

Do Soul-saving
Work on the Sabbath

*I will make a mortal more rare than fine gold, a man more
than the golden wedge of Ophir. Isaiah 13:12, NKJV.*

IF IT WAS RIGHT for David to satisfy his hunger by eating of the bread
that had been set apart to a holy use, then it was right for the disciples to
supply their need by plucking the grain upon the sacred hours of the
Sabbath. Again, the priests in the Temple performed greater labor on the
Sabbath than upon other days. The same labor in secular business would
be sinful; but the work of the priests was in the service of God. They were
performing those rites that pointed to the redeeming power of Christ, and
their labor was in harmony with the object of the Sabbath. But now Christ
Himself had come. The disciples, in doing the work of Christ, were engaged in God's service, and that which was necessary for the accomplishment of this work it was right to do on the Sabbath day.

Christ would teach His disciples and His enemies that the service of
God is first of all. The object of God's work in this world is the redemption of humankind; therefore that which is necessary to be done on the
Sabbath in the accomplishment of this work is in accord with the Sabbath
law. Jesus then crowned His argument by declaring Himself the "Lord of
the Sabbath," One above all question and above all law. This infinite Judge
acquits the disciples of blame, appealing to the very statutes they are accused of violating. . . .

Upon another Sabbath, as Jesus entered a synagogue, He saw there a
man who had a withered hand. The Pharisees watched Him, eager to see
what He would do. The Savior well knew that in healing on the Sabbath
He would be regarded as a transgressor, but He did not hesitate to break
down the wall of traditional requirements that barricaded the Sabbath.
Jesus bade the afflicted man stand forth, and then asked, "Is it lawful to do
good on the sabbath days, or to do evil? to save life, or to kill?" It was a
maxim among the Jews that a failure to do good, when one had opportunity, was to do evil; to neglect to save life was to kill. Thus Jesus met
the rabbis on their own ground. "But they held their peace. And when
he had looked round about on them with anger, being grieved for the
hardness of their hearts, he saith unto the man, Stretch forth thine hand.
And he stretched it out: and his hand was restored whole as the other"
(Mark 3:4, 5).—*The Desire of Ages,* pp. 285, 286.

Doing Well on the Sabbath Honors the Day

*Of how much more value then is a man than a sheep? Therefore
it is lawful to do good on the Sabbath. Matthew 12:12, NKJV.*

WHEN QUESTIONED, "Is it lawful to heal on the sabbath days?" Jesus
answered, "What man shall there be among *you*, that shall have one sheep,
and if it fall into a pit on the sabbath day, will he not lay hold on it, and
lift it out? How much then is a man better than a sheep? Wherefore it is
lawful to do well on the sabbath days" (Matt. 12:10-12).

The spies dared not answer Christ in the presence of the multitude, for
fear of involving themselves in difficulty. They knew that He had spoken
the truth. Rather than violate their traditions, they would leave a human
being to suffer, while they would relieve a brute because of the loss to the
owner if it were neglected. Thus greater care was shown for a dumb animal than for a person, who is made in the image of God.

This illustrates the working of all false religions. They originate in
the human desire to exalt self above God, but they result in degrading
humanity below the brute. Every religion that wars against the
sovereignty of God defrauds human beings of the glory which was theirs
at the creation, and which is to be restored to them in Christ. Every false
religion teaches its adherents to be careless of human needs, sufferings,
and rights. The gospel places a high value upon humanity as the purchase
of the blood of Christ, and it teaches a tender regard for the wants and
woes of humankind. . . .

When Jesus turned upon the Pharisees with the question whether it
was lawful on the Sabbath day to do good or to do evil, to save life or to
kill, He confronted them with their own wicked purposes. They were
hunting His life with bitter hatred, while He was saving life and bringing
happiness to multitudes. Was it better to slay upon the Sabbath, as they
were planning to do, than to heal the afflicted, as He had done? Was it
more righteous to have murder in the heart upon God's holy day rather
than love, which finds expression in deeds of mercy?

In the healing of the withered hand, Jesus condemned the custom of
the Jews, and left the fourth commandment standing as God had given it.
"It is lawful to do well on the sabbath days," He declared. By sweeping
away the senseless restrictions of the Jews, Christ honored the Sabbath,
while those who complained of Him were dishonoring God's holy day.—
The Desire of Ages, pp. 286, 287.

The Sabbath Designed to Bring Us Into Harmony With God

And He said to them, "The Sabbath was made for man,
and not man for the Sabbath." Mark 2:27, NKJV.

WHEN ACCUSED OF Sabbathbreaking at Bethesda, Jesus defended Himself by affirming His Sonship to God, and declaring that He worked in harmony with the Father. Now that the disciples are attacked, He cites His accusers to examples from the Old Testament, acts performed on the Sabbath by those who were in the service of God.

The Jewish teachers prided themselves on their knowledge of the Scriptures, and in the Savior's answer there was an implied rebuke for their ignorance of the Sacred Writings. "Have ye not read so much as this," He said, "what David did, when himself was an hungred, and they which were with him; how he went into the house of God, and did take and eat the shewbread . . . ; which it is not lawful to eat but for the priests alone?" (Luke 6:3, 4). "And he said unto them, The sabbath was made for man, and not man for the sabbath" (Mark 2:27). "Have ye not read in the law, how that on the sabbath days the priests in the temple profane the sabbath, and are blameless? But I say unto you, That in this place is one greater than the temple" (Matt. 12:5, 6). "The Son of man is Lord also of the sabbath" (Mark 2:28). . . .

Jesus did not let the matter pass without administering a rebuke to His enemies. He declared that in their blindness they had mistaken the object of the Sabbath. He said, "If ye had known what this meaneth, I will have mercy, and not sacrifice, ye would not have condemned the guiltless" (Matt. 12:7). Their many heartless rites could not supply the lack of that truthful integrity and tender love which will ever characterize the true worshiper of God. . . .

It is the service of love that God values. When this is lacking, the mere round of ceremony is an offense to Him. So with the Sabbath. It was designed to bring men and women into communion with God; but when the mind was absorbed with wearisome rites, the object of the Sabbath was thwarted. Its mere outward observance was a mockery.—*The Desire of Ages,* pp. 284-286.

The Sabbath a Sign
of Covenant Relationship

It is a sign between Me and the children of Israel forever;
for in six days the Lord made the heavens and the earth, and on
the seventh day He rested and was refreshed. Exodus 31:17, NKJV.

IF MEN AND WOMEN would acknowledge the true Sabbath, they would not, as they now do, despise the Word of God. The observance of the seventh day would be a golden chain binding them to their Creator. But the commandment which points out who the true God is—the Creator and Ruler of the earth—is dishonored and disobeyed. This is the reason why there is so little stability in the world. The churches have refused God's sign and misrepresented His character. They have torn down God's sacred rest day, exalting a spurious sabbath in its place. Oh, that men and women would cease to lock themselves out of heaven by their own perversities.—*Manuscript Releases,* vol. 5, p. 82.

A breach has been made in the law of God, and He is calling for a people that will repair this breach. A spurious sabbath has been exalted instead of the Sabbath of Jehovah. Soon laws will be passed compelling all to observe the first day of the week instead of the seventh. We must meet this difficulty, and we shall find trouble enough, without stirring up contention among those who profess to be keeping God's commandments.— *Ibid.,* pp. 82, 83.

With these plain words [Exodus 31:16, 17] before us, who of those who know the truth will dare to make less prominent the distinguishing features of our faith? It is an established fact, to be made prominent before all nations, kindreds, tongues, and peoples, that the Lord God made the world in six days, and rested on the seventh day. "Thus the heavens and the earth were finished, and all the host of them. And on the seventh day God ended his work which he had made; and he rested on the seventh day from all his work which he had made."—*Ibid.,* p. 83.

The Sabbath was God's sign between Him and His people, and evidence of His kindness, mercy, and love, a token by which His people are distinguished from all false religionists of the world. And God has pledged Himself that He will bless them in their obedience, showing Himself that He is their God, and has taken them into covenant relation with Himself, and that He will fulfill His promise to all that are obedient.—*Ibid.,* p. 84.

147

A Day of
Healing and Joy

*But the ruler of the synagogue answered with indignation, because Jesus
had healed on the Sabbath; and he said to the crowd, "There are six
days on which men ought to work; therefore come and be healed
on them, and not on the Sabbath day." Luke 13:14, NKJV.*

"AND HE WAS teaching in one of the synagogues on the sabbath. And,
behold, there was a woman which had a spirit of infirmity eighteen years,
and was bowed together, and could in no wise lift up herself. And when
Jesus saw her, he called her to him, and said unto her, Woman, thou art
loosed from thine infirmity. And he laid his hands on her; and immediately
she was made straight, and glorified God."

The compassionate heart of Christ was touched at the sight of this suffering woman, and we should suppose that every human being who looked
upon her would have rejoiced that she was loosed from her bondage, and
healed of an affliction that had bowed her down for eighteen years. But
Jesus perceived by the lowering, angry countenances of the priests and rabbis that they felt no joy at her deliverance. They were not ready to utter
thankful words because one who had been suffering and deformed by disease was restored to health and symmetry. They felt no gratitude that her
deformed body was made comely, and that the Holy Spirit made glad her
heart till it overflowed with thankfulness, and she glorified God.

The psalmist says, "Whoso offereth praise glorifieth me." But in the
midst of the words of gratitude is heard a discordant note. "And the ruler
of the synagogue answered with indignation, because that Jesus had healed
on the sabbath day." He was indignant that Christ had caused an unhappy
woman to sound a note of joy upon the Sabbath. In a loud voice, harsh
with passion, he said to the people, "There are six days in which men
ought to work; in them therefore come and be healed, and not on the sabbath day."

If this man had really had conscientious scruples in regard to the true
observance of the Sabbath, he would have discerned the nature and character of the work that Christ had performed. . . . The work that Christ had
done was in harmony with the sanctification of the Sabbath day. The people on this side and that side wondered and were glad at the work that had
been wrought for the suffering woman; and there were those whose hearts
were touched, whose minds were enlightened, who would have acknowledged themselves the disciples of Christ, had it not been for the lowering,
angry countenances of the rabbis.—*Signs of the Times, Apr. 23, 1896.*

A Day on
Which to Show Mercy

*Also to You, O Lord, belongs mercy; for You render to
each one according to his work. Psalm 62:12, NKJV.*

THE LORD GOD of Sabaoth will hear earnest prayer. He will lead those
who feel their dependence upon Him, and will so guide the workers that
many souls shall come to a knowledge of the truth.

Truth as it is in Jesus exercises a transforming influence upon the minds
of its receivers. Let no one forget that God is always a majority, and that
with Him success is bound to crown all missionary effort. Those who have
a living connection with God know that divinity works through humanity. Every soul that cooperates with God will do justly, love mercy, and
walk humbly with God.

The Lord is a God of mercy, and cares even for the dumb beasts He
has created. When He healed on the Sabbath day, and was accused of
breaking the law of God, He said to His accusers: "Doth not each one of
you on the sabbath loose his ox or his ass from the stall, and lead him away
to watering? And ought not this woman, being a daughter of Abraham,
whom Satan hath bound, lo, these eighteen years, be loosed from this bond
on the sabbath day? And when he had said these things, all his adversaries
were ashamed; and all the people rejoiced for all the glorious things that
were done by him."

The Lord looks upon the creatures He has made with compassion, no
matter to what race they may belong. God "hath made of one blood all
nations of men for to dwell on all the face of the earth, and hath determined the times before appointed, and the bounds of their habitation; that
they should seek the Lord, if haply they might feel after him, and find him,
though he be not far from every one of us; for in him we live, and move,
and have our being; as certain also of your own poets have said, For we
are also his offspring."

Speaking to His disciples, the Savior said, "All ye are brethren." God
is our common Father, and each one of us is our brother's keeper.—*Review
and Herald,* Jan. 21, 1896.

Set Example of Sabbath Sacredness, and Teach It

These words which I command you today shall be in your heart; you shall teach them diligently to your children, and shall talk of them when you sit in your house, when you walk by the way, when you lie down, and when you rise up. Deuteronomy 6:6, 7, NKJV.

YOU HAVE FAILED in your family to appreciate the sacredness of the Sabbath and to teach it to your children and enjoin upon them the importance of keeping it according to the commandment. Your sensibilities are not clear and ready to discern the high standard that we must reach in order to be commandment keepers. But God will assist you in your efforts when you take hold of the work earnestly. You should possess perfect control over yourself; then you can have better success in controlling your children when they are unruly.

There is a great work before you to repair past neglects; but you are not required to perform it in your own strength. Ministering angels will aid you in the work. Do not give up the work nor lay aside the burden, but take hold of it with a will and repair your long neglect. You must have higher views of God's claims upon you in regard to His holy day. Everything that can possibly be done on the six days which God has given to you should be done. You should not rob God of one hour of holy time.

Great blessings are promised to those who place a high estimate upon the Sabbath and realize the obligations resting upon them in regard to its observance: "If thou turn away thy foot from the sabbath [from trampling upon it, setting it at naught], from doing thy pleasure on my holy day; and call the sabbath a delight, the holy of the Lord, honourable; . . . I will cause thee to ride upon the high places of the earth, and feed thee with the heritage of Jacob thy father: for the mouth of the Lord hath spoken it."

When the Sabbath commences, we should place a guard upon ourselves, upon our acts and our words, lest we rob God by appropriating to our own use that time which is strictly the Lord's. . . .

Nothing which will in the sight of Heaven be regarded as a violation of the holy Sabbath should be left unsaid or undone, to be said or done upon the Sabbath. God requires not only that we refrain from physical labor upon the Sabbath, but that the mind be disciplined to dwell upon sacred themes.—*Testimonies for the Church*, vol. 2, pp. 701-703.

The Commandments Are for All

Also the sons of the foreigner who join themselves to the Lord,
to serve Him, and to love the name of the Lord, to be His servants—
everyone who keeps from defiling the Sabbath, and holds fast My
covenant—even them I will bring to My holy mountain. Isaiah 56:6, 7, NKJV.

UNDER THE MOSAIC law, strangers and eunuchs were excluded from the full enjoyment of the privileges granted to Israel. But the prophet declares that a time is coming when these restrictions will cease. The holy oracles were especially committed to the Jews; not to be an Israelite was not to belong to the favored people of God. The Jews had come more and more to regard themselves as superior by divine right to every other people upon the earth; yet they had not been careful to maintain their separate and holy character by rendering obedience to all the commandments of God.

Now the prophet declares that the stranger who will love and obey God shall enjoy the privileges that have belonged exclusively to the chosen people. Hitherto, circumcision and a strict observance of the ceremonial law had been the conditions upon which Gentiles could be admitted to the congregation of Israel; but these distinctions were to be abolished by the gospel. [Isaiah 56:6-8 quoted.] . . .

The first part of [Isaiah 58] brings to view a people who apparently delight in the service of God; they seek Him daily, "as a nation that did righteousness, and forsook not the ordinance of their God." Yet their lives are not right before the Lord; for He commands His prophet, "Cry aloud, spare not, lift up thy voice like a trumpet, and shew my people their transgression, and the house of Jacob their sins." . . .

This prophecy reaches down the centuries to the time when the man of sin attempted to make void one of the precepts of God's law, to trample under foot the original Sabbath of Jehovah, and in its stead exalt one of his own creation. And when the Christian world set aside God's holy Sabbath, and in its place accept a common working day, unsanctioned by a single "Thus saith the Lord," they are encouraging infidelity, and virtually acknowledging the supremacy of that power by whose authority alone the change has been effected. The rejection of the Sabbath has led to the rejection of the whole law, and thousands of professed Christians now boldly declare it void.—*Signs of the Times,* Feb. 28, 1884.

Jesus Kept the
Sabbath by Doing Good

*Then Jesus said to them, "I will ask you one thing: is it lawful on the Sabbath
to do good or to do evil, to save life or to destroy it?" Luke 6:9, NKJV.*

IT IS NO VIOLATION of the Sabbath to perform works of necessity, as
ministering to the sick or aged, and relieving distress. Such works are in perfect harmony with the Sabbath law. Our great Exemplar was ever active upon
the Sabbath, when the necessities of the sick and suffering came before Him.
The Pharisees, because of this, accused Him of Sabbathbreaking, as do many
ministers today who are in opposition to the law of God. But we say, Let God
be true, and every man a liar who dares make this charge against the Savior.

Jesus answered the accusation of the Jews thus, "If ye had known what
this meaneth, I will have mercy, and not sacrifice, ye would not have condemned the guiltless." He had already declared to them that He had kept
His Father's commandments. When He was accused of Sabbathbreaking in
the matter of healing the withered hand, He turned upon His accusers with
the question "Is it lawful to do good on the sabbath days, or to do evil? to
save life, or to kill?" In summing up His answer to the questioning of the
Pharisees He said, "Wherefore it is lawful to do well on the sabbath days."
Here Christ justified His work as in perfect harmony with the Sabbath
law.—*Signs of the Times,* Feb. 28, 1878.

Those who hold that Christ abolished the law teach that He broke the
Sabbath and justified His disciples in doing the same. Thus they are really
taking the same ground as did the caviling Jews. In this they contradict the
testimony of Christ Himself, who declared, "I have kept my Father's commandments, and abide in his love" (John 15:10).

Neither the Savior nor His followers broke the law of the Sabbath.
Christ was a living representative of the law. No violation of its holy precepts was found in His life.

Looking upon a nation of witnesses who were seeking occasion to
condemn Him, He could say unchallenged, "Which of you convicteth me
of sin?" (John 8:46, RV). . . .

"The sabbath was made for man, and not man for the sabbath," Jesus
said. The institutions that God has established are for the benefit of humankind. . . . The law of Ten Commandments, of which the Sabbath
forms a part, God gave to His people as a blessing. "The Lord commanded
us," said Moses, "to do all these statutes, to fear the Lord our God, for our
good always, that he might preserve us alive" (Deut. 6:24).—*The Desire of
Ages,* pp. 287, 288.

The Sabbath Memorializes a Literal Day

God thunders marvelously with His voice; He does great
things which we cannot comprehend. Job 37:5, NKJV.

WHEN GOD SPOKE His law with an audible voice from Sinai, He introduced the Sabbath by saying, "Remember the sabbath day, to keep it holy." He then declares definitely what shall be done on the six days, and what shall not be done on the seventh. He next gives the reason for thus observing the week, by pointing us back to His example on the first seven days of time. "For in six days the Lord made heaven and earth, the sea, and all that in them is, and rested the seventh day: wherefore the Lord blessed the sabbath day, and hallowed it." This reason appears beautiful and forcible when we understand the record of Creation to mean literal days.

The first six days of each week are given to us in which to labor, because God employed the same period of the first week in the work of Creation. The seventh day God has reserved as a day of rest, in commemoration of His rest during the same period of time after He had performed the work of Creation in six days.

But the infidel supposition, that the events of the first week required seven vast, indefinite periods for their accomplishment, strikes directly at the foundation of the Sabbath of the fourth commandment. It makes indefinite and obscure that which God has made very plain. It is the worst kind of infidelity; for with many who profess to believe the record of Creation, it is infidelity in disguise. It charges God with commanding us to observe the week of seven literal days in commemoration of seven indefinite periods, which is unlike His dealings with us, and is an impeachment of His wisdom. . . .

The Word of God is given as a lamp unto our feet, and a light unto our path. Those who cast His Word behind them, and seek by their own blind philosophy to penetrate the mysteries of Jehovah, will stumble in darkness. A guide has been given to mortals whereby they may trace His works as far as will be for their good. Inspiration, in giving us the history of the Flood, has explained wonderful mysteries that geology alone could never fathom.—*Signs of the Times,* Mar. 20, 1879.

The Sabbath Reminds
Us of God's Creative Power

*Great is the Lord, and greatly to be praised; and His
greatness is unsearchable. Psalm 145:3, NKJV.*

INFIDEL GEOLOGISTS claim that the world is very much older than the
Bible record makes it. They reject the testimony of God's Word because
of those things which are to them evidences from the earth itself that it has
existed tens of thousands of years. And many who profess to believe the
Bible are at a loss to account for wonderful things which are found in the
earth, with the view that Creation week was only seven literal days, and
that the world is now only about six thousand years old. These, to free
themselves from difficulties thrown in their way by infidel geologists,
adopt the view that the six days of Creation were six vast, indefinite periods, and the day of God's rest was another indefinite period; making senseless the fourth commandment of God's holy law. Some eagerly receive this
position; for it destroys the force of the fourth commandment, and they
feel a freedom from its claims upon them.

Bones of human beings and animals are found in the earth, in mountains and in valleys, showing that much larger humans and beasts once existed. Instruments of warfare are sometimes found; also petrified wood.
Because the bones found are so much larger than those of humans and animals now living, or that have existed for many generations past, some
conclude that the earth was populated long before the record of Creation
by a race of beings vastly superior in size to those now living. Those who
reason in this manner have limited ideas of the size of people, animals, and
trees, before the Flood, and of the great changes which then took place in
the earth.

Without Bible history, geology can prove nothing. . . . When human
beings leave the Word of God, and seek to account for His creative works
upon natural principles, they are upon a boundless ocean of uncertainty.
Just how God accomplished the work of Creation in six literal days, He
has never revealed to mortals. His creative works are as incomprehensible
as His existence.—*Signs of the Times,* Mar. 20, 1879.

Believe God's Word,
Not Human Reasoning

*The secret things belong to the Lord our God, but those
things which are revealed belong to us and to our children forever, that
we may do all the words of this law. Deuteronomy 29:29, NKJV.*

IT HAS BEEN the special work of Satan to lead fallen humanity to rebel against God's government, and he has succeeded too well in his efforts. He has tried to obscure the law of God, which in itself is very plain. He has manifested a special hatred against the fourth precept of the Decalogue, because it defines the living God, the maker of the heavens and the earth. Yielding to his devices, people have turned from the plainest precepts of Jehovah to receive infidel fables.

They will be left without excuse. God has given sufficient evidence upon which to base faith, if one wishes to believe. In the last days, the earth will be almost destitute of true faith. Upon the merest pretense, the Word of God will be considered unreliable, while human reasoning will be received, though it be in opposition to plain Scripture facts. Men and women will endeavor to explain from natural causes the work of Creation. But just how God wrought in the work of Creation He has never revealed to mortals. Human science cannot search out the secrets of the God of heaven. . . .

Human beings professing to be ministers of God raise their voices against the investigation of prophecy, and tell the people that the prophecies, especially of Daniel and John, are obscure, and that we cannot understand them. Yet some of these very ones eagerly receive the suppositions of geologists, which dispute the Mosaic record. But if God's revealed will is so difficult to be understood, certainly people should not rest their faith upon mere suppositions in regard to that which He has not revealed. God's ways are not as our ways, neither are His thoughts as our thoughts. . . . Humans, with their vain reasoning, make a wrong use of these things which God designed should lead them to exalt Him. They fall into the same error as did the people before the Flood—those things which God gave them as a benefit, they turned into a curse, by making a wrong use of them.—*Signs of the Times,* Mar. 20, 1879.

The Sabbath Was
Kept Anciently, and Is Today

"Fear God and give glory to Him, for the hour of His judgment has come; and worship Him who made heaven and earth, the sea and springs of water." . . . "Here are those who keep the commandments of God and the faith of Jesus." Revelation 14:7-12, NKJV.

THE PROPHET . . . points out the ordinance which has been forsaken: "Thou shalt raise up the foundations of many generations; and thou shalt be called, The repairer of the breach, The restorer of paths to dwell in. If thou turn away thy foot from the sabbath, from doing thy pleasure on my holy day; and call the sabbath a delight, the holy of the Lord, honourable; and shalt honour him, not doing thine own ways, nor finding thine own pleasure, nor speaking thine own words: then shalt thou delight thyself in the Lord" (Isa. 58:12-14). . . .

Hallowed by the Creator's rest and blessing, the Sabbath was kept by Adam in his innocence in holy Eden; by Adam, fallen yet repentant, when he was driven from his happy estate. It was kept by all the patriarchs, from Abel to righteous Noah, to Abraham, to Jacob. When the chosen people were in bondage in Egypt, many, in the midst of prevailing idolatry, lost their knowledge of God's law; but when the Lord delivered Israel, He proclaimed His law in awful grandeur to the assembled multitude, that they might know His will and fear and obey Him forever.

From that day to the present the knowledge of God's law has been preserved in the earth, and the Sabbath of the fourth commandment has been kept. Though the "man of sin" succeeded in trampling underfoot God's holy day, yet even in the period of his supremacy there were, hidden in secret places, faithful souls who paid it honor. Since the Reformation, there have been some in every generation to maintain its observance. Though often in the midst of reproach and persecution, a constant testimony has been borne to the perpetuity of the law of God and the sacred obligation of the creation Sabbath.

These truths, as presented in Revelation 14 in connection with "the everlasting gospel," will distinguish the church of Christ at the time of His appearing. For as the result of the threefold message it is announced: "Here are they that keep the commandments of God, and the faith of Jesus." And this message is the last to be given before the coming of the Lord. Immediately following its proclamation the Son of man is seen by the prophet, coming in glory to reap the harvest of the earth.—*The Great Controversy*, pp. 452-454.

Keeping the
Sabbath as a Family

Therefore know that the Lord your God, He is God, the faithful
God who keeps covenant and mercy for a thousand generations with those
who love Him and keep His commandments. Deuteronomy 7:9, NKJV.

SEARCH THE SCRIPTURES, parents. Be not only hearers, but doers of the Word. Meet God's standard in the education of your children. Let them see that you are preparing for the Sabbath on the working days of the week. All preparation should be made, every stitch taken, on the six working days; all cooking for the Sabbath should be done on the preparation day. It is possible to do this, and if you make it a rule, you can do it. . . .

Explain your work and its purpose to your children, and let them help themselves and their parents in their preparation to keep the Sabbath according to the commandment. Lead your children to consider the Sabbath a delight, the day of days, the holy of the Lord, honorable. . . .

On Friday the clothing of the children . . . should all be laid out by their own hands under the direction of the mother, so that they can dress quickly, without any confusion or rushing about, and hasty speeches. . . . This is God's holy day; the day that He has set apart to commemorate His creative works; a day which He has sanctified and hallowed. . . .

On the Sabbath, parents should give all the time they can to their children, thus making it a delight. I have seen many families where father, mother, and the older members of the household take themselves away from the younger children, and leave them to amuse themselves as best they can. After a while, the children become weary and go out of doors, and engage in play or some kind of mischief. Thus the Sabbath has no sacred significance to them. In pleasant weather the parents can take their children out for a walk in the fields and forest, and talk to them of the lofty trees, the shrubs and flowers, and teach them that God is the Maker of all these things. Then teach them the reasons for the Sabbath, that it is to commemorate God's created works. After working six days, He rested the seventh, and blessed and hallowed the day of His rest. Thus the most profitable instruction can be given.—*Lake Union Herald*, Apr. 14, 1909.

Good Works
Continue on the Sabbath

For this reason the Jews persecuted Jesus, and sought to kill Him, because He had done these things on the Sabbath. But Jesus answered them, "My Father has been working until now, and I have been working." John 5:16, 17, NKJV.

AT JERUSALEM, where the Savior now was, many of the learned rabbis lived. Here their false ideas about the Sabbath were taught to the people. Great numbers came to worship at the Temple, and thus the rabbis' teaching was spread far and wide. Christ wished to correct these errors. This was why He healed the man on the Sabbath day, and told him to carry his bed. He knew that this act would attract the attention of the rabbis, and thus would give Him an opportunity to instruct them. So it proved. The Pharisees brought Christ before the Sanhedrin, the chief council of the Jews, to answer the charge of Sabbathbreaking.

The Savior declared that His action was in harmony with the Sabbath law. It was in harmony with the will and the work of God. "My Father worketh hitherto," He said, "and I work" (John 5:17).

God works continually in sustaining every living thing. Was His work to cease upon the Sabbath day? Should God forbid the sun to fulfill its office on the Sabbath? Should He cut off its rays from warming the earth and nourishing vegetation?

Should the brooks stay from watering the fields, and the waves of the sea still their ebbing and flowing? Must the wheat and maize stop growing, and the trees and flowers put forth no bud or blossom on the Sabbath?

Then people would miss the fruits of the earth, and the blessings that sustain their life. Nature must continue its work, or mortals would die. And they also have a work to do on this day. The necessities of life must be attended to, the sick must be cared for, the wants of the needy must be supplied. God does not desire His creatures to suffer an hour's pain that may be relieved on the Sabbath or any other day.

Heaven's work never ceases, and we should never rest from doing good. Our own work the law forbids us to do on the rest day of the Lord. The toil for a livelihood must cease; no labor for worldly pleasure or profit is lawful upon that day. But the Sabbath is not to be spent in useless inactivity. As God ceased from His labor of creating, and rested upon the Sabbath, so we are to rest. He bids us lay aside our daily occupations, and devote those sacred hours to healthful rest, to worship, and to holy deeds.—*The Story of Jesus*, pp. 73, 74.

A Vision of the
Sabbath Commandment

The seventh day is the Sabbath of the Lord your God. In it you shall not do any work: you, nor your son, nor your daughter, nor your manservant, nor your maidservant, nor your ox, nor your donkey, nor any of your cattle, nor your stranger who is within your gates, that your manservant and your maidservant may rest as well as you. Deuteronomy 5:14, NKJV.

JESUS STOOD BY the ark, and as the saints' prayers came up to Him, the incense in the censer would smoke, and He would offer up their prayers with the smoke of the incense to His Father.

In the ark was the golden pot of manna, Aaron's rod that budded, and the tables of stone, which folded together like a book. Jesus opened them, and I saw the ten commandments written on them with the finger of God. On one table were four, and on the other six. The four on the first table shone brighter than the other six. But the fourth, the Sabbath commandment, shone above them all; for the Sabbath was set apart to be kept in honor of God's holy name. The holy Sabbath looked glorious—a halo of glory was all around it. . . .

And I saw that if God had changed the Sabbath from the seventh to the first day, He would have changed the writing of the Sabbath commandment, written on the tables of stone, which are now in the ark in the most holy place of the temple in heaven; and it would read thus: The first day is the Sabbath of the Lord thy God. But I saw that it read the same as when written on the tables of stone by the finger of God, and delivered to Moses on Sinai, "But the seventh day is the sabbath of the Lord thy God." I saw that the holy Sabbath is, and will be, the separating wall between the true Israel of God and unbelievers; and that the Sabbath is the great question to unite the hearts of God's dear, waiting saints.

I saw that God had children who do not see and keep the Sabbath. They have not rejected the light upon it. And at the commencement of the time of trouble, we were filled with the Holy Ghost as we went forth and proclaimed the Sabbath more fully.—*Life Sketches of Ellen G. White,* pp. 100, 101.

Why Worship
Is Due God

*Hallow My Sabbaths, and they will be a sign between Me and you, that
you may know that I am the Lord your God. Ezekiel 20:20, NKJV.*

IN REVELATION 14, human beings are called upon to worship the
Creator; and the prophecy brings to view a class that, as the result of the
threefold message, are keeping the commandments of God. One of these
commandments points directly to God as the Creator. The fourth precept
declares: "The seventh day is the sabbath of the Lord thy God: . . . for in
six days the Lord made heaven and earth, the sea, and all that in them is,
and rested the seventh day: wherefore the Lord blessed the sabbath day,
and hallowed it" (Ex. 20:10, 11). . . .

"The importance of the Sabbath as the memorial of creation is that it
keeps ever present the true reason why worship is due to God"—because
He is the Creator, and we are His creatures. "The Sabbath therefore lies at
the very foundation of divine worship, for it teaches this great truth in the
most impressive manner, and no other institution does this. The true
ground of divine worship, not of that on the seventh day merely, but of all
worship, is found in the distinction between the Creator and His creatures.
This great fact can never become obsolete, and must never be forgotten."—J. N. Andrews, *History of the Sabbath,* chap. 27.

It was to keep this truth ever before the minds of people that God instituted the Sabbath in Eden; and so long as the fact that He is our Creator
continues to be a reason why we should worship Him, so long the Sabbath
will continue as its sign and memorial. Had the Sabbath been universally
kept, the thoughts and affections of humans would have been led to the
Creator as the object of reverence and worship, and there would never
have been an idolater, an atheist, or an infidel.

The keeping of the Sabbath is a sign of loyalty to the true God, "him
that made heaven, and earth, and the sea, and the fountains of waters." It
follows that the message which commands mortals to worship God and
keep His commandments will especially call upon them to keep the fourth
commandment.—*The Great Controversy,* pp. 437, 438.

The Sabbath Not
Jewish but Christ's Holy Day

So He came to Nazareth, where He had been brought up. And as His custom was, He went into the synagogue on the Sabbath day, and stood up to read. Luke 4:16, NKJV.

HOW CAN WE account for the observance of the first day of the week by the majority of professed Christians, when the Bible presents no authority for this change either in the precepts or in the example of Christ or His followers? We can account for it in the fact that the world has followed the traditions of human beings instead of a "Thus saith the Lord." This has been the work that Satan has always sought to accomplish—lead people away from the commandments of God to the veneration and obedience of the traditions of the world. Through human instrumentalities he has cast contempt upon the Sabbath of Jehovah, and has stigmatized it as "the old Jewish Sabbath."

Thousands have thoughtlessly echoed this reproach, as though it were something to which was attached great weight of argument; but they have lost sight of the fact that the Jewish people were especially chosen of God as the guardians of His truth, the keepers of His law, the depositary of His sacred oracles. They received the lively oracles to give unto us. The Old and New Testaments both came through the Jews to us. Every promise in the Bible, every ray of light which has shone upon us from the Word of God, has come through the Jewish nation.

Christ was the leader of the Hebrews as they marched from Egypt to Canaan. In union with the Father, Christ proclaimed the law amid the thunders of Sinai to the Jews, and when He appeared on earth as a man, He came as a descendant of Abraham. Shall we use the same argument concerning the Bible and Christ, and reject them as Jewish, as is done in rejecting the Sabbath of the Lord our God? The Sabbath institution is as closely identified with the Jews as is the Bible, and there is the same reason for the rejection of one as of the other. But the Sabbath is not Jewish in its origin. It was instituted in Eden before there were such a people known as the Jews. The Sabbath was made for all humanity, and was instituted in Eden before the fall of Adam and Eve. The Creator called it "my holy day." Christ announced Himself as the "Lord . . . of the sabbath." Beginning with creation, it is as old as the human race, and having been made for human beings it will exist as long as they shall exist.— *Signs of the Times,* Nov. 12, 1894.

Sabbath Rest
and Joy in Eternity

"And it shall come to pass that from one New Moon to another, and from one Sabbath to another, all flesh shall come to worship before Me," says the Lord. Isaiah 66:23, NKJV.

AT LAST JESUS was at rest. The long day of shame and torture was ended. As the last rays of the setting sun ushered in the Sabbath, the Son of God lay in quietude in Joseph's tomb. His work completed, His hands folded in peace, He rested through the sacred hours of the Sabbath day.

In the beginning the Father and the Son had rested upon the Sabbath after Their work of creation. When "the heavens and the earth were finished, and all the host of them" (Gen. 2:1), the Creator and all heavenly beings rejoiced in contemplation of the glorious scene. "The morning stars sang together, and all the sons of God shouted for joy" (Job 38:7).

Now Jesus rested from the work of redemption; and though there was grief among those who loved Him on earth, yet there was joy in heaven. Glorious to the eyes of heavenly beings was the promise of the future. . . . With this scene the day upon which Jesus rested is forever linked. For "his work is perfect" (Deut. 32:4); and "whatsoever God doeth, it shall be for ever" (Eccl. 3:14). When there shall be a "restitution of all things, which God hath spoken by the mouth of all his holy prophets since the world began" (Acts 3:21), the creation Sabbath, the day on which Jesus lay at rest in Joseph's tomb, will still be a day of rest and rejoicing. Heaven and earth will unite in praise, as "from one sabbath to another" (Isa. 66:23) the nations of the saved shall bow in joyful worship to God and the Lamb.

In the closing events of the crucifixion day, fresh evidence was given of the fulfillment of prophecy, and new witness borne to Christ's divinity. When the darkness had lifted from the cross, and the Savior's dying cry had been uttered, immediately another voice was heard, saying, "Truly this was the Son of God" (Matt. 27:54).—*The Desire of Ages*, pp. 769, 770.

JUNE

∾

Doing the King's Business

Be Like Jesus, Not Like the World

You shall not have in your bag differing weights, a heavy and a light. You shall not have in your house differing measures, a large and a small. Deuteronomy 25:13, 14, NKJV.

THOSE WHO PROFESS to love and fear God should cherish sympathy and love for one another, and should guard the interests of others as their own. Christians should not regulate their conduct by the world's standard. In all ages the people of God are as distinct from worldlings as their profession is higher than that of the ungodly. From the beginning to the end of time, God's people are one body.

The love of money is the root of all evil. In this generation the desire for gain is the absorbing passion. If wealth cannot be secured by honest industry, human beings seek to obtain it by fraud. Widows and orphans are robbed of their scanty pittance, and poor people are made to suffer for the necessaries of life. And all this that the rich may support their extravagance, or indulge their desire to hoard.

The terrible record of crime daily committed for the sake of gain is enough to chill the blood and fill the soul with horror. The fact that even among those who profess godliness the same sins exist to a greater or less extent calls for deep humiliation of soul and earnest action on the part of the followers of Christ. Love of display and love of money have made this world a den of thieves and robbers. But Christians are professedly not dwellers upon the earth; they are in a strange country, stopping, as it were, only for a night. They should not be actuated by the same motives and desires as are those who have their home and treasure here. God designed that our lives should represent the life of our great Pattern: that, like Jesus, we should live to do others good. . . .

Every wrong done to the children of God is done to Christ Himself in the person of His saints. Every attempt to advantage one's self by the ignorance, weakness, or misfortune of another is registered as fraud in the ledger of heaven.—*Southern Watchman,* May 10, 1904.

Do Right in Business, Not Just in Church

In everything do to others as you would have them do to you;
for this is the law and the prophets. Matthew 7:12, NRSV.

THOSE WHO TRULY fear God would rather toil day and night, and eat the bread of poverty, than to indulge a passion for gain which would oppress the widow and the fatherless, or turn strangers from their right. Our Savior sought to impress upon His hearers that the person who would venture to defraud a neighbor in the smallest item would, if the opportunity were favorable, overreach in larger matters. The slightest departure from rectitude breaks down the barriers, and prepares the heart to do greater injustice. By precept and example Christ taught that the strictest integrity should govern our conduct toward our fellow beings. Said the divine Teacher, "Whatsoever ye would that men should do to you, do ye even so to them."

Just to the extent that people would advantage themselves at the disadvantage of others will their souls become insensible to the influence of the Spirit of God. Gain obtained at such a cost is a fearful loss. It is better to want than to lie; better to hunger than to defraud; better to die than to sin. Extravagance, overreaching, extortion indulged by those professing godliness, are corrupting their faith and destroying their spirituality. The church is in a great degree responsible for the sins of its members. It gives countenance to the evil if it fails to lift its voice against it. The influence from which it has most to fear is not that of open opposers, infidels, and blasphemers, but of inconsistent professors of Christ. These are the ones who keep back the blessing of the God of Israel. . . .

The business world does not lie outside the limits of God's government. True religion is not to be merely paraded on the Sabbath and displayed in the sanctuary; it is for every day and for every place. Its claims must be recognized and obeyed in every act of life. Those who possess the genuine article will in all their business affairs show as clear a perception of right as when offering their supplications at the throne of grace.—*Southern Watchman,* May 10, 1904.

Be Honest With Others and With God

You shall have a perfect and just weight, a perfect and just measure, that your days may be lengthened in the land which the Lord your God is giving you. Deuteronomy 25:15, NKJV.

IT IS BEST to deal honestly with your fellow beings and with God. You are dependent upon Christ for every favor you enjoy; you are dependent upon Him for the future, immortal life; and you cannot afford to be without respect unto the recompense of reward. Those who realize their dependence upon God will feel that they must be honest with others, and, above all, they must be honest with God, from whom come all the blessings of life. The evasion of the positive commands of God concerning tithes and offerings is registered in the books of heaven as robbery toward Him.

No one who is dishonest with God or with others can truly prosper. . . . The Lord has bought us with His own precious blood, and it is because of His mercy and grace that we may hope for the great gift of salvation. And we are enjoined to deal justly, to love mercy, and to walk humbly with our God. Yet the Lord declares, "Ye have robbed me, even this whole nation." When we deal unjustly with other human beings or with our God, we despise the authority of God and ignore the fact that Christ has purchased us with His own life.

The world is robbing God upon the wholesale plan. The more He imparts of wealth, the more thoroughly do people claim it as their own, to be used as they shall please. But shall the professed followers of Christ follow the customs of the world? Shall we forfeit peace of conscience, communion with God, and fellowship with our brethren and sisters because we fail to devote to His cause the portion He has claimed as His own?

Let those who claim to be Christians bear in mind that they are trading on the capital entrusted them of God, and that they are required to faithfully follow the directions of the Scriptures in regard to its disposal. If your heart is right with God, you will not embezzle your Lord's goods and invest them in your own selfish enterprises.—*Review and Herald,* Dec. 17, 1889.

Imitate Jesus
and His Ethics

Let each of you look out not only for his own interests, but also for the interests of others. Let this mind be in you which was also in Christ Jesus. Philippians 2:4, 5, NKJV.

THE ETHICS INCULCATED by the gospel acknowledge no standard but the perfection of God's mind, God's will. God requires from His creatures conformity to His will. Imperfection of character is sin, and sin is the transgression of the law. All righteous attributes of character dwell in God as a perfect, harmonious whole. All those who receive Christ as their personal Savior are privileged to possess these attributes. This is the science of holiness.

How glorious are the possibilities set before the fallen race! Through His Son, God has revealed the excellency to which human beings are capable of attaining. Through the merits of Christ, they are lifted from their depraved state, purified, and made more precious than the golden wedge of Ophir. It is possible for them to become companions of the angels in glory, and to reflect the image of Jesus Christ, shining even in the bright splendor of the eternal throne. It is their privilege to have faith that through the power of Christ they shall be made immortal. Yet how seldom they realize to what heights they could attain if they would allow God to direct their every step!

God permits every human being to exercise individuality. He desires no one to submerge his or her mind in the mind of a fellow mortal. Those who desire to be transformed in mind and character are not to look to others, but to the divine Example. . . .

As our Example we have One who is all and in all, the chiefest among ten thousand, One whose excellency is beyond comparison. He graciously adapted His life for universal imitation. United in Christ were wealth and poverty; majesty and abasement; unlimited power, and meekness and lowliness which in every soul who receives Him will be reflected. In Him, through the qualities and powers of the human mind, the wisdom of the greatest Teacher the world has ever known was revealed.—*Signs of the Times,* Sept. 3, 1902.

Never Take Advantage
of Another's Misfortune

*You shall not pervert justice due the stranger or the fatherless, nor
take a widow's garment as a pledge. Deuteronomy 24:17, NKJV.*

GOD'S WORD SANCTIONS no policy that will enrich one class by the oppression and suffering of another. In all our business transactions it teaches us to put ourselves in the place of those with whom we are dealing, to look not only on our own things, but also on the things of others. Those who would take advantage of another's misfortunes in order to benefit themselves, or who seek to profit themselves through another's weakness or incompetence, are transgressors both of the principles and of the precepts of the Word of God.

"Thou shalt not pervert the judgment of the stranger, nor of the fatherless; nor take a widow's raiment to pledge" (Deut. 24:17). "When thou dost lend thy brother any thing, thou shalt not go into his house to fetch his pledge. Thou shalt stand abroad, and the man to whom thou dost lend shall bring out the pledge abroad unto thee. And if the man be poor, thou shalt not sleep with his pledge" (verses 10-12). "If thou at all take thy neighbour's raiment to pledge, thou shalt deliver it unto him by that the sun goeth down: for that is his covering only . . . : wherein shall he sleep? and it shall come to pass, when he crieth unto me, that I will hear; for I am gracious" (Ex. 22:26, 27). "If thou sell aught unto thy neighbour, or buyest aught of thy neighbour's hand, ye shall not oppress one another" (Lev. 25:14).

"Ye shall do no unrighteousness in judgment, in measures of length, of weight, or of quantity" (Lev. 19:35, ARV). "Thou shalt not have in thy bag diverse weights, a great and a small. Thou shalt not have in thy house diverse measures, a great and a small" (Deut. 25:13, 14, ARV). "Just balances, just weights, a just ephah, and a just hin, shall ye have" (Lev. 19:36, ARV).

"Give to him that asketh thee, and from him that would borrow of thee turn not thou away" (Matt. 5:42). "The wicked borroweth, and payeth not again: but the righteous sheweth mercy, and giveth" (Ps. 37:21). . . .

The plan of life that God gave to Israel was intended as an object lesson for all humankind. If these principles were carried out today, what a different place this world would be!—*The Ministry of Healing*, pp. 187, 188.

Character Tested by Presence of the Less Fortunate

When you reap your harvest in your field, and forget a sheaf in the field, you shall not go back to get it; it shall be for the stranger, the fatherless, and the widow, that the Lord your God may bless you in all the work of your hands. Deuteronomy 24:19, NKJV.

I SAW THAT it is in the providence of God that widows and orphans, the blind, the deaf, the lame, and persons afflicted in a variety of ways, have been placed in close Christian relationship to His church; it is to prove His people and develop their true character. Angels of God are watching to see how we treat these persons who need our sympathy, love, and disinterested benevolence. This is God's test of our character.

If we have the true religion of the Bible we shall feel that a debt of love, kindness, and interest is due to Christ in behalf of His children; and we can do no less than to show our gratitude for His immeasurable love to us while we were sinners unworthy of His grace, by having a deep interest and unselfish love for fellow believers who are less fortunate than ourselves.

The two great principles of the law of God are supreme love to God and unselfish love to our neighbor. The first four commandments and the last six hang upon, or grow out of, these two principles. Christ explained to the lawyer who his neighbor was in the illustration of the man who was traveling from Jerusalem to Jericho and who fell among thieves and was robbed and beaten and left half dead.

The priest and the Levite saw this man suffering, but their hearts did not respond to his wants. They avoided him by passing by on the other side. The Samaritan came that way, and when he saw the stranger's need of help he did not question whether he was a relative or was of his country or creed; but he went to work to help the sufferer because there was work which needed to be done. He relieved him as best he could, put him upon his own beast, and carried him to an inn and made provision for his wants at his own expense.

This Samaritan, said Christ, was neighbor to him who fell among thieves. The Levite and the priest represent a class in the church who manifest an indifference to the very ones who need their sympathy and help. This class, notwithstanding their position in the church, are commandment breakers. The Samaritan represents a class who are true helpers with Christ and who are imitating His example in doing good.—*Testimonies for the Church*, vol. 3, pp. 511, 512.

The Golden Rule
to Govern Business Dealings

What does the Lord require of you but to do justly, to love
mercy, and to walk humbly with your God? Micah 6:8, NKJV.

THE LAWS OF the nations bear marks of the infirmities and passions of
the unrenewed heart; but God's laws bear the stamp of the divine, and if
they are obeyed, they will lead to a tender regard for the rights and privileges of others. . . . His watchful care is over all the interests of His children, and He declares He will undertake the cause of the afflicted and the
oppressed. If they cry unto Him, He says, "I will hear; for I am gracious."

A man of means, if he possesses strict integrity, and loves and fears
God, may be a benefactor to the poor. He can help them, and take no
more interest [on the money he lends] than can be mercifully exacted. He
thus meets with no loss himself, and his unfortunate neighbor is greatly
benefited, for he is saved from the hands of the dishonest schemer. The
principles of the golden rule are not to be lost sight of for a moment in any
business transaction. . . . God never designed that one person should prey
upon another. He jealously guards the rights of His children, and in the
books of Heaven great loss is set down on the side of the unjust dealer.

In the Holy Scriptures fearful denunciations are pronounced against
the sin of covetousness. "No . . . covetous man, who is an idolater, hath
any inheritance in the kingdom of Christ and of God." The psalmist says,
"The wicked boasteth of his heart's desire, and blesseth the covetous,
whom the Lord abhorreth." Paul ranks covetous people with idolaters,
adulterers, thieves, drunkards, revilers, and extortioners, none of whom
shall inherit the kingdom of God. These are the fruits of a corrupt tree, and
God is dishonored by them. We are not to make the customs and maxims
of the world our criterion. Reforms must take place; all injustice must be
put away.

We are commanded to "search the scriptures." The whole Word of
God is our rule of action. We are to carry out its principles in our daily
lives; there is no surer mark of Christianity than this. We must carry out
the great principles of justice and mercy in our relations with one another.
We must be daily cultivating those qualities that will fit us for the society
of heaven. If we do these things, God becomes our surety, and promises
to bless all that we undertake; and we "shall never be moved."—*Signs of the*
Times, Feb. 7, 1884.

God's Plan to Prevent Poverty

*That fiftieth year shall be a Jubilee to you; in it you shall neither
sow nor reap what grows of its own accord, nor gather the grapes of your
untended vine. . . . And if you sell anything to your neighbor or buy from
your neighbor's hand, you shall not oppress one another. Leviticus 25:11-14, NKJV.*

IN GOD'S PLAN for Israel every family had a home on the land, with sufficient ground for tilling. Thus were provided both the means and the incentive for a useful, industrious, and self-supporting life. And no devising
of human beings has ever improved upon that plan. To the world's departure from it is owing, to a large degree, the poverty and wretchedness that
exist today.

At the settlement of Israel in Canaan, the land was divided among the
whole people, the Levites only, as ministers of the sanctuary, being excepted
from the equal distribution. The tribes were numbered by families, and to
each family, according to its numbers, was apportioned an inheritance.

And although some might for a time dispose of their possessions, they
could not permanently barter away the inheritance of their children. When
able to redeem their land, they were at liberty at any time to do so. Debts
were remitted every seventh year, and in the fiftieth, or year of jubilee, all
landed property reverted to the original owner.

"The land shall not be sold for ever" was the Lord's direction: "for the
land is mine; for ye are strangers and sojourners with me. And in all the
land of your possession ye shall grant a redemption for the land. If thy
brother be waxen poor, and hath sold away some of his possession, and if
any of his kin come to redeem it, then shall he redeem that which his
brother sold. And if the man . . . himself be able to redeem it; . . . he may
return unto his possession. But if he be not able to restore it to him, then
that which is sold shall remain in the hand of him that hath bought it until
the year of jubile" (Lev. 25:23-28). . . . Thus every family was secured in
its possession, and a safeguard was afforded against the extremes of either
wealth or want.—*The Ministry of Healing,* pp. 183-185.

God's Grace
Needed to Polish Us

Therefore you shall not oppress one another, but you shall fear
your God; for I am the Lord your God. Leviticus 25:17, NKJV.

YOU ARE IN danger of making grave mistakes in your business transactions. God warns you to be on your guard lest you indulge a spirit of crowding one another. Be careful not to cultivate the sharper's tact, for this will not stand the test of the day of God. Shrewdness and close calculation are needed, for you have all classes to deal with. . . . But let not these traits become a ruling power. Under proper control, they are essential elements in the character; and if you keep the fear of God before you, and His love in the heart, you will be safe.

It is far better to yield some advantages that might be gained than to cultivate an avaricious spirit and thus make it a law of nature. Petty sharpness is unworthy of a Christian. We have been separated from the world by the great cleaver of truth. Our wrong traits of character are not always visible to ourselves, although they may be very apparent to others. But time and circumstances will surely prove us and bring to light the gold of character or discover the baser metal. . . .

Every base thought, every wrong action, reveals some defect in the character. These rugged traits must be brought under the chisel and hammer in God's great workshop, and the grace of God must smooth and polish before we can be fitted for a place in the glorious temple.

God can make these [leaders in our church institutions] more precious than fine gold, even the golden wedge of Ophir, if they will yield themselves to His transforming hand. They should be determined to make the noblest use of every faculty and every opportunity. The Word of God should be their study and their guide in deciding what is the highest and best in all cases. . . .

The weakest follower of Christ has entered into alliance with infinite power. In many cases God can do little with men and women of learning because they feel no need of leaning upon Him who is the Source of all wisdom; therefore, after a trial, He sets them aside for people of inferior talent who have learned to rely upon Him, whose souls are fortified by goodness, truth, and unwavering fidelity, and who will not stoop to anything that will leave a stain upon the conscience.—*Testimonies for the Church,* vol. 4, pp. 540, 541.

Principles of the
Gospel Must Control Us

*Then he said to the keeper of his vineyard, "Look, for three
years I have come seeking fruit on this fig tree and find none.
Cut it down; why does it use up the ground?" Luke 13:7, NKJV.*

THE LORD WOULD be pleased to have His people more considerate than they now are, more merciful and more helpful to one another. When the love of Christ is in the heart, each will be tenderly regardful of the interests of others. Brothers and sisters will not take advantage of each other in business transactions. They will not charge exorbitant interest because they see their brothers or sisters in a close place where they must have help.

Those who will take advantage of the necessities of another prove conclusively that they are not governed by the principles of the gospel of Christ. Their course is recorded in the books of heaven as fraud and dishonesty; and wherever these principles rule, the blessing of the Lord will not come into the heart. Such persons are receiving the impress of the great adversary rather than that of the Spirit of God. But those who shall finally inherit the heavenly kingdom must be transformed by divine grace. They must be pure in heart and life and possess symmetrical characters. . . .

All the means you may accumulate, even though it should be millions, will not be sufficient to pay a ransom for your soul. Then do not remain in impenitence and unbelief, and . . . defeat the gracious purposes of God; do not force from His reluctant hand destruction of your property or affliction of your person.

How many there are who are now taking a course which must erelong lead to just such visitations of judgment. They live on day by day, week by week, year by year, for their own selfish interest. Their influence and means, accumulated through God-given skill and tact, are used upon themselves and their families without thought of their gracious Benefactor. Nothing is allowed to flow back to the Giver. . . .

At last His patience with these unfaithful stewards is exhausted; and He brings all their selfish, worldly schemes to an abrupt termination, showing them that as they have gathered for their own glory, He can scatter; and they are helpless to resist His power.—*Testimonies for the Church,* vol. 5, pp. 350, 351.

Our Business Standards Reveal Our Character

Shall I count pure those with the wicked balances,
and with the bag of deceitful weights? Micah 6:11, NKJV.

AN HONEST PERSON, according to Christ's measurement, is one who will manifest unbending integrity. Deceitful weights and false balances, with which many seek to advance their interests in the world, are abomination in the sight of God. Yet many who profess to keep the commandments of God are dealing with false weights and false balances. When men or women are indeed connected with God, and are keeping His law in truth, their lives will reveal the fact; for all their actions will be in harmony with the teachings of Christ. They will not sell their honor for gain. Their principles are built upon the sure foundation, and their conduct in worldly matters is a transcript of their principles.

Firm integrity shines forth as gold amid the dross and rubbish of the world. Deceit, falsehood, and unfaithfulness may be glossed over and hidden from the eyes of humanity, but not from the eyes of God. The angels of God, who watch the development of character and weigh moral worth, record in the books of heaven these minor transactions which reveal character. If working people in the daily vocations of life are unfaithful and slight their work, the world will not judge incorrectly if they estimate their standard in religion according to their standard in business.

"He that is faithful in that which is least is faithful also in much: and he that is unjust in the least is unjust also in much." It is not the magnitude of the matter that makes it fair or unfair. As men and women deal with their fellow citizens, so will they deal with God. Those who are unfaithful in the mammon of unrighteousness will never be entrusted with the true riches. The children of God should not fail to remember that in all their business transactions they are being proved, weighed in the balances of the sanctuary.—*Testimonies for the Church,* vol. 4, pp. 310, 311.

Even "Small" Sins
Have Big Consequences

The integrity of the upright will guide them, but the perversity
of the unfaithful will destroy them. Proverbs 11:3, NKJV.

CHRIST HAS SAID: "A good tree cannot bring forth evil fruit, neither can a corrupt tree bring forth good fruit." "Wherefore by their fruits ye shall know them." The deeds of people's lives are the fruit they bear. If they are unfaithful and dishonest in temporal matters, they are bringing forth briers and thorns; they will be unfaithful in the religious life and will rob God in tithes and offerings.

The Bible condemns in the strongest terms all falsehood, false dealing, and dishonesty. Right and wrong are plainly stated. But I was shown that God's people have placed themselves on the enemy's ground; they have yielded to his temptations and followed his devices until their sensibilities have become fearfully blunted. A slight deviation from truth, a little variation from the requirements of God, is thought to be, after all, not so very sinful, when pecuniary gain or loss is involved. But sin is sin, whether committed by the possessor of millions or by the beggar in the streets. Those who secure property by false representations are bringing condemnation on their souls. All that is obtained by deceit and fraud will be only a curse to the receiver.

Adam and Eve suffered the terrible consequences of disobeying the express command of God. They might have reasoned: This is a very small sin, and will never be taken into account. But God treated the matter as a fearful evil, and the woe of their transgression will be felt through all time. In the times in which we live, sins of far greater magnitude are often committed by those who profess to be God's children. In the transaction of business, falsehoods are uttered and acted by God's professed people that bring His frown upon them and a reproach upon His cause.

The least departure from truthfulness and rectitude is a transgression of the law of God. Continual indulgence in sin accustoms the person to a habit of wrongdoing, but does not lessen the aggravated character of the sin. God has established immutable principles, which He cannot change without a revision of His whole nature. If the Word of God were faithfully studied by all who profess to believe the truth, they would not be dwarfs in spiritual things. Those who disregard the requirements of God in this life would not respect His authority were they in heaven.—*Testimonies for the Church*, vol. 4, pp. 311, 312.

Build Character
on Jesus, the Rock

I was envious of the boastful, when I saw the prosperity of the wicked. . . . Until I went into the sanctuary of God; then I understood their end. Psalm 73:3-17, NKJV.

THE VERY FIRST step in the path to life is to keep the mind stayed on God, to have His fear continually before the eyes. A single departure from moral integrity blunts the conscience, and opens the door to the next temptation. "He that walketh uprightly walketh surely; but he that perverteth his ways shall be known" (Prov. 10:9).

We are commanded to love God supremely, and our neighbor as ourselves; but the daily experience of life shows that this law is disregarded. Uprightness in deal and moral integrity will secure the favor of God, and make men and women a blessing to themselves and to society; but amid the varied temptations that assail them whichever way they may turn, it is impossible to keep a clear conscience and the approval of heaven without divine aid and a principle to love honesty for the sake of the right.

A character that is approved of God and humanity is to be preferred to wealth. The foundation should be laid broad and deep, resting on the rock Christ Jesus. There are too many who profess to work from the true foundation, whose loose dealing shows them to be building on sliding sand; but the great tempest will sweep away their foundation, and they will have no refuge.

Many plead that unless they are sharp, and watch to advantage themselves, they will meet with loss. Their unscrupulous neighbors, who take selfish advantages, are prospered; while they, although trying to deal strictly in accordance with Bible principles, are not so highly favored. Do these persons see the future? Or are their eyes too dim to see, through the miasma-laden fogs of worldliness, that honor and integrity are not rewarded in the coin of this world? Will God reward virtue with mere worldly success? He has their names graven on the palms of His hands, as heirs to enduring honors, riches that are imperishable.—*The Seventh-day Adventist Bible Commentary,* Ellen G. White Comments, vol. 3, p. 1158.

Public Service
Demands Strict Integrity

It is not for kings to drink wine, nor for princes intoxicating drink; lest they drink and forget the law, and pervert the justice of all the afflicted. Proverbs 31:4, 5, NKJV.

INTEMPERATE PERSONS should not by vote of the people be placed in positions of trust. Their influence corrupts others, and grave responsibilities are involved. With brain and nerve narcotized by tobacco and stimulus they make a law of their nature, and when the immediate influence is gone there is a collapse. Frequently human life is hanging in the balance; on the decision of those in these positions of trust depends life and liberty, or bondage and despair. How necessary that all who take part in these transactions should be those who are proved, those of self-culture, those of honesty and truth, of staunch integrity, who will spurn a bribe, who will not allow their judgment or convictions of right to be swerved by partiality or prejudice.

Thus saith the Lord, "Thou shalt not wrest the judgment of thy poor in his cause. Keep thee far from a false matter; and the innocent and righteous slay thou not: for I will not justify the wicked. And thou shalt take no gift: for the gift blindeth the wise, and perverteth the words of the righteous."—*Signs of the Times,* July 8, 1880.

Only men and women of strict temperance and integrity should be admitted to our legislative halls and chosen to preside in our courts of justice. Property, reputation, and even life itself are insecure when left to the judgment of those who are intemperate and immoral. How many innocent persons have been condemned to death, how many more have been robbed of all their earthly possessions, by the injustice of drinking jurors, lawyers, witnesses, and even judges! . . .

There is need now of people like Daniel—men and women who have the self-denial and the courage to be radical temperance reformers. Let every Christian see that his or her example and influence are on the side of reform. Let ministers of the gospel be faithful in instructing and warning the people. And let all remember that our happiness in two worlds depends upon the right improvement of one.—*Signs of the Times,* Feb. 11, 1886.

God's Word Approves
the Judicial Oath

You shall not circulate a false report. Do not put your hand with
the wicked to be an unrighteous witness. Exodus 23:1, NKJV.

I SAW THAT the Lord still has something to do with the laws of the land. While Jesus is in the sanctuary, God's restraining Spirit is felt by rulers and people. But Satan controls to a great extent the mass of the world, and were it not for the laws of the land, we should experience much suffering. I was shown that when it is actually necessary, and they are called upon to testify in a lawful manner, it is no violation of God's Word for His children to solemnly take God to witness that what they say is the truth, and nothing but the truth.

Human beings are so corrupt that laws are made to throw the responsibility upon their own heads. Some men and women do not fear to lie to other people; but they have been taught, and the restraining Spirit of God has impressed them, that it is a fearful thing to lie to God. The case of Ananias and Sapphira his wife is given for an example. The matter is carried from humans to God, so that if one bears false witness, it is not to mortals, but to the great God, who reads the heart, and knows the exact truth in every case. Our laws make it a high crime to take a false oath. God has often visited judgment upon false swearers, and even while the oath was on their lips, the destroying angel has cut them down. This was to prove a terror to evildoers.

I saw that if there is anyone on earth who can consistently testify under oath, it is Christians. They live in the light of God's countenance. They grow strong in His strength. And when matters of importance must be decided by law, there is no one who can so well appeal to God as the Christian. . . .

Jesus submitted to the oath in the hour of His trial. The high priest said unto Him: "I adjure thee by the living God, that thou tell us whether thou be the Christ, the Son of God." Jesus said unto him: "Thou hast said." If Jesus in His teachings to His disciples referred to the judicial oath, He would have reproved the high priest, and there enforced His teachings, for the good of His followers present.

Satan has been pleased that some have viewed oath taking in a wrong light; for it has given him opportunity to oppress them and take from them their Lord's money. The stewards of God must be more wise, lay their plans, and prepare themselves to withstand Satan's devices; for he is to make greater efforts than ever before.—*Testimonies for the Church,* vol. 1, pp. 202, 203.

Choices Being Made Between Two Sides

You shall not pervert the judgment of your poor in his dispute.
Keep yourself far from a false matter; do not kill the innocent and
righteous. For I will not justify the wicked. Exodus 23:6, 7, NKJV.

CHRIST PRONOUNCES A woe upon all who transgress the law of God. He pronounced a woe upon the lawyers in His day because they exercised their power to afflict those who looked to them for justice and judgment. All the terrible consequences of sin will come to those who, even though they may be nominal church members, regard it as a light matter to set aside the law of Jehovah, and to make no distinction between good and evil.

In the representations the Lord has given me, I have seen those who follow their own desires misrepresenting the truth, oppressing their brethren, and placing difficulties before them. Characters are now being developed, and many are taking sides, some on the side of the Lord Jesus Christ, some on the side of Satan and his angels. The Lord calls for all who will be true and obedient to His law to come out of and away from all connection with those who have placed themselves on the side of the enemy. Against their names is written, "TEKEL; Thou art weighed in the balances, and art found wanting" (Dan. 5:27). . . .

There are many men and women, apparently moral, but who are not Christians. They are deceived in their estimate of what constitutes true Christians. They possess an alloy of character that destroys the value of the gold, and they cannot be stamped with the impress of divine approval. They must be rejected as impure, worthless metal.

We cannot, of ourselves, perfect a true moral character, but we can accept of Christ's righteousness. We can be partakers of the divine nature, and escape the corruptions that are in the world through lust. Christ has left before us a perfect pattern of what we are to be as sons and daughters of God.—*This Day With God,* p. 222.

Handling Money to Meet God's Approval

Lay up for yourselves treasures in heaven, where neither moth
nor rust destroys and where thieves do not break in and steal. For where
your treasure is, there your heart will be also. Matthew 6:20, 21, NKJV.

MANY FATHERS AND mothers are poor in the midst of abundance. They abridge, in a degree, their own personal comforts and frequently deny themselves of those things that are necessary for the enjoyment of life and health, while they have ample means at their command. They feel forbidden, as it were, to appropriate their means for their own comfort or for charitable purposes. They have one object before them, and that is to save property to leave for their children.

This idea is so prominent, so interwoven with all their actions, that their children learn to look forward to the time when this property will be theirs. They depend upon it, and this prospect has an important but not a favorable influence upon their characters. Some become spendthrifts, others become selfish and avaricious, and still others grow indolent and reckless. Many do not cultivate habits of economy; they do not seek to become self-reliant. They are aimless, and have but little stability of character. The impressions received in childhood and youth are wrought in the texture of character and become the principle of action in mature life. . . .

With the light of God's Word, so plain and clear in reference to the money lent to stewards, and with the warnings and reproofs which God has given through the *Testimonies* in regard to the disposition of means—if, with all this light before them, children either directly or indirectly influence their parents to divide their property while living, or to will it mainly to the children to come into their hands after the death of their parents, they take upon themselves fearful responsibilities.

Children of aged parents who profess to believe the truth should, in the fear of God, advise and entreat their parents to be true to their profession of faith, and take a course in regard to their means which God can approve. Parents should lay up for themselves treasures in heaven by appropriating their means themselves to the advancement of the cause of God. They should not rob themselves of heavenly treasure by leaving a surplus of means to those who have enough; for by so doing they not only deprive themselves of the precious privilege of laying up a treasure in the heavens that faileth not, but they rob the treasury of God.—*Testimonies for the Church*, vol. 3, pp. 119, 120.

To Win Souls,
Forgo Personal Gain

I know how to be abased, and I know how to abound. Everywhere and in all things I have learned both to be full and to be hungry, both to abound and to suffer need. I can do all things through Christ who strengthens me. Philippians 4:12, 13, NKJV.

IN EVERY AGE Satan has sought to impair the efforts of God's servants by introducing into the church a spirit of fanaticism. Thus it was in Paul's day, and thus it was in later centuries during the time of the Reformation. Wycliffe, Luther, and many others who blessed the world by their influence and their faith encountered the wiles by which the enemy seeks to lead into fanaticism overzealous, unbalanced, and unsanctified minds.

Misguided souls have taught that the attainment of true holiness carries the mind above all earthly thoughts and leads men and women to refrain wholly from labor. Others, taking extreme views of certain texts of Scripture, have taught that it is a sin to work—that Christians should take no thought concerning the temporal welfare of themselves or their families, but should devote their lives wholly to spiritual things. The teaching and example of the apostle Paul are a rebuke to such extreme views. . . .

When Paul first visited Corinth, he found himself among a people who were suspicious of the motives of strangers. The Greeks on the seacoast were keen traders. So long had they trained themselves in sharp business practices, that they had come to believe that gain was godliness, and that to make money, whether by fair means or foul, was commendable. Paul was acquainted with their characteristics, and he would give them no occasion for saying that he preached the gospel in order to enrich himself. He might justly have claimed support from his Corinthian hearers; but this right he was willing to forgo, lest his usefulness and success as a minister should be injured by the unjust suspicion that he was preaching the gospel for gain. He would seek to remove all occasion for misrepresentation, that the force of his message might not be lost.—*The Acts of the Apostles,* pp. 348, 349.

Set Right
Priorities in Life

*Seek first the kingdom of God and His righteousness, and all
these things shall be added to you. Matthew 6:33, NKJV.*

ON EVERY HAND there is that which would tempt the Christian to forsake the narrow way; but those who would perfect a character fit for eternity must take the will of God as their standard, separating entirely from
everything that is displeasing to Him. Thousands are betrayed into sin because they leave the citadel of the heart unguarded. They become en-
grossed with the cares of this world, and true godliness is driven from their
hearts. They rush eagerly into speculation, seeking to accumulate more of
this world's treasure. Thus they place themselves where it is impossible for
them to advance in the Christian life. "Be ye therefore sober, and watch
unto prayer." And while you pray, strive earnestly to guard your heart
from all pollution; for prayer without effort is a solemn mockery.

"Love not the world, neither the things that are in the world. If any
man love the world, the love of the Father is not in him." Every moment
of our time belongs to God, and we have no right so to burden ourselves
with cares that there is no room in our hearts for His love. At the same
time, we are to obey the injunction "Not slothful in business." We are to
labor, that we may have to give to him that needs. God does not desire us
to allow our powers to rust through inaction. Christians must work; they
must engage in business; and they can go a certain length in this line, and
commit no sin against God.

But too often Christians allow the cares of life to take the time that belongs to God. They devote their precious moments to business or to
amusement. Their whole energies are employed in acquiring earthly treasure. In so doing they place themselves on forbidden ground.

Many professing Christians are very careful that all their business transactions shall bear the stamp of strict honesty, but dishonesty marks their relations with God. Absorbed in worldly business, they fail to perform the
duties they owe to those around them. Their children are not brought up
in the nurture and admonition of the Lord. The family altar is neglected;
private devotion is forgotten. Eternal interests, instead of being put first, are
given only the second place. God is robbed because their best thoughts are
given to the world, because their time is spent on things of minor importance. Thus they are ruined, not because of their dishonesty in dealing with
others, but because they have defrauded God of what is rightfully His
own.—*Signs of the Times,* Dec. 17, 1896.

Christians Must Never Depart From Integrity

He said to them, "You are those who justify yourselves in the sight of others; but God knows your hearts; for what is prized by human beings is an abomination in the sight of God." Luke 16:15, NRSV.

IN ALL THE details of life the strictest principles of honesty are to be maintained. These are not the principles which govern our world, for Satan—deceiver, liar, and oppressor—is the master, and his subjects follow him and carry out his purposes. But Christians serve under a different Master, and their actions must be wrought in God, irrespective of all selfish gain.

Deviation from perfect fairness in business deals may appear as a small thing in the estimation of some, but our Savior did not thus regard it. His words on this point are plain and explicit: "He that is faithful in that which is least is faithful also in much" (Luke 16:10). People who will overreach their neighbors on a small scale will overreach in a larger scale if the temptation is brought to bear upon them. A false representation in a small matter is as much dishonesty in the sight of God as falsity in a larger matter.

In the Christian world today fraud is practiced to a fearful extent. God's commandment-keeping people should show that they are above all these things. The dishonest practices which mar the dealing of men and women with their fellow human beings should never be practiced by one who professes to be a believer in present truth. God's people do great harm to the truth by the least departure from integrity.

Some persons may not have a pleasant exterior, they may be deficient in many respects, but if they have a reputation for straightforward honesty, they will be respected. Stern integrity covers many objectionable traits of character. Those who steadfastly adhere to truth will win the confidence of all. Not only will fellow believers in the faith trust them, but unbelievers will be constrained to acknowledge them as persons of honor.—*Mind, Character, and Personality,* vol. 2, p. 437.

The servants of God are obliged to be more or less connected with the worldly by business transactions, but they should buy and sell with a realization that the eye of God is upon them. No false balances or deceitful weights are to be used, for these are an abomination to the Lord. In every business transaction Christians will be just what they want their church friends to think they are. Their course of action is guided by underlying principles. They do not scheme; therefore they have nothing to conceal, nothing to gloss over.—*Ibid.,* pp. 437, 438.

Reveal Love While Doing God's Business

Dead flies putrefy the perfumer's ointment, and cause it to give off a foul odor;
so does a little folly to one respected for wisdom and honor. Ecclesiastes 10:1, NKJV.

I APPEAL TO my brothers and sisters in faith, and urge them to cultivate tenderness of heart. Whatever may be your calling or position, if you cherish selfishness and covetousness, the displeasure of the Lord will be upon you. Do not make the work and cause of God an excuse for dealing closely and selfishly with anyone, even if transacting business that has to do with His work. God will accept nothing in the line of gain that is brought into His treasury through selfish transactions.

Every act in connection with His work is to bear divine inspection. Every sharp transaction, every attempt to take advantage of persons who are under pressure of circumstances, every plan to purchase their land or property for a sum beneath its value, will not be acceptable to God, even though the money gained is made an offering to His cause. The price of the blood of the only-begotten Son of God has been paid for every human being, and it is necessary to deal honestly, to deal with equity with every person, in order to carry out the principles of the law of God. . . .

If a brother or sister who has labored disinterestedly for the cause of God becomes enfeebled in body and is unable to work, let him or her not be dismissed and be obliged to get along the best way they can. Give them wages sufficient to support themselves, for remember they belong to God's family, and that you are all brothers and sisters. . . .

We are commanded to love our neighbors as ourselves. This command is not that we shall simply love those who think and believe exactly as we think and believe. Christ illustrated the meaning of the commandment by the parable of the good Samaritan. But how strangely these precious words are neglected, and how frequently people oppress their fellow human beings, and lift up their souls unto vanity.—*Review and Herald,* Dec. 18, 1894.

Imitate Christ,
Not the World

*For the love of money is a root of all kinds of evil, for which
some have strayed from the faith in their greediness, and pierced
themselves through with many sorrows. 1 Timothy 6:10, NKJV.*

I SAW THAT God's people are in great peril; many are dwellers upon the earth; their interest and affections are centered in the world. Their example is not right. The world is deceived by the course pursued by many who profess great and noble truths. Our responsibility is in accordance with the light given, the graces and gifts bestowed. On the workers whose talents, whose means, whose opportunities and abilities, are greatest rests the heaviest responsibility. . . .

Brother A was presented before me to represent a class who are in a similar position. They have never been indifferent to the smallest worldly advantage. By diligent business tact and successful investments, by trading, not on pounds, but on pence and farthings, they have accumulated property. But in doing this they have educated faculties inconsistent with the development of Christian character. Their lives in no way represent Christ; for they love the world and its gain better than they love God or the truth. "If any man love the world, the love of the Father is not in him."

All the abilities which men and women possess belong to God. Worldly conformity and attachments are emphatically forbidden in His Word. When the power of the transforming grace of God is felt upon the heart, it will send a person, hitherto worldly, into every pathway of beneficence. Those who have in their hearts a determination to lay up treasure in the world will "fall into temptation and a snare, and into many foolish and hurtful lusts, which drown men in destruction and perdition. For the love of money is the root of all evil [the foundation of all avarice and worldliness]: which while some coveted after, they have erred from the faith, and pierced themselves through with many sorrows." . . .

Jesus has opened to everyone a way by which wisdom, grace, and power may be obtained. He is our example in all things, and nothing should divert the mind from the main object in life, which is to have Christ in the soul, melting and subduing the heart. When this is the case, every member of the church, every professor of the truth, will be Christlike in character, in words, in actions.—*Testimonies for the Church,* vol. 5, pp. 277, 278.

Be Compassionate When
Poverty Is Unavoidable

Poverty and shame will come to him who disdains correction,
but he who regards reproof will be honored. Proverbs 13:18, NKJV.

IN THE PARABLE [Matthew 18:32] the lord summoned the unmerciful debtor, and "said unto him, O thou wicked servant, I forgave thee all that debt, because thou desiredst me; shouldest not thou also have had compassion on thy fellowservant, even as I had pity on thee? And his lord was wroth, and delivered him to the tormentors, till he should pay all that was due unto him." "So likewise," said Jesus, "shall my heavenly Father do also unto you, if ye from your hearts forgive not every one his brother their trespasses." Those who refuse to forgive are thereby casting away their own hope of pardon.

But the teaching of this parable should not be misapplied. God's forgiveness toward us lessens in no wise our duty to obey Him. So the spirit of forgiveness toward our fellow beings does not lessen the claim of just obligation. In the prayer which Christ taught His disciples He said, "Forgive us our debts, as we forgive our debtors" (Matt. 6:12).

By this He did not mean that in order to be forgiven our sins we must not require our just dues from our debtors. If they cannot pay, even though this may be the result of unwise management, they are not to be cast into prison, oppressed, or even treated harshly; but the parable does not teach us to encourage indolence. The Word of God declares that "anyone unwilling to work should not eat" (2 Thess. 3:10, NRSV).

The Lord does not require the hardworking man or woman to support others in idleness. With many there is a waste of time, a lack of effort, which brings to poverty and want. If these faults are not corrected by those who indulge them, all that might be done in their behalf would be like putting treasure into a bag with holes. Yet there is an unavoidable poverty, and we are to manifest tenderness and compassion toward those who are unfortunate. We should treat others just as we ourselves, in like circumstances, would wish to be treated.—*Christ's Object Lessons*, pp. 247, 248.

Show Divine Love
by Being Merciful

But the mercy of the Lord is from everlasting to everlasting on those who fear Him, and His righteousness to children's children, to such as keep His covenant, and to those who remember His commandments to do them. Psalm 103:17, 18, NKJV.

MERCY IS AN attribute that the human agent may share with God. As did Christ, so one may lay hold on the divine arm and be in communication with divine power. To us has been given a service of mercy to perform for our fellow human beings. In performing this service, we are laboring together with God. We do well, then, to be merciful, even as our Father in heaven is merciful.

"I will have mercy," God says, "and not sacrifice." Mercy is kind, pitiful. Mercy and the love of God purify the soul, beautify the heart, and cleanse the life from selfishness. Mercy is a manifestation of divine love, and is shown by those who, identified with God, serve Him by reflecting the light of heaven upon the pathway of their fellow creatures.

The condition of many persons calls for the exercise of genuine mercy. Christians, in their dealing with one another, are to be controlled by principles of mercy and love. They are to improve every opportunity for helping fellow beings in distress. The duty of every Christian is plainly outlined in the words: "Judge not, and ye shall not be judged: condemn not, and ye shall not be condemned: forgive, and ye shall be forgiven: give, and it shall be given unto you; good measure, pressed down, and shaken together, and running over." "As ye would that men should do to you, do ye also to them likewise." These are the principles that we shall do well to cherish.

Let those who desire to perfect a Christlike character ever keep in view the cross on which Christ died a cruel death in order to redeem humankind. Let them ever cherish the same merciful spirit that led the Savior to make an infinite sacrifice for our redemption.—*Signs of the Times,* May 21, 1902.

Seek Divine Wisdom
in Handling Money

His lord said to him, "Well done, good and faithful servant;
you were faithful over a few things, I will make you ruler over many
things. Enter into the joy of your lord." Matthew 25:21, NKJV.

[BROTHER C] IS IN a responsible position, but if the members of the family to which he has allied himself in marriage will prove true to him, they will influence him to become a wise steward of his Lord's goods. Then he will bestow his means as if in the view of the whole universe of heaven. He will not participate in any unlawful scheme for making money, but will move with an eye single to the glory of God. He will eschew all petty tricks and avoid all mean, dishonest devices, and will do nothing that will [in] any way work against the cultivation of true piety. He will realize that all his business transactions lie within the domain of God.

We must not lose sight of the fact that stewards are to trade with their Lord's goods, and that they are handling a sacred responsibility. The Bible requires that people buy and sell and transact all their business with as keen a sense of their religious obligation as they have when offering up petitions to their heavenly Father, asking for strength and grace. The Lord has not left any to do as they please with their goods, and to give as impulse shall dictate, or as friends may demand. The money they handle is not theirs, and is not to be expended unnecessarily, for the vineyard of the Lord is to be worked, and its working requires the expenditure of means.

Now is our day of trust, and the day of reckoning is yet to come. The Lord has entrusted means to His stewards to be used wisely, for all are moral agents and are required to bear responsibilities. Our varied trusts are given in proportion to our ability to use, but we are not to use God's means merely for the gratification of selfish desires, and as inclination may dictate.

[Brother C] has failed at times in the past in handling his Lord's goods, and has not always considered whether he was using the money entrusted to him in a way that would please his Master and advance the cause of truth. He must give an account of how he disposes of the means given in trust to him. He cannot study his own will in this matter. He must seek wisdom from God.—*Testimonies on Sexual Behavior, Adultery, and Divorce,* pp. 70, 71.

Invest to Glorify God, Not Self

Talk no more so very proudly; let no arrogance come from your mouth, for the Lord is the God of knowledge; and by Him actions are weighed. 1 Samuel 2:3, NKJV.

I WAS IN THE night season called upon to behold buildings rising story after story toward heaven. These buildings were warranted to be fireproof, and they were erected to glorify the owners and builders. . . . Those to whom these buildings belonged were not asking themselves: "How can we best glorify God?" The Lord was not in their thoughts.

I thought: "Oh, that those who are thus investing their means could see their course as God sees it! They are piling up magnificent buildings, but how foolish in the sight of the Ruler of the universe is their planning and devising. They are not studying with all the powers of heart and mind how they may glorify God. They have lost sight of this, the first duty of human beings."

As these lofty buildings went up, the owners rejoiced with ambitious pride that they had money to use in gratifying self and provoking the envy of their neighbors. Much of the money that they thus invested had been obtained through exaction, through grinding down the poor. They forgot that in heaven an account of every business transaction is kept; every unjust deal, every fraudulent act, is there recorded. The time is coming when in their fraud and insolence men and women will reach a point that the Lord will not permit them to pass, and they will learn that there is a limit to the forbearance of Jehovah. . . .

There are not many, even among educators and statesmen, who comprehend the causes that underlie the present state of society. Those who hold the reins of government are not able to solve the problem of moral corruption, poverty, pauperism, and increasing crime. They are struggling in vain to place business operations on a more secure basis. If men and women would give more heed to the teaching of God's Word, they would find a solution of the problems that perplex them.—*Testimonies for the Church*, vol. 9, pp. 12, 13.

Represent Christ in Every Circumstance

For by the grace given to me I say to everyone among you not to think of yourself more highly than you ought to think, but to think with sober judgment, each according to the measure of faith that God has assigned. Romans 12:3, NRSV.

LIVE FOR SOMETHING besides self. If your motives are pure and unselfish, if you are looking out to do work that somebody must do, to show kind attentions and to do courteous acts, you are unconsciously building your own monument. In the home life, in the church, and in the world you are representing Christ in character. This is the work the Lord calls upon all . . . to do. . . .

Let your aspirations and your motives be pure. In every business transaction be rigidly honest. However tempted, never deceive or prevaricate in the least matter. At times a natural impulse may bring temptation to diverge from the straightforward path of honesty, but do not vary one hair's breadth. If in any matter you make a statement as to what you will do, and afterward find that you have favored others to your own loss, do not vary from principle. Carry out your agreement.

By seeking to change your plans you would show that you could not be depended on. And should you draw back in little transactions, you would draw back in larger ones. Under such circumstances some are tempted to deceive, saying, I was not understood. My words have been taken to mean more than I intended. The fact is, they meant just what they said, but lost the good impulse, and then wanted to draw back from their agreement, lest it prove a loss to them. The Lord requires us to do justice, to love mercy, and truth, and righteousness. . . .

Men and women are destitute of the stern virtues required to build up the church. They are not capable of devising methods and plans of a healthful, solid character. They are deficient in the very qualifications essential to the prosperity of the church. It is this kind of education that needs to be changed to an education that is sound and sensible, in harmony with Bible principles.—*Manuscript Releases,* vol. 20, pp. 343, 344.

In Planning, Consider
the Unending Future

For bodily exercise profits a little, but godliness is profitable for all things, having promise of the life that now is and of that which is to come. 1 Timothy 4:8, NKJV.

THE ACCOUNTS OF every business, the details of every transaction, pass the scrutiny of unseen auditors, agents of Him who never compromises with injustice, never overlooks evil, never palliates wrong. . . .

Against all evildoers God's law utters condemnation. They may disregard that voice, they may seek to drown its warning, but in vain. It follows them. It makes itself heard. It destroys their peace. If unheeded, it pursues them to the grave. It bears witness against them at the judgment. A quenchless fire, it consumes at last soul and body.

"What shall it profit a man, if he shall gain the whole world, and lose his own soul? Or what shall a man give in exchange for his soul?" (Mark 8:36, 37).

This is a question that demands consideration by every parent, every teacher, every student—by every human being, young or old. No scheme of business or plan of life can be sound or complete that embraces only the brief years of this present life and makes no provision for the unending future. Let the youth be taught to take eternity into their reckoning. Let them be taught to choose the principles and seek the possessions that are enduring—to lay up for themselves that "treasure in the heavens that faileth not, where no thief approacheth, neither moth corrupteth" (Luke 12:33). . . .

All who do this are making the best possible preparation for life in this world. No man or woman can lay up treasure in heaven without finding life on earth thereby enriched and ennobled.

"Godliness is profitable unto all things, having promise of the life that now is, and of that which is to come" (1 Tim. 4:8).—*Education,* pp. 144, 145.

Never Dishonor God
by Violating Righteous Principles

*So are the ways of everyone who is greedy for gain; it
takes away the life of its owners. Proverbs 1:19, NKJV.*

TO EVERY PERSON is given his or her work. Each has a place in the
eternal plan of heaven. It is the duty of fathers and mothers to overcome
their own lawlessness, their untidy habits. Truth is clean and pure and of
great value and needs to be brought into the character building. Those
who have the truth, the love of the truth in their hearts, will make any and
every sacrifice that this truth may have the first place in everything. . . .

There are those in our churches who have much to say in regard to
Christianity, but in whose presence we should always be guarded, for they
dismiss the Word of God from their business transactions. When there is
buying and selling to be done, God is not by their side. The enemy is on
the ground, and he takes possession of them. Christian brotherhood and
love is laid a sacrifice on the altar of greed. God, heaven, the precepts of
Jehovah, His oft-repeated injunctions, are obliterated from the soul. They
know not what it means to practice the principles laid down in the Word
of God. They sell their souls for unlawful gain. So thick is the veil which
blinds their eyes that they can see only the fraudulent gain. So hard is the
incrustation that envelops the heart that it feels not the love and tenderness
and pity of Christ for their fellow beings. The holiness and truth of God
are shut out from their souls.

Will the people of God frown down all this corrupting influence? Will
they give their hearts to God? Will they deal mercifully with their fellow
mortals? Will Seventh-day Adventists bear in mind that they cannot
swerve from truth in their dealings with their fellow beings, that they cannot violate justice or let go their integrity without forsaking God?
Anything that dishonors Him will never benefit you. People who expect
to prosper by violating the eternal principles of righteousness are laying up
for themselves a harvest they will not care to reap. They place themselves
in the enemy's ranks and bring degradation upon themselves. Although for
a time they may seem to prosper, they can never help to compose the family of God.—*Sermons and Talks,* vol. 2, pp. 133, 134.

Faithful Stewards
Provide for God's Work

I, the Lord, have called You in righteousness, and will hold Your hand; I will keep You and give You as a covenant to the people, as a light to the Gentiles. Isaiah 42:6, NKJV.

I HAD BEEN shown that some people who are shrewd, prudent, and sharp in regard to the transaction of business generally, some who are distinguished for promptness and thoroughness, manifest a want of foresight and promptness in regard to a proper disposal of their property while they are living. They know not how soon their probation may close; yet they pass on from year to year with their business unsettled, and frequently their lives finally close without their having the use of their reason. Or they may die suddenly, without a moment's warning, and their property be disposed of in a manner that they would not have approved. These are guilty of negligence; they are unfaithful stewards.

Christians who believe the present truth should manifest wisdom and foresight. They should not neglect the disposition of their means, expecting a favorable opportunity to adjust their business during a long illness. They should have their business in such a shape that, were they called at any hour to leave it, and should they have no voice in its arrangement, it might be settled as they would have had it were they alive.

Many families have been dishonestly robbed of all their property and have been subjected to poverty because the work that might have been well done in an hour had been neglected. Those who make their wills should not spare pains or expense to obtain legal advice and to have them drawn up in a manner to stand the test.

I saw that those who profess to believe the truth should show their faith by their works. They should, with the unrighteous mammon, make friends, that they may finally be received into everlasting habitations. God has made men and women stewards of means. He has placed in their hands the money with which to carry forward the great work for the salvation of souls for whom Christ left His home, His riches, His glory, and became poor that He might, by His own humiliation and sacrifice, bring many sons and daughters of Adam to God.

In His providence the Lord has ordained that the work in His vineyard should be sustained by the means entrusted to the hands of His stewards. A neglect on their part to answer the calls of the cause of God in carrying forward His work shows them to be unfaithful and slothful servants.—*Testimonies for the Church,* vol. 3, pp. 116, 117.

JULY

❧

Practicing the End-time Lifestyle

The New Lifestyle
Through Jesus

I have been crucified with Christ; it is no longer I who live, but Christ lives in me; and the life which I now live in the flesh I live by faith in the Son of God, who loved me and gave Himself for me. Galatians 2:20, NKJV.

SELF MUST DIE if we would be counted as the followers of Christ. The apostle says, "If ye then be risen with Christ, seek those things which are above, where Christ sitteth on the right hand of God. . . . For ye are dead, and your life is hid with Christ in God." "If any man be in Christ, he is a new creature: old things are passed away; behold, all things are become new."

When men and women are converted to God, a new moral taste is created; and they love the things that God loves; for their lives are bound up by the golden chain of the immutable promises, to the life of Jesus. Their hearts are drawn out after God. Their prayer is "Open thou mine eyes, that I may behold wondrous things out of thy law." In the immutable standard they see the character of the Redeemer, and know that though they have sinned, they are not to be saved in their sins, but from their sins; for Jesus is the Lamb of God which taketh away the sin of the world. It is through the blood of Christ that they are brought nigh unto God.

As they behold the righteousness of Christ in the divine precepts, they exclaim, "The law of the Lord is perfect, converting the soul." As sinners are pardoned for their transgressions through the merits of Christ, as they are clothed with the righteousness of Christ through faith in Him, they declare with the psalmist, "How sweet are thy words unto my taste! yea, sweeter than honey to my mouth!" "More to be desired are they than gold, yea, than much fine gold: sweeter also than honey and the honeycomb." This is conversion.

When the Spirit of God controls the mind and heart, it turns the hearts of the fathers to the children, and the disobedient to the wisdom of the just. The law of Jehovah will then be regarded as a transcript of the divine character, and a new song bursts forth from hearts that have been touched by divine grace; for they realize that the promise of God has been fulfilled in their experience, that their transgressions are forgiven, their sins covered. They have exercised repentance toward God for the violation of His law, and faith toward our Lord Jesus Christ, who has died for their justification.—*Review and Herald*, June 21, 1892.

Jesus Requires Wholehearted Commitment

"You shall love the Lord your God with all your heart,
with all your soul, with all your strength, and with all your mind,"
and "your neighbor as yourself." Luke 10:27, NKJV.

THE LORD IS testing and proving you. He has counseled, admonished, and entreated. All these solemn admonitions will either make the church better or decidedly worse. The oftener the Lord speaks to correct or counsel, and you disregard His voice, the more disposed will you be to reject it again and again, till God says: "Because I have called, and ye refused; I have stretched out my hand, and no man regarded; but ye have set at nought all my counsel, and would none of my reproof. . . . Then shall they call upon me, but I will not answer; they shall seek me early, but they shall not find me; for that they hated knowledge, and did not choose the fear of the Lord: they would none of my counsel: they despised all my reproof. Therefore shall they eat of the fruit of their own way, and be filled with their own devices."

Are you not halting between two opinions? Are you not neglecting to heed the light which God has given you? Take heed lest there be in any of you an evil heart of unbelief in departing from the living God. You know not the time of your visitation. The great sin of the Jews was that of neglecting and rejecting present opportunities. As Jesus views the state of His professed followers today, He sees base ingratitude, hollow formalism, hypocritical insincerity, pharisaical pride, and apostasy.

The tears which Christ shed on the crest of Olivet were for the impenitence and ingratitude of every individual to the close of time. He sees His love despised. The soul's temple courts have been converted into places of unholy traffic. Selfishness, mammon, malice, envy, pride, passion, are all cherished in the human heart. His warnings are rejected and ridiculed, His ambassadors are treated with indifference, their words seem as idle tales. Jesus has spoken by mercies, but these mercies have been unacknowledged; He has spoken by solemn warnings, but these warnings have been rejected.

I entreat you who have long professed the faith and who still pay outward homage to Christ: Do not deceive your own souls. It is the whole heart that Jesus prizes. The loyalty of the soul is alone of value in the sight of God. "If thou hadst known, even thou, at least in this thy day, the things which belong unto thy peace!" *"Thou . . . even thou"*—Christ is at this moment addressing you personally, stooping from His throne, yearning with pitying tenderness over those who feel not their danger, who have no pity for themselves.—*Testimonies for the Church*, vol. 5, pp. 72, 73.

God Has Sent
Warnings, but Few Listen

And it shall come to pass at that time that I will search Jerusalem with lamps, and punish the men who are settled in complacency, who say in their heart, "The Lord will not do good, nor will He do evil." Zephaniah 1:12, NKJV.

WE ARE NEAR the close of time. I have been shown that the retributive judgments of God are already in the land. The Lord has given us warning of the events about to take place. Light is shining from His Word; yet darkness covers the earth, and gross darkness the people. "When they shall say, Peace and safety; then sudden destruction cometh upon them . . . ; and they shall not escape."

It is our duty to inquire the cause of this terrible darkness, that we may shun the course by which men and women have brought upon themselves so great delusion. God has given the world an opportunity to learn and to obey His will. He has given them, in His Word, the light of truth; He has sent them warning, counsel, and admonition; but few will obey His voice. Like the Jewish nation, the majority, even of professed Christians, pride themselves on their superior advantages, but make no returns to God for these great blessings.

In infinite mercy a last warning message has been sent to the world, announcing that Christ is at the door and calling attention to God's broken law. But as the antediluvians rejected with scorn the warning of Noah, so will the pleasure lovers of today reject the message of God's faithful servants. The world pursues its unvarying round, absorbed as ever in its business and its pleasures, while the wrath of God is about to be visited on the transgressors of His law.

Our compassionate Redeemer, foreseeing the perils that would surround His followers at this time, has given them special warning: "Take heed to yourselves, lest at any time your hearts be overcharged with surfeiting, and drunkenness, and cares of this life, and so that day come upon you unawares. For as a snare shall it come on all them that dwell on the face of the whole earth. Watch ye therefore, and pray always, that ye may be accounted worthy to escape all these things that shall come to pass, and to stand before the Son of man."—*Testimonies for the Church,* vol. 5, pp. 99, 100.

Fanaticism and Noise
No Evidence of Faith

Thanks be to God, I speak in tongues more than all of you; but in the congregation I would rather speak five words intelligibly to instruct others than a myriad of words in a tongue. 1 Corinthians 14:18, 19, MLB.

ERROR MUST FIRST be rooted up, then the soil is prepared for the good seed to spring up and bear fruit to the glory of God.

The only remedy . . . is thorough discipline and organization. A spirit of fanaticism has ruled a certain class of Sabbathkeepers . . . ; they have sipped but lightly at the fountain of truth and are unacquainted with the spirit of the message of the third angel. Nothing can be done for this class until their fanatical views are corrected. Some who were in the 1854 movement have brought along with them erroneous views, such as the nonresurrection of the wicked, and the future age, and they are seeking to unite these views and their past experience with the message of the third angel. They cannot do this; there is no concord between Christ and Belial.

The nonresurrection of the wicked and their peculiar views of the age to come are gross errors which Satan has worked in among the last-day heresies to serve his own purpose to ruin souls. These errors can have no harmony with the message of heavenly origin.

Some of these persons have exercises which they call gifts and say that the Lord has placed them in the church. They have an unmeaning gibberish which they call the unknown tongue, which is unknown not only by human beings but by the Lord and all heaven. Such gifts are manufactured by men and women, aided by the great deceiver. Fanaticism, false excitement, false talking in tongues, and noisy exercises have been considered gifts which God has placed in the church. Some have been deceived here. The fruits of all this have not been good. "Ye shall know them by their fruits."

Fanaticism and noise have been considered special evidences of faith. Some are not satisfied with a meeting unless they have a powerful and happy time. They work for this and get up an excitement of feeling. But the influence of such meetings is not beneficial. When the happy flight of feeling is gone, they sink lower than before the meeting because their happiness did not come from the right source. The most profitable meetings for spiritual advancement are those which are characterized with solemnity and deep searching of heart; each seeking to know themselves, and earnestly, and in deep humility, seeking to learn of Christ.—*Testimonies for the Church,* vol. 1, pp. 411, 412.

God Not Pleased
With Tasteless Disorder

Then the Lord said to Moses, "Go to the people and sanctify them
today and tomorrow, and let them wash their clothes." . . . And Moses
brought the people out of the camp to meet with God. Exodus 19:10-17, NKJV.

SOME RECEIVE THE idea that in order to carry out that separation from the world which the Word of God requires, they must be neglectful of their apparel. There is a class of sisters who think that they are carrying out the principle of nonconformity to the world by wearing . . . the same dress worn by them through the week, upon the Sabbath, to appear in the assembly of the saints to engage in the worship of God.

And some men who profess to be Christians view the matter of dress in the same light. They assemble with God's people upon the Sabbath, with their clothing dusty, and soiled, and even with gaping rents in them, and placed upon their persons in a slovenly manner.

This class, if they had an engagement to meet a friend honored by the world, and they wished to be especially favored by him or her, would exert themselves to appear . . . with the best apparel that could be obtained; for this friend would feel insulted were they to come . . . with hair uncombed, and garments uncleanly, and in disorder.

Yet these persons think that it is no matter in what dress they appear, or what is the condition of their persons, when they meet upon the Sabbath to worship the great God. They assemble in His house, which is as the audience chamber of the Most High, where heavenly angels are in attendance, with but little respect, or reverence, as their persons and clothing indicate. Their whole appearance typifies the character of such men and women.

The favorite theme of this class is pride of dress. Decency, taste, and order, they regard as pride. And according to the dress of these mistaken souls will be their conversation, their acts, and their deal. They are careless, and often low in their conversation at their homes, among their brethren and sisters, and before the world. The dress, and its arrangement upon the person, is generally found to be the index of the man or the woman. Those who are careless and untidy in dress are seldom elevated in their conversation, and possess but little refinement of feelings. They sometimes consider oddity and coarseness, humility. . . .

Our God is a God of order, and He is not in any degree pleased with distraction, with filthiness, or with sin.—*Selected Messages,* book 2, pp. 475, 476.

Follow Christ and Defeat the Enemy

For all that is in the world—the lust of the flesh, the lust of the eyes, and the pride of life—is not of the Father but is of the world. 1 John 2:16, NKJV.

MANY OF THE people of God are stupefied by the spirit of the world, and are denying their faith by their works. They cultivate a love for money, for houses and lands, until it absorbs the powers of mind and being, and shuts out love for the Creator and for souls for whom Christ died. The god of this world has blinded their eyes; their eternal interests are made secondary; and brain, bone, and muscle are taxed to the utmost to increase their worldly possessions. And all this accumulation of cares and burdens is borne in direct violation of the injunction of Christ, who said, "Lay not up for yourselves treasures upon earth, where moth and rust doth corrupt, and where thieves break through and steal."

They forget that He said also, "Lay up *for yourselves* treasures in heaven"; that in so doing they are working for their own interest. The treasure laid up in heaven is safe; no thief can approach nor moth corrupt it. But their treasure is upon the earth, and their affections are upon their treasure.

In the wilderness, Christ met the great leading temptations that would assail humanity. There, singlehanded, He encountered the wily, subtle foe, and overcame him. The first great temptation was upon appetite; the second, presumption; the third, love of the world. The thrones and kingdoms of the world, and the glory of them, were offered to Christ. Satan came with worldly honor, wealth, and the pleasures of life, and presented them in the most attractive light to allure and deceive. "All these things," said he to Christ, "will I give thee, if thou wilt fall down and worship me." Yet Christ repelled the wily foe, and came off victor. . . .

The example of Christ is before us. He overcame Satan, showing us how we also may overcome. Christ resisted Satan with Scripture. He might have had recourse to His own divine power, and used His own words; but He said, "It is written, Man shall not live by bread alone, but by every word that proceedeth out of the mouth of God." If the Sacred Scriptures were studied and followed, the Christian would be fortified to meet the wily foe; but the Word of God is neglected, and disaster and defeat follow.—*Counsels on Stewardship,* pp. 209, 210.

Decided Efforts Must Be Made Against Sin

Whoever heeds instruction is on the path to life, but one who rejects a rebuke goes astray. Proverbs 10:17, NRSV.

MANY APOLOGIZE for their spiritual weakness, for their outbursts of passion, for the lack of love they show their brethren and sisters. They feel a sense of estrangement from God, a realization of their bondage to self and sin; but their desire to do God's will is based upon their own inclination, not upon the deep, inward conviction of the Holy Spirit. They believe that the law of God is binding; but they do not, with the eager interest of judgment-bound souls, compare their actions with that law. They admit that God should be worshiped and loved supremely, but God is not in all their thoughts. They believe that the precepts which enjoin love to others should be observed; but they treat their associates with cold indifference, and sometimes with injustice. Thus they walk away from the path of willing obedience. They do not carry the work of repentance far enough. The sense of their wrong should lead them to seek God most earnestly for power to reveal Christ by kindness and forbearance.

Many spasmodic efforts to reform are made, but those who make these efforts do not crucify self. They do not give themselves entirely into the hands of Christ, seeking for divine power to do His will. They are not willing to be molded after the divine similitude. In a general way they acknowledge their imperfections, but the particular sins are not given up. "We have done the things we ought not to have done," they say, "and have left undone the things we ought to have done." But their acts of selfishness, so offensive to God, are not seen in the light of His law. Full contrition is not expressed for the victories that self has gained.

The enemy is willing that these spasmodic efforts should be made; for those who make them engage in no decided warfare against evil. A soothing plaster, as it were, is placed over their minds, and in self-sufficiency they make a fresh start to do the will of God.

But a general conviction of sin is not reformative. We may have a vague, disagreeable sense of imperfection, but this will avail us nothing unless we make a decided effort to obtain the victory over sin. If we wish to cooperate with Christ, to overcome as He overcame, we must, in His strength, make the most determined resistance against self and selfishness.—*Signs of the Times*, Mar. 11, 1897.

Seek to Be
Temperate in All Things

*In the way of righteousness is life, and in its
pathway there is no death. Proverbs 12:28, NKJV.*

GOD HAS PERMITTED the light of health reform to shine upon us in these last days, that by walking in the light we may escape many of the dangers to which we shall be exposed. Satan is working with great power to lead men and women to indulge appetite, gratify inclination, and spend their days in heedless folly. He presents attractions in a life of selfish enjoyment and of sensual indulgence.

Intemperance saps the energies of both mind and body. Those who are thus overcome have placed themselves upon Satan's ground, where they will be tempted and annoyed, and finally controlled at pleasure by the enemy of all righteousness.

Parents need to be impressed with their obligation to give to the world children having well-developed characters—children who will have moral power to resist temptation, and whose life will be an honor to God and a blessing to others. Those who enter upon active life with firm principles will be prepared to stand unsullied amid the moral pollutions of this corrupt age. Let mothers improve every opportunity to educate their children for usefulness.

The work of the mother is sacred and important. She should teach her children, from the cradle up, habits of self-denial and self-control. Her time, in a special sense, belongs to her children. But if it is mostly occupied with the follies of this degenerate age, if society, dress, and amusements absorb her attention, her children will fail to be suitably educated. . . .

Intemperance begins at the table, and, with the majority, appetite is indulged until indulgence becomes second nature. Whoever eats too much, or of food which is not healthful, is weakening the power to resist the clamors of other appetites and passions.

Many parents, to avoid the task of patiently educating their children to habits of self-denial, indulge them in eating and drinking whenever they please. The desire to satisfy the taste and to gratify inclination does not lessen with the increase of years; and these indulged youth, as they grow up, are governed by impulse, slaves to appetite. When they take their places in society, and begin life for themselves, they are powerless to resist temptation.—*Christian Education*, pp. 175-177.

Training Children
a Sacred Responsibility

"Come out from among them, and be separate, says the Lord. Do not touch what is unclean, and I will receive you." "I will be a Father to you, and you shall be My sons and daughters, says the Lord Almighty." 2 Corinthians 6:17, 18, NKJV.

WHEN PARENTS AND children meet at the final reckoning, what a scene will be presented! Thousands of children who have been slaves to appetite and debasing vice, whose lives are moral wrecks, will stand face to face with the parents who made them what they are. Who but the parents must bear this fearful responsibility? Did the Lord make these youth corrupt? Oh, no! Who, then, has done this fearful work? Were not the sins of the parents transmitted to the children in perverted appetites and passions? And was not the work completed by those who neglected to train them according to the pattern which God has given? Just as surely as they exist, all these parents will pass in review before God.

Satan is ready to do his work; he will not neglect to present allurements which the children have no will or moral power to resist. I saw that, through his temptations, he is instituting ever-changing fashions, and attractive parties and amusements, that mothers may be led to devote their time to frivolous matters, instead of to the education and training of their children. Our youth need mothers who will teach them from the cradle to control passion, to deny appetite, and to overcome selfishness. They need line upon line, precept upon precept, here a little and there a little. . . .

Woman should fill the position which God originally designed for her, as her husband's equal. The world needs mothers who are mothers not merely in name, but in every sense of the word. We may safely say that the distinctive duties of woman are more sacred, more holy, than those of man. Let woman realize the sacredness of her work, and in the strength and fear of God take up her life mission. Let her educate her children for usefulness in this world, and for a home in the better world. . . .

I entreat Christian mothers to realize their responsibility, and to live, not to please themselves, but to glorify God. Christ pleased not Himself, but took upon Him the form of a servant. He left the royal courts, and clothed His divinity with humanity, that by His own example He might teach us how we may be exalted to the position of sons and daughters in the royal family, children of the heavenly King.—*Christian Education*, pp. 177-179.

Work and Exercise
Contribute to Health

*You are wearied in the length of your way; yet you
did not say, "There is no hope." You have found the life of
your hand; therefore you were not grieved. Isaiah 57:10, NKJV.*

RICHES AND IDLENESS are thought by some to be blessings indeed. But when some persons have acquired wealth, or inherited it unexpectedly, their active habits have been broken up, their time is unemployed, they live at ease, and their usefulness seems at an end; they become restless, anxious, and unhappy, and their lives soon close.

Those who are always busy, and go cheerfully about the performance of their daily tasks, are the most happy and healthy. The rest and composure of night brings to their wearied frames unbroken slumber. The Lord knew what was for the happiness of human beings when He gave them work to do. The sentence that they must toil for their bread, and the promise of future happiness and glory, came from the same throne. Both are blessings. . . .

Exercise will aid the work of digestion. To walk out after a meal, hold the head erect, put back the shoulders, and exercise moderately will be a great benefit. The mind will be diverted from self to the beauties of nature. The less the attention is called to the stomach after a meal, the better. If you are in constant fear that your food will hurt you, it most assuredly will. Forget self, and think of something cheerful. . . .

The lungs should not be deprived of pure, fresh air. If pure air is ever necessary, it is when any part of the system, [such] as the lungs or stomach, is diseased. Judicious exercise would induce the blood to the surface, and thus relieve the internal organs. Brisk, yet not violent exercise in the open air, with cheerfulness of spirits, will promote the circulation, giving a healthful glow to the skin, and sending the blood, vitalized by the pure air, to the extremities.

The diseased stomach will find relief by exercise. Physicians frequently advise invalids to visit foreign countries, to go to the springs, or to ride upon the ocean, in order to regain health; when, in nine cases out of ten, if they would eat temperately and engage in healthful exercise with a cheerful spirit, they would regain health and save time and money. Exercise, and a free and abundant use of the air and sunlight—blessings which Heaven has freely bestowed upon all—would give life and strength to the emaciated invalid.—*Testimonies for the Church,* vol. 2, pp. 529-531.

When Trials Come,
Cling to Jesus

*Fear not, for I am with you; be not dismayed, for I am
your God. I will strengthen you, yes, I will help you, I will
uphold you with My righteous right hand. Isaiah 41:10, NKJV.*

PARENTS SHOULD devise ways and means for keeping their children
usefully busy. . . . Parents must never forget that they must work earnestly
for themselves and their little ones, if they with them are gathered into the
ark of safety. We are still in the enemy's country. Let parents strive to reach
a higher standard, and to carry their children with them. Let them cast off
the works of darkness and put on the armor of light.

Prove your willingness to make every effort in your power to place
your children in the most favorable situation for forming the character that
God requires His servants to form. Exercise every spiritual sinew and muscle to save your little flock. The powers of hell will conspire for your destruction. Pray much more than you do. Lovingly, tenderly teach your
children to come to God as a heavenly Father.

By your example in the management of the home, teach them self-
control. Teach them to be helpful in the home. Tell them that Christ lived
not to please Himself. The Holy Spirit will fill your mind with the most
precious thoughts as you work for your own salvation and the salvation of
your children.

Parents, gather the rays of divine light which are shining upon your
pathway. Walk in the light as Christ is in the light. As you take up the
work of saving your children and maintaining your position on the highway of holiness, the most provoking trials will come. But do not lose your
hold. Cling to Jesus. He says, "Let him take hold of my strength, that he
may make peace with me; and he shall make peace with me."

Difficulties will arise. You will meet with obstacles. Look constantly to
Jesus. When an emergency arises, ask, "Lord, what shall I do now?" If you
refuse to storm or fret or scold, the Lord will show you the way through.
He will help you to use the talent of speech in such a Christlike way that
the precious attributes of patience, comfort, and love will be brought into
the home. . . .

Do all in your power to stand on vantage ground before your children.
By following a Christlike course of action, holding firmly to the promises
of God, you may be evangelists in the home, ministers of grace to your
children.—*Spalding and Magan Collection*, p. 185.

For Every Difficulty, God's Grace Is Sufficient

And He said to me, "My grace is sufficient for you, for My strength is made perfect in weakness." 2 Corinthians 12:9, NKJV.

NONE CAN BE so situated that they cannot obey God. There is too little faith with Christians of today. They are willing to work for Christ and His cause only when they themselves can see a prospect of favorable results. Divine grace will aid the efforts of every true believer. That grace is sufficient for us under all circumstances. The Spirit of Christ will exert His renewing, perfecting power upon the character of all who will be obedient and faithful.

God is the great I AM, the source of being, the center of authority and power. Whatever the condition or situation of His creatures, they can have no sufficient excuse for refusing to answer the claims of God. The Lord holds us responsible for the light shining upon our pathway. We may be surrounded by difficulties that appear formidable to us, and because of these we may excuse ourselves for not obeying the truth as it is in Jesus; but there can be no excuse that will bear investigation. Could there be an excuse for disobedience, it would prove our heavenly Father unjust, in that He had given us conditions of salvation with which we could not comply. . . .

Christians should not array before their imagination all the trials which may occur before the end of the race. They have but to begin to serve God, and each day live and labor for the glory of God that day, and obstacles which appeared insurmountable will gradually grow less and less; or, should they encounter all that they have feared, the grace of Christ will be imparted to them according to their need. Strength increases with the difficulties met and overcome. . . .

Those whose hearts are fixed to serve God will find opportunity to serve Him. They will pray, they will read the Word of God, they will seek virtue and forsake vice. They can brave contempt and derision while looking unto Jesus, the author and finisher of our faith, who endured the contradiction of sinners against Himself. Help and grace are promised by Him whose words are truth. God will not fail to fulfill His promise to all who trust in Him.—*Sketches From the Life of Paul*, pp. 296-298.

Husbands Are to
Be Thoughtful and Cheerful

Husbands, likewise, dwell with them with understanding,
giving honor to the wife, as to the weaker vessel, and as being heirs together
of the grace of life, that your prayers may not be hindered. 1 Peter 3:7, NKJV.

THE HUSBAND SHOULD manifest great interest in his family. Especially should he be very tender of the feelings of a feeble wife. He can shut the door against much disease. Kind, cheerful, and encouraging words will prove more effective than the most healing medicines. These will bring courage to the heart of the desponding and discouraged, and the happiness and sunshine brought into the family by kind acts and encouraging words will repay the effort tenfold.

The husband should remember that much of the burden of training his children rests upon the mother, that she has much to do with molding their minds. This should call into exercise his tenderest feelings, and with care should he lighten her burdens. He should encourage her to lean upon his large affections and direct her mind to heaven, where there is strength and peace and a final rest for the weary. He should not come to his home with a clouded brow, but should with his presence bring sunlight into the family and should encourage his wife to look up and believe in God. Unitedly they can claim the promises of God and bring His rich blessing into the family.—*Testimonies for the Church,* vol. 1, pp. 306, 307.

Many a husband and father might learn a helpful lesson from the carefulness of the faithful shepherd. Jacob, when urged to undertake a rapid and difficult journey, made answer: "The children are tender, and the flocks and herds with young are with me: and if men should overdrive them one day, all the flock will die. . . . I will lead on softly, according as the cattle that goeth before me and the children be able to endure."

In life's toilsome way let the husband and father "lead on softly," as the companion of his journey is able to endure. Amidst the world's eager rush for wealth and power, let him learn to stay his steps, to comfort and support the one who is called to walk by his side.—*The Ministry of Healing,* p. 374.

Bible Holiness
Is Our Great Need

To them God willed to make known what are the riches of the glory of this mystery among the Gentiles: which is Christ in you, the hope of glory. Colossians 1:27, NKJV.

IT IS DIFFICULT for those who feel secure in their attainments, and who believe themselves to be rich in spiritual knowledge, to receive the message [to the Laodiceans] which declares that they are deceived and in need of every spiritual grace. The unsanctified heart is "deceitful above all things, and desperately wicked." I was shown that many are flattering themselves that they are good Christians, who have not a ray of light from Jesus. They have not a living experience for themselves in the divine life. They need a deep and thorough work of self-abasement before God before they will feel their true need of earnest, persevering effort to secure the precious graces of the Spirit.

God leads His people on step by step. The Christian life is a constant battle and a march. There is no rest from the warfare. It is by constant, unceasing effort that we maintain the victory over the temptations of Satan. As a people we are triumphing in the clearness and strength of the truth. We are fully sustained in our positions by an overwhelming amount of plain scriptural testimony. But we are very much wanting in Bible humility, patience, faith, love, self-denial, watchfulness, and the spirit of sacrifice. We need to cultivate Bible holiness. Sin prevails among the people of God. The plain message of rebuke to the Laodiceans is not received. Many cling to their doubts and their darling sins while they are in so great a deception as to talk and feel that they are in need of nothing. They think the testimony of the Spirit of God in reproof is uncalled for or that it does not mean them.

Such are in the greatest need of the grace of God and spiritual discernment that they may discover their deficiency in spiritual knowledge. They lack almost every qualification necessary to perfect Christian character. They have not a practical knowledge of Bible truth, which leads to lowliness of life and a conformity of their will to the will of Christ. They are not living in obedience to all God's requirements.

It is not enough to merely profess to believe the truth. All the soldiers of the cross of Christ virtually obligate themselves to enter the crusade against the adversary of souls, to condemn wrong and sustain righteousness. But the message of the True Witness reveals the fact that a terrible deception is upon our people, which makes it necessary to come to them with warnings, to break their spiritual slumber, and arouse them to decided action.—*Testimonies for the Church,* vol. 3, pp. 253, 254.

Be Faithful in
Small, Common Tasks

Be diligent to present yourself approved to God, a worker who does not need to be ashamed, rightly dividing the word of truth. 2 Timothy 2:15, NKJV.

BY FAITHFULNESS in little things, Elisha was preparing for weightier trusts. Day by day, through practical experience, he gained a fitness for a broader, higher work. He learned to serve; and in learning this, he learned also how to instruct and lead. The lesson is for all. None can know what may be God's purpose in His discipline; but all may be certain that faithfulness in little things is the evidence of fitness for greater responsibilities. . . .

Those who feel that it is of no consequence how they perform the smaller tasks prove themselves unfit for a more honored position. They may think themselves fully competent to take up the larger duties; but God looks deeper than the surface. After test and trial, there is written against them the sentence "Thou art weighed in the balances, and art found wanting." Their unfaithfulness reacts upon themselves. They fail of gaining the grace, the power, the force of character, which is received through unreserved surrender.

Because they are not connected with some directly religious work, many feel that their lives are useless, that they are doing nothing for the advancement of God's kingdom. If they could do some great thing, how gladly they would undertake it! But because they can serve only in little things, they think themselves justified in doing nothing. In this they err. . . .

Many long for special talent with which to do a wonderful work, while the duties lying close at hand, the performance of which would make the life fragrant, are lost sight of. Let such ones take up the duties lying directly in their pathway. Success depends not so much on talent as on energy and willingness. It is not the possession of splendid talents that enables us to render acceptable service, but the conscientious performance of daily duties, the contented spirit, the unaffected, sincere interest in the welfare of others. In the humblest lot true excellence may be found. The commonest tasks, wrought with loving faithfulness, are beautiful in God's sight.—*Prophets and Kings,* pp. 218, 219.

Meeting Difficulties
Develops Spiritual Muscle

The Lord is not slack concerning His promise, as some count
slackness, but is longsuffering toward us, not willing that any should
perish but that all should come to repentance. 2 Peter 3:9, NKJV.

IN SEASONS OF temptations we seem to lose sight of the fact that God tests us that our faith may be tried, and be found unto praise and honor and glory at the appearing of Jesus. The Lord places us in different positions to develop us. If we have defects of character of which we are not aware, He gives us discipline that will bring those defects to our knowledge, that we may overcome them.

It is His providence that brings us into varying circumstances. In each new position, we meet a different class of temptations. How many times, when we are placed in some trying situation, we think, "This is a wonderful mistake. How I wish I had stayed where I was before." But why is it that you are not satisfied? It is because your circumstances have served to bring new defects in your character to your notice; but nothing is revealed but that which was in you. What should you do when you are tried by the providences of the Lord? You should rise to the emergency of the case, and overcome your defects of character.

It is coming in contact with difficulties that will give you spiritual muscle and sinew. You will become strong in Christ if you endure the testing process and the proving of God. But if you find fault with your situation and with everybody around you, you will only grow weaker. I have seen people who were always finding fault with everything and everybody around them, but the fault was in themselves. They had need to fall upon the Rock and be broken. They felt whole in their own self-righteousness. The trials that come upon us come to prove us. The enemy of our souls is working against us continually, but our defects of character will be made manifest to us, and when they are made plain, instead of finding fault with others, let us say, "I will arise and go to my father."

When we begin to realize that we are sinners, and fall on the Rock to be broken, the everlasting arms are placed about us, and we are brought close to the heart of Jesus. Then we shall be charmed with His loveliness, and disgusted with our own righteousness. We need to come close to the foot of the cross. The more we humble ourselves there, the more exalted will God's love appear.—*Review and Herald,* Aug. 6, 1889.

Maintain Integrity, Whatever the Cost

Remember those who rule over you, who have spoken the word of God to you, whose faith follow, considering the outcome of their conduct. Hebrews 13:7, NKJV.

EVERY PLAN AND purpose of life should be subjected to this unerring test [the Word of God]. The Word of inspiration is the wisdom of God applied to human affairs. However advantageous a certain course may appear to finite judgment, if denounced by that Word it will be only evil in its results.

It may be a difficult matter for those in high positions to pursue the path of undeviating integrity whether they shall receive praise or censure. Yet this is the only safe course. All the rewards which they might gain by selling their honor would be only as the breath from polluted lips, as dross to be consumed in the fire. Those who have moral courage to stand in opposition to the vices and errors of their fellow beings—it may be of those whom the world honors—will receive hatred, insult, and abusive falsehood. They may be thrust down from their high position, because they would not be bought or sold, because they could not be induced by bribes or threats to stain their hands with iniquity.

Everything on earth may seem to conspire against them; but God has set His seal upon His own work. They may be regarded by other people as weak, . . . unfit to hold office; but how differently does the Most High regard them. Those who despise them are the really ignorant. While the storms of calumny and reviling may pursue persons of integrity through life, and beat upon their graves, God has the "well done" prepared for them. Folly and iniquity will at best yield only a life of unrest and discontent, and at its close a thorny dying pillow. And how many, as they view their course of action and its results, are led to end with their own hands their disgraceful career. And beyond all this waits the judgment, and the final, irrevocable doom, Depart! . . .

The Son of God has set an example for all His followers. They are not to court praise from others, not to seek for themselves ease or wealth, but to emulate His life of purity and self-denial at whatever cost. . . . They will not manifest a disregard for the rights of others. God's law commands us to love our neighbor as ourselves, to suffer no evil to be instituted against them which we can hinder. But the rule which Christ has given extends still further. Said the world's Redeemer, "Love one another, as I have loved you." Nothing short of this can reach the standard of Christianity.— *Signs of the Times*, Feb. 2, 1882.

Motive Determines
Value of Our Acts

*So He called His disciples to Him and said to them, "Assuredly,
I say to you that this poor widow has put in more than all those who have
given to the treasury; for they all put in out of their abundance, but she out of her
poverty put in all that she had, her whole livelihood." Mark 12:43, 44, NKJV.*

IT IS THE MOTIVE that gives character to our acts, stamping them with ignominy or with high moral worth. Not the great things which every eye sees and every tongue praises does God account most precious. The little duties cheerfully done, the little gifts which make no show, and which to human eyes may appear worthless, often stand highest in His sight. A heart of faith and love is dearer to God than the most costly gift.

The poor widow gave her living to do the little that she did. She deprived herself of food in order to give those two mites to the cause she loved. And she did it in faith, believing that her heavenly Father would not overlook her great need. It was this unselfish spirit and childlike faith that won the Savior's commendation.

Among the poor there are many who long to show their gratitude to God for His grace and truth. They greatly desire to share with their more prosperous fellow church members in sustaining His service. These souls should not be repulsed. Let them lay up their mites in the bank of heaven. If given from a heart filled with love for God, these seeming trifles become consecrated gifts, priceless offerings, which God smiles upon and blesses.

When Jesus said of the widow, She "hath cast in more than they all," His words were true, not only of the motive, but of the results of her gift. The "two mites, which make a farthing" have brought to God's treasury an amount of money far greater than the contributions of those rich Jews. The influence of that little gift has been like a stream, small in its beginning, but widening and deepening as it flowed down through the ages. In a thousand ways it has contributed to the relief of the poor and the spread of the gospel.

Her example of self-sacrifice has acted and reacted upon thousands of hearts in every land and in every age. It has appealed to both the rich and the poor, and their offerings have swelled the value of her gift. God's blessing upon the widow's mite has made it the source of great results. So with every gift bestowed and every act performed with a sincere desire for God's glory. It is linked with the purposes of Omnipotence. Its results for good no one can measure.—*The Desire of Ages,* pp. 615, 616.

Stay Close to Jesus and Become Like Him

You will show me the path of life; in Your presence is fullness of joy; at Your right hand are pleasures forevermore. Psalm 16:11, NKJV.

THIS WORLD IS our school—a school of discipline and training. We are placed here to form characters like the character of Christ, and to acquire the habits and the language of the higher life. Influences opposed to good abound on every hand. The developments of sin are becoming so full, so deep, so abhorrent to God, that soon He will arise in majesty to shake terribly the earth.

So artful are the plans of the enemy, so specious the complications which he brings about, that those who are weak in the faith do not discern his deceptions. They fall into the snares prepared by Satan, who works through human instrumentalities to deceive if possible the very elect. Those only who are closely connected with God will be able to discern the falsehoods and the intrigues of the enemy.

There are in this world only two classes, those who serve God, and those who stand under the black banner of the prince of darkness. Those who enter the gates of the City of God must, in this world, live in union with Christ.

The principles of God's government—the only principles that will endure from everlasting to everlasting—are to be followed by those who are seeking for entrance into the kingdom of heaven. The line of demarcation between those who serve God and those who serve Him not is to be kept clear and distinct.

Let us allow God to control our minds. Let us not say or do anything that will turn a fellow being from the right way. I feel very sad as I think of how few there are who show that they have tasted the deep blessedness of communion with a risen, ascended Savior. Men and women of the world are striving for the supremacy. God's followers are to keep Christ ever in view, inquiring at every step, "Is this the way of the Lord?" A holy desire to live the life of Christ is to fill their hearts. In Him dwells all the fullness of the Godhead. In Him are hid all the treasures of wisdom and knowledge.

Oh, that our people could realize what advantages would be theirs if they would look constantly to Jesus. . . . He is our Alpha and our Omega. Pressing close to Him, and holding communion with Him, we become like Him. Through the transforming power of the Spirit of Christ, we are changed in heart and life.—*Australasian Union Conference Record,* Feb. 1, 1904.

To Find True
Happiness, Obey God

This is my happy way of life: obeying your commandments. Psalm 119:56, NLT.

HAPPINESS MUST BE sought in the right way, and from the right source. Some think they may surely find happiness in a course of indulgence in sinful pleasures, or in deceptive worldly attractions. And some sacrifice physical and moral obligations, thinking to find happiness, and they lose both soul and body. Others will seek their happiness in the indulgence of an unnatural appetite, and consider the indulgence of taste more desirable than health and life. Many suffer themselves to be enchained by sensual passions, and will sacrifice physical strength, intellect, and moral powers to the gratification of lust. They will bring themselves to untimely graves, and in the judgment will be charged with self-murder.

Is this . . . happiness desirable which is to be found in the path of disobedience and transgression of physical and moral law? Christ's life points out the true source of happiness, and how it is to be attained. His life points the direct and only path to heaven. Let the voice of wisdom be heard. Let it mark out the path. "Her ways are ways of pleasantness, and all her paths are peace."

Temptations are on every side to allure the steps of youth to their ruin. The sad deficiency in the education of children leaves them weak and unguarded, vacillating in character, feeble in intellect, and deficient in moral strength, so that so far from imitating the life of Christ, the youth generally are like a reed trembling in the wind. They have not physical constitution or moral power, because they yield to temptations. Through sinful indulgences, they stain their purity, and their manners are corrupted. They are impatient of restraint, and flatter themselves if they could only have their own way they should then be very happy. . . .

If children and youth would seek their highest earthly good, they must look for it in the path of faithful obedience. A sound constitution, which is the greatest earthly prize, can only be obtained by a denial of unnatural appetite. If they would be happy indeed, they should cheerfully seek to be found at the post of duty, doing the work which devolves upon them with fidelity, conforming their hearts and lives to the perfect pattern.—*Youth's Instructor,* April 1872.

When in Trial,
Review God's Great Mercy

Uphold my steps in Your paths, that my footsteps may not slip.
I have called upon You, for You will hear me, O God; incline
Your ear to me, and hear my speech. Psalm 17:5, 6, NKJV.

THE LORD DIRECTED Moses to recount to the children of Israel His dealings with them in their deliverance from Egypt and their wonderful preservation in the wilderness. He was to call to mind their unbelief and murmuring when brought into trial, and the Lord's great mercy and loving-kindness, which had never forsaken them. This would stimulate their faith and strengthen their courage. . . .

It is just as essential that the people of God in this day should bear in mind how and when they have been tested, and where their faith has failed; where they have imperiled His cause by their unbelief and also by their self-confidence. God's mercy, His sustaining providence, His never-to-be-forgotten deliverances, are to be recounted, step by step.

As God's people thus review the past, they should see that the Lord is ever repeating His dealings. They should understand the warnings given, and should beware not to repeat their mistakes. Renouncing all self-dependence, they are to trust in Him to save them from again dishonoring His name. In every victory that Satan gains, souls are imperiled. Some become the subjects of his temptations, never to recover themselves. . . .

God sends trials to prove who will stand faithful under temptation. He brings all into trying positions to see if they will trust in a power out of and above themselves. Everyone has undiscovered traits of character that must come to light through trial. God allows those who are self-sufficient to be sorely tempted, that they may understand their helplessness.

When trials come to us; when we can see before us, not an increase of prosperity, but a pressure necessitating sacrifice on the part of all, how shall we receive Satan's insinuation that we are to have a very hard time? If we listen to his suggestions, unbelief in God will spring up. . . . We should look at the work He has done, the reforms He has wrought. We should gather up the evidences of Heaven's blessings, the tokens for good, saying: "Lord, we believe in Thee, in Thy servants, and in Thy work."—*Testimonies for the Church*, vol. 7, pp. 210, 211.

Receive Light,
and Walk in It

*You are the light of the world. A city that is set on
a hill cannot be hidden. Matthew 5:14, NKJV.*

THERE IS ONE thing in this world which is the greatest object of Christ's
solicitude. It is His church on earth; for its members should be representatives, in spirit and character, of Him. The world is to recognize in them
the representatives of Christianity, the depository of sacred truths in which
is stored the most precious jewels for the enrichment of others. Through
the ages of moral darkness and error, through centuries of strife and persecution, the church of Christ has been as a city set on a hill. From age to
age, through successive generations to the present time, the pure doctrines
of the Bible have been unfolding within its borders.

But in order that the church on earth may be an educating power in
the world, it must cooperate with the church in heaven. The hearts of
those who are members of the church must be open to receive every ray
of light that God shall choose to impart. God has light to impart to us according to our ability to receive, and as we receive the light, we shall be
capable of receiving more and more of the rays of the Sun of
Righteousness. . . .

Every one of us is upon probation, in school, where we are required
to be diligent students. It is enjoined upon us to walk in the light, as Christ
is in the light. It is by walking in the light that we learn of God, and "this
is life eternal, that they might know thee the only true God, and Jesus
Christ, whom thou hast sent" (John 17:3). These are the words of Him
who was with the Father before the world was, and He uttered these
words while praying for all those who should believe in God through the
words of His disciples. To know God in His works is true science. Let us
follow on to know the Lord till we shall know that His goings forth are
prepared as the morning. . . .

Faithful souls have constituted the church of God on earth, and He has
taken them into covenant relation with Himself, uniting His church on
earth with His church in heaven. He has sent forth heavenly angels to minister to His church, and the gates of hell have not been able to prevail
against His people.—*Manuscript Releases,* vol. 2, pp. 265, 266.

Reveal Love, Compassion, and Tenderness

And whatever you do in word or deed, do all in the name of the Lord Jesus, giving thanks to God the Father through Him. Colossians 3:17, NKJV.

GREAT RESPONSIBILITY comes to those who have been baptized in the name of the Father, the Son, and the Holy Spirit. Strive to understand the meaning of the words "Ye are dead, and your life is hid with Christ in God." In the new life upon which you have entered, you are pledged to represent the life of Christ. . . .

The old sinful life is dead, the new life entered into with Christ by the pledge of baptism. Practice the virtues of the Savior's character. Let His word "dwell in you richly in all wisdom; teaching and admonishing one another in psalms and hymns and spiritual songs, singing with grace in your hearts to the Lord." . . .

These things are to be presented in the churches. Love, compassion, and tenderness are to be revealed among us. Put on, as the elect of God, mercy and kindness. The sins that were practiced before conversion are to be put off with the old man. With the new man, Christ Jesus, are to be put on "kindness, humbleness of mind, meekness, longsuffering."

Those who have risen with Christ to walk in newness of life are the elect of God. They are holy unto the Lord, and are acknowledged by Him as His beloved. As such, they are under solemn covenant to distinguish themselves by showing humility of mind. They are to clothe themselves in garments of righteousness. They are separate from the world, from its spirit, its practices, and they are to reveal that they are learning of Him who says, "I am meek and lowly in heart."

If they realize that they have died with Christ, if they keep their baptismal vow, the world will have no power to draw them aside to deny Christ. If they live the life of Christ in this world, they are partakers of the divine nature. Then, when Christ, who is our life, shall appear, they also will appear with Him in glory.—*Manuscript Releases,* vol. 19, pp. 236, 237.

Do Not Accuse Others, but Intercede for Them

Therefore, in all things He had to be made like His brethren,
that He might be a merciful and faithful High Priest in things pertaining to
God, to make propitiation for the sins of the people. Hebrews 2:17, NKJV.

LET HUMAN BEINGS, subject to temptation, remember that in the heavenly courts they have a High Priest who is touched with the feeling of their infirmities, because He Himself was tempted, even as they are. And let those in positions of responsibility, especially, remember that they are subject to temptation, and wholly dependent on the merits of the Savior. However sacred the work to which they may be called, they are still sinners, who can be saved only through the grace of Christ. One day they must stand before the throne of God, saved by the blood of the Lamb, or condemned to the punishment of the wicked. . . .

How grieved Christ is by the lack of love and tenderness manifested by His people in their dealings with one another! He notes the words, the tones of the voice. He hears the harsh, severe judgment passed on those whom He, in infinite love, is presenting to the Father. He hears every sigh of pain and sorrow caused by human harshness, and His Spirit is grieved.

Apart from Christ we can do no good thing. How inconsistent, then, it is for human beings to exalt themselves! How strange that any should forget that they must repent, in common with their fellow beings, and that those whom they condemn with severity may stand justified before God, receiving the sympathy of Christ and the angels.

Let God's messengers act as wise men and women. Let them not lift up their souls unto vanity, but cherish humility. "Thus saith the high and lofty One that inhabiteth eternity, whose name is Holy; I dwell in the high and holy place, with him also that is of a contrite and humble spirit, to revive the spirit of the humble, and to revive the heart of the contrite ones." . . .

Christ is pleading the case of every tempted soul, but while He is doing this, many of His people are grieving Him by taking their stand with Satan to accuse their brethren and sisters, pointing to their polluted garments.

Let not the criticized ones become discouraged; for while others are condemning them, Christ is saying of them, I have graven thee upon the palms of My hands. By creation and by redemption thou art Mine.—*Review and Herald*, Mar. 17, 1903.

Live Unselfishly, and
Teach People to Love Jesus

You shall walk in all the ways which the Lord your God has commanded you, that you may live and that it may be well with you, and that you may prolong your days in the land which you shall possess. Deuteronomy 5:33, NKJV.

CHRIST IS THE way, the truth, and the life. I ask you to study His life. . . . He came to bring to lost souls the gift of eternal life. In the sacrifice of His Son, the Father revealed how much He desires that sinners shall be saved. "Therefore doth my Father love me," Christ declared, "because I lay down my life." The Father loves us with a love that is but feebly comprehended.

It is because men and women lack the spirit of self-denial and self-sacrifice that they cannot comprehend the sacrifice made by Heaven in giving Christ to the world. Their religious experience is mingled with selfishness and self-exaltation. How can such professors have anything but a meager hope of sharing the inheritance of Christ? "Verily I say unto you," He said to His disciples, "Except ye be converted, and become as little children, ye shall not enter into the kingdom of heaven."

There are many who, while professing godliness, measure themselves among themselves, and in consequence grow weak in spiritual life. Pride is not overcome. Not until these souls fall on the Rock and are broken will they understand their need. Oh, that they might confess their wrongs before God, and plead for the presence of the Holy Spirit in their lives! Truth and righteousness will flow into the hearts that are cleansed from selfishness and sin, and through the lives of those in whose souls truth occupies the first place. . . .

The wickedness of the world is not abating. Every year evil becomes more prevalent, and is more lightly regarded. Let our gatherings together be made seasons of heart searching and confession. It is the privilege of this people who have had such great blessings to be trees of righteousness, shedding forth comfort and blessing. They are to be living stones, emitting light. Those who have received pardon for their sins should with earnest purpose lead those who are in the ways of sin into paths of righteousness. Partaking of Christ's self-denial and self-sacrifice, they will teach men and women to give up selfishness and sin, and accept in their place the lovely attributes of the divine nature.—*Review and Herald,* July 22, 1909.

Bring the Lower
Passions Into Subjection

Beloved, I beg you as sojourners and pilgrims, abstain from fleshly
lusts which war against the soul, having your conduct honorable among
the Gentiles, that . . . they may, by your good works which they
observe, glorify God in the day of visitation. 1 Peter 2:11, 12, NKJV.

NEAR THE CLOSE of this earth's history Satan will work with all his powers in the same manner and with the same temptations wherewith he tempted ancient Israel just before their entering the Land of Promise. He will lay snares for those who claim to keep the commandments of God, and who are almost on the borders of the heavenly Canaan. He will use his powers to their utmost in order to entrap souls, and to take God's professed people upon their weakest points.

Those who have not brought the lower passions into subjection to the higher powers of their being, those who have allowed their minds to flow in a channel of carnal indulgence of the baser passions, Satan is determined to destroy with his temptations—to pollute their souls with licentiousness. He is not aiming especially at the lower and less important marks, but he makes use of his snares through those whom he can enlist as his agents to allure or attract men and women to take liberties which are condemned in the law of God.

And those in responsible positions, teaching the claims of God's law, whose mouths are filled with arguments in vindication of His law, against which Satan has made such a raid—over such he sets his hellish powers and his agencies at work, and overthrows them upon the weak points in their character, knowing that those who offend on one point are guilty of all, thus obtaining complete mastery over the entire person. Mind, soul, body, and conscience are involved in the ruin. If they be messengers of righteousness, and have had great light, or if the Lord has used them as His special workers in the cause of truth, then how great is the triumph of Satan! How he exults! How God is dishonored! . . .

Satan knows it is his time. He has but little time left now in which to work, and he will work with tremendous power to ensnare the people of God upon their weak points of character. . . . It is necessary to guard the thoughts; to fence the soul about with the injunctions of God's Word; and to be very careful in every thought, word, and action not to be betrayed into sin.—*Review and Herald*, May 17, 1887.

Seek to Reflect
the Image of Jesus

Whoever says, "I abide in him," ought to
walk just as he walked. 1 John 2:6, NRSV.

WHAT SURPASSING LOVE and condescension, that when we had no
claim on divine mercy, Christ was willing to undertake our redemption!
But our great Physician requires of every soul unquestioning obedience.
We are never to prescribe for our own case. Christ must have the entire
control of our will and action, or He will not undertake in our behalf.

Many are not sensible of their condition and their danger; and there is
much in the nature of the Christian religion that is averse to every worldly
feeling and principle, and opposed to the pride of the human heart. We
may flatter ourselves, as did Nicodemus, that our lives and our moral character have been correct, and think that we need not humble our heart before God, like the common sinner; but we must be content to enter into
life in the very same way as the chief of sinners. Self must die. We must
not trust to our own righteousness, but depend on the righteousness of
Christ. He is our strength and our hope.

Genuine faith is followed by love—love that is manifested in the
home, in society, and in all the relations of life—love which smooths away
difficulties, and lifts us above the disagreeable trifles that Satan places in our
way to annoy us. And love will be followed by obedience. All the powers
and the passions of the converted person are brought under the control of
Christ. His Spirit is a renewing power, transforming to the divine image
all who will receive it.

To become a disciple of Christ is to deny self, and follow Jesus through
evil as well as through good report. It is to close the door to pride, envy,
doubt, and other sins, and thus shut out strife, hatred, and every evil work.
It is to welcome into our hearts Jesus, the meek and lowly one, who is
seeking admittance as our guest. . . .

Jesus is a pattern for humanity, complete, perfect. He proposes to make
us like Himself—true in every purpose, feeling, and thought—true in
heart, soul, and life. The man or woman who cherishes the most of the
love of Christ in the soul, who reflects the image of Christ most perfectly,
is, in the sight of God, the truest, most noble, and most honorable person.
But those who have not the Spirit of Christ are "none of his."—*Signs of the
Times,* July 14, 1887.

We Should Give
Hope to the Fallen

And to be renewed in the spirit of your minds, and to clothe
yourselves with the new self, created according to the likeness of God,
in true righteousness and holiness. Ephesians 4:23, 24, NRSV.

CHRIST WAS A faithful reprover. Never lived there another who so hated evil; never another whose denunciation of it was so fearless. To all things untrue and base His very presence was a rebuke. In the light of His purity, people saw themselves unclean, their life's aims mean and false. Yet He drew them. He who had created them understood the value of humanity. Evil He denounced as the foe of those whom He was seeking to bless and to save. In every human being, however fallen, He beheld a child of God, one who might be restored to the privilege of divine relationship.

"God sent not his Son into the world to condemn the world; but that the world through him might be saved" (John 3:17). Looking upon people in their suffering and degradation, Christ perceived ground for hope where appeared only despair and ruin. Wherever there existed a sense of need, there He saw opportunity for uplifting. Souls tempted, defeated, feeling themselves lost, ready to perish, He met, not with denunciation, but with blessing.

The beatitudes were His greeting to the whole human family. Looking upon the vast throng gathered to listen to the Sermon on the Mount, He seemed for the moment to have forgotten that He was not in heaven, and He used the familiar salutation of the world of light. From His lips flowed blessings as the gushing forth of a long-sealed fountain.

Turning from the ambitious, self-satisfied favorites of this world, He declared that those were blessed who, however great their need, would receive His light and love. To the poor in spirit, the sorrowing, the persecuted, He stretched out His arms, saying, "Come unto me, . . . and I will give you rest" (Matt. 11:28).

In every human being He discerned infinite possibilities. He saw men and women as they might be, transfigured by His grace—in "the beauty of the Lord our God" (Ps. 90:17). Looking upon them with hope, He inspired hope. Meeting them with confidence, He inspired trust. . . . In many a heart that seemed dead to all things holy were awakened new impulses. To many a despairing one there opened the possibility of a new life.—*Education,* pp. 79, 80.

Take Time for Prayer and the Word

These are the ones sown among thorns; they are the ones who hear the word, and the cares of this world, the deceitfulness of riches, and the desires for other things entering in choke the word, and it becomes unfruitful. Mark 4:18, 19, NKJV.

CHRIST SPECIFIED THE things that are dangerous to the soul. As recorded by Mark, He mentions the cares of this world, the deceitfulness of riches, and the lusts of other things. Luke specifies the cares, riches, and pleasures of this life. These are what choke the word, the growing spiritual seed. The soul ceases to draw nourishment from Christ, and spirituality dies out of the heart.

"The cares of this world." No class is free from the temptation to worldly care. To the poor, toil and deprivation and the fear of want bring perplexities and burdens. To the rich come fear of loss and a multitude of anxious cares. Many of Christ's followers forget the lesson He has bidden us learn from the flowers of the field. They do not trust to His constant care. Christ cannot carry their burden, because they do not cast it upon Him. . . .

Many who might be fruitful in God's service become bent on acquiring wealth. Their whole energy is absorbed in business enterprises, and they feel obliged to neglect things of a spiritual nature. Thus they separate themselves from God. . . . We are to labor that we may impart to those in need. Christians must work, they must engage in business, and they can do this without committing sin. But many become so absorbed in business that they have no time for prayer, no time for the study of the Bible, no time to seek and serve God.

At times the longings of the soul go out for holiness and heaven; but there is no time to turn aside from the din of the world to listen to the majestic and authoritative utterances of the Spirit of God. The things of eternity are made subordinate, the things of the world supreme. It is impossible for the seed of the Word to bring forth fruit; for the life of the soul is given to nourish the thorns of worldliness.

And many who are working with a very different purpose fall into a like error. They are working for others' good; their duties are pressing, their responsibilities are many, and they allow their labor to crowd out devotion. . . . They walk apart from Christ, their life is not pervaded by His grace, and the characteristics of self are revealed.—*Christ's Object Lessons,* pp. 51, 52.

Study Christ's Words, Not Human Opinions

*For the law was given through Moses, but grace and
truth came through Jesus Christ. John 1:17, NKJV.*

JESUS WAS THE LIGHT of the world. He came forth from God with a
message of hope and salvation to the fallen children of Adam. If men and
women would but receive Him as their personal Savior, He promised to
restore to them the image of God, and to redeem all that had been lost
through sin. He presented to human beings the truth, without one thread
of interwoven error. When He taught, His words came with authority; for
He spoke with positive knowledge of the truth.

The teaching of mortals is wholly different from the teaching of
Christ. There is a constant tendency on the part of humans to present their
own theories and opinions as matter worthy of attention, even when they
have no foundation in truth. They are very tenacious for their erroneous
ideas and idle opinions. They will hold firmly to the traditions of humanity, and defend them as vigorously as if they were the veritable truth. Jesus
declared that everyone that was of the truth would hear His voice.

How much more power would attend the preaching of the Word
today if ministers dwelt less upon human theories and arguments and far
more upon the lessons of Christ and upon practical godliness. He who had
stood in the counsel of God, who had dwelt in His presence, was well acquainted with the origin and elements of truth, and understood its relation
and importance to humanity. He presented to the world the plan of salvation, and unfolded truth of the highest order, even the words of eternal life.

Patriarchs, prophets, and apostles spoke as they were moved upon by
the Holy Ghost, and they plainly stated that they spoke not by their own
power, nor in their own name. They desired that no credit might be as-
cribed to them, that no one might regard them as the originators of anything whereof they might glory. They were jealous for the honor of God,
to whom all praise belongs. They declared that their ability and the messages they brought were given them as delegates of the power of God. God
was their authority and sufficiency. . . .

Christ is the Author of all truth. Every brilliant conception, every
thought of wisdom, every capacity and talent of human beings, is the gift
of Christ. He borrowed no new ideas from humanity; for He originated
all.—*Review and Herald,* Jan. 7, 1890.

Be Used by the
Spirit in Christ's Service

Great and marvelous are Your works, Lord God Almighty!
Just and true are Your ways, O King of the saints! Who shall not
fear You, O Lord, and glorify Your name? For You alone are holy. For
all nations shall come and worship before You. Revelation 15:3, 4, NKJV.

GOD WILL MOVE upon those in humble positions to declare the message of present truth. Many such will be seen hastening hither and thither, constrained by the Spirit of God to give the light to those in darkness. The truth is as a fire in their bones, filling them with a burning desire to enlighten those who sit in darkness. Many, even among the uneducated, will proclaim the Word of the Lord. Children will be impelled by the Holy Spirit to go forth to declare the message of heaven. The Spirit will be poured out upon those who yield to His promptings. Casting off humanity's binding rules and cautious movements, they will join the army of the Lord.

In the future, those in the common walks of life will be impressed by the Spirit of the Lord to leave their ordinary employment and go forth to proclaim the last message of mercy. As rapidly as possible they are to be prepared for labor, that success may crown their efforts. They cooperate with heavenly agencies, for they are willing to spend and be spent in the service of the Master. No one is authorized to hinder these workers. They are to be bidden Godspeed as they go forth to fulfill the great commission. No taunting word is to be spoken of them as in the rough places of the earth they sow the gospel seed.

Life's best things—simplicity, honesty, truthfulness, purity, unsullied integrity—cannot be bought or sold; they are as free to the ignorant as to the educated, to the black person as to the white person, to the humble peasant as to the king upon his throne.

Humble workers, who do not trust in their own strength, but who labor in simplicity, trusting always in God, will share in the joy of the Savior. Their persevering prayers will bring souls to the cross. In cooperation with their self-sacrificing efforts Jesus will move upon hearts, working miracles in the conversion of souls. Men and women will be gathered into church fellowship. Meetinghouses will be built and schools established. The hearts of the workers will be filled with joy as they see the salvation of God.—*Testimonies for the Church*, vol. 7, pp. 26-28.

AUGUST

❦

Relating to the Natural World

Happiness to Be Found in Natural Surroundings

And God called the dry land Earth, and the gathering together of the waters He called Seas. And God saw that it was good. Genesis 1:10, NKJV.

THE FATHER AND the Son engaged in the mighty, wondrous work they had contemplated, of creating the world. The earth came forth from the hand of the Creator exceedingly beautiful. There were mountains and hills and plains; and interspersed among them were rivers and other bodies of water. The earth was not one extensive plain. Its surface was diversified with hills and mountains. These, however, were not high and ragged as they now are, but regular and beautiful in shape. The bare, high rocks were never seen upon them, but lay beneath the surface, answering as bones to the earth.

The waters were regularly dispersed. The hills, mountains, and very beautiful plains were adorned with plants and flowers, and tall, majestic trees of every description, which were many times larger, and much more beautiful, than trees now are. The air was pure and healthful, and the earth seemed like a noble palace. Angels beheld and rejoiced at the wonderful and beautiful works of God.

After the earth was created, and the beasts upon it, the Father and Son carried out their purpose, which was designed, before the fall of Satan, to make human beings in their own image. They had wrought together in the creation of the earth and every living thing upon it. And now God says to His Son, "Let us make man in our image." As Adam came forth from the hand of his Creator, he was of noble height and of beautiful symmetry. He was more than twice as tall as men now living upon the earth, and was well proportioned. His features were perfect and beautiful. His complexion was neither white nor sallow, but ruddy, glowing with the rich tint of health. Eve was not quite as tall as Adam. Her head reached a little above his shoulders. She, too, was noble—perfect in symmetry, and very beautiful.

This sinless pair wore no artificial garments. They were clothed with a covering of light and glory, such as the angels wear. While they lived in obedience to God, this circle of light enshrouded them. Although everything God had made was in the perfection of beauty, and there seemed nothing wanting upon the earth which God had created to make Adam and Eve happy, yet He manifested His great love to them by planting a garden especially for them. . . . This beautiful garden was to be their home, their special residence.—*Signs of the Times,* Jan. 9, 1897.

All Nature Entrusted
to Adam and Eve

Then God said, "Let Us make man in Our image, according to Our likeness; let them have dominion over the fish of the sea, over the birds of the air, and over the cattle, over all the earth and over every creeping thing that creeps on the earth." Genesis 1:26, NKJV.

WHILE THEY REMAINED true to God, Adam and his companion were to bear rule over the earth. Unlimited control was given them over every living thing. The lion and the lamb sported peacefully around them or lay down together at their feet. The happy birds flitted about them without fear; and as their glad songs ascended to the praise of their Creator, Adam and Eve united with them in thanksgiving to the Father and the Son.

The holy pair were not only children under the fatherly care of God but students receiving instruction from the all-wise Creator. They were visited by angels, and were granted communion with their Maker, with no obscuring veil between. They were full of the vigor imparted by the tree of life, and their intellectual power was but little less than that of the angels. The mysteries of the visible universe—"the wondrous works of him which is perfect in knowledge" (Job 37:16)—afforded them an exhaustless source of instruction and delight.

The laws and operations of nature, which have engaged humanity's study for six thousand years, were opened to their minds by the infinite Framer and Upholder of all. They held converse with leaf and flower and tree, gathering from each the secrets of its life. With every living creature, from the mighty leviathan that playeth among the waters to the insect mote that floats in the sunbeam, Adam was familiar. He had given to each its name, and he was acquainted with the nature and habits of all.

God's glory in the heavens, the innumerable worlds in their orderly revolutions, "the balancings of the clouds," the mysteries of light and sound, of day and night—all were open to the study of our first parents. On every leaf of the forest or stone of the mountains, in every shining star, in earth and air and sky, God's name was written. The order and harmony of creation spoke to them of infinite wisdom and power. They were ever discovering some attraction that filled their hearts with deeper love and called forth fresh expressions of gratitude.—*Patriarchs and Prophets,* pp. 50, 51.

God's Wisdom and Love Revealed in Nature

Then God blessed them, and God said to them, "Be fruitful and multiply; fill the earth and subdue it; have dominion over the fish of the sea, over the birds of the air, and over every living thing that moves on the earth." Genesis 1:28, NKJV.

THE HOLY PAIR looked upon nature as a picture of unsurpassed loveliness. The brown earth was clothed with a carpet of living green, diversified with an endless variety of self-propagating, self-perpetuating flowers. Shrubs, flowers, and trailing vines regaled the senses with their beauty and fragrance. The many varieties of lofty trees were laden with fruit of every kind, and of delicious flavor, adapted to please the taste and meet the wants of the happy Adam and Eve. This Eden home God provided for our first parents, giving them unmistakable evidences of His great love and care for them.

Adam was crowned as king in Eden. To him was given dominion over every living thing that God had created. The Lord blessed Adam and Eve with intelligence such as He had not given to the animal creation. He made Adam the rightful sovereign over all the works of His hands. . . .

Adam and Eve could trace the skill and glory of God in every spire of grass, and in every shrub and flower. The natural loveliness which surrounded them like a mirror reflected the wisdom, excellence, and love of their heavenly Father. And their songs of affection and praise rose sweetly and reverentially to heaven, harmonizing with the songs of the exalted angels, and with the happy birds who were caroling forth their music without a care. There was no disease, decay, nor death anywhere. Life, life was in everything the eye rested upon. The atmosphere was impregnated with life. Life was in every leaf, in every flower, and in every tree.

The Lord knew that Adam could not be happy without labor, therefore He gave him the pleasant employment of dressing the garden. And as he tended the things of beauty and usefulness around him, he could behold the goodness and glory of God in His created works. Adam had themes for contemplation in the works of God in Eden, which was heaven in miniature.

God did not form human beings merely to contemplate His glorious works; therefore He gave them hands for labor, as well as minds and hearts for contemplation. If the happiness of humans consisted in doing nothing, the Creator would not have given Adam his appointed work. In labor, humanity was to find happiness as well as in meditation.—*Review and Herald,* Feb. 24, 1874.

Work Given as a Source of Happiness

Then the Lord God took the man and put him in the garden of Eden to tend and keep it. Genesis 2:15, NKJV.

GOD PLACED HUMAN beings under law, as an indispensable condition of their very existence. They were subjects of the divine government, and there can be no government without law. God might have created humans without the power to transgress His law; He might have withheld the hand of Adam from touching the forbidden fruit; but in that case people would have been, not free moral agents, but mere automatons. Without freedom of choice, their obedience would not have been voluntary, but forced. There could have been no development of character. Such a course would have been contrary to God's plan in dealing with the inhabitants of other worlds. It would have been unworthy of humans as intelligent beings, and would have sustained Satan's charge of God's arbitrary rule. . . .

The home of our first parents was to be a pattern for other homes as their children should go forth to occupy the earth. That home, beautified by the hand of God Himself, was not a gorgeous palace. Men and women, in their pride, delight in magnificent and costly edifices, and glory in the works of their own hands; but God placed Adam and Eve in a garden. This was their dwelling. The blue heavens were its dome; the earth, with its delicate flowers and carpet of living green, was its floor; and the leafy branches of the goodly trees were its canopy. Its walls were hung with the most magnificent adornings—the handiwork of the great Master Artist.

In the surroundings of the holy pair was a lesson for all time—that true happiness is found, not in the indulgence of pride and luxury, but in communion with God through His created works. If people would give less attention to the artificial, and would cultivate greater simplicity, they would come far nearer to answering the purpose of God in their creation. Pride and ambition are never satisfied, but those who are truly wise will find substantial and elevating pleasure in the sources of enjoyment that God has placed within the reach of all.

To the dwellers in Eden was committed the care of the garden, "to dress it and to keep it." Their occupation was not wearisome, but pleasant and invigorating. God appointed labor as a blessing to our first parents, to occupy their minds, to strengthen their bodies, and to develop their faculties.—*Patriarchs and Prophets,* pp. 49, 50.

The Earth Will Produce
Abundantly for Diligent Workers

Then the trees of the field shall yield their fruit, and the earth shall
yield her increase. They shall be safe in their land; and they shall know
that I am the Lord, when I have broken the bands of their yoke and delivered
them from the hand of those who enslaved them. Ezekiel 34:27, NKJV.

THERE IS NEED of much more extensive knowledge in regard to the preparation of the soil. There is not sufficient breadth of view as to what can be realized from the earth. A narrow and unvarying routine is followed with discouraging results.—*Fundamentals of Christian Education*, p. 317.

Let the educated ability be employed in devising improved methods of work. This is what the Lord wants. . . .

There is need of intelligent and educated ability to devise the best methods in farming, in building, and in every other department, that the worker may not labor in vain. . . . God, who has made the world for the benefit of human beings, will provide means from the earth to sustain the diligent worker.

The seed placed in thoroughly prepared soil will produce its harvest. God can spread a table for His people in the wilderness. . . . There is much mourning over unproductive soil, when, if people would read the Old Testament Scriptures, they would see that the Lord knew much better than they in regard to the proper treatment of land. After being cultivated for several years, and giving its treasures to the possession of humankind, portions of the land should be allowed to rest, and then the crops should be changed. We might learn much also from the Old Testament in regard to the labor problem. . . .

The earth has its concealed treasures, and the Lord would have thousands and tens of thousands working upon the soil who are crowded into the cities to watch for a chance to earn a trifle. . . . The earth is to be made to give forth its strength; but without the blessing of God it could do nothing.

In the beginning, God looked upon all He had made, and pronounced it very good. The curse was brought upon the earth in consequence of sin. But shall this curse be multiplied by increasing sin? Ignorance is doing its baleful work. Slothful servants are increasing the evil by their lazy habits. . . . But the earth has blessings hidden in its depths for those who have courage and will and perseverance to gather its treasures.—*Ibid.*, pp. 315-327.

Who will be missionaries to do this work, to teach proper methods to the youth and to all who feel willing and humble enough to learn?—*Ibid.*, p. 324.

Work and Study Benefit
Both the Earth and the Mind

Indeed heaven and the highest heavens belong to the Lord your God,
also the earth with all that is in it. Deuteronomy 10:14, NKJV.

IN ITSELF THE beauty of nature leads the soul away from sin and worldly attractions, and toward purity, peace, and God. For this reason the cultivation of the soil is good work for children and youth. It brings them into direct contact with nature and nature's God. And that they may have this advantage, there should be, as far as possible, in connection with our schools, large flower gardens and extensive lands for cultivation.—*Counsels to Parents, Teachers, and Students,* pp. 186, 187.

In the school that is started here in Cooranbong [Australia], we look to see real success in agricultural lines, combined with the study of the sciences. We mean for this place to be a center, from which shall radiate light, precious advanced knowledge that shall result in the working of unimproved lands, so that hills and valleys shall blossom as the rose. For both children and adults, labor combined with mental taxation will give the right kind of all-round education. The cultivation of the mind will bring tact and fresh incentive to the cultivation of the soil.—*Testimonies to Ministers,* p. 244.

The school has made an excellent beginning. The students are learning how to plant trees, strawberries, etc.; how they must keep every spangle and fiber of the roots uncramped in order to give them a chance to grow. Is not this a most precious lesson as to how to treat the human mind, and the body as well—not to cramp any of the organs of the body, but to give them ample room to do their work? . . .

We should work the soil cheerfully, hopefully, gratefully, believing that the earth holds in its bosom rich stores for the faithful worker to garner, richer than gold or silver. . . . With proper, intelligent cultivation the earth will yield its treasures for the benefit of humanity. . . .

The cultivation of our land requires the exercise of all the brainpower and tact we possess. The lands around us testify to the indolence of human beings. We hope to arouse to action the dormant senses. We hope to see intelligent farmers who will be rewarded for their earnest labor. The hand and heart must cooperate, bringing new and sensible plans into operation in the cultivation of the soil.—*Ibid.,* pp. 242-244.

Cooperating With God in Work Promotes Happiness

And we labor, working with our own hands. Being reviled, we bless; being persecuted, we endure. 1 Corinthians 4:12, NKJV.

AT THE CREATION, labor was appointed as a blessing. It meant development, power, happiness. The changed condition of the earth through the curse of sin has brought a change in the conditions of labor; yet though now attended with anxiety, weariness, and pain, it is still a source of happiness and development. And it is a safeguard against temptation. Its discipline places a check on self-indulgence, and promotes industry, purity, and firmness. Thus it becomes a part of God's great plan for our recovery from the Fall.

The youth [and others] should be led to see the true dignity of labor. Show them that God is a constant worker. All things in nature do their allotted work. Action pervades the whole creation, and in order to fulfill our mission we, too, must be active.

In our labor we are to be workers together with God. He gives us the earth and its treasures; but we must adapt them to our use and comfort. He causes the trees to grow; but we prepare the timber and build the house. He has hidden in the earth the gold and silver, the iron and coal; but it is only through toil that we can obtain them. . . .

While God has created and constantly controls all things, He has endowed us with a power not wholly unlike His. To us has been given a degree of control over the forces of nature. As God called forth the earth in its beauty out of chaos, so we can bring order and beauty out of confusion. And though all things are now marred with evil, yet in our completed work we feel a joy akin to His when, looking on the fair earth, He pronounced it "very good."

As a rule, the exercise most beneficial to the youth will be found in useful employment. The little children find both diversion and development in play; and their sports should be such as to promote not only physical, but mental and spiritual growth. As they gain strength and intelligence, the best recreation will be found in some line of effort that is useful. That which trains the hand to helpfulness, and teaches the young to bear their share of life's burdens, is most effective in promoting the growth of mind and character.—*Education*, pp. 214, 215.

Well-regulated Work
Aids All-around Development

For the earth which drinks in the rain that often comes upon it, and bears herbs useful for those by whom it is cultivated, receives blessing from God; but if it bears thorns and briers, it is rejected and near to being cursed, whose end is to be burned. Hebrews 6:7, 8, NKJV.

THE YOUTH NEED to be taught that life means earnest work, responsibility, care-taking. They need a training that will make them practical—men and women who can cope with emergencies. They should be taught that the discipline of systematic, well-regulated labor is essential, not only as a safeguard against the vicissitudes of life, but as an aid to all-around development.

Notwithstanding all that has been said and written concerning the dignity of labor, the feeling prevails that it is degrading. Young men are anxious to become teachers, clerks, merchants, physicians, lawyers, or to occupy some other position that does not require physical toil. Young women shun housework and seek an education in other lines. These need to learn that no man or woman is degraded by honest toil. That which degrades is idleness and selfish dependence. Idleness fosters self-indulgence, and the result is a life empty and barren—a field inviting the growth of every evil. . . .

Since both men and women have a part in homemaking, boys as well as girls should gain a knowledge of household duties. . . . Let the children and youth learn from the Bible how God has honored the work of the everyday toiler.

Let them read of "the sons of the prophets" (2 Kings 6:1-7), students at school, who were building a house for themselves, and for whom a miracle was wrought to save from loss the ax that was borrowed. Let them read of Jesus the carpenter, and Paul the tentmaker, who with the toil of the craftsman linked the highest ministry, human and divine. Let them read of the lad whose five loaves were used by the Savior in that wonderful miracle for the feeding of the multitude; of Dorcas the seamstress, called back from death, that she might continue to make garments for the poor; of the wise woman described in the Proverbs, who "seeketh wool, and flax, and worketh willingly with her hands"; who "looketh well to the ways of her household, and eateth not the bread of idleness" (Prov. 31:13, 27).—*Education,* pp. 215-217.

The Beauty of Nature
Reveals God's Character

I will lift up my eyes to the hills—from whence comes my help? My help comes from the Lord, who made heaven and earth. Psalm 121:1, 2, NKJV.

I ONCE HAD the pleasure of beholding one of Colorado's most beautiful sunsets. The great Master Artist had hung out on the shifting canvas of the heavens, for the benefit of all, both rich and poor, one of His finest paintings. It almost seemed that the gates of heaven were ajar that we might see the beauty there was within. Oh! thought I, as one after another passed without noticing the scene, if it had been painted by human hands, how many would have been ready to fall down and worship it!

God is a lover of the beautiful. He loves beauty of character, and He would have us cultivate purity and simplicity, the quiet graces of the flowers. We are to seek for the ornament of a meek and quiet spirit, which is in the sight of God of great price.

Parents, what kind of education are you giving your children? Are you teaching them to cherish that which is pure and lovely, or are you seeking to place their hands in that of the world? Are you spending time and means that they may learn the outward proprieties of life, and secure the superficial, the deceptive adornments of the world?

From their earliest childhood, open before them the great book of nature. Teach them the ministry of the flowers. Show them that if Jesus had not come to earth and died, we should have had none of the beautiful things which we now enjoy. Call their attention to the fact that the color and even the arrangement of every delicate bud and flower is an expression of the love of God to human beings, and that affection and gratitude to their heavenly Father should be awakened in their hearts for all these gifts.

Jesus, the greatest teacher the world ever knew, drew the most valuable illustrations of truth from scenes in nature. Parents, imitate His example, and use the things that delight the senses to impress important truths upon the minds of your children. Take them out in the morning, and let them hear the birds caroling forth their songs of praise. Teach them that we too should return thanks to the bountiful Giver of all for the blessings we daily receive. Teach them that it is not dress that makes the man or the woman, but that it is true goodness of heart.—*Review and Herald,* Oct. 27, 1885.

God's Love and
Glory Seen in Nature

What are human beings that you are mindful of them, mortals
that you care for them? Yet you have made them a little lower than angels
[margin], and crowned them with glory and honor. Psalm 8:4, 5, NRSV.

OUR KIND HEAVENLY Father would have His children trust in Him as a child trusts in earthly parents. But we too often see poor, feeble mortals loading themselves down with cares and perplexities that God never intended them to bear. They have reversed the order; they are seeking the world first, and making the kingdom of heaven secondary. If even the little sparrow, which has no thought of future need, is cared for, why should the time and attention of human beings, who are made in the image of God, be wholly absorbed with these things?

God has given us every evidence of His love and care, yet how often we fail to discern the divine hand in our manifold blessings. Every faculty of our being, every breath we draw, every comfort we enjoy, comes from Him. Every time we gather around the family board to partake of refreshments, we should remember that all this is an expression of the love of God. And shall we take the gift, and deny the Giver? . . .

When Adam and Eve were placed in their Eden home, they had everything that a benevolent Creator could give them to add to their comfort and happiness. But they ventured to disobey God, and were therefore expelled from their lovely home. Then it was that the great love of God was expressed to us in one gift, that of His dear Son. If our first parents had not accepted the gift, the race would today be in hopeless misery. But how gladly did they hail the promise of the Messiah.

It is the privilege of all to accept this Savior, to become children of God, members of the royal family, and to sit at last at God's right hand. What love, what marvelous love, is this! John calls upon us to behold it: "Behold, what manner of love the Father hath bestowed upon us, that we should be called the sons of God."

Notwithstanding the curse was pronounced upon the earth that it should bring forth thorns and thistles, there is a flower upon the thistle. This world is not all sorrow and misery. God's great book of nature is open for us to study, and from it we are to gain more exalted ideas of His greatness and unexcelled love and glory.—*Review and Herald,* Oct. 27, 1885.

God's Power Exercised
Constantly in Nature

Who has measured the waters in the hollow of His hand, measured
heaven with a span and calculated the dust of the earth in a measure?
Weighed the mountains in scales and the hills in a balance? Isaiah 40:12, NKJV.

THE PSALMIST SAYS: "The heavens declare the glory of God; and the firmament sheweth his handiwork. Day unto day uttereth speech, and night unto night sheweth knowledge. There is no speech nor language, where their voice is not heard." Some may suppose that these grand things in the natural world are God. They are not God. All these wonders in the heavens are only doing the work appointed them. They are the Lord's agencies. God is the superintendent, as well as the Creator, of all things. The divine Being is engaged in upholding the things that He has created. The same hand that holds the mountains and balances them in position guides the worlds in their mysterious march around the sun.

There is scarcely an operation of nature to which we may not find reference in the Word of God. The Word declares that "he maketh his sun to rise," and the rain to descend. He "maketh grass to grow upon the mountains. . . . He giveth snow like wool: he scattereth the hoarfrost like ashes. He casteth forth his ice like morsels. . . . He sendeth out his word, and melteth them: he causeth his wind to blow, and the waters flow." "He maketh lightnings for the rain; and bringeth the wind out of his treasuries."

These words of Holy Writ say nothing of the independent laws of nature. God furnishes the matter and the properties with which to carry out His plans. He employs His agencies that vegetation may flourish. He sends the dew and the rain and the sunshine, that verdure may spring forth, and spread its carpet over the earth; that the shrubs and fruit trees may bud and blossom and bring forth.

It is not to be supposed that a law is set in motion for the seed to work itself, that the leaf appears because it must do so of itself. God has laws that He has instituted, but they are only the servants through which He effects results. It is through the immediate agency of God that every tiny seed breaks through the earth, and springs into life. Every leaf grows, every flower blooms, by the power of God.—*Review and Herald,* Mar. 17, 1904.

Appreciate Earth's
Natural, Quiet Beauty

*Who has divided a channel for the overflowing water, or a
path for the thunderbolt, to cause it to rain on a land where there is
no one, a wilderness in which there is no man; to satisfy the desolate waste,
and cause to spring forth the growth of tender grass? Job 38:25-27, NKJV.*

HE WHO LAID the foundation of the earth, who garnished the heavens and marshaled the stars in their order, He who has clothed the earth with a living carpet, and beautified it with lovely flowers of every shade and variety, would have His children appreciate His works and delight in the simple, quiet beauty with which He has adorned their earthly home.

Christ sought to draw the attention of His disciples away from the artificial to the natural: "If God so clothe the grass of the field, which today is, and to morrow is cast into the oven, shall he not much more clothe you, O ye of little faith?"

Why did not our heavenly Father carpet the earth with brown or gray? He chose the color that was most restful, the most acceptable to the senses. How it cheers the heart and refreshes the weary spirit to look upon the earth, clad in its garments of living green! Without this covering the air would be filled with dust, and the earth would appear like a desert. Every spire of grass, every opening bud and blooming flower, is a token of God's love, and should teach us a lesson of faith and trust in Him. Christ calls our attention to their natural loveliness, and assures us that the most gorgeous array of the greatest king that ever wielded an earthly scepter was not equal to that worn by the humblest flower. . . .

I would present before you Christ and Him crucified. Give Him your heart's best affections. Give Him your intellect; it belongs to Him. Give Him your talents of means and of influence; they were only lent to you for improvement. Jesus laid aside His robes of royalty, stepped down from His eternal throne, clothed His divinity with humanity, and for our sakes became poor, that we through His poverty might become rich. Rich in money? in lands? in bank stock? No; that we might secure eternal riches.

There is no salvation except that which comes through Christ. He came to earth to lift up the fallen. With His human arm He encircles the race, while with His divine arm He grasps the throne of the infinite, thus connecting finite humans to the infinite God, and uniting earth to heaven.—*Review and Herald,* Oct. 27, 1885.

Nature Offers Messages
of Hope and Comfort

He sends the springs into the valleys, which flow among the hills. They give drink to
every beast of the field; the wild donkeys quench their thirst. Psalm 104:10, 11, NKJV.

NATURE AND REVELATION alike testify of God's love. Our Father in
heaven is the source of life, of wisdom, and of joy. Look at the wonderful
and beautiful things of nature. Think of their marvelous adaptation to the
needs and happiness, not only of human beings, but of all living creatures.
The sunshine and the rain, that gladden and refresh the earth, the hills and
seas and plains, all speak to us of the Creator's love. It is God who supplies
the daily needs of all His creatures.

In the beautiful words of the psalmist: "The eyes of all wait upon thee;
and thou givest them their meat in due season. Thou openest thine hand,
and satisfiest the desire of every living thing" (Ps. 145:15, 16).

God made Adam and Eve perfectly holy and happy; and the fair earth,
as it came from the Creator's hand, bore no blight of decay or shadow of
the curse. It is transgression of God's law—the law of love—that has
brought woe and death.

Yet even amid the suffering that results from sin, God's love is revealed. It is written that God cursed the ground for man's sake (Gen. 3:17).
The thorn and the thistle—the difficulties and trials that make life one of
toil and care—were appointed for our good as a part of the training needful in God's plan for our uplifting from the ruin and degradation that sin
has wrought.

The world, though fallen, is not all sorrow and misery. In nature itself
are messages of hope and comfort. There are flowers upon the thistles, and
the thorns are covered with roses.

"God is love" is written upon every opening bud, upon every spire of
springing grass. The lovely birds making the air vocal with their happy
songs, the delicately tinted flowers in their perfection perfuming the air,
the lofty trees of the forest with their rich foliage of living green—all testify to the tender, fatherly care of our God and to His desire to make His
children happy.—*Steps to Christ,* pp. 9, 10.

Draw Spiritual Lessons
and Health Benefits From Trees

He causes the grass to grow for the cattle, and vegetation for the service of man, that he may bring forth food from the earth. Psalm 104:14, NKJV.

IN A CERTAIN place, preparations were being made to clear the land for the erection of a sanitarium. Light was given that there is health in the fragrance of the pine, the cedar, and the fir. And there are several other kinds of trees that have medicinal properties that are health-promoting.

Let not such trees be ruthlessly cut down. Better change the site of the [sanitarium] building than cut down these evergreen trees. There are lessons for us in these trees. God's Word declares, "The righteous shall flourish like the palm tree; he shall grow like a cedar in Lebanon." David says, "I am like a green olive tree in the house of God: I trust in the mercy of God for ever and ever."

The Christian is likened to the cedar of Lebanon. I have read that this tree does more than send down a few short roots into the yielding loam. It sends strong roots deep down into the earth, and strikes down further and still further in search of a still stronger hold. And in the fierce blast of the tempest, it stands firm, held by its network of cables beneath.

So Christians strike roots deep into Christ. They have faith in their Redeemer. They know in whom they believe. They are fully persuaded that Jesus is the Son of God and the Savior of sinners. The goodly sound of the gospel is received without conflicting doubts. The roots of faith strike deep down. Genuine Christians, like the cedar of Lebanon, do not grow in the soft surface soil, but are rooted in God, riveted in the clefts of the mountain rocks.

Study these lessons from the trees. I could dwell long on this subject, but I must not just now. I ask you not to cut away your pine trees. They will be a blessing to many. Let them live.

I want to say to you, my brethren and sisters, that you have my prayers and my sympathy in your work. Remember that you are trees in the garden of the Lord, and that the divine protection is round about you. The more visible the line of demarcation between the flowers of God and the briar and thorn of Satan's planting, the more the Lord is glorified.—*Spalding and Magan Collection*, pp. 228, 229.

Nature Is Guided and Upheld by the Creator

Sing to the Lord with thanksgiving; sing praises on the harp to our
God, who covers the heavens with clouds, who prepares rain for the earth,
who makes grass to grow on the mountains. Psalm 147:7, 8, NKJV.

MANY TEACH THAT matter possesses vital power. They hold that certain properties are imparted to matter, and it is then left to act through its own inherent power; and that the operations of nature are carried on in harmony with fixed laws that God Himself cannot interfere with. This is false science, and is sustained by nothing in the Word of God.

Nature is not self-acting; it is the servant of its Creator. God does not annul His laws nor work contrary to them; but He is continually using them as His instruments. Nature testifies of an intelligence, a presence, an active agency, that works in, and through, and above its laws. There is in nature the continual working of the Father and the Son. Said Christ, "My Father worketh hitherto, and I work."

God has finished His creative work, but His energy is still exerted in upholding the objects of His creation. It is not because the mechanism that has once been set in motion continues its work by its own inherent energy that the pulse beats and breath follows breath; but every breath, every pulsation of the heart, is an evidence of the all-pervading care of Him in whom we live and have our being.

It is not because of inherent power that year by year the earth produces its bounties and continues its motion around the sun. The hand of God guides the planets, and keeps them in position in their orderly march through the heavens. It is through His power that vegetation flourishes, that the leaves appear and the flowers bloom. His word controls the elements, and by Him the valleys are made fruitful. He covers the heavens with clouds, and prepares rain for the earth; He "maketh grass to grow upon the mountains." "He giveth snow like wool: he scattereth the hoarfrost like ashes." "When he uttereth his voice, there is a multitude of waters in the heavens, and he causeth the vapours to ascend from the ends of the earth; he maketh lightnings with rain, and bringeth forth the wind out of his treasures." . . .

His care is over all the works of His hands. Nothing is too great to be directed by Him; nothing is too small to escape His notice.—*Signs of the Times,* Mar. 20, 1884.

Christ Points Us to a More Glorious World

We do not look at the things which are seen, but at the things which are not seen. For the things which are seen are temporary, but the things which are not seen are eternal. 2 Corinthians 4:18, NKJV.

EARTH AND EARTHLY things will perish with the using. A few years will pass by, and death will come. Your eternal destiny will be fixed, eternally fixed. If your soul is lost, what will compensate you for its loss? Christ the Life Giver, Christ the Redeemer, Christ the Lamb of God, who taketh away the sins of the world, points you to a nobler world. He brings it within range of your vision. He takes you to the threshold of heaven, and brings you to contemplate the glories of eternal realities, that your aspirations may be quickened to grasp the far more exceeding and eternal weight of glory. As you contemplate heavenly scenes, desire is kindled in your heart to have friendship with God, to be wholly reconciled to Him.

Our Savior's work is to adjust the claims between earthly and heavenly interests, to put the duties and responsibilities of the life that now is in proper relation to those that pertain to eternal life. The fear and love of God are the first things that should claim our attention. We cannot afford to put off that which concerns our soul's interest till tomorrow. The life which we now live we are to live by faith in the Son of God. We are redeemed from the beggarly elements of the world with a redemption that is full and complete, that cannot be increased by any supplement from human sources.

But in the midst of this flood of mercies, this plentitude of divine love, many hearts continue in indifference, careless, and unimpressed by the provisions of God's grace. Shall we who claim to be Christians make no effort to break the spell which Satan has cast upon these souls? Shall we let them go on in hardness of heart, without God, and without hope in the world? No; although every appeal we may make may be slighted and refused, we cannot cease to pray for them and to make tender entreaty for their souls. We must do all we can, through the aid of God's Holy Spirit, to break down the barriers by which they have sought to make themselves impregnable to the light of God's truth. We must seek to open their eyes to their blindness, to loose them from the captivity of Satan.—*Signs of the Times,* July 17, 1893.

Many Lessons to Be Learned From Nature

Let them praise the name of the Lord, for He commanded
and they were created. He has also established them forever and ever;
He has made a decree which shall not pass away. Psalm 148:5, 6, NKJV.

HOW BEAUTIFUL THE psalmist's description of God's care for the creatures of the woods: "The high hills are a refuge for the wild goats; and the rocks for the conies" (Ps. 104:18). He sends the springs to run among the hills, where the birds have their habitation and "sing among the branches" (verse 12). All the creatures of the woods and hills are a part of His great household. He opens His hand, and satisfies "the desire of every living thing" (Ps. 145:16).

The eagle of the Alps is sometimes beaten down by the tempest into the narrow defiles of the mountains. Storm clouds shut in this mighty bird of the forest, their dark masses separating her from the sunny heights where she has made her home. Her efforts to escape seem fruitless. She dashes to and fro, beating the air with her strong wings, and waking the mountain echoes with her cries. At length, with a note of triumph, she darts upward, and, piercing the clouds, is once more in the clear sunlight, with the darkness and tempest far beneath.

So we may be surrounded with difficulties, discouragement, and darkness. Falsehood, calamity, injustice, shut us in. There are clouds that we cannot dispel. We battle with circumstances in vain. There is one, and but one, way of escape. The mists and fogs cling to the earth; beyond the clouds God's light is shining. Into the sunlight of His presence we may rise on the wings of faith.

Many are the lessons that may thus be learned. Self-reliance, from the tree that, growing alone on plain or mountainside, strikes down its roots deep into the earth, and in its rugged strength defies the tempest. The power of early influence, from the gnarled, shapeless trunk, bent as a sapling, to which no earthly power can afterward restore its lost symmetry. The secret of a holy life from the water lily, that, on the bosom of some slimy pool, surrounded by weeds and rubbish, strikes down its channeled stem to the pure sands beneath, and, drawing thence its life, lifts up its fragrant blossoms to the light in spotless purity.—*Education*, pp. 118, 119.

How to Learn From Nature Its Deepest Lessons

*Who among all these does not know that the hand of the Lord
has done this, in whose hand is the life of every living thing,
and the breath of all mankind? Job 12:9, 10, NKJV.*

WHILE THE CHILDREN and youth gain a knowledge of facts from teachers and textbooks, let them learn to draw lessons and discern truth for themselves. In their gardening, question them as to what they learn from the care of their plants. As they look on a beautiful landscape, ask them why God clothed the fields and woods with such lovely and varied hues. Why was not all colored a somber brown? When they gather the flowers, lead them to think why He spared us the beauty of these wanderers from Eden. Teach them to notice the evidences everywhere manifest in nature of God's thought for us, the wonderful adaptation of all things to our need and happiness.

Those alone who recognize in nature their Father's handiwork, who in the richness and beauty of the earth read the Father's handwriting— those alone learn from the things of nature their deepest lessons, and receive their highest ministry. Only those can fully appreciate the significance of hill and vale, river and sea, who look upon them as an expression of the thought of God, a revelation of the Creator.

Many illustrations from nature are used by the Bible writers, and as we observe the things of the natural world, we shall be enabled, under the guiding of the Holy Spirit, more fully to understand the lessons of God's Word. It is thus that nature becomes a key to the treasure-house of the Word.

Children should be encouraged to search out in nature the objects that illustrate Bible teachings, and to trace in the Bible the similitudes drawn from nature. They should search out, both in nature and in Holy Writ, every object representing Christ, and those also that He employed in illustrating truth. Thus may they learn to see Him in tree and vine, in lily and rose, in sun and star. They may learn to hear His voice in the song of birds, in the sighing of the trees, in the rolling thunder, and in the music of the sea. And every object in nature will repeat to them His precious lessons.

To those who thus acquaint themselves with Christ, the earth will nevermore be a lonely and desolate place. It will be their Father's house, filled with the presence of Him who once dwelt among us.—*Education,* pp. 119, 120.

Nature Teaches the Value of Obedience to Law

Are not two sparrows sold for a copper coin? And not one of them falls to the ground apart from your Father's will. Matthew 10:29, NKJV.

THE GREAT TEACHER brought His hearers in contact with nature, that they might listen to the voice which speaks in all created things; and as their hearts became tender and their minds receptive, He helped them to interpret the spiritual teaching of the scenes upon which their eyes rested. The parables, by means of which He loved to teach lessons of truth, show how open His spirit was to the influences of nature and how He delighted to gather the spiritual teaching from the surroundings of daily life.

The birds of the air, the lilies of the field, the sower and the seed, the shepherd and the sheep—with these Christ illustrated immortal truth. He drew illustrations also from the events of life, facts of experience familiar to the hearers—the leaven, the hid treasure, the pearl, the fishing net, the lost coin, the prodigal son, the houses on the rock and the sand. In His lessons there was something to interest every mind, to appeal to every heart. Thus the daily task, instead of being a mere round of toil, bereft of higher thoughts, was brightened and uplifted by constant reminders of the spiritual and the unseen.

So we should teach. Let the children learn to see in nature an expression of the love and the wisdom of God; let the thought of Him be linked with bird and flower and tree; let all things seen become to them the interpreters of the unseen, and all the events of life be a means of divine teaching.

As they learn thus to study the lessons in all created things, and in all life's experiences, show that the same laws which govern the things of nature and the events of life are to control us; that they are given for our good; and that only in obedience to them can we find true happiness and success.—*Education*, pp. 102, 103.

Valuable Objects in Nature
Are Pruned or Refined

*Behold, I have refined you, but not as silver; I have tested
you in the furnace of affliction. Isaiah 48:10, NKJV.*

THE FURNACE FIRES are not to destroy, but to refine, ennoble, sanctify. Without trial we would not feel so much our need of God and His help; and we would become proud and self-sufficient. In the trials that come to us we should see the evidences that the Lord's eye is upon us, and that He means to draw us to Himself. It is not the whole, but the wounded, who need a physician; it is those who are pressed almost beyond the point of endurance who need a Helper.

The fact that we are called upon to endure trial proves that the Lord sees something in us very precious, which He desires to develop. If He saw in us nothing whereby He might glorify His name, He would not spend time in refining us. We do not take special pains in pruning brambles. Christ does not cast worthless stones into His furnace. It is valuable ore that He tests.

The blacksmith puts the iron and steel into the fire that he may know what manner of metal they are. The Lord allows His chosen ones to be placed in the furnace of affliction, in order that He may see what temper they are of, and whether He can mold and fashion them for His work.

It may be that much work needs to be done in your character-building, that you are a rough stone which must be squared and polished before it can fill a place in God's temple. You need not be surprised if, with chisel and hammer, God cuts away the sharp corners of your character, until you are prepared to fill the place He has for you. No human being can accomplish this work. Only by God can it be done. And be assured that He will not strike one useless blow. His every blow is struck in love, for your eternal happiness. He knows your infirmities, and works to restore, not to destroy.

When trials arise that seem unexplainable, we should not allow our peace to be spoiled. However unjustly we may be treated, let not passion arise. By indulging a spirit of retaliation, we injure ourselves. We destroy our own confidence in God, and grieve the Holy Spirit. There is by our side a witness, a heavenly messenger, who will lift up for us a standard against the enemy. He will shut us in with the bright beams of the Sun of Righteousness. Beyond this, Satan cannot penetrate. He cannot pass this shield of holy light.—*Signs of the Times,* Aug. 18, 1909.

Nature Testifies of a
Master Artist and Designer

Day unto day utters speech, and night unto night reveals knowledge. There is
no speech nor language where their voice is not heard. Psalm 19:2, 3, NKJV.

THE THINGS OF nature that we now behold give us but a faint conception of Eden's glory. Sin has marred earth's beauty; on all things may be
seen traces of the work of evil. Yet much that is beautiful remains. Nature
testifies that One infinite in power, great in goodness, mercy, and love, created the earth, and filled it with life and gladness. Even in their blighted
state, all things reveal the handiwork of the great Master Artist. Wherever
we turn, we may hear the voice of God, and see evidences of His goodness.

From the solemn roll of the deep-toned thunder and old ocean's
ceaseless roar, to the glad songs that make the forests vocal with melody,
nature's ten thousand voices speak His praise. In earth and sea and sky,
with their marvelous tint and color, varying in gorgeous contrast or
blended in harmony, we behold His glory.

The everlasting hills tell us of His power. The trees that wave their
green banners in the sunlight, and the flowers in their delicate beauty, point
to their Creator. The living green that carpets the brown earth tells of God's
care for the humblest of His creatures. The caves of the sea and the depths
of the earth reveal His treasures. He who placed the pearls in the ocean and
the amethyst and chrysolite among the rocks is a lover of the beautiful. The
sun rising in the heavens is a representative of Him who is the life and light
of all that He has made. All the brightness and beauty that adorn the earth
and light up the heavens speak of God. . . . All things tell of His tender, fatherly care and of His desire to make His children happy.

The mighty power that works through all nature and sustains all things
is not, as some proponents of science represent, merely an all-pervading
principle, an actuating energy. God is a Spirit; yet He is a personal Being;
for so He has revealed Himself: "The Lord is the true God, he is the living God, and an everlasting king" (Jer. 10:10). . . .

God's handiwork in nature is not God Himself in nature. The things of
nature are an expression of God's character and power; but we are not to regard nature as God. The artistic skill of human beings produces very beautiful workmanship, things that delight the eye, and these things reveal to us
something of the thought of the designer; but the thing made is not the
maker. It is not the work, but the workman, that is counted worthy of honor.
So while nature is an expression of God's thought, it is not nature, but the
God of nature, that is to be exalted.—*The Ministry of Healing,* pp. 411-413.

Earth's Bounties Give Evidence of God's Love

Now may He who supplies seed to the sower, and bread for food,
supply and multiply the seed you have sown and increase the fruits
of your righteousness, while you are enriched in everything for all liberality,
which causes thanksgiving through us to God. 2 Corinthians 9:10, 11, NKJV.

AS WE ARE continually receiving the blessings of God, so are we to be continually giving. When the heavenly Benefactor ceases to give to us, then we may be excused; for we shall have nothing to bestow. God has never left us without evidence of His love, in that He did us good. He gives us rain from heaven and fruitful seasons, providing us abundantly with His bounties, and filling our hearts with gladness. He has declared that "while the earth remaineth, seedtime and harvest, and cold and heat, and summer and winter, and day and night shall not cease."

We are sustained every moment by God's care, and upheld by His power. He spreads our tables with food. He gives us peaceful and refreshing sleep. Weekly He brings to us the Sabbath, that we may rest from our temporal labors, and worship Him in His own house. He has given us His Word to be a lamp to our feet and a light to our path. In its sacred pages we find the counsels of wisdom; and as oft as we lift our hearts to Him in penitence and faith, He grants us the blessings of His grace. Above all else is the infinite gift of God's dear Son, through whom flow all other blessings for this life and for the life to come.

Surely goodness and mercy attend us at every step. Not till we wish the infinite Father to cease bestowing His gifts on us, should we impatiently exclaim, Is there no end of giving? Not only should we faithfully render to God our tithes, which He claims as His own, but we should bring a tribute to His treasury as an offering of gratitude. Let us with joyful hearts bring to our Creator the firstfruits of all His bounties—our choicest possessions, our best and holiest service.—*Review and Herald,* Feb. 9, 1886.

The Natural World
Speaks of the Creator

Let heaven and earth praise Him, the seas and everything that
moves in them. For God will save Zion and build the cities of Judah,
that they may dwell there and possess it. Psalm 69:34, 35, NKJV.

THE SAME CREATIVE energy that brought the world into existence is still exerted in upholding the universe and continuing the operations of nature. The hand of God guides the planets in their orderly march through the heavens. It is not because of inherent power that year by year the earth continues its motion round the sun, and produces its bounties. The word of God controls the elements. He covers the heavens with clouds, and prepares rain for the earth. He makes the valleys fruitful, and "grass to grow upon the mountains." It is through His power that vegetation flourishes; that the leaves appear and the flowers bloom.

The whole natural world is designed to be an interpreter of the things of God. To Adam and Eve in their Eden home, nature was full of the knowledge of God, teeming with divine instruction. It was vocal with the voice of wisdom to their attentive ears. Wisdom spoke to the eye, and was received into the heart; for they communed with God in His created works. As soon as the holy pair transgressed the law of the Most High, the brightness from the face of God departed from the face of nature. Nature is now marred and defiled by sin. But God's object lessons are not obliterated; even now, rightly studied and interpreted, [nature] speaks of the Creator.

As divine truth is revealed in Holy Writ, so it is reflected, as from a mirror, in the face of nature; and through His creation we become acquainted with the Creator. And so the book of nature becomes a great lesson book, which instructors who are wise can use, in connection with the Scriptures, to guide lost sheep back to the fold of God. As the works of God are studied, the Holy Spirit flashes conviction into the mind. It is not the conviction which logical reasoning produces; but unless the mind has become too dark to know God, the eye too dim to see Him, the ear too dull to hear His voice, a deeper meaning is grasped, and the sublime, spiritual truths of the written Word are impressed on the heart.

The most effective way to teach the heathen who know not God is through His works. In this way, far more readily than by any other method, they can be made to realize the difference between their idols, the works of their own hands, and the true God, the Maker of heaven and earth.—*Special Testimonies on Education,* pp. 58-60.

Rich Blessings From
a Sabbath for the Land

*Six years you shall sow your field, and six years you shall
prune your vineyard, and gather in its fruit; but in the seventh year there
shall be a sabbath of solemn rest for the land, a sabbath to the Lord. You shall
neither sow your field nor prune your vineyard. Leviticus 25:3, 4, NKJV.*

THE FEAST OF TABERNACLES, or harvest festival, with its offerings
from orchard and field, its week's encampment in the leafy booths, its social reunions, the sacred memorial service, and the generous hospitality to
God's workers, the Levites of the sanctuary, and to His children, the
strangers and the poor, uplifted all minds in gratitude to Him who had
crowned the year with His goodness, and whose paths dropped fatness.

By the devout in Israel, fully a month of every year was occupied in
this way. It was a period free from care and labor, and almost wholly devoted, in the truest sense, to purposes of education.

In apportioning the inheritance of His people, it was God's purpose to
teach them, and through them the people of after generations, correct
principles concerning the ownership of the land. The land of Canaan was
divided among the whole people, the Levites only, as ministers of the sanctuary, being excepted. Though one might for a season dispose of his possession, he could not barter away the inheritance of his children. When
able to do so, he was at liberty at any time to redeem it; debts were remitted every seventh year, and in the fiftieth, or year of jubilee, all landed
property reverted to the original owner. Thus every family was secured in
its possession, and a safeguard was afforded against the extremes either of
wealth or of poverty.

By the distribution of the land among the people, God provided for
them, as for the dwellers in Eden, the occupation most favorable to development—the care of plants and animals. A further provision for education
was the suspension of agricultural labor every seventh year, the land lying
fallow, and its spontaneous products being left to the poor. Thus was given
opportunity for more extended study, for social interaction and worship,
and for the exercise of benevolence, so often crowded out by life's cares
and labors.

Were the principles of God's laws regarding the distribution of property carried out in the world today, how different would be the condition
of the people!—*Education*, pp. 42-44.

The Poor Have Rights in God's World

The earth is the Lord's, and all its fullness, the world
and those who dwell therein. Psalm 24:1, NKJV.

"ON THE TENTH day of the seventh month, in the day of atonement," the trumpet of the jubilee was sounded. Throughout the land, wherever the Jewish people dwelt, the sound was heard, calling upon all the children of Jacob to welcome the year of release. On the great Day of Atonement satisfaction was made for the sins of Israel, and with gladness of heart the people would welcome the jubilee.

As in the sabbatical year, the land was not to be sown or reaped, and all that it produced was to be regarded as the rightful property of the poor. Certain classes of Hebrew slaves—all who did not receive their liberty in the sabbatical year—were now set free.

But that which especially distinguished the year of jubilee was the reversion of all landed property to the family of the original possessor. By the special direction of God the land had been divided by lot. After the division was made no one was at liberty to trade his estate. Neither was he to sell his land unless poverty compelled him to do so, and then, whenever he or any of his kindred might desire to redeem it, the purchaser must not refuse to sell it; and if unredeemed, it would revert to its first possessor or his heirs in the year of jubilee. . . .

The people were to be impressed with the fact that it was God's land which they were permitted to possess for a time; that He was the rightful owner, the original proprietor, and that He would have special consideration made for the poor and unfortunate. It was to be impressed upon the minds of all that the poor have as much right to a place in God's world as have the more wealthy.

Such were the provisions made by our merciful Creator, to lessen suffering, to bring some ray of hope, to flash some gleam of sunshine, into the life of the destitute and distressed.—*Patriarchs and Prophets*, pp. 533, 534.

Work, for Earth's
Night Is Coming

*Those who are wise shall shine like the brightness of the firmament, and those
who turn many to righteousness like the stars forever and ever. Daniel 12:3, NKJV.*

THE WORK GIVEN us is a great and important one, and in it are needed
wise, unselfish workers, workers who understand what it means to give
themselves to unselfish effort to save souls. But there is no need for the service of men and women who are lukewarm, for such Christ cannot use.
Workers are needed whose hearts are touched with human suffering and
whose lives give evidence that they are receiving and imparting light and
life and grace.

The people of God are to come close to Christ in self-denial and sacrifice, their one aim being to give the message of mercy to all the world.
Some will work in one way and some in another, as the Lord shall call and
lead them. But they are all to strive together, seeking to make the work a
perfect whole. With pen and voice they are to labor for Him. The printed
word of truth is to be translated into different languages and carried to the
ends of the earth.

My heart is often burdened because so many who might work are
doing nothing. They are the sport of Satan's temptations. Every church
member who has a knowledge of the truth is expected to work while the
day lasts; for the night cometh, wherein no one can work. Erelong we shall
understand what that night means. The Spirit of God is being grieved away
from the earth. The nations are angry with one another. Widespread
preparations are being made for war. The night is at hand. Let the church
arouse and go forth to do its appointed work. Every believer, educated or
uneducated, can bear the message.

Eternity stretches before us. The curtain is about to be lifted. What are
we thinking of, that we cling to our selfish love of ease, while all around us
souls are perishing? Have our hearts become utterly callous? Can we not see
and understand that we have a work to do in behalf of others? My brethren
and sisters, are you among those who, having eyes, see not, and having ears,
hear not? Is it in vain that God has given you a knowledge of His will? Is
it in vain that He has sent you warning after warning of the nearness of the
end? Do you believe the declarations of His Word concerning what is coming upon the world? Do you believe that God's judgments are hanging over
the inhabitants of the earth? How, then, can you sit at ease, careless and indifferent?—*Testimonies for the Church*, vol. 9, pp. 26, 27.

Cultivating the Soil
Is Doing God's Service

"And behold, this vine" "was planted in good soil by many waters, to bring forth branches, bear fruit, and become a majestic vine." Ezekiel 17:7, 8, NKJV.

THE TITHING SYSTEM was instituted by the Lord as the very best arrangement to help the people in carrying out the principles of the law. If this law were obeyed, the people would be entrusted with the entire vineyard, the whole earth. . . .

Human beings were to cooperate with God in restoring the diseased land to health, that it might be a praise and a glory to His name. And as the land they possessed would, if managed with skill and earnestness, produce its treasures, so their hearts, if controlled by God, would reflect His character. . . .

In the laws which God gave for the cultivation of the soil, He was giving the people opportunity to overcome their selfishness and become heavenly-minded. Canaan would be to them as Eden if they obeyed the word of the Lord. Through them the Lord designed to teach all the nations of the world how to cultivate the soil so that it would yield healthy fruit, free from disease. The earth is the Lord's vineyard, and is to be treated according to His plan. Those who cultivated the soil were to realize that they were doing God service. They were as truly in their lot and place as were the men appointed to minister in the priesthood and in work connected with the tabernacle. God told the people that the Levites were a gift to them, and no matter what their trade, they were to help to support them.—*The Seventh-day Adventist Bible Commentary,* Ellen G. White Comments, vol. 1, p. 1112.

Through disobedience to God, Adam and Eve had lost Eden, and because of sin the whole earth was cursed. But if God's people followed His instruction, their land would be restored to fertility and beauty. God Himself gave them directions in regard to the culture of the soil, and they were to cooperate with Him in its restoration. Thus the whole land, under God's control, would become an object lesson of spiritual truth. As in obedience to His natural laws the earth should produce its treasures, so in obedience to His moral law the hearts of the people were to reflect the attributes of His character. Even the heathen would recognize the superiority of those who served and worshiped the living God.—*Christ's Object Lessons,* p. 289.

An Exhaustless Source
of Instruction and Delight

Where were you when I laid the foundations of the earth?
Tell Me, if you have understanding. Who determined its measurements?
Surely you know! Or who stretched the line upon it? Job 38:4, 5, NKJV.

TO ADAM AND EVE was committed the care of the garden, "to dress it and to keep it" (Gen. 2:15). Though rich in all that the Owner of the universe could supply, they were not to be idle. Useful occupation was appointed them as a blessing, to strengthen the body, to expand the mind, and to develop the character.

The book of nature, which spread its living lessons before them, afforded an exhaustless source of instruction and delight. On every leaf of the forest and stone of the mountains, in every shining star, in earth and sea and sky, God's name was written. With both the animate and the inanimate creation—with leaf and flower and tree, and with every living creature, from the leviathan of the waters to the mote in the sunbeam—the dwellers in Eden held converse, gathering from each the secrets of its life. God's glory in the heavens, the innumerable worlds in their orderly revolutions, "the balancings of the clouds" (Job 37:16), the mysteries of light and sound, of day and night—all were objects of study by the pupils of earth's first school.

The laws and operations of nature, and the great principles of truth that govern the spiritual universe, were opened to their minds by the infinite Author of all. In "the light of the knowledge of the glory of God" (2 Cor. 4:6), their mental and spiritual powers developed, and they realized the highest pleasures of their holy existence.

As it came from the Creator's hand, not only the Garden of Eden but the whole earth was exceedingly beautiful. No taint of sin, or shadow of death, marred the fair creation. God's glory "covered the heavens, and the earth was full of his praise." . . .

The Garden of Eden was a representation of what God desired the whole earth to become, and it was His purpose that, as the human family increased in numbers, they should establish other homes and schools like the one He had given. Thus in course of time the whole earth might be occupied with homes and schools where the words and the works of God should be studied, and where the students should thus be fitted more and more fully to reflect, throughout endless ages, the light of the knowledge of His glory.—*Education,* pp. 21, 22.

Fallow Ground of the
Human Heart Should Be Worked

*Sow for yourselves righteousness; reap in mercy; break up
your fallow ground, for it is time to seek the Lord, till He
comes and rains righteousness on you. Hosea 10:12, NKJV.*

I WANT TO exhort those who are in positions of responsibility to waken to their duty, and not imperil the cause of present truth by engaging inefficient men and women to do the work of God. We want those who are willing to go into new fields, and to do hard service for the Lord.

I remember visiting in Iowa when the country was new, and I saw the farmers breaking the new ground. I noticed that they had heavy teams, and made tremendous efforts to make deep furrows, but the laborers gained strength and muscle by the exercise of their physical powers. It will make our young workers strong to go into new fields, and break up the fallow ground of human hearts. This work will drive them nearer to God. It will help them to see that they are altogether inefficient in themselves.

They must be wholly the Lord's. They must put away their self-esteem and self-importance, and put on the Lord Jesus Christ. When they do this, they will be willing to go without the camp, and bear the burden as good soldiers of the cross. They will gain efficiency and ability by mastering difficulties and overcoming obstacles. Workers are wanted for responsible positions, but they must be those who have given full proof of their ministry in willingness to wear the yoke of Christ. Heaven regards this class with approval.

I exhort you to have the eyesalve, that you may discern what God would have you do. There are too many Christless sermons preached. An array of powerless words only confirms the people in their backslidings. May God help us that His Spirit may be made manifest among us. We should not wait until we go home to obtain the blessing of Heaven. The ministers should begin right here with the people to seek God, and to work from the right standpoint. Those who have been long in the work have been far too content to wait for the showers of the latter rain to revive them.

We are the people who, like John, are to prepare the way of the Lord; and if we are prepared for the second coming of Christ, we must work with all diligence to prepare others for Christ's second advent, as did the forerunner of Christ for His first advent, calling men and women to repentance. . . . May God help us to search the Scriptures for ourselves, and when we are all filled with the truth of God, it will flow out as water from a living spring.—*Review and Herald,* Oct. 8, 1889.

Greater Efficiency and
Deeper Consecration Needed

*However, when He, the Spirit of truth, has come, He will guide you
into all truth; for He will not speak on His own authority, but whatever He
hears He will speak; and He will tell you things to come. John 16:13, NKJV.*

EVERY DAY THAT passes brings us nearer the end. Does it bring us also
near to God? Are we watching unto prayer? Those with whom we associate day by day need our help, our guidance. They may be in such a condition of mind that a word in season will be sent home by the Holy Spirit
as a nail in a sure place. Tomorrow some of these souls may be where we
can never reach them again. What is our influence over these fellow travelers? What effort do we make to win them to Christ?

Time is short, and our forces must be organized to do a larger work.
Laborers are needed who comprehend the greatness of the work and who
will engage in it, not for the wages they receive, but from a realization of
the nearness of the end. The time demands greater efficiency and deeper
consecration. Oh, I am so full of this subject that I cry to God: "Raise up
and send forth messengers filled with a sense of their responsibility, messengers in whose hearts self-idolatry, which lies at the foundation of all sin,
has been crucified." . . .

Putting our trust in God, we are to move steadily forward, doing
His work with unselfishness, in humble dependence upon Him, committing ourselves and our present and future to His wise providence,
holding the beginning of our confidence firm unto the end, remember-
ing that it is not because of our worthiness that we receive the blessings
of heaven, but because of the worthiness of Christ, and our acceptance,
through faith in Him, of God's abounding grace.—*Testimonies for the
Church,* vol. 9, pp. 27-29.

Keep Streams of
Beneficence in Constant Circulation

*Do you not say, "There are still four months and then comes
the harvest"? Behold, I say to you, lift up your eyes and look at
the fields, for they are already white for harvest! John 4:35, NKJV.*

HUMAN POWER DID not establish the work of God, neither can human power destroy it. To those who carry forward His work in face of difficulty and opposition, God will give the constant guidance and guardianship of His holy angels. His work on earth will never cease. The building of His spiritual temple will be carried forward until it shall stand complete, and the headstone shall be brought forth with shoutings: "Grace, grace unto it."

Christians are to be a benefit to others. Thus they themselves are benefited. "He that watereth shall be watered also himself" (Prov. 11:25). This is a law of the divine administration, a law by which God designs that the streams of beneficence shall be kept, like the waters of the great deep, in constant circulation, perpetually returning to their source. In the fulfilling of this law is the power of Christian missions.

I have been instructed that wherever by self-sacrifice and urgent efforts facilities for the establishment and advancement of the cause have been provided, and the Lord has prospered the work, those in that place should give of their means to help His servants who have been sent to new fields. Wherever the work has been established on a good foundation, the believers should feel themselves under obligation to help those in need by transferring, even at great sacrifice, a portion or all of the means which in former years was invested in behalf of the work in their locality. Thus the Lord designs that His work shall increase. This is the law of restitution in right lines.—*Testimonies for the Church,* vol. 7, p. 170.

SEPTEMBER

❧

Sharing the Good News

Tell Others to
Love and Obey Christ

*"You are My witnesses," says the Lord, "and My servant whom I have chosen,
that you may know and believe Me, and understand that I am He. Before Me
there was no God formed, nor shall there be after Me." Isaiah 43:10, NKJV.*

SATAN IS CONSTANTLY alluring away from faithfulness and thoroughness in the essential works of preparedness for the great event that will try
every person's soul. The work in the heavenly sanctuary is going forward.
Jesus is cleansing the sanctuary. The work on earth corresponds with the
work in heaven. The heavenly angels are at work constantly to draw
human beings, the living agents, to look to Jesus, to contemplate and meditate upon Jesus, that they may, in viewing the perfection of Christ, be impressed with the imperfections of their own characters. The promised
Comforter, Christ . . . declared, "shall testify of me." This is the burden of
the message for this time. . . .

Talk as Christ talked. Work as Christ worked. We must look to Christ
and live. Catching sight of His loveliness, we long to practice the virtues
and righteousness of Christ. It is by beholding Christ that we become
changed into His image, and by renouncing self, giving our hearts up
wholly to Jesus for His Spirit to refine, ennoble, and elevate, we will be in
close connection with the future world, bathed in the bright beams of the
Sun of Righteousness. We rejoice with joy unspeakable and full of glory.
Then we are commanded to go into other cities and towns and tell them
the good news with hearts all aglow with divine love, even to them that
are afar off, even as many as the Lord your God shall call.

Tell to others the blessed truths of His Word, and in obeying the words
of Christ, continue in His love. [Tell them] how He urges us by the love
we bear to Him to keep His commandments. He does this, not to urge us
to do impossible things, but because He knows what it means to keep His
Father's commandments. He wants every soul that heareth His invitation to
say the same to others, and to receive His richest gifts, for He knows that
in keeping the commandments of God, we are not brought into servile
bondage, but are made free through the blood of Jesus Christ. "And in
keeping of them [His commandments] there is great reward" (Ps. 19:11).

Tell it to others with pen and voice, with piety, with humility, with
love, representing the character of Christ. "And the Spirit and the bride
say, Come. And let him that heareth say, Come. And let him that is athirst
come. And whosoever will, let him take the water of life freely" (Rev.
22:17).—*The Upward Look,* p. 344.

All Have a
Duty to Witness

You shall receive power when the Holy Spirit has come
upon you; and you shall be witnesses to Me in Jerusalem, and in all
Judea and Samaria, and to the end of the earth. Acts 1:8, NKJV.

MY HEART WAS rejoiced to see among the converts so many young men
and women, with hearts softened and subdued by the love of Jesus, acknowledging the good work wrought by God for their souls. It was indeed
a precious season. "With the heart man believeth unto righteousness; and
with the mouth confession is made unto salvation." God forbid that these
souls should ever lose the ardor of their first love, that a strange coldness,
through pride and love of the world, should take possession of their minds
and hearts.

It is essential that these who have newly come to the faith should have
a sense of their obligation to God, who has called them to a knowledge of
the truth, and filled their hearts with His sacred peace, that they may exert
a sanctifying influence over all with whom they associate. "Ye are my witnesses, saith the Lord."

To every one God has committed a work, to make known His salvation to the world. In true religion there is nothing selfish or exclusive. The
gospel of Christ is diffusive and aggressive. It is described as the salt of the
earth, the transforming leaven, the light which shineth in darkness. It is impossible for one to retain the favor and love of God, and enjoy communion with Him, and still feel no responsibility for the souls for whom
Christ died, who are in error and darkness, perishing in their sins.

If those who profess to be followers of Christ neglect to shine as lights
in the world, the vital power will leave them, and they will become cold
and Christless. The spell of indifference will be upon them, a deathlike
sluggishness of soul, which will make them bodies of death instead of living representatives of Jesus. All must lift the cross and in modesty, meekness, and lowliness of mind take up their God-given duties, engaging in
personal effort for those around them who need help and light.

All who accept these duties will have a rich and varied experience,
their own hearts will glow with fervor, and they will be strengthened and
stimulated to renewed, persevering efforts to work out their own salvation
with fear and trembling, because it is God that worketh in them both to
will and to do of His good pleasure.—*Review and Herald,* July 21, 1891.

Carry Light and Hope Everywhere

Let your light so shine before men, that they may see your good works and glorify your Father in heaven. Matthew 5:16, NKJV.

PRACTICAL WORK WILL have far more effect than mere sermonizing. We are to give food to the hungry, clothing to the naked, and shelter to the homeless. And we are called to do more than this. The wants of the soul, only the love of Christ can satisfy. If Christ is abiding in us, our hearts will be full of divine sympathy. The sealed fountains of earnest, Christlike love will be unsealed.

God calls not only for our gifts for the needy, but for our cheerful countenance, our hopeful words, our kindly handclasp. When Christ healed the sick, He laid His hands upon them. So should we come in close touch with those whom we seek to benefit.

There are many from whom hope has departed. Bring back the sunshine to them. Many have lost their courage. Speak to them words of cheer. Pray for them. There are those who need the bread of life. Read to them from the Word of God. Upon many is a soul sickness which no earthly balm can reach nor physician heal. Pray for these souls, bring them to Jesus. Tell them that there is a balm in Gilead and a Physician there.

Light is a blessing, a universal blessing, pouring forth its treasures on a world unthankful, unholy, demoralized. So it is with the light of the Sun of Righteousness. The whole earth, wrapped as it is in the darkness of sin, and sorrow, and pain, is to be lighted with the knowledge of God's love. From no sect, rank, or class of people is the light shining from heaven's throne to be excluded.

The message of hope and mercy is to be carried to the ends of the earth. . . . No longer are the heathen to be wrapped in midnight darkness. The gloom is to disappear before the bright beams of the Sun of Righteousness. The power of hell has been overcome.

But no one can impart that which he or she has not received. In the work of God, humanity can originate nothing. . . . It was the golden oil emptied by the heavenly messengers into the golden tubes, to be conducted from the golden bowl into the lamps of the sanctuary, that produced a continuous bright and shining light. It is the love of God continually transferred to men and women that enables them to impart light. Into the hearts of all who are united to God by faith the golden oil of love flows freely, to shine out again in good works, in real, heartfelt service for God.—*Christ's Object Lessons*, pp. 417-419.

Sharing the Good News

To Witness Successfully, First Crucify Self

There was a man sent from God, whose name was John. This man came for a witness, to bear witness of the Light, that all through him might believe. John 1:6, 7, NKJV.

GOD'S WORD TO us is "Be ye therefore perfect, even as your Father which is in heaven is perfect." He calls upon everyone to crucify self. Those who respond grow strong in Him. They learn daily from Christ, and the more they learn, the greater is their desire to build up God's kingdom by helping their fellow beings. The more enlightenment they have, the greater is their desire to enlighten others. The more they talk with God, the less they live to themselves. The greater their privileges, opportunities, and facilities for Christian work, the greater is the obligation they feel to work for others.

Human nature is ever struggling for expression. A person who is made complete in Christ must first be emptied of pride, of self-sufficiency. Then there is silence in the soul, and God's voice can be heard. Then the Spirit can find unobstructed entrance. Let God work in and through you. Then with Paul you can say, "I live; yet not I, but Christ liveth in me." But until self is laid on the altar, until we let the Holy Spirit mold and fashion us according to the divine similitude, we cannot reach God's ideal for us.

Christ said, "I am come that they might have life, and that they might have it more abundantly." This life is what we must have in order to work for Christ, and we must have it "more abundantly." God will breathe this life into every soul that dies to self. But entire self-renunciation is required. Unless this takes place, we carry with us that which destroys our happiness and usefulness.

The Lord needs men and women who carry with them into the daily life the light of a godly example, men and women whose words and actions show that Christ is abiding in the heart, teaching, leading, and guiding. He needs men and women of prayer, who, by wrestling alone with God, obtain the victory over self, and then go forth to impart to others that which they have received from the Source of power.

God accepts those who crucify self, and makes them vessels unto honor. They are in His hands as clay in the hands of the potter, and He works His will through them. Such men and women receive spiritual power. Christ lives in them, and the power of His Spirit attends their efforts. They realize that they are to live in this world the life that Jesus lived—a life free from all selfishness; and He enables them to bear witness for Him that draws souls to the cross of Calvary.—*Signs of the Times,* Apr. 9, 1902.

Invite People to
Become Children of God

Behold what manner of love the Father has bestowed on us,
that we should be called children of God! Therefore the world does
not know us, because it did not know Him. 1 John 3:1, NKJV.

"BELOVED, NOW ARE we the sons of God, and it doth not yet appear what we shall be; but we know that, when he shall appear, we shall be like him; for we shall see him as he is. And every man that hath this hope in him purifieth himself, even as he is pure."

In this scripture are portrayed Christian privileges that are comprehended by but comparatively few. Everyone should become familiar with the blessings that God has offered us in His Word. He has given us many assurances as to what He will do for us. And all that He has promised is made possible by Christ's sacrifice in our behalf.

John the Baptist bore witness of the One through whom we may become sons and daughters of God. . . . "As many as received him, to them gave he power to become the sons of God, even to them that believe on his name."

Divine sonship is not something that we may gain of ourselves. Only to those who receive Christ as their Savior is given the power to become sons and daughters of God. Sinners cannot, by any power of their own, rid themselves of sin. For the accomplishment of this result, they must look to a higher Power. John exclaimed, "Behold the Lamb of God, which taketh away the sin of the world." Christ alone has power to cleanse the heart. He who is seeking for forgiveness and acceptance can say only: "Nothing in my hand I bring; simply to Thy cross I cling."

But the promise of sonship is made to all who "believe on his name." Everyone who comes to Jesus in faith will receive pardon. As soon as the penitent one looks to the Savior for help to turn from sin, the Holy Spirit begins His transforming work upon the heart. "As many as received him, to them gave he power to become the sons of God."

What an incentive to greater effort this should be to all who are trying to set the hope of the gospel before those who are still in the darkness of error.—*Review and Herald,* Sept. 3, 1903.

Angels Cooperate
With Soul Winners

To Him all the prophets witness that, through His name, whoever
believes in Him will receive remission of sins. Acts 10:43, NKJV.

GOD WORKS THROUGH heavenly instrumentalities that those who
know the truth may be brought in connection with souls who need light
and knowledge. Read the tenth chapter of Acts. The God of heaven beheld the devotion and piety of Cornelius. He witnessed his prayers and his
almsgiving, and marked the power of his influence. He desired to give him
light in regard to Christ's mission and to connect him with His work.

The Lord sent His angel to signify this to Cornelius, and to place him
in connection with the apostle Peter. The angel told Cornelius just where
Peter lived, and assured him, "He shall tell thee what thou oughtest to do."
Then an angel was sent to Peter to remove his doubt as to the propriety of
working for the Gentiles. "What God has cleansed, that call not thou common." While Peter was pondering in regard to the mysterious revelation
that had been given him, the Spirit said unto him, "Behold, three men
seek thee. Arise therefore, and . . . go with them, doubting nothing; for I
have sent them."

What a history is this to show that Heaven is in close connection with
our world. On the ladder that Jacob saw, angels of God are ascending and
descending. God is above the ladder, and beams of light and glory are shining the whole length from heaven to earth. This line of communication is
still open.

And what was the outcome of God's dealing with Cornelius? Read the
precious history, and learn, and praise God; for its lesson is for us. . . . And
God "commanded us to preach unto the people, and to testify that it is he
which was ordained of God to be the Judge of quick and dead. To him
give all the prophets witness, that through his name whosoever believeth
in him shall receive remission of sins."

As Peter spoke these things, the Holy Spirit fell upon the assembly, and
they were baptized in the name of the Lord. Thus in Caesarea a company
of Christian believers was established to hold up the light of truth.

This is the work to be done today. We have a message to give to the
people. . . . Christ declares, "I am the bread of life: he that cometh to me
shall never hunger; and he that believeth on me shall never thirst. . . . All
that the Father giveth me shall come to me; and him that cometh to me I
will in no wise cast out."—*Australasian Union Conference Record*, Jan. 1, 1900.

Guard Your Words and Be Tactful as You Witness

*Walk in wisdom toward those who are outside, redeeming the
time. Let your speech always be with grace, seasoned with salt, that you
may know how you ought to answer each one. Colossians 4:5, 6, NKJV.*

IT IS TRUE that we are commanded to "cry aloud, spare not, lift up thy voice like a trumpet, and shew my people their transgression, and the house of Jacob their sins" (Isa. 58:1). This message must be given; but while it must be given, we should be careful not to thrust and crowd and condemn those who have not the light that we have. . . .

Those who have had great privileges and opportunities, and who have failed to improve their physical, mental, and moral powers, but who have lived to please themselves and have refused to bear their responsibility, are in greater danger and in greater condemnation before God than those who are in error upon doctrinal points, yet who seek to live to do good to others. Do not censure others; do not condemn them.

If we allow selfish considerations, false reasoning, and false excuses to bring us into a perverse state of mind and heart, so that we shall not know the ways and will of God, we shall be far more guilty than the open sinner. We need to be very cautious in order that we may not condemn those who, before God, are less guilty than ourselves.

Let everyone bear in mind that we are in no case to invite persecution. We are not to use harsh and cutting words. Keep them out of every article written, drop them out of every address given. Let the Word of God do the cutting, the rebuking; let finite men and women hide and abide in Jesus Christ. Let the spirit of Christ appear. Let all be guarded in their words, lest they place those not of our faith in deadly opposition against us and give Satan an opportunity to use the unadvised words to hedge up our way.

There is to be a time of trouble such as never was since there was a nation. Our work is to study to weed out of all our discourses everything that savors of retaliation and defiance and making a drive against churches and individuals, because this is not Christ's way and method.

The fact that God's people, who know the truth, have failed to do their duty according to the light given in the Word of God makes it a necessity for us to be the more guarded, lest we offend unbelievers before they have heard the reasons for our faith in regard to the Sabbath and Sunday.—*Testimonies for the Church,* vol. 9, pp. 243, 244.

Now Is the Time to Work for Christ

I charge you therefore before God and the Lord Jesus Christ,
who will judge the living and the dead at His appearing and His kingdom:
Preach the word! Be ready in season and out of season. Convince, rebuke,
exhort, with all longsuffering and teaching. 2 Timothy 4:1, 2, NKJV.

WHAT USE HAVE you made of the gift of God? He has supplied you with the motive force of action, that with patience and hope and untiring vigilance you might set forth Christ and Him crucified, calling the lost to repent of their sins, sounding the note of warning that Christ is soon to come with power and great glory.

If the members of the . . . church do not arouse now and go to work in missionary fields, they will fall back into deathlike slumber. How did the Holy Spirit work upon your hearts? . . . Were you not inspired to exercise the talents God has given you, that every man and woman and youth should employ them to set forth the truth for this time, making personal efforts, going into the cities where the truth has never been proclaimed, and lifting up the standard?

Have not your energies been quickened by the blessing that God has bestowed upon you? Has not the truth been more deeply impressed upon your soul? Can you not see more clearly its relative importance to those who are perishing out of Christ? Since the manifest revealing of God's blessing, are you witnessing for Christ more distinctly and decidedly than ever before?

The Holy Spirit has brought decidedly to your minds the important, vital truths for this time. Is this knowledge to be bound up in a napkin and hidden in the earth? No, no. It is to be put out to the exchangers. As a person uses his or her talents, however small, with faithfulness, the Holy Spirit takes the things of God, and presents them anew to the mind. Through His Spirit God makes His Word a vivifying power. It is quick and powerful, exerting a strong influence upon minds, not because of the learning or intelligence of the human agent, but because divine power is working with the human power. And it is to the divine power that all praise is to be given.—*Testimonies for the Church,* vol. 8, pp. 54, 55.

Practical Christianity
Important in Witnesses

You know the commandments: "Do not commit adultery,"
"Do not murder," "Do not steal," "Do not bear false witness,"
"Do not defraud," "Honor your father and mother." Mark 10:19, NKJV.

PEOPLE WHO WILL not admit the claims of God's law, which are so very plain, will generally take a lawless course; for they have so long taken sides with the great rebel in warring against the law of God, which is the foundation of His government in heaven and earth, that they are trained in this labor. In their warfare they will not open their eyes or consciences to light. They close their eyes, lest they shall become enlightened.

Their case is as hopeless as was that of the Jews who would not see the light which Christ brought to them. The wonderful evidences which He gave them of His Messiahship in the miracles that He performed, in healing the sick, raising the dead, and doing the works which no other had done or could do, instead of melting and subduing their hearts, and overcoming their wicked prejudices, inspired them with satanic hatred and fury such as Satan possessed when he was thrust out of heaven. The greater light and evidence they had, the greater was their hatred. They were determined to extinguish the light by putting Christ to death. . . .

Our work should be to embrace every opportunity to present the truth in its purity and simplicity where there is any desire or interest to hear the reasons of our faith. Those who have dwelt mostly upon the prophecies and the theoretical points of our faith should without delay become Bible students upon practical subjects. They should take a deeper draft at the fountain of divine truth. They should carefully study the life of Christ and His lessons of practical godliness, given for the benefit of all and to be the rule of right living for all who should believe on His name. They should be imbued with the spirit of their great Exemplar and have a high sense of the sacred life of a follower of Christ.—*Testimonies for the Church,* vol. 3, pp. 213, 214.

Witness Wherever Jesus Calls You

The Lord stood with me and strengthened me, so that the message might be preached fully through me, and that all the Gentiles might hear. 2 Timothy 4:17, NKJV.

RESOLVE, NOT IN your own strength, but in the strength and grace given of God, that you will consecrate to Him now, just now, every power, every ability. You will then follow Jesus because He bids you, and you will not ask where, or what reward will be given. It will be well with you as you obey the word: "Follow me." Your part is to lead others to the light by judicious, faithful efforts. Under the guardianship of the divine Leader, will to do, resolve to act, without a moment's hesitation.

When you die to self, when you surrender to God, to do His work, to let the light that He has given you shine forth in good works, you will not labor alone. God's grace stands forth to cooperate with every effort to enlighten the ignorant and those who do not know that the end of all things is at hand.

But God will not do your work. Light may shine in abundance, but the grace given will convert your soul only as it arouses you to cooperate with divine agencies. You are called upon to put on the Christian armor and enter the Lord's service as active soldiers. Divine power is to cooperate with human effort to break the spell of worldly enchantment that the enemy has cast upon souls. . . .

Let your hearts be drawn out in love for perishing souls. Obey the impulse given by High Heaven. Grieve not the Holy Spirit by delay. Resist not God's methods of recovering souls from the thralldom of sin. To everyone, according to their several ability, is given their work. Do your best, and God will accept your efforts.—*Testimonies for the Church,* vol. 8, pp. 55, 56.

Jesus Identifies Himself With the Needy

And the King will answer them and say to them,
"Assuredly, I say to you, inasmuch as you did it to one of the least
of these My brethren, you did it to Me." Matthew 25:40, NKJV.

WHILE GOD IN His providence has laden the earth with His bounties and filled its storehouses with the luxuries of life, there is no excuse whatever for allowing the treasury of God to remain empty. Christians are not excusable for permitting the widow's cries and the orphan's prayers to ascend to Heaven because of their suffering want, while a liberal Providence has placed in the hands of these Christians abundance to supply their need.

Let not the cries of the widow and fatherless call down the vengeance of Heaven upon us as a people. In the professed Christian world, there is enough expended in extravagant display, for jewels and ornaments, to supply the wants of all the hungry and clothe the naked in our towns and cities; and yet these professed followers of the meek and lowly Jesus need not deprive themselves of suitable food or comfortable clothing.

What will these church members say when confronted in the day of God by the worthy poor, the afflicted, the widows and fatherless, who have known pinching want for the meager necessities of life, while there was expended by these professed followers of Christ, for superfluous clothing, and needless ornaments expressly forbidden in the Word of God, enough to supply all their wants?

We see ladies professing godliness wear elegant gold chains, necklaces, rings, and other jewelry . . . while want stalks in the streets, and the suffering and destitute are on every side. These do not interest them, nor awaken their sympathy; but they will weep over the imaginary suffering depicted in the last novel. They have no ears for the cries of the needy, no eyes to behold the cold and almost naked forms of women and children around them. They look upon real want as a species of crime, and withdraw from suffering humanity as from a contagious disease. To such, Christ will say, "I was an hungred, and ye gave me no meat: I was thirsty, and ye gave me no drink: . . . sick, and in prison, and ye visited me not."

But on the other hand Christ says to the righteous: "For I was an hungred, and ye gave me meat: I was thirsty, and ye gave me drink: I was a stranger, and ye took me in: naked, and ye clothed me: I was sick, and ye visited me: I was in prison, and ye came unto me.". . . Thus Christ identifies His interest with that of suffering humanity. Deeds of love and charity done to the suffering are as though done to Himself.—*Review and Herald,* Nov. 21, 1878.

The Holy Spirit Will Empower for Witnessing

And with great power the apostles gave witness to the resurrection of the Lord Jesus. And great grace was upon them all. Acts 4:33, NKJV.

WHAT WAS THE result of the outpouring of the Spirit on the day of Pentecost? The glad tidings of a risen Savior were carried to the uttermost parts of the inhabited world. The hearts of the disciples were surcharged with a benevolence so full, so deep, so far-reaching, that it impelled them to go to the ends of the earth, testifying, God forbid that we should glory, save in the cross of our Lord Jesus Christ.

As they proclaimed the truth as it is in Jesus, hearts yielded to the power of the message. The church beheld converts flocking to it from all directions. Believers were reconverted. Sinners united with Christians in seeking the pearl of great price. Those who had been the bitterest opponents of the gospel became its champions. . . . The only ambition of the believers was to reveal the likeness of Christ's character, and to labor for the enlargement of His kingdom. . . .

Under their labors there were added to the church chosen ones, who, receiving the word of life, consecrated their lives to the work of giving to others the hope that had filled their hearts with peace and joy. Hundreds proclaimed the message "The kingdom of God is at hand." They could not be restrained or intimidated by threatenings. The Lord spoke through them, and wherever they went, the sick were healed, and the poor had the gospel preached unto them. So mightily can God work when human beings give themselves up to the control of His Spirit.

To us today, as verily as to the first disciples, the promise of the Spirit belongs. God will today endow men and women with power from above, as He endowed those who on the day of Pentecost heard the message of salvation. At this very hour His Spirit and His grace are for all who need them and who will take Him at His word.

Notice that it was after the disciples had come into perfect unity, when they were no longer striving for the highest place, that the Spirit was poured out. They were of one accord. All differences had been put away. And the testimony borne of them after the Spirit had been given is the same. Mark the word: "The multitude of them that believed were of one heart and of one soul." The Spirit of Him who died that sinners might live animated the entire company of believers.—*Australasian Union Conference Record,* June 1, 1904.

God Gives Grace to Those Who Believe His Word

But without faith it is impossible to please Him, for he who comes to God must believe that He is, and that He is a rewarder of those who diligently seek Him. Hebrews 11:6, NKJV.

I HAVE BEEN shown that many have confused ideas in regard to conversion. They have often heard the words repeated from the pulpit, "Ye must be born again." "You must have a new heart." These expressions have perplexed them. They could not comprehend the plan of salvation.

Many have stumbled to ruin because of the erroneous doctrines taught by some ministers concerning the change that takes place at conversion. Some have lived in sadness for years, waiting for some marked evidence that they were accepted by God. They have separated themselves in a large measure from the world, and find pleasure in associating with the people of God; yet they dare not profess Christ, because they fear it would be presumption to say that they are children of God. They are waiting for that peculiar change that they have been led to believe is connected with conversion.

After a time some of these do receive evidence of their acceptance with God, and are then led to identify themselves with His people. And they date their conversion from this time. But I have been shown that they were adopted into the family of God before that time. God accepted them when they became weary of sin, and having lost their desire for worldly pleasures, resolved to seek God earnestly. But, failing to understand the simplicity of the plan of salvation, they lost many privileges and blessings which they might have claimed had they only believed, when they first turned to God, that He had accepted them.

Others fall into a more dangerous error. They are governed by impulse. Their sympathies are stirred, and they regard this flight of feeling as an evidence that they are accepted by God and are converted. But the principles of their life are not changed. The evidences of a genuine work of grace on the heart are to be found not in feeling, but in the life. "By their fruits," Christ declared, "ye shall know them." . . .

The work of grace upon the heart is not an instantaneous work. It is effected by continuous, daily watching and believing the promises of God. The repentant, believing ones, who cherish faith and earnestly desire the renewing grace of Christ, God will not turn away empty. He will give them grace. And ministering angels will aid them as they persevere in their efforts to advance.—*Evangelism,* pp. 286, 287.

One Small Book
Produced Big Results

Behold, a sower went out to sow. And as he sowed, some seed fell by the wayside. . . . But others fell on good ground and yielded a crop: some a hundredfold, some sixty, some thirty. He who has ears to hear, let him hear! Matthew 13:3-9, NKJV.

AFTER THE MEETING closed [a service at the Michigan camp meeting], a sister took me heartily by the hand, expressing great joy at meeting Sister White again. She inquired if I remembered calling at a log house in the woods twenty-two years before. She gave us refreshments, and I left with them a little book, *Experience and Views*.

She stated that she had lent that little book to her neighbors, as new families had settled around her, until there was very little left of it; and she expressed a great desire to obtain another copy of the work. Her neighbors were deeply interested in it, and were desirous of seeing the writer. She said that when I called upon her I talked to her of Jesus and the beauties of heaven, and that the words were spoken with such fervor that she was charmed, and had never forgotten them.

Since that time the Lord had sent ministers to preach the truth to them, and now there was quite a company observing the Sabbath. The influence of that little book, now worn out with perusing, had extended from one to another, performing its silent work, until the soil was ready for the seeds of truth.

I well remember the long journey we took twenty-two years ago, in Michigan. We were on our way to hold a meeting in Vergennes. We were fifteen miles from our destination. Our driver had passed over the road repeatedly and was well acquainted with it, but was compelled to acknowledge that he had lost the way. We traveled forty miles that day, through the woods, over logs and fallen trees, where there was scarcely a trace of road. . . .

We could not understand why we should be left to this singular wandering in the wilderness. We were never more pleased than when we came in sight of a little clearing on which was a log cabin, where we found the sister I have mentioned. She kindly welcomed us to her home, and provided us with refreshments, which were gratefully received. As we rested, I talked with the family and left them the little book. She gladly accepted it, and has preserved it until the present time.

For twenty-two years our wanderings on this journey have seemed indeed mysterious to us, but here we met quite a company who are now believers in the truth, and who date their first experience from the influence of that little book.—*Signs of the Times*, Oct. 19, 1876.

Personal Ministry Is Key to Winning Souls

Then they came to Him, bringing a paralytic who was carried by four men. . . . When Jesus saw their faith, He said to the paralytic, "Son, your sins are forgiven you." Mark 2:3-5, NKJV.

THERE IS NEED of coming close to the people by personal effort. If less time were given to sermonizing, and more time were spent in personal ministry, greater results would be seen. The poor are to be relieved, the sick cared for, the sorrowing and the bereaved comforted, the ignorant instructed, the inexperienced counseled. We are to weep with those that weep, and rejoice with those that rejoice. Accompanied by the power of persuasion, the power of prayer, the power of the love of God, this work will not, cannot, be without fruit.

We should ever remember that the object of the medical missionary work is to point sin-sick men and women to the Man of Calvary, who taketh away the sin of the world. By beholding Him, they will be changed into His likeness. We are to encourage the sick and suffering to look to Jesus and live. Let the workers keep Christ, the Great Physician, constantly before those to whom disease of body and soul has brought discouragement. . . . Encourage them to place themselves in the care of Him who gave His life to make it possible for them to have life eternal. Talk of His love; tell of His power to save.

This is the high duty and precious privilege of the medical missionary. And personal ministry often prepares the way for this. God often reaches hearts through our efforts to relieve physical suffering. . . .

In almost every community there are large numbers who do not listen to the preaching of God's Word or attend any religious service. If they are reached by the gospel, it must be carried to their homes. Often the relief of their physical needs is the only avenue by which they can be approached.

Missionary nurses who care for the sick and relieve the distress of the poor will find many opportunities to pray with them, to read to them from God's Word, and to speak of the Savior. They can pray with and for the helpless ones who have not strength of will to control the appetites that passion has degraded. They can bring a ray of hope into the lives of the defeated and disheartened. Their unselfish love, manifested in acts of disinterested kindness, will make it easier for these suffering ones to believe in the love of Christ.—*The Ministry of Healing,* pp. 143-145.

Make Clear the Worth of the Soul

Take heed to yourself and to the doctrine. Continue in them, for in doing this you will save both yourself and those who hear you. 1 Timothy 4:16, NKJV.

THE WORK YOU are doing to help our sisters feel their individual accountability to God is a good and necessary work. Long has it been neglected; but when this work has been laid out in clear lines, simple and definite, we may expect that the essential duties of the home, instead of being neglected, will be done much more intelligently. The Lord would ever have us urge, upon those who do not understand, the worth of the human soul.

If we can arrange, as you are now working, to have regularly organized companies intelligently instructed in regard to the part they should act as servants of the Master, our churches will have life and vitality such as have been so long needed.

Christ our Savior appreciated the excellency of the soul. Our sisters have generally a very hard time, with their increasing families and their unappreciated trials. I have so longed for women who could be educators to help them to arise from their discouragement, and to feel that they could do a work for the Lord. And this effort is bringing rays of sunshine into their lives, and is being reflected upon the hearts of others. God will bless you, and all who shall unite with you, in this grand work.

Many youth as well as our older sisters manifest themselves shy of religious conversation. They do not take in the matter as it is. The Word of God must be their assurance, their hope, their peace. They close the windows that should open heavenward, and open the windows wide earthward. But when they shall see the excellency of the human soul, they will close the windows earthward, cease depending on earthly amusements and associations, break away from folly and sin, and will open the windows heavenward, that they may behold spiritual things. Then can they say, I will receive the light of the Sun of Righteousness, that I may shine forth to others.

The most successful toilers are those who will cheerfully work to serve God in small things. Every human being is to work with his or her own individual thread, weave it into the fabric that composes the web, and complete the pattern.—*Review and Herald,* May 9, 1899.

Music Can Attract
People to God's Message

Oh, sing to the Lord a new song! Sing to the Lord,
all the earth. Sing to the Lord, bless His name; proclaim the good
news of His salvation from day to day. Psalm 96:1, 2, NKJV.

A FEW NIGHTS since, my mind was much troubled in contemplating what we could do to get the truth before the people in these large cities. We are sure if they would only hear the message, some would receive the truth and in their turn communicate it to others.

The ministers warn their congregations and say it is dangerous doctrine that is presented, and if they go out to hear they will be deceived and deluded with this strange doctrine. The prejudices would be removed if we could get the people out to hear. We are praying over this matter and believe that the Lord will make a place for the message of warning and instruction to come to the people in these last days.

One night I seemed to be in a council meeting where these matters were being talked over. And a very grave, dignified man said, "You are praying for the Lord to raise up men and women of talent to give themselves to the work. You have talent in your midst which needs to be recognized."

Several wise propositions were made and then words were spoken in substance as I write them. He said, "I call your attention to the singing talent which should be cultivated; for the human voice in singing is one of God's entrusted talents to be employed to His glory. The enemy of righteousness makes a great account of this talent in his service. And that which is the gift of God, to be a blessing to souls, is perverted, misapplied, and serves the purpose of Satan.

"This talent of voice is a blessing if consecrated to the Lord to serve His cause. [Carrie Gribble] has talent, but it is not appreciated. Her position should be considered and her talent will attract the people, and they will hear the message of truth."—*Evangelism*, pp. 497, 498.

Truth Is to Be Lived, Not Merely Spoken

Say among the nations, "The Lord reigns; the world also is firmly established, it shall not be moved; He shall judge the peoples righteously." Psalm 96:10, NKJV.

MEN AND WOMEN are not to be spiritually dwarfed by a connection with the church, but strengthened, elevated, ennobled, prepared for the most sacred work ever committed to mortals. It is the Lord's purpose to have a well-trained army, ready to be called into action at a moment's notice. This army will be made up of well-disciplined men and women who have placed themselves under influences that have prepared them for service.

God's workers are to watch for souls as they that must give an account, and they need the abiding presence of Christ in their hearts, in order that they may win sinners to Him. They must themselves have surrendered all to God, that they may tell those for whom they labor the need and meaning of unreserved surrender. They must remember that they are laborers together with God, and must guard against dilatory, uncertain movements. Satan watches untiringly for opportunities to gain control of those whom they are seeking to win to Christ. Only through ceaseless vigilance can the workers for Jesus beat back the enemy. Only in the strength of the Redeemer can they lead the tempted one to the cross. It is not learning nor eloquence that will accomplish this, but the presentation of the truth of God, spoken in simplicity and with the power of the Spirit.

There is only one power that can turn the sinner from sin to holiness—the power of Christ. Our Redeemer is the only one who can take away sin. He alone can forgive sin. He alone can make men and women steadfast, and keep them so.

The truth is not merely to be spoken by those who work for Christ; it is to be lived. People are watching and weighing those who claim to believe the special truths for this time. They are watching to see wherein their life represents Christ. By humbly and earnestly engaging in the work of doing good to all, God's people will exert an influence that will tell on all with whom they are brought in contact. If those who know the truth will take hold of this work as opportunities are presented, day by day doing deeds of love and kindness in the neighborhood where they live, Christ will be revealed in their lives.—*Review and Herald,* June 2, 1903.

Aim High and Attempt Much for God

By faith Enoch was taken away so that he did not see death,
"and was not found, because God had taken him"; for before he was
taken he had this testimony, that he pleased God. Hebrews 11:5, NKJV.

THE LORD HAS a great work to be done, and He will bequeath the most in the future life to those who do the most faithful, willing service in the present life. The Lord chooses His own agents, and each day under different circumstances He gives them a trial in His plan of operation. In each truehearted endeavor to work out His plan, He chooses His agents not because they are perfect but because, through a connection with Him, they may gain perfection.

God will accept only those who are determined to aim high. He places every human agent under obligation to do his or her best. Moral perfection is required of all. Never should we lower the standard of righteousness in order to accommodate inherited or cultivated tendencies to wrongdoing. We need to understand that imperfection of character is sin. All righteous attributes of character dwell in God as a perfect, harmonious whole, and everyone who receives Christ as a personal Savior is privileged to possess these attributes. . . .

Let no one say, I cannot remedy my defects of character. If you come to this decision, you will certainly fail of obtaining everlasting life. The impossibility lies in your own will. If you will not, then you cannot overcome. The real difficulty arises from the corruption of an unsanctified heart, and an unwillingness to submit to the control of God.

Many whom God has qualified to do excellent work accomplish very little, because they attempt little. Thousands pass through life as if they had no definite object for which to live, no standard to reach. Such will obtain a reward proportionate to their works. . . .

Be ambitious, for the Master's glory, to cultivate every grace of character. In every phase of your character building you are to please God. This you may do; for Enoch pleased Him though living in a degenerate age. And there are Enochs in this our day.—*Christ's Object Lessons*, pp. 330-332.

Witness at Every
Large Gathering in Cities

*And they were astonished at His teaching, for
His word was with authority. Luke 4:32, NKJV.*

I WAS GIVEN instruction that as we approach the end, there will be large gatherings in our cities . . . and that preparations must be made to present the truth at these gatherings. When Christ was upon this earth, He took advantage of such opportunities. Wherever a large number of people were gathered for any purpose, His voice was heard, clear and distinct, giving His message. And as a result, after His crucifixion and ascension, thousands were converted in a day. The seed sown by Christ sank deep into hearts, and germinated, and when the disciples received the gift of the Holy Spirit, the harvest was gathered in.

The disciples went forth and preached the Word everywhere with such power that fear fell upon their opposers, and they dared not do that which they would have done had not the evidence been so plain that God was working.

At every large gathering some of our ministers should be in attendance. They should work wisely to obtain a hearing and to get the light of the truth before as many as possible. . . .

At all such gatherings there should be present men and women whom God can use. Leaflets containing the light of present truth should be scattered among the people like the leaves of autumn. To many who attend these gatherings these leaflets would be as the leaves of the tree of life, which are for the healing of the nations.

I send you this, my brethren, that you may give it to others. Those who go forth to proclaim the truth shall be blessed by Him who has given them the burden of proclaiming this truth. . . .

The time has come when, as never before, Seventh-day Adventists are to arise and shine, because their light has come, and the glory of the Lord has risen upon them.—*Evangelism*, pp. 35, 36.

Christ's Followers to Differ From the World

But you are a chosen generation, a royal priesthood, a holy nation,
His own special people, that you may proclaim the praises of Him who
called you out of darkness into His marvelous light. 1 Peter 2:9, NKJV.

AS WE READ the Word of God, how plain it appears that His people are to be peculiar and distinct from the unbelieving world around them. Our position is interesting and fearful; living in the last days, how important that we imitate the example of Christ, and walk even as He walked. "If any man will come after me, let him deny himself, and take up his cross, and follow me." The opinions and wisdom of mortals must not guide or govern us. They always lead away from the cross.

The servants of Christ have neither their home nor their treasure here. Would that all of them could understand that it is only because the Lord reigns that we are even permitted to dwell in peace and safety among our enemies. It is not our privilege to claim special favors of the world. We must consent to be poor and despised among men and women, until the warfare is finished and the victory won. The members of Christ are called to come out and be separate from the friendship and spirit of the world; their strength and power consists in being chosen and accepted of God. . . .

The world is ripening for its destruction. God can bear with sinners but a little longer. They must drink the dregs of the cup of His wrath unmixed with mercy. Those who will be heirs of God, and joint heirs with Christ to the immortal inheritance, will be peculiar. Yes, so peculiar that God places a mark upon them as His, wholly His. Think ye that God will receive, honor, and acknowledge a people so mixed up with the world that they differ from them only in name? Read again Titus 2:13-15. It is soon to be known who is on the Lord's side, who will not be ashamed of Jesus. Those who have not moral courage to conscientiously take their position in the face of unbelievers, leave the fashions of the world, and imitate the self-denying life of Christ are ashamed of Him, and do not love His example.—*Testimonies for the Church,* vol. 1, pp. 286, 287.

Win Souls Through the Sabbath School

Jesus answered and said to him, "Most assuredly, I say to you, unless one is born again, he cannot see the kingdom of God." John 3:3, NKJV.

THE SABBATH SCHOOL teacher should be a laborer together with God, cooperating with Christ. Do not be content with a lifeless, formal religion. The object of Sabbath school work should be the ingathering of souls. The order of working may be faultless, the facilities all that could be desired; but if the children and youth are not brought to Christ, the school is a failure; for unless souls are drawn to Christ, they become more and more unimpressionable under the influence of a formal religion.

The teacher should cooperate, as He knocks at the door of the heart of those who need help. If pupils respond to the pleading of the Spirit, and open the door of the heart, that Jesus may come in, He will open their understanding, that they may comprehend the things of God. The teacher's work is simple work, but if it is done in the Spirit of Jesus, depth and efficiency will be added to it by the operation of the Spirit of God.

There should be much personal work done in the Sabbath school. The necessity of this kind of work is not recognized and appreciated as it should be. From a heart filled with gratitude for the love of God, which has been imparted to the soul, the teacher should labor tenderly and earnestly for the conversion of the scholars.

What evidence can we give to the world that the Sabbath school work is not a mere pretense? It will be judged by its fruits. It will be estimated by the character and work of the pupils. In our Sabbath schools the Christian youth should be entrusted with responsibilities, that they may develop their abilities and gain spiritual power.

Let the youth first give themselves to God, and then let them in their early experience be taught to help others. This work will bring their faculties into exercise and enable them to learn how to plan and how to execute their plans for the good of their associates. Let them seek the company of those who need help, not to engage in foolish conversation, but to represent Christian character, to be laborers together with God, winning those who have not given themselves to God.—*Testimonies on Sabbath School Work*, pp. 47, 48.

Work to Be
Done in Large Cities

*The people who walked in darkness have seen a great light; those who dwelt in
the land of the shadow of death, upon them a light has shined. Isaiah 9:2, NKJV.*

EVERY CHRISTIAN WILL have a missionary spirit. To bear fruit is to
work as Christ worked, to love souls as He has loved us. The very first
impulse of the renewed heart is to bring others also to the Savior: and
just as soon as a person is converted to the truth, he or she feels an earnest
desire that those in darkness should see the precious light shining from
God's Word. . . .

Missionaries are needed to spread the light of truth in . . . great cities,
and the children of God—those whom He calls the light of the world—
ought to be doing all they can in this direction. You will meet with discouragements; you will have opposition. The enemy will whisper, What
can these few poor people do in this great city? But if you walk in the light,
you can every one be light bearers to the world.

Do not seek to accomplish some great work, and neglect the little
opportunities close at hand. We can do very much by exemplifying the
truth in our daily life. The influence which we may thus exert cannot be
easily withstood.

People may combat and defy our logic; they may resist our appeals; but
a life of holy purpose, of disinterested love in their behalf, is an argument
in favor of the truth that they cannot gainsay. Far more can be accomplished by humble, devoted, virtuous lives than can be effected by preaching when a godly example is lacking. You can labor to build up the
church, to encourage your fellow believers, and to make the social meetings interesting; and you can let your prayers go out, like sharp sickles,
with the laborers into the harvest field. Each should have a personal interest, a burden of soul, to watch and pray for the success of the work.

You can also in meekness call the attention of others to the precious
truths of God's Word. Young men should be instructed that they may
labor in these cities. They may never be able to present the truth from the
desk, but they could go from house to house, and point the people to the
Lamb of God that taketh away the sin of the world. The dust and rubbish
of error have buried the precious jewels of truth; but the Lord's workers
can uncover these treasures, so that many will look upon them with delight and awe.—*Historical Sketches of the Foreign Missions of the Seventh-day
Adventists,* pp. 181, 182.

Expressions of Sympathy
Open Hearts to the Gospel

Love never fails. But whether there are prophecies,
they will fail; whether there are tongues, they will cease; whether
there is knowledge, it will vanish away. 1 Corinthians 13:8, NKJV.

GOD EXPECTS PERSONAL service from everyone to whom He has entrusted a knowledge of the truth for this time. Not all can go as missionaries to foreign lands, but all can be home missionaries in their families and neighborhoods. There are many ways in which church members may give the message to those around them. One of the most successful is by living helpful, unselfish, Christian lives.

Those who are fighting the battle of life at great odds may be refreshed and strengthened by little attentions which cost nothing. Kindly words simply spoken, little attentions simply bestowed, will sweep away the clouds of temptation and doubt that gather over the soul. The true heart expression of Christlike sympathy, given in simplicity, has power to open the door of hearts that need the simple, delicate touch of the spirit of Christ.

Christ accepts, oh, so gladly, every human agency that is surrendered to Him. He brings the human into union with the divine, that He may communicate to the world the mysteries of incarnate love. Talk it, pray it, sing it, fill the world with the message of His truth, and keep pressing on into the regions beyond.

Heavenly intelligences are waiting to cooperate with human instrumentalities, that they may reveal to the world what human beings may become and what, through their influence, they may accomplish for the saving of souls that are ready to perish. Those who are truly converted will be so filled with the love of God that they will long to impart to others the joy that they themselves possess.

The Lord desires His church to show forth to the world the beauty of holiness. It is to demonstrate the power of Christian religion. Heaven is to be reflected in the character of the Christian. The song of gratitude and praise is to be heard by those in darkness.

For the good tidings of the gospel, for its promises and assurances, we are to express our gratitude by seeking to do others good. The doing of this work will bring rays of heavenly righteousness to wearied, perplexed, suffering souls. It is as a fountain opened for the wayworn, thirsty traveler. At every work of mercy, every work of love, angels of God are present.—
Testimonies for the Church, vol. 9, pp. 30, 31.

Soul Winning Creates
Demand for Holy Spirit

Arise, shine; for your light has come! And the glory of the Lord is risen upon you.
For behold, the darkness shall cover the earth, and deep darkness the people; but the
Lord will arise over you, and His glory will be seen upon you. Isaiah 60:1, 2, NKJV.

OUR REDEEMER spent whole nights in prayer to His Father; and the foundation of the Christian church and missionary activity was laid in the very element of prayer. The disciples were of one accord in one place, calling upon the Lord that the outpouring of His Holy Spirit might come upon them.

While the Holy Spirit is given richly through various channels, the more we seek it the wider will be the diffusion. Thus, earnest work being done to save souls, there will be constantly furnished us a necessity for renewed application to the Source of all power; and thus there will be established an habitual communication between the soul and God. The fountain of the water of life is constantly drawn upon by faith, and is never exhausted.

The work is progressive—action and reaction. Love and devotion to God will give activity to benevolence, and benevolence will increase faith and spirituality. Oh, how much we need heavenly wisdom! Well, is it not promised us? "If any of you lack wisdom, let him ask of God, that giveth to all men liberally, and upbraideth not; and it shall be given him. But let him ask in faith, nothing wavering. For he that wavereth is like a wave of the sea driven with the wind and tossed. For let not that man think that he shall receive any thing of the Lord." Oh, what an assurance is this! How full and broad! Let us take the promise just as it reads. The Lord wants us to come unto Him with full assurance of faith, believing His word, that He will do just as He said He would.

Would that we might feel the importance of educating every individual member of the church to do something. We should individually sense the solemn obligation of Christians to bring into activity all their divinely entrusted resources and capabilities, to do to the utmost of their power the work the Lord expects them to do. . . .

We need more faith, more sanctified ability. High and ennobling motives are before us. We have no time, no words to spend in controversy. . . . There is need of sanctified energy. The armies of heaven are on the move, and where is the human agent to cooperate with God?—*Testimonies to Southern Africa, pp. 43, 44.*

Consecrated Workers Could Do Great Work in Short Time

*Now the whole group of those who believed were of one heart
and one soul, and no one claimed private ownership of any possessions,
but everything they owned was held in common. Acts 4:32, NRSV.*

THE WORLD NEEDS missionaries, consecrated home missionaries, and no one will be registered in the books of heaven as a Christian who has not a missionary spirit. But we can do nothing without sanctified energy. Just as soon as the missionary spirit is lost from the heart, and zeal for the cause of God begins to wane, the burden of our testimonies and plans is a cry for prudence and economy, and real backsliding begins in the missionary work.

Instead of diminishing the work, let all the councils be conducted in such a manner that increased purpose may be manifested to carry forward the great work of warning the world, though it may cost self-denial and sacrifice. If every member of the church was constantly impressed with the thought, I am not my own, but have been bought with a price, all would feel that they are under the most sacred obligation to improve every ability given of God, to double their usefulness year by year, and have no excuse for spiritual negligence. Then there would be no lack of sympathy with the Master in the great work of saving souls.

Who are there among us that with spiritual perception can discern the stirring conflict that is going on in the world between the forces of good and evil? Do you understand the nature of the great controversy between Christ, the Prince of life, and Satan, the prince of darkness? Does the conflict appear the same to you as it appears to the heavenly intelligences?

Oh, if all who professed to be followers of Christ were indeed living channels of light to the world, imbued by the Spirit of God, with hearts full to overflowing with the gospel message, with the very countenance beaming with devotion to God and love to others, what a work might be accomplished in a short time! The messengers of the truth would not speak with hesitation, with uncertainty, but with fearlessness and confidence. Their words and the very tones of the voice would strike conviction to the hearts of the hearers.—*Review and Herald,* Aug. 23, 1892.

Workers to Reveal
the Spirit of Jesus

The night is far spent, the day is at hand. Therefore let us cast off the works of darkness, and let us put on the armor of light. Romans 13:12, NKJV.

AFTER MOST EARNEST efforts have been made to bring the truth before those whom God has entrusted with large responsibilities, be not discouraged if they reject it. Truth was rejected in the days of Christ. Be sure to maintain the dignity of the work by well-ordered plans and a godly conversation.

Never be afraid of elevating the standard too high. The families who engage in this missionary work should come close to hearts. The spirit of Jesus should pervade the souls of the workers; for it is the pleasant, sympathetic words, the manifestation of disinterested love for souls, that will break down the barriers of pride and selfishness, and show to unbelievers that we have the love of Christ, and then the truth will find its way to their hearts. This is our work and the fulfilling of God's plans.

All coarseness and roughness must be purged from us. Courtesy, refinement, and Christian politeness must be cherished. Guard against being abrupt and blunt. Do not regard such peculiarities as virtues, for God does not so regard them. But seek in all things not to offend those who are not of our faith. Never make the most objectionable features of our faith stand out prominently, when there is no call for it. Such a course is only an injury to the cause.

All should seek to have the softening, subduing influence of the Spirit of God in the heart—Christlike tenderness and love for souls. Those who are sent out to labor together should put away their peculiar notions and set ideas, and seek to labor together, heart and soul, to carry out God's will. They must plan to work in harmony in order to work to advantage.

We want more, much more, of the Spirit of Christ, and less, much less, of self and the peculiarities of character which build up a wall to keep us apart from our fellow beings. We can do much to break down these barriers by revealing the graces of Christ in our lives. Jesus has been trusting His goods to the church, age after age. One generation after another for century after century have been gathering up their hereditary trust until the increasing responsibilities have descended to our time. . . . We want to be clothed, not in our own garments, but in the whole armor of Christ's righteousness.—*Atlantic Canvasser,* Dec. 18, 1890.

285

Consecrate Self, Then Search for Perishing Souls

The voice of one crying in the wilderness: "Prepare the way of the Lord; make straight in the desert a highway for our God." Isaiah 40:3, NKJV.

DO YOU FEEL the sanctifying power of sacred truth in heart and life and character? Have you the assurance that God, for the sake of His dear Son, has forgiven your sins? Are you striving to live with a conscience void of offense toward God and humanity? Do you often plead with God in behalf of your friends and neighbors? If you have made your peace with God, and have placed all upon the altar, you may engage with profit in soul-winning service.

In following any plan that may be set in operation for carrying to others a knowledge of present truth and of the marvelous providences connected with the advancing cause, let us first consecrate ourselves fully to Him whose name we wish to exalt. Let us also pray earnestly in behalf of those whom we expect to visit, by living faith bringing them, one by one, into the presence of God.

The Lord knows our thoughts and purposes, and how easily can He melt us! How His Spirit, like a fire, can subdue the flinty heart! How He can fill the soul with love and tenderness! How He can give us the graces of His Spirit, and fit us to go in and out, in laboring for souls!

The power of overcoming grace should be felt throughout the church today; and it may be felt, if we take heed to the counsels of Christ to His followers. As we learn to adorn the doctrine of Christ our Savior, we shall surely see of the salvation of God.

To all who are about to take up special missionary work . . . I would say: Be diligent in your efforts; live under the guidance of the Holy Spirit. Add daily to your Christian experience. Let those who have special aptitude work for unbelievers in the high places as well as in the low places of life. Search diligently for perishing souls. Oh, think of the yearning desire Christ has to bring to His fold again those who have gone astray!

Watch for souls as they that must give an account. In your church and neighborhood missionary work, let your light shine forth in such clear, steady rays that no one can stand up in the judgment and say, "Why did you not tell me about this truth? Why did you not care for my soul?"—*Church Officers' Gazette*, September 1914.

Unselfish Service Gives Joy to Both Christ and Us

Let us not grow weary while doing good, for in due season
we shall reap if we do not lose heart. Galatians 6:9, NKJV.

IN THIS LIFE our work for God often seems to be almost fruitless. Our efforts to do good may be earnest and persevering, yet we may not be permitted to witness their results. To us the effort may seem to be lost. But the Savior assures us that our work is noted in heaven, and that the recompense cannot fail. . . . In the words of the psalmist we read: "He that goeth forth and weepeth, bearing precious seed, shall doubtless come again with rejoicing, bringing his sheaves with him" (Ps. 126:6).

And while the great final reward is given at Christ's coming, true-hearted service for God brings a reward even in this life. Obstacles, opposition, and bitter, heartbreaking discouragements the workers will have to meet. They may not see the fruit of their toil. But in face of all this they find in their labor a blessed recompense.

All who surrender themselves to God in unselfish service for humanity are in cooperation with the Lord of glory. This thought sweetens all toil, it braces the will, it nerves the spirit for whatever may befall. Working with unselfish heart, ennobled by being partakers of Christ's sufferings, sharing His sympathies, they help to swell the tide of His joy, and bring honor and praise to His exalted name.

In fellowship with God, with Christ, and with holy angels they are surrounded with a heavenly atmosphere, an atmosphere that brings health to the body, vigor to the intellect, and joy to the soul.

All who consecrate body, soul, and spirit to God's service will be constantly receiving a new endowment of physical, mental, and spiritual power. The inexhaustible supplies of heaven are at their command. Christ gives them the breath of His own Spirit, the life of His own life. The Holy Spirit puts forth its highest energies to work in heart and mind.—*Testimonies for the Church,* vol. 6, pp. 305, 306.

Every Member to Help Spread the Gospel

Then Jesus spoke to them again, saying, "I am the light of the world. He who follows Me shall not walk in darkness, but have the light of life." John 8:12, NKJV.

THOSE WHO FOLLOW Jesus will be laborers together with God. They will not walk in darkness, but will find the true path where Jesus, the Light of the world, leads the way; and as they bend their steps Zionward, moving on in faith, they will attain unto a bright experience in the things of God. The mission of Christ, so dimly understood, so faintly comprehended, that called Him from the throne of God to the mystery of the altar of the cross of Calvary, will more and more unfold to the mind, and it will be seen that in the sacrifice of Christ are found the spring and principle of every other mission of love. It is the love of Christ which has been the incentive of every true missionary worker in cities, in towns, in the highways and the byways of the world.

The church of Christ has been organized on earth for missionary purposes, and it is of the highest importance that every individual member of the church should be a sincere laborer together with God, filled with the Spirit, having the mind of Christ, perfected in sympathy with Christ, and therefore bending every energy according to his or her entrusted ability to the saving of souls. Christ requires that everyone who would be called by His name should make His work the first and highest consideration, and disinterestedly cooperate with heavenly intelligences in saving the perishing for whom Christ has died.

To misapply means or influence or any entrusted capital of mind or body is to rob God and to rob the world; for it is turning the energies into another channel than that in which God designed they should move for the salvation of the world. When Christ was here upon earth, He sent out His disciples to proclaim the kingdom of God throughout Judea, and in this example He clearly revealed that it is the duty of His people throughout all time to impart to others the knowledge they have of the way, the life, and the truth. In all His labors Jesus sought to train His church for missionary work, and as their numbers increased, their mission would extend, until eventually the gospel message would belt the world through their ministrations.—*Review and Herald,* Oct. 30, 1894.

OCTOBER

∾

Enjoying Good Health

Everyone Should Know
and Obey the Laws of Life

My son, give attention to my words; incline your ear to my sayings. Do not let them depart from your eyes; keep them in the midst of your heart; for they are life to those who find them, and health to all their flesh. Proverbs 4:20-22, NKJV.

PURE AIR, SUNLIGHT, abstemiousness, rest, exercise, proper diet, the use of water, trust in divine power—these are the true remedies. Every person should have a knowledge of nature's remedial agencies and how to apply them. It is essential both to understand the principles involved in the treatment of the sick and to have a practical training that will enable one rightly to use this knowledge.

The use of natural remedies requires an amount of care and effort that many are not willing to give. Nature's process of healing and upbuilding is gradual, and to the impatient it seems slow. The surrender of hurtful indulgences requires sacrifice. But in the end it will be found that nature, untrammeled, does its work wisely and well. Those who persevere in obedience to its laws will reap the reward in health of body and health of mind.

Too little attention is generally given to the preservation of health. It is far better to prevent disease than to know how to treat it when contracted. It is the duty of every person, for one's own sake, and for the sake of humanity, to inform himself or herself in regard to the laws of life and conscientiously to obey them. All need to become acquainted with that most wonderful of all organisms, the human body. They should understand the functions of the various organs and the dependence of one upon another for the healthy action of all. They should study the influence of the mind upon the body, and of the body upon the mind, and the laws by which they are governed.

We cannot be too often reminded that health does not depend on chance. It is a result of obedience to law. This is recognized by the contestants in athletic games and trials of strength. These men and women make the most careful preparation. They submit to thorough training and strict discipline. Every physical habit is carefully regulated. They know that neglect, excess, or carelessness, which weakens or cripples any organ or function of the body, would ensure defeat. . . .

In view of the issues at stake, nothing with which we have to do is small. Every act casts its weight into the scale that determines life's victory or defeat. The scriptures bid us, "So run, that ye may obtain."—*The Ministry of Healing*, pp. 127-129.

Leaders to Practice
and Teach Health Reform

Come and see what God has done: he is awesome
in his deeds among mortals. Psalm 66:5, NRSV.

THE CHURCH IS making history. Every day is a battle and a march. On every side we are beset by invisible foes, and we either conquer through the grace given us by God or we are conquered. I urge that those who are taking a neutral position in regard to health reform be converted. This light is precious, and the Lord gives me the message to urge that all who bear responsibilities in any line in the work of God take heed that truth is in the ascendancy in the heart and life. Only thus can any meet the temptations they are sure to encounter in the world.

Why do some of our ministers manifest so little interest in health reform? It is because instruction on temperance in all things is opposed to their practice of self-indulgence. In some places this has been the great stumblingblock in the way of our bringing the people to investigate and practice and teach health reform. No one should be set apart as a teacher of the people while his or her own teaching or example contradicts the testimony God has given His servants to bear in regard to diet, for this will bring confusion. Disregard of health reform unfits one to stand as the Lord's messenger.

The light that the Lord has given on this subject in His Word is plain, and leaders will be tested and tried in many ways to see if they will heed it. Every church, every family, needs to be instructed in regard to Christian temperance. All should know how to eat and drink in order to preserve health. We are amid the closing scenes of this world's history; and there should be harmonious action in the ranks of Sabbathkeepers. Those who stand aloof from the great work of instructing the people upon this question do not follow where the Great Physician leads the way. "If any man will come after me," Christ said, "let him deny himself, and take up his cross, and follow me" (Matt. 16:24).

The Lord has presented before me that many, many will be rescued from physical, mental, and moral degeneracy through the practical influence of health reform. Health talks will be given; publications will be multiplied. The principles of health reform will be received with favor; and many will be enlightened. The influences that are associated with health reform will commend it to the judgment of all who want light; and they will advance step by step to receive the special truths for this time. Thus truth and righteousness will meet together.—*Review and Herald*, June 18, 1914.

It's Time to Give Up
Health-destroying Indulgences

Trust in the Lord with all your heart, and lean not on your own understanding; in all your ways acknowledge Him, and He shall direct your paths. Proverbs 3:5, 6, NKJV.

THERE IS A message regarding health reform to be borne in every church. There is a work to be done in every school. Neither principal nor teachers should be entrusted with the education of the youth until they have a practical knowledge of this subject. Some have felt at liberty to criticize and question and find fault with health reform principles of which they knew little by experience. They should stand shoulder to shoulder, heart to heart, with those who are working in right lines.

The subject of health reform has been presented in the churches; but the light has not been heartily received. The selfish, health-destroying indulgences of men and women have counteracted the influence of the message that is to prepare a people for the great day of God. If the churches expect strength, they must live the truth which God has given them. If the members of our churches disregard the light on this subject, they will reap the sure result in both spiritual and physical degeneracy. And the influence of these older church members will leaven those newly come to the faith.

The Lord does not now work to bring many souls into the truth, because of the church members who have never been converted and those who were once converted but who have backslidden. What influence would these unconsecrated members have on new converts? Would they not make of no effect the God-given message which His people are to bear?

Let all examine their own practices to see if they are not indulging in that which is a positive injury to them. Let them dispense with every unhealthful gratification in eating and drinking. Some go to distant countries to seek a better climate; but wherever they may be, the stomach creates for them a malarious atmosphere. They bring upon themselves suffering that no one can alleviate. Let them bring their daily practice into harmony with nature's laws; and by doing as well as believing, an atmosphere may be created about both soul and body that will be a savor of life unto life.—*Testimonies for the Church,* vol. 6, pp. 370, 371.

Share the Light
on Healthful Living

Then your light shall break forth like the morning, your healing
shall spring forth speedily, and your righteousness shall go before you;
the glory of the Lord shall be your rear guard. Isaiah 58:8, NKJV.

OUR MINISTERS SHOULD become intelligent on health reform. They need to become acquainted with physiology and hygiene; they should understand the laws that govern physical life, and their bearing upon the health of mind and soul.

Thousands upon thousands know little of the wonderful body God has given them or of the care it should receive; and they consider it of more importance to study subjects of far less consequence. The ministers have a work to do here. When they take a right position on this subject, much will be gained. In their own lives and homes they should obey the laws of life, practicing right principles and living healthfully. Then they will be able to speak correctly on this subject, leading the people higher and still higher in the work of reform. Living in the light themselves, they can bear a message of great value to those who are in need of just such a testimony.

There are precious blessings and a rich experience to be gained if ministers will combine the presentation of the health question with all their labors in the churches. The people must have the light on health reform. This work has been neglected, and many are ready to die because they need the light which they ought to have and must have before they will give up selfish indulgence.

The presidents of our conferences need to realize that it is high time they were placing themselves on the right side of this question. Ministers and teachers are to give to others the light they have received. Their work in every line is needed. God will help them; He will strengthen His servants who stand firmly, and will not be swayed from truth and righteousness in order to accommodate self-indulgence.

The work of educating in medical missionary lines is an advance step of great importance in awakening men and women to their moral responsibilities. Had the ministers taken hold of this work in its various departments in accordance with the light which God has given, there would have been a most decided reformation in eating, drinking, and dressing. . . . They themselves and a large number of others have been sufferers unto death, but all have not yet learned wisdom.—*Counsels on Diet and Foods*, pp. 452, 453.

Nutritious Diet Important
for Intellectual Vigor

Daniel purposed in his heart that he would not defile himself with the portion of the king's delicacies, nor with the wine which he drank; therefore he requested of the chief of the eunuchs that he might not defile himself. Daniel 1:8, NKJV.

THE HUMAN INTELLECT must gain expansion and vigor and acuteness and activity. It must be taxed to do hard work, or it will become weak and inefficient. Brainpower is required to think most earnestly; it must be put to the stretch to solve hard problems and master them, else the mind decreases in power and aptitude to think. The mind must invent, work, and wrestle, in order to give hardness and vigor to the intellect; and if the physical organs are not kept in the most healthful condition by substantial, nourishing food, the brain does not receive its portion of nutrition to work.

Daniel understood this, and he brought himself to a plain, simple, nutritious diet, and refused the luxuries of the king's table. The desserts which take so much time to prepare are, many of them, detrimental to health. Solid foods requiring mastication will be far better than mush or liquid foods. I dwell upon this as essential. . . .

The intellect is to be kept thoroughly awake with new, earnest, wholehearted work. How is it to be done? The power of the Holy Spirit must purify the thoughts and cleanse the soul of its moral defilement. Defiling habits not only abase the soul, but debase the intellect. Memory suffers, laid on the altar of base, hurtful practices. . . .

When teachers and learners shall consecrate soul, body, and spirit to God, and purify their thoughts by obedience to the laws of God, they will continually receive a new endowment of physical and mental power. Then will there be heart-yearnings after God, and earnest prayer for clear perception to discern. . . .

Diligent study is essential, and diligent hard work. . . . A well-balanced mind is not usually obtained in the devotion of the physical powers to amusements. Physical labor that is combined with mental taxation for usefulness is a discipline in practical life, sweetened always by the reflection that it is qualifying and educating the mind and body better to perform the work God designs us to do in various lines. . . . The mind thus educated to enjoy physical taxation in practical life becomes enlarged and, through culture and training, well disciplined and richly furnished for usefulness, and acquires a knowledge essential to be a help and blessing to themselves and to others.—*Fundamentals of Christian Education,* pp. 226-229.

Higher Powers to Control Physical Nature

Everyone who competes for the prize is temperate in all things. Now
they do it to obtain a perishable crown, but we for an imperishable crown. . . .
But I discipline my body and bring it into subjection, lest, when I have preached
to others, I myself should become disqualified. 1 Corinthians 9:25-27, NKJV.

THE PROGRESS OF reform depends upon a clear recognition of fundamental truth. While, on the one hand, danger lurks in a narrow philosophy and a hard, cold orthodoxy, on the other hand there is great danger in a careless liberalism. The foundation of all enduring reform is the law of God. We are to present in clear, distinct lines the need of obeying this law. Its principles must be kept before the people. They are as everlasting and inexorable as God Himself.

One of the most deplorable effects of the original apostasy was that people lost the power of self-control. Only as this power is regained can there be real progress.

The body is the only medium through which the mind and the soul are developed for the upbuilding of character. Hence it is that the adversary of souls directs his temptations to the enfeebling and degrading of the physical powers. His success here means the surrender to evil of the whole being. The tendencies of our physical nature, unless under the dominion of a higher power, will surely work ruin and death.

The body is to be brought into subjection. The higher powers of the being are to rule. The passions are to be controlled by the will, which is itself to be under the control of God. The kingly power of reason, sanctified by divine grace, is to bear sway in our lives.

The requirements of God must be brought home to the conscience. Men and women must be awakened to the duty of self-mastery, the need of purity, freedom from every depraving appetite and defiling habit. They need to be impressed with the fact that all their powers of mind and body are the gift of God, and are to be preserved in the best possible condition for His service.

In that ancient ritual which was the gospel in symbol, no blemished offering could be brought to God's altar. The sacrifice that was to represent Christ must be spotless. The Word of God points to this as an illustration of what His children are to be—"a living sacrifice," "holy and without blemish."—*The Ministry of Healing*, pp. 129, 130.

Good Health Needed
to Achieve Success

I will seek what was lost and bring back what was driven away,
bind up the broken and strengthen what was sick; but I will destroy the
fat and the strong, and feed them in judgment. Ezekiel 34:16, NKJV.

SINCE THE MIND and the soul find expression through the body, both mental and spiritual vigor are in great degree dependent upon physical strength and activity; whatever promotes physical health promotes the development of a strong mind and a well-balanced character. Without health no one can as distinctly understand or as completely fulfill his or her obligations to oneself, to other persons, or to the Creator. Therefore the health should be as faithfully guarded as the character. A knowledge of physiology and hygiene should be the basis of all educational effort.

Though the facts of physiology are now so generally understood, there is an alarming indifference in regard to the principles of health. Even of those who have a knowledge of these principles, there are few who put them in practice. Inclination or impulse is followed as blindly as if life were controlled by mere chance rather than by definite and unvarying laws.

The youth, in the freshness and vigor of life, little realize the value of their abounding energy. A treasure more precious than gold, more essential to advancement than learning or rank or riches—how lightly it is held! how rashly squandered! How many men and women, sacrificing health in the struggle for riches or power, have almost reached the object of their desire, only to fall helpless, while others, possessing superior physical endurance, grasped the longed-for prize! Through morbid conditions, the result of neglecting the laws of health, how many have been led into evil practices, to the sacrifice of every hope for this world and the next!

In the study of physiology, pupils should be led to see the value of physical energy and how it can be so preserved and developed as to contribute in the highest degree to success in life's great struggle.

Children should be early taught, in simple, easy lessons, the rudiments of physiology and hygiene. . . . They should understand the importance of guarding against disease by preserving the vigor of every organ and should also be taught how to deal with common diseases and accidents. Every school should give instruction in both physiology and hygiene, and, so far as possible, should be provided with facilities for illustrating the structure, use, and care of the body.—*Education,* pp. 195, 196.

Aim for Holiness,
Not Merely Health

I appeal to you therefore, brothers and sisters, by the
mercies of God, to present your bodies as a living sacrifice, holy and
acceptable to God, which is your spiritual worship. Romans 12:1, NRSV.

SHOULD THOSE CONNECTED with this enterprise [the Health Institute at Battle Creek] cease to look at their work from a high religious standpoint, and descend from the exalted principles of present truth to imitate in theory and practice those at the head of institutions where the sick are treated only for the recovery of health, the special blessing of God would not rest upon our institution more than upon those where corrupt theories are taught and practiced.

I saw that a very extensive work could not be accomplished in a short time, as it would not be an easy matter to find physicians whom God could approve and who would work together harmoniously, disinterestedly, and zealously for the good of suffering humanity. It should ever be kept prominent that the great object to be attained through this channel is not only health, but perfection, and the spirit of holiness, which cannot be attained with diseased bodies and minds. This object cannot be secured by working merely from the worldling's standpoint. God will raise up men and women and qualify them to engage in the work, not only as physicians of the body, but of the sin-sick soul, as spiritual parents to the young and inexperienced. . . .

The view that those who have abused both their physical and mental powers, or who have broken down in either mind or body, must suspend activity in order to regain health is a great error. In a very few cases entire rest for a short period may be necessary, but these instances are very rare. In most cases the change would be too great.

Those who have broken down by intense mental labor should have rest from wearing thought, yet to teach them that it is wrong and even dangerous for them to exercise their mental powers to a degree leads them to view their condition as worse than it really is. . . .

Those who have broken down by physical exertion must have less labor, and that which is light and pleasant. But to shut them away from all labor and exercise would in many cases prove their ruin. . . . Inactivity is the greatest curse that could come upon such. Their powers become so dormant that it is impossible for them to resist disease and languor, as they must do in order to regain health.—*Testimonies for the Church*, vol. 1, pp. 554-556.

Health Reform and
Third Angel's Message Closely Allied

Who gives food to all flesh, for His mercy endures forever. Oh, give thanks
to the God of heaven! For His mercy endures forever. Psalm 136:25, 26, NKJV.

THE LORD HAD in His providence given light in regard to the establishment of sanitariums where the sick should be treated upon hygienic principles. The people must be taught to depend on the Lord's remedies, pure
air, pure water, simple, healthful foods.

Every effort made for the physical and moral health of the people
should be based on moral principles. The advocates of reform who are laboring with the glory of God in view will plant their feet firmly upon the
principles of hygiene; they will adopt a correct practice. The people need
true knowledge. By their wrong habits of life, men and women of this
generation are bringing upon themselves untold suffering.

Physicians have a work to do to bring about reform by educating the
people, that they may understand the laws which govern their physical life.
They should know how to eat properly, to work intelligently, to dress
healthfully, and should be taught to bring all their habits into harmony
with the laws of life and health, and to discard drugs. There is a great work
to be done. If the principles of health reform are carried out, the work will
indeed be as closely allied to that of the third angel's message as the hand
is to the body.

Why is there so much dissension? Why so much independent action,
so much selfish ambition in this great missionary field? God is dishonored.
There should be concentrated, united action. This is as necessary in the
physician's work as in any other branch of the work of preparation for the
great day of God. . . .

Teach the people how to prevent disease. Tell them to cease rebelling
against nature's laws, and by removing every obstruction give it a chance
to put forth its very best efforts to set things right. Nature must have a fair
chance to employ its healing agencies. We must make earnest efforts to
reach a higher platform in regard to the methods of treating the sick. If
the light which God has given prevails, if truth overcomes error, advanced
steps will be taken in health reform. This must be.—*Manuscript Releases,*
vol. 13, pp. 177, 178.

Advent Message to Sanctify Body and Soul

Beloved, I pray that you may prosper in all things and be in health, just as your soul prospers. 3 John 2, NKJV.

GOD'S PURPOSE FOR His children is that they shall grow up to the full stature of men and women in Christ. In order to do this they must use aright every power of mind, soul, and body. They cannot afford to waste any mental or physical strength.

The question of how to preserve the health is one of primary importance. When we study this question in the fear of God, we shall learn that it is best, for both our physical health and our spiritual advancement, to observe simplicity in diet. Let us patiently study this question. We need knowledge and judgment in order to move wisely in this matter. Nature's laws are not to be resisted, but obeyed.

Those who have received instruction regarding the evils of the use of flesh meats, tea and coffee, and rich and unhealthful food preparations, and who are determined to make a covenant with God by sacrifice, will not continue to indulge their appetite for food that they know to be unhealthful. God demands that the appetite be cleansed, and that self-denial be practiced in regard to those things which are not good. This is a work that will have to be done before His people can stand before Him a perfected people.

The remnant people of God must be a converted people. The presentation of this message is to result in the conversion and sanctification of souls. We are to feel the power of the Spirit of God in this movement. This is a wonderful, definite message; it means everything to the receiver, and it is to be proclaimed with a loud cry. We must have a true, abiding faith that this message will go forth with increasing importance till the close of time. . . .

A solemn responsibility rests upon those who know the truth, that all their works shall correspond with their faith, and that their lives shall be refined and sanctified, and they be prepared for the work that must rapidly be done in these closing days of the message. They have no time or strength to spend in the indulgence of appetite. The words should come to us now with impelling earnestness, "Repent . . . , and be converted, that your sins may be blotted out, when the times of refreshing shall come from the presence of the Lord."—*Review and Herald,* Feb. 24, 1910.

Conditions for Good
Health Must Be Observed

*If you diligently heed the voice of the Lord your God and do
what is right in His sight, give ear to His commandments and keep
all His statutes, I will put none of the diseases on you which I have brought
on the Egyptians. For I am the Lord who heals you. Exodus 15:26, NKJV.*

CHRIST HAD BEEN the guide and teacher of ancient Israel, and He taught them that health is the reward of obedience to the laws of God. The Great Physician who healed the sick in Palestine had spoken to His people from the pillar of cloud, telling them what they must do, and what God would do for them. [Exodus 15:26 quoted.] Christ gave to Israel definite instruction in regard to their habits of life, and He assured them, "The Lord will take away from thee all sickness" (Deut. 7:15). When they fulfilled the conditions, the promise was verified to them. "There was not one feeble person among their tribes" (Ps. 105:37).

These lessons are for us. There are conditions to be observed by all who would preserve health. All should learn what these conditions are. The Lord is not pleased with ignorance in regard to His laws, either natural or spiritual. We are to be workers together with God for the restoration of health to the body as well as to the soul.

And we should teach others how to preserve and to recover health. For the sick we should use the remedies which God has provided in nature, and we should point them to Him who alone can restore. It is our work to present the sick and suffering to Christ in the arms of our faith. We should teach them to believe in the Great Healer. We should lay hold on His promise, and pray for the manifestation of His power. The very essence of the gospel is restoration, and the Savior would have us bid the sick, the hopeless, and the afflicted take hold upon His strength.

The power of love was in all Christ's healing, and only by partaking of that love, through faith, can we be instruments for His work. If we neglect to link ourselves in divine connection with Christ, the current of life-giving energy cannot flow in rich streams from us to the people. . . .

To take His yoke is one of the first conditions of receiving His power. The very life of the church depends upon its faithfulness in fulfilling the Lord's commission. To neglect this work is surely to invite spiritual feebleness and decay. Where there is no active labor for others, love wanes, and faith grows dim.—*The Desire of Ages,* pp. 824, 825.

Self-development Essential to Accomplish Most Good

Those who want to save their life will lose it, and those who lose their life for my sake will save it. What does it profit them if they gain the whole world, but lose or forfeit themselves? Luke 9:24, 25, NRSV.

ONLY ONE LEASE of life is granted us; and the inquiry with everyone should be "How can I invest my powers so that they may yield the greatest profit? How can I do most for the glory of God and the benefit of my fellow beings?" For life is valuable only as it is used for the attainment of these ends.

Our first duty toward God and our fellow humans is that of self-development. Every faculty with which the Creator has endowed us should be cultivated to the highest degree of perfection, that we may be able to do the greatest amount of good of which we are capable. Hence that time is spent to good account which is used in the establishment and preservation of physical and mental health. We cannot afford to dwarf or cripple any function of body or mind. As surely as we do this, we must suffer the consequences.

Every person has the opportunity, to a great extent, of making himself or herself whatever he or she chooses to be. The blessings of this life, and also of the immortal state, are within their reach. They may build up a character of solid worth, gaining new strength at every step. They may advance daily in knowledge and wisdom, conscious of new delights as they progress, adding virtue to virtue, grace to grace. . . . Their intelligence, knowledge, and virtue will thus develop into greater strength and more perfect symmetry.

On the other hand, they may allow their powers to rust out for want of use, or to be perverted through evil habits, lack of self-control, or moral and religious stamina. Their course then tends downward; they are disobedient to the law of God and to the laws of health. Appetite conquers them; inclination carries them away. It is easier for them to allow the powers of evil, which are always active, to drag them backward, than to struggle against them and go forward. Dissipation, disease, and death follow. This is the history of many lives that might have been useful in the cause of God and humanity.—*Christian Temperance and Bible Hygiene,* pp. 41, 42.

Temperate Habits and
Physical Exercise Produce Vigor

Therefore, having these promises, beloved, let us cleanse ourselves from all filthiness of the flesh and spirit, perfecting holiness in the fear of God. 2 Corinthians 7:1, NKJV.

MANY HAVE SUFFERED from severe mental taxation, unrelieved by physical exercise. The result is a deterioration of their powers, and they are inclined to shun responsibilities. What they need is more active labor. This condition is not confined to those whose heads are white with the frost of time; those young in years have fallen into the same state, and have become mentally feeble.

Strictly temperate habits, combined with exercise of the muscles as well as of the mind, will preserve both mental and physical vigor, and give power of endurance to those engaged in the ministry, to editors, and to all others whose habits are sedentary.

Ministers, teachers, and students do not become as intelligent as they should in regard to the necessity of physical exercise in the open air. They neglect this duty, a duty which is most essential to the preservation of health. They closely apply their minds to study, and yet eat the allowance of a laboring man. Under such habits, some grow corpulent, because the system is clogged. Others become thin and feeble, because their vital powers are exhausted in throwing off the excess of food. . . . If physical exercise were combined with mental exertion, the circulation of the blood would be quickened, the action of the heart would be more perfect, impure matter would be thrown off, and new life and vigor would be felt in every part of the body. . . .

It is a sacred work in which we are engaged. . . . It is a duty that we owe to God to keep the spirit pure, as a temple for the Holy Ghost. If the heart and mind are devoted to the service of God, obeying all His commandments, loving Him with all the heart, might, mind, and strength, and our neighbor as ourselves, we shall be found loyal and true to the requirements of Heaven.

We are now in God's workshop. Many of us are rough stones from the quarry. But as the truth of God is brought to bear upon us, every imperfection is removed, and we are prepared to shine as lively stones in the heavenly temple, where we shall be brought into association not only with the holy angels but with the King of heaven Himself.

The consciousness of rightdoing is the best medicine for diseased bodies and minds. The special blessing of God resting upon the receiver is health and strength. A person whose mind is quiet and satisfied in God is in the pathway to health.—*Christian Temperance and Bible Hygiene,* pp. 160-162.

Follow the Example
Set by the Four Hebrews

"Then let our countenances be examined before you, and the countenances of the young men who eat the portion of the king's delicacies; and as you see fit, so deal with your servants." . . . And at the end of ten days their countenance appeared better and fatter in flesh than all the young men who ate the portion of the king's delicacies. Daniel 1:13-15, NKJV.

"AS FOR THESE four children, God gave them knowledge and skill in all learning and wisdom: and Daniel had understanding in all visions and dreams. Now at the end of the days that the king had said he should bring them in, then the prince of the eunuchs brought them in before Nebuchadnezzar. And the king communed with them; and among them all was found none like Daniel, Hananiah, Mishael, and Azariah: therefore stood they before the king. And in all matters of wisdom and understanding, that the king inquired of them, he found them ten times better than all the magicians and astrologers that were in all his realm."

This record contains much of importance on the subject of health reform. In the experience of the four Hebrew children a lesson is given regarding the need of abstaining from all spirituous liquors, and from indulgence of perverted appetite. The position taken by these Hebrew youth was vindicated, and at the end of ten days they were found fairer in flesh and better in knowledge than all the rest whom the king was proving.

In this our day, the Lord would be pleased to have those who are preparing for the future, immortal life follow the example of Daniel and his companions in seeking to maintain strength of body and clearness of mind. The more careful we learn to be in treating our bodies, the more readily shall we be able to escape the evils that are in the world through lust. . . .

Let us ask, What is the object of true higher education? Is it not that we may stand in right relation to God? The test of all education should be Is it fitting us to keep our minds fixed upon the mark of the prize of the high calling of God in Christ Jesus? . . .

We are to learn how to equalize the labor done by brain, bone, and muscle. If you put to task the faculties of the mind, loading them with heavy burdens, while you leave the muscles unexercised, this course will tell its story just as surely as the wise course of the Hebrew youth told its story. Parents should follow a consistent course in the education of their children. Our youth should be taught from their very childhood how to exercise the body and the mind proportionately.—*General Conference Bulletin,* May 30, 1909.

Control the Appetite
Through Christ's Power

Repent therefore and be converted, that your sins may be blotted out, so that times of refreshing may come from the presence of the Lord. Acts 3:19, NKJV.

THE POWER OF Christ alone can work the transformation in heart and mind that all must experience who would partake with Him of the new life in the kingdom of God. . . . In order to serve Him aright, we must be born of the divine Spirit. This will lead to watchfulness. It will purify the heart and renew the mind, and give us a new capacity for knowing and loving God. It will give us willing obedience to all His requirements. This is true worship.

God requires continual advancement from His people. They need to learn that indulged appetite is the greatest hindrance to mental improvement and soul sanctification. With all our profession of health reform, many of us eat improperly. Indulgence of appetite is the greatest cause of physical and mental debility, and lies largely at the foundation of feebleness and premature death. Let the individual who is seeking to possess purity of spirit bear in mind that in Christ there is power to control the appetite. . . .

Flesh foods are injurious to the physical well-being, and we should learn to do without them. Those who are in a position where it is possible to secure a vegetarian diet, but who choose to follow their own preferences in this matter, eating and drinking as they please, will gradually grow careless of the instruction the Lord has given regarding other phases of the present truth, and will lose their perception of what is truth; they will surely reap as they have sown. . . .

I appeal to old and young and to middle-aged: Deny your appetite of those things that are doing you injury. Serve the Lord by sacrifice. Let the children have an intelligent part in this work. We are all members of the Lord's family, and the Lord would have His children, young and old, determine to deny appetite, and to save the means needed for the building of meetinghouses and the support of missionaries.

I am instructed to say to parents: Place yourselves, soul and spirit, on the Lord's side of this question. We need ever to bear in mind that in these days of probation we are on trial before the Lord of the universe. Will you not give up indulgences that are doing you injury? Words of profession are cheap; let your acts of self-denial testify that you will be obedient to the demands that God makes on His peculiar people.—*Review and Herald*, Feb. 24, 1910.

Christians to Be Strictly
Temperate, Governed by Principle

Therefore, whether you eat or drink, or whatever you do,
do all to the glory of God. 1 Corinthians 10:31, NKJV.

THE APOSTLE PAUL writes: "Know ye not that they which run in a race run all, but one receiveth the prize? So run, that ye may obtain. And every man that striveth for the mastery is temperate in all things. Now they do it to obtain a corruptible crown; but we an incorruptible. I therefore so run, not as uncertainly; so fight I, not as one that beateth the air; but I keep under my body, and bring it into subjection; lest that by any means, when I have preached to others, I myself should be a castaway" (1 Cor. 9:24-27).

There are many in the world who indulge pernicious habits. Appetite is the law that governs them; and because of their wrong habits, the moral sense is clouded and the power to discern sacred things is to a great extent destroyed. But it is necessary for Christians to be strictly temperate. They should place their standard high. Temperance in eating, drinking, and dressing is essential. Principle should rule instead of appetite or fancy. Those who eat too much, or whose food is of an objectionable quality, are easily led into dissipation, and into other "foolish and hurtful lusts, which drown men in destruction and perdition" (1 Tim. 6:9). The "labourers together with God" should use every jot of their influence to encourage the spread of true temperance principles.

It means much to be true to God. He has claims upon all who are engaged in His service. He desires that mind and body be preserved in the best condition of health, every power and endowment under the divine control, and as vigorous as careful, strictly temperate habits can make them. We are under obligation to God to make an unreserved consecration of ourselves to Him, body and soul, with all the faculties appreciated as His entrusted gifts, to be employed in His service.

All our energies and capabilities are to be constantly strengthened and improved during this probationary period. Only those who appreciate these principles, and have been trained to care for their bodies intelligently and in the fear of God, should be chosen to take responsibilities in this work. . . . Every church needs a clear, sharp testimony, giving the trumpet a certain sound.—*Counsels on Diet and Foods*, pp. 156, 157.

Food to Be
Wholesome and Palatable

*Why do you spend money for what is not bread, and your
wages for what does not satisfy? Listen diligently to Me, and eat what is
good, and let your soul delight itself in abundance. Isaiah 55:2, NKJV.*

SOME OF OUR people, while conscientiously abstaining from eating improper foods, neglect to supply themselves with the elements necessary for the sustenance of the body. Those who take an extreme view of health reform are in danger of preparing tasteless dishes, making them so insipid that they are not satisfying. Food should be prepared in such a way that it will be appetizing as well as nourishing. It should not be robbed of that which the system needs. I use some salt, and always have, because salt, instead of being deleterious, is actually essential for the blood. Vegetables should be made palatable with a little milk or cream, or something equivalent.

While warnings have been given regarding the dangers of disease through butter, and the evil of the free use of eggs by small children, yet we should not consider it a violation of principle to use eggs from hens which are well cared for and suitably fed. Eggs contain properties which are remedial agencies in counteracting certain poisons.

Some, in abstaining from milk, eggs, and butter, have failed to supply the system with proper nourishment, and as a consequence have become weak and unable to work. Thus health reform is brought into disrepute. The work that we have tried to build up solidly is confused with strange things that God has not required, and the energies of the church are crippled. But God will interfere to prevent the results of these too strenuous ideas. The gospel is to harmonize the sinful race. It is to bring the rich and poor together at the feet of Jesus.

The time will come when we may have to discard some of the articles of diet we now use, such as milk and cream and eggs; but it is not necessary to bring upon ourselves perplexity by premature and extreme restrictions. Wait until the circumstances demand it, and the Lord prepares the way for it. . . .

Let us never bear a testimony against health reform by failing to use wholesome, palatable food in place of the harmful articles of diet that we have discarded. Do not in any way encourage an appetite for stimulants. Eat only plain, simple, wholesome food, and thank God constantly for the principles of health reform. In all things be true and upright, and you will gain precious victories.—*Review and Herald,* Mar. 3, 1910.

Control of Appetite
to Begin in Childhood

The fear of the Lord is the beginning of knowledge, but
fools despise wisdom and instruction. Proverbs 1:7, NKJV.

NOT ONLY HAS disease been transmitted from generation to generation, but parents bequeath to their children their own wrong habits, their perverted appetites, and corrupt passions. Men and women are slow to learn wisdom from the history of the past. The strange absence of principle that characterizes the present generation, the disregard of the laws of life and health, is astonishing. Although a knowledge of these things can be readily obtained, a deplorable ignorance prevails.

With the majority, the principal anxiety is "What shall I eat? what shall I drink? and wherewithal shall I be clothed?" Notwithstanding all that has been said and written upon the importance of health and the means to preserve it, appetite is the great law which governs men and women generally.

What can be done to stay the tide of disease and crime that is sweeping our race down to ruin and to death? As the great cause of the evil is to be found in the indulgence of appetite and passion, so the first and great work of reform must be to learn and practice the lessons of temperance and self-control.

To effect a permanent change for the better in society, the education of the masses must begin in early life. The habits formed in childhood and youth, the tastes acquired, the self-control gained, the principles inculcated from the cradle, are almost certain to determine the future of the man or woman. The crime and corruption occasioned by intemperance and lax morals might be prevented by the proper training of the youth.

One of the greatest aids in perfecting pure and noble characters in the young, strengthening them to control appetite and refrain from debasing excesses, is sound physical health. And, on the other hand, these very habits of self-control are essential to the maintenance of health. . . .

Especially is youth the time to lay up a stock of knowledge to be put in daily practice through life. Youth is the time to establish good habits, to correct wrong ones already contracted, to gain and to hold the power of self-control, and to lay the plan and accustom one's self to the practice of ordering all the acts of life with reference to the will of God and the welfare of our fellow creatures.—*Review and Herald,* Dec. 13, 1881.

Stimulants Eventually
Produce Evil Results

No testing has overtaken you that is not common to everyone. God is faithful, and he will
not let you be tested beyond your strength, but with the testing he will also provide
the way out so that you may be able to endure it. 1 Corinthians 10:13, NRSV.

AS A PEOPLE, with all our profession of health reform, we eat too much. Indulgence of appetite is the greatest cause of physical and mental debility, and lies at the foundation of the feebleness which is apparent everywhere.

Intemperance commences at our tables in the use of unhealthful food. After a time, through continued indulgence, the digestive organs become weakened, and the food taken does not satisfy the appetite. Unhealthy conditions are established, and there is a craving for more stimulating food. Tea, coffee, and flesh meats produce an immediate effect. Under the influence of these poisons the nervous system is excited, and, in some cases, for the time being, the intellect seems to be invigorated and the imagination to be more vivid. Because these stimulants produce for the time being such agreeable results, many conclude that they really need them and continue their use.

But there is always a reaction. The nervous system, having been unduly excited, borrowed power for present use from its future resources of strength. All this temporary invigoration of the system is followed by depression. In proportion as these stimulants temporarily invigorate the system will be the letting down of the power of the excited organs after the stimulus has lost its force. The appetite is educated to crave something stronger which will have a tendency to keep up and increase the agreeable excitement, until indulgence becomes habit, and there is a continual craving for stronger stimulus, as tobacco, wines, and liquors. . . .

The great end for which Christ endured that long fast in the wilderness was to teach us the necessity of self-denial and temperance. This work should commence at our tables and should be strictly carried out in all the concerns of life. The Redeemer of the world came from heaven to help us in our weakness, that, in the power which Jesus came to bring us, we might become strong to overcome appetite and passion, and might be victor on every point.—*Testimonies for the Church*, vol. 3, pp. 487, 488.

Through Jesus Comes
Health and Relief From Perplexities

Now when they came to Marah, they could not drink the waters of Marah, for they were bitter. Therefore the name of it was called Marah. And the people complained against Moses, saying, "What shall we drink?" Exodus 15:23, 24, NKJV.

THE LORD HAD a lesson to teach the children of Israel. The waters of Marah were an object lesson, representing the diseases brought upon human beings because of sin. It is no mystery that the inhabitants of the earth are suffering from disease of every stripe and type. It is because they transgress the law of God.

Thus did the children of Israel. They broke down the barriers which God in His providence had erected to preserve them from disease, that they might live in health and holiness, and so learn obedience in their journeyings through the wilderness. They journeyed under the special direction of Christ, who had given Himself as a sacrifice to preserve a people who would ever keep God in their remembrance, notwithstanding Satan's masterly temptations. Enshrouded in the pillar of cloud, it was Christ's desire to keep under His sheltering wing of preservation all who would do His will.

It was not by chance that in their journey the children of Israel came to Marah. Before they left Egypt the Lord began His lessons of instruction, that He might lead them to realize that He was their God, their Deliverer, their Protector. They murmured against Moses and against God, but still the Lord sought to show them that He would relieve all their perplexities if they would look to Him. The evils they met and passed through were part of God's great plan, whereby He desired to prove them.

When they came to the waters of Marah, "the people murmured against Moses, saying, What shall we drink? And he cried unto the Lord; and the Lord shewed him a tree, which when he had cast into the waters, the waters were made sweet: there he made for them a statute and an ordinance, and there he proved them." . . . Though invisible to human eyes, God was the leader of the Israelites, their mighty Healer. He it was who put into the tree the properties which sweetened the waters. Thus He desired to show them that by His power He could cure the evils of the human heart.

Christ is the great Physician, not only of the body, but of the soul. He restores us to our God. God permitted His only begotten Son to be bruised, that healing properties might flow forth from Him to cure all our diseases.—*Manuscript Releases,* vol. 15, pp. 29-31.

Obey Nature's Laws
to Enjoy Health

*Let no one despise your youth, but be an example to the believers in word,
in conduct, in love, in spirit, in faith, in purity. 1 Timothy 4:12, NKJV.*

THERE IS NOT one in a thousand, married or unmarried, who realizes the
importance of purity of habits, in preserving cleanliness of the body and purity of thought. Sickness and disease is the sure consequence of disobedience
to nature's laws, and neglect of the laws of life and health. It is the house in
which we live that we need to preserve, that it may do honor to God, who
has redeemed us. We need to know how to preserve the living machinery,
that our soul, body, and spirit may be consecrated to His service.

As rational beings we are deplorably ignorant of the body and its requirements. While the schools we have established have taken up the study
of physiology, they have not taken hold of the matter with that decided
energy which they should. They have not practiced intelligently that
which they have received in knowledge. And they do not realize that unless it is practiced, the body will decay.

Notwithstanding all the light shining forth from the Scriptures on this
subject; notwithstanding the lessons given in the history of Daniel, Shadrach,
Meshach, and Abednego; notwithstanding the result of plain healthful diet,
there is little regard for the lessons penned by those inspired of God. The
dietetic habits of the people generally are neglected; there is an increase of
tobacco using, liquor drinking, and subsisting on flesh meats. . . .

You are the Lord's property—His by creation and His by redemption.
"Thou shalt love . . . thy neighbour as thyself." The law of self-respect, for
the property of the Lord is here brought to view. And this will lead to respect for the obligations which every human being is under to preserve the
living machinery that is so fearfully and wonderfully made. This living machinery is to be understood. Every part of its wonderful mechanism is to
be carefully studied. Self-preservation is to be practiced. . . .

The transgression of the physical law is the transgression of God's law.
Our Creator is Jesus Christ. He is the Author of our being. He has created
the human structure. He is the Author of physical laws as He is the Author
of the moral law. And human beings who are careless and reckless of the
habits and practices that concern their physical life and health sin against
God.—*The Kress Collection*, pp. 45, 46.

Follow Divine Counsel
to Preserve Health

So Moses' father-in-law said to him, "The thing that you do is not good. Both you and these people who are with you will surely wear yourselves out. For this thing is too much for you; you are not able to perform it by yourself." Exodus 18:17, 18, NKJV.

WHEN WE DO all we can on our part to have health, then may we expect that the blessed results will follow, and we can ask God in faith to bless our efforts for the preservation of health. He will then answer our prayer, if His name can be glorified thereby. But let all understand that they have a work to do. God will not work in a miraculous manner to preserve the health of persons who are taking a sure course to make themselves sick.—*Counsels on Diet and Foods,* p. 26.

A careful conformity to the laws God has implanted in our being will ensure health, and there will not be a breaking down of the constitution.—*Ibid.,* p. 20.

Many have inquired of me, What course shall I take best to preserve my health? My answer is Cease to transgress the laws of your being; cease to gratify a depraved appetite, eat simple food, dress healthfully, which will require modest simplicity, work healthfully, and you will not be sick. . . . Many are suffering in consequence of the transgression of their parents. They cannot be censured for their parents' sin; but it is nevertheless their duty to ascertain wherein their parents violated the laws of their being . . . ; and wherein their parents' habits were wrong, they should change their own course, and place themselves, by correct habits, in a better relation to health.—*Health Reformer,* August 1866.

The harmonious, healthy action of all the powers of body and mind results in happiness; the more elevated and refined the powers, the more pure and unalloyed the happiness. An aimless life is a living death. The mind should dwell upon themes relating to our eternal interests. This will be conducive to health of body and mind.—*Review and Herald,* July 29, 1884.

God has pledged Himself to keep this living machinery in healthful action if the human agent will obey His laws and cooperate with God.—*Counsels on Diet and Foods,* p. 17.

The Lord has given His people a message in regard to health reform. This light has been shining upon their pathway for [many] years; and the Lord cannot sustain His servants in a course which will counteract it. . . . The light which God has given upon health reform cannot be trifled with without injury to those who attempt it; and no human being can hope to succeed in the work of God while, by precept and example, they act in opposition to the light which God has sent.—*Ibid.,* p. 38.

Effect Follows Cause, Producing Health or Disease

Either make the tree good and its fruit good, or else make the tree bad and its fruit bad; for a tree is known by its fruit. Matthew 12:33, NKJV.

ADAM AND EVE in Eden were noble in stature, and perfect in symmetry and beauty. They were sinless, and in perfect health. What a contrast to the human race now! Beauty is gone. Perfect health is not known. Everywhere we look we see disease, deformity, and imbecility. . . .

Since the fall, intemperance in almost every form has existed. The appetite has controlled reason. The human family have followed in a course of disobedience and, like Eve, have been beguiled by Satan to disregard the prohibitions God has made, flattering themselves that the consequence would not be as fearful as had been apprehended. The human family have violated the laws of health, and have run to excess in almost everything. Disease has been steadily increasing. The cause has been followed by the effect.

God gave our first parents the food He designed that the race should eat. It was contrary to His plan to have the life of any creature taken. There was to be no death in Eden. The fruit of the trees in the garden was the food their wants required. God gave no one permission to eat animal food until after the Flood. . . .

Many marvel that the human race has so degenerated, physically, mentally, and morally. They do not understand that it is the violation of God's constitution and laws and the violation of the laws of health that have produced this sad degeneracy. The transgression of God's commandments has caused His prospering hand to be removed. Intemperance in eating and in drinking, and the indulgence of base passions, have benumbed the fine sensibilities, so that sacred things have been placed upon a level with common things. . . .

Many have expected that God would keep them from sickness merely because they have asked Him to do so. But God did not regard their prayers, because their faith was not made perfect by works. God will not work a miracle to keep those from sickness who have no care for themselves, but are continually violating the laws of health, and make no effort to prevent disease. . . . God will not work in a miraculous manner to preserve the health of persons who are taking a sure course to make themselves sick, by their careless inattention to the laws of health.—*Review and Herald,* Apr. 2, 1914.

To Have a Clear Mind, Follow Temperance Principles

Now may the God of peace Himself sanctify you completely;
and may your whole spirit, soul, and body be preserved blameless
at the coming of our Lord Jesus Christ. 1 Thessalonians 5:23, NKJV.

THE APOSTLE THUS entreats, "I beseech you therefore, brethren, by the mercies of God, that ye present your bodies a living sacrifice, holy, acceptable unto God, which is your reasonable service." . . .

When we pursue a course of eating and drinking that lessens physical and mental vigor, or become the prey of habits that tend to the same results, we dishonor God, for we rob Him of the service He claims from us. Those who acquire and indulge the unnatural appetite for tobacco do this at the expense of health. They are destroying nervous energy, lessening vital force and sacrificing mental strength.

Those who profess to be the followers of Christ yet have this terrible sin at their door cannot have a high appreciation of the atonement and an elevated estimate of eternal things. Minds that are clouded and partially paralyzed by narcotics are easily overcome by temptation, and cannot enjoy communion with God.

Those who use tobacco can make but a poor plea to the liquor inebriate. Two thirds of the drunkards in our land created an appetite for liquor by the use of tobacco. Those who claim that tobacco does not injure them can be convinced of their mistake by depriving themselves of it for a few days; the trembling nerves, the giddy head, the irritability they feel, will prove to them that this sinful indulgence has bound them in slavery. It has overcome willpower. They are in bondage to a vice that is fearful in its results. . . .

God requires that His people should be temperate in all things. The example of Christ, during that long fast in the wilderness, should teach His followers to repulse Satan when he comes under the guise of appetite. Then may they have influence to reform those who have been led astray by indulgence, and have lost moral power to overcome the weakness and sin that has taken possession of them. Thus may Christians secure health and happiness, in a pure, well-ordered life and a mind clear and untainted before God.—*Signs of the Times,* Jan. 6, 1876.

Physical Work Helps
to Develop Mind and Character

*They shall build houses and inhabit them; they shall plant vineyards
and eat their fruit. They shall not build and another inhabit; they shall not
plant and another eat; for as the days of a tree, so shall be the days of My people,
and My elect shall long enjoy the work of their hands. Isaiah 65:21, 22, NKJV.*

NOW, AS IN the days of Israel, every youth should be instructed in the duties of practical life. Each should acquire a knowledge of some branch of manual labor by which, if need be, to obtain a livelihood. This is essential, not only as a safeguard against the vicissitudes of life, but from its bearing upon physical, mental, and moral development. Even if it were certain that one would never need to resort to manual labor for support, still they should be taught to work. Without physical exercise no one can have a sound constitution and vigorous health; and the discipline of well-regulated labor is no less essential to the securing of a strong, active mind and a noble character.

Students who have gained book knowledge without gaining a knowledge of practical work cannot lay claim to a symmetrical education. The energies that should have been devoted to business of various lines have been neglected. Education does not consist in using the brain alone. Physical employment is a part of the training essential for every youth. An important phase of education is lacking if the student is not taught how to engage in useful labor.

The healthful exercise of the whole being will give an education that is broad and comprehensive. Every student should devote a portion of each day to active labor. Thus habits of industry will be formed and a spirit of self-reliance encouraged, while the youth will be shielded from many evil and degrading practices that are so often the result of idleness. And this is all in keeping with the primary object of education; for in encouraging activity, diligence, and purity, we are coming into harmony with the Creator. . . .

The discipline for practical life that is gained by physical labor combined with mental taxation is sweetened by the reflection that it is qualifying mind and body better to perform the work that God designs human beings to do. The more perfectly the youth understand how to perform the duties of practical life, the greater will be their enjoyment day by day in being of use to others. The mind educated to enjoy useful labor becomes enlarged; through training and discipline it is fitted for usefulness; for it has acquired the knowledge essential to make its possessor a blessing to others.—*Messages to Young People*, pp. 177–179.

Temperance in All Things Is Essential

According to my earnest expectation and hope that in nothing I shall
be ashamed, but that with all boldness, as always, so now also Christ will
be magnified in my body, whether by life or by death. Philippians 1:20, NKJV.

THERE ARE MANY now under the shadow of death who have prepared to do a work for the Master, but who have not felt that a sacred obligation rested upon them to observe the laws of health. The laws of the physical system are indeed the laws of God; but this fact seems to have been forgotten.

Some have limited themselves to a diet that cannot sustain them in health. They have not provided nourishing food to take the place of injurious articles; and they have not considered that tact and ingenuity must be exercised in preparing food in the most healthful manner. The system must be properly nourished in order to perform its work. . . .

There are many in the world who indulge pernicious habits. Appetite is the law that governs them; and because of their wrong habits, the moral sense is clouded, and the power to discern sacred things is to a great extent destroyed. But it is necessary for Christians to be strictly temperate. They should place their standard high. Temperance in eating, drinking, and dressing is essential. Principle should rule instead of appetite or fancy. . . .

It means much to be true to God. He has claims upon all who are engaged in His service. He desires that mind and body be preserved in the best condition of health, every power and endowment under the divine control, and as vigorous as careful, strictly temperate habits can make them. We are under obligation to God to make an unreserved consecration of ourselves to Him, body and soul, with all the faculties appreciated as His entrusted gifts, to be employed in His service. All our energies and capabilities are to be constantly strengthened and improved during this probationary period. . . .

If we can arouse the moral sensibilities of our people on the subject of temperance, a great victory will be gained. Temperance in all things of this life is to be taught and practiced. Temperance in eating, drinking, sleeping, and dressing is one of the grand principles of the religious life. Truth brought into the sanctuary of the soul will guide in the treatment of the body. Nothing that concerns the health of the human agent is to be regarded with indifference. Our eternal welfare depends upon the use we make during this life of our time, strength, and influence.—*Review and Herald,* June 11, 1914.

Our Thinking Is Affected by Our Eating

Behold, I will bring it health and healing; I will heal them and reveal to them the abundance of peace and truth. Jeremiah 33:6, NKJV.

THE PRINCIPLES OF healthful living mean a great deal to us individually and as a people. When the message of health reform first came to me, I was weak and feeble, subject to frequent fainting spells. I was pleading with God for help, and He opened before me the great subject of health reform. He instructed me that those who are keeping His commandments must be brought into sacred relation to Himself, and that by temperance in eating and drinking they must keep mind and body in the most favorable condition for service. . . .

We do not mark out any precise line to be followed in diet; but we do say that in countries where there are fruits, grains, and nuts in abundance, flesh meat is not the right food for God's people. I have been instructed that flesh meat has a tendency to animalize the nature, to rob men and women of that love and sympathy which they should feel for everyone, and to give the lower passions control over the higher powers of the being. If meat eating was ever healthful, it is not safe now. Cancers, tumors, and pulmonary diseases are largely caused by meat eating.

We are not to make the use of flesh meat a test of fellowship, but we should consider the influence that professed believers who use flesh meats have over others. As God's messengers, shall we not say to the people, "Whether therefore ye eat, or drink, or whatsoever ye do, do all to the glory of God"?

Shall we not bear a decided testimony against the indulgence of perverted appetite? Will any who are ministers of the gospel, proclaiming the most solemn truth ever given to mortals, set an example in returning to the fleshpots of Egypt? Will those who are supported by the tithe from God's storehouse permit themselves by self-indulgence to poison the life-giving current flowing through their veins? Will they disregard the light and warnings that God has given them?

The health of the body is to be regarded as essential to growth in grace and the acquirement of an even temper. If the stomach is not properly cared for, the formation of an upright moral character will be hindered. The brain and nerves are in sympathy with the stomach. Erroneous eating and drinking result in erroneous thinking and acting.—*Review and Herald,* Mar. 3, 1910.

Prepare Wholesome Diet Without Flesh Meats

Is there no balm in Gilead, is there no physician there? Why then is there no recovery for the health of the daughter of my people? Jeremiah 8:22, NKJV.

ALL ARE NOW being tested and proved. We have been baptized into Christ, and if we will act our part by separating from everything that would drag us down and make us what we ought not to be, strength to grow into Christ, who is our living head, will be given us, and we shall see the salvation of God.

Only when we are intelligent in regard to the principles of healthful living can we be fully aroused to see the evils resulting from improper diet. Those who, after seeing their mistakes, have courage to change their habits will find that the reformatory process requires a struggle and much perseverance; but when correct tastes are once formed, they will realize that the use of the food which they formerly regarded as harmless was slowly but surely laying the foundation for dyspepsia and other diseases.

Fathers and mothers, watch unto prayer. Guard strictly against intemperance in every form. Teach your children the principles of true health reform. Teach them what things to avoid in order to preserve health. Already the wrath of God has begun to be visited on the children of disobedience. What crimes, what sins, what iniquitous practices, are now being revealed on every hand! As a people we are to exercise great care in guarding our children against depraved associates.

Greater efforts should be put forth to educate the people in the principles of health reform. Cooking schools should be established, and house-to-house instruction should be given in the art of cooking wholesome food. Old and young should learn how to cook more simply. Wherever the truth is presented, the people are to be taught how to prepare food in a simple yet appetizing way. They are to be shown that a nourishing diet can be provided without the use of flesh meats. . . .

Much tact and discretion should be employed in preparing nourishing food to take the place of that which has formerly constituted the diet of those who are learning to be health reformers. Faith in God, earnestness of purpose, and a willingness to help one another will be required. A diet lacking in the proper elements of nutrition brings reproach upon the cause of health reform. We are mortal, and must supply ourselves with food that will give proper nourishment to the body.—*Review and Herald,* Mar. 3, 1910.

Both Physical and Mental Faculties to Be Cultivated

Do you not know that your body is the temple of the Holy Spirit who is in you, whom you have from God, and you are not your own? 1 Corinthians 6:19, NKJV.

HEALTH IS A great treasure. It is the richest possession mortals can have. Wealth, honor, or learning is dearly purchased, if it be at the loss of the vigor of health. None of these attainments can secure happiness if health is wanting. It is a terrible sin to abuse the health that God has given us. Every abuse of health enfeebles us for life and makes us losers, even if we gain any amount of education. . . .

Poverty, in many cases, is a blessing; for it prevents youth and children from being ruined by inaction. The physical as well as the mental powers should be cultivated and properly developed. The first and constant care of parents should be that their children may have firm constitutions, that they may be sound men and women. It is impossible to attain this object without physical exercise.

For their own physical health and moral good, children should be taught to work, even if there is no necessity as far as want is concerned. If they would have pure and virtuous characters they must have the discipline of well-regulated labor, which will bring into exercise all the muscles. The satisfaction that children will have in being useful, and in denying themselves to help others, will be the most healthful pleasure they ever enjoyed. . . .

Physical labor will not prevent the cultivation of the intellect. Far from it. The advantages gained by physical labor will balance a person and prevent the mind from being overworked. The toil will come upon the muscles and relieve the wearied brain. . . .

It does not require a frail, helpless, overdressed, simpering thing to make a lady. A sound body is required for a sound intellect. Physical soundness and a practical knowledge of all the necessary household duties will never be hindrances to a well-developed intellect; both are highly important for a lady.

All the powers of the mind should be called into use and developed in order for men and women to have well-balanced minds. The world is full of one-sided men and women who have become such because one set of their faculties is cultivated while others were dwarfed from inaction. . . .

The human mind will have action. If it is not active in the right direction, it will be active in the wrong. And in order to preserve the balance of the mind, labor and study should be united in the schools.—*Testimonies for the Church*, vol. 3, pp. 150-153.

Pure, Fresh Air Promotes
Health of Mind and Body

*Do not be wise in your own eyes; fear the Lord and depart from evil. It will
be health to your flesh, and strength to your bones. Proverbs 3:7, 8, NKJV.*

A CONTENTED MIND, a cheerful spirit, is health to the body and
strength to the soul. Nothing is so fruitful a cause of disease as depression,
gloominess, and sadness. Mental depression is terrible. . . .

Air, air, the precious boon of heaven which all may have, will bless you
with its invigorating influence if you will not refuse it entrance. Welcome
it, cultivate a love for it, and it will prove a precious soother of the nerves.
Air must be in constant circulation to be kept pure. The influence of pure,
fresh air is to cause the blood to circulate healthfully through the system. It
refreshes the body and tends to render it strong and healthy, while at the
same time its influence is decidedly felt upon the mind, imparting a degree
of composure and serenity. It excites the appetite, and renders the digestion
of food more perfect, and induces sound and sweet sleep.

The effects produced by living in close, ill-ventilated rooms are these:
The system becomes weak and unhealthy, the circulation is depressed, the
blood moves sluggishly through the system because it is not purified and
vitalized by the pure, invigorating air of heaven. . . .

Do you believe that the end of all things is at hand, that the scenes of this
earth's history are fast closing? If so, show your faith by your works. . . .

"Faith, if it hath not works, is dead, being alone." Few have that genuine faith which works by love and purifies the soul. But all who are accounted worthy of everlasting life must obtain a moral fitness for the same.
"Beloved, now are we the sons of God, and it doth not yet appear what
we shall be: but we know that, when he shall appear, we shall be like him;
for we shall see him as he is. And every man that hath this hope in him
purifieth himself, even as he is pure." This is the work before you, and you
have none too much time if you engage in the work with all your soul.—
Testimonies for the Church, vol. 1, pp. 702-705.

Love for God Is
Essential for Perfect Health

For you were bought at a price; therefore glorify God in your body and in your spirit, which are God's. 1 Corinthians 6:20, NKJV.

OUR BODIES BELONG to God. He paid the price of redemption for the body as well as for the soul. . . . The Creator watches over the human machinery, keeping it in motion. Were it not for His constant care, the pulse would not beat, the action of the heart would cease, the brain would no longer act its part.

The brain is the organ and instrument of the mind, and controls the whole body. In order for the other parts of the system to be healthy, the brain must be healthy. And in order for the brain to be healthy, the blood must be pure. If by correct habits of eating and drinking the blood is kept pure, the brain will be properly nourished.

It is the lack of harmonious action in the human organism that brings disease. The imagination may control the other parts of the body to their injury. All parts of the system must work harmoniously. The different parts of the body, especially those remote from the heart, should receive a free circulation of blood. The limbs act an important part, and should receive proper attention.

God is the great caretaker of the human machinery. In the care of our bodies we must cooperate with Him. Love for God is essential for life and health. . . . In order to have perfect health our hearts must be filled with love and hope and joy. . . .

Those who put their whole souls into the medical missionary work, who labor untiringly in peril, in privation, in watchings oft, in weariness and painfulness, are in danger of forgetting that they must be faithful guardians of their own mental and physical powers. They are not to allow themselves to be overtaxed. But they are filled with zeal and earnestness, and they sometimes move unadvisedly, putting themselves under too heavy a strain. Unless such workers make a change, the result will be that sickness will come upon them and they will break down. . . .

We have a calling as much higher than common, selfish interests as the heavens are higher than the earth. But this thought should not lead the willing, hardworking servants of God to carry all the burdens they can possibly bear, without periods of rest.—*Medical Ministry,* pp. 291-293.

NOVEMBER

❧

Worshiping at Home

Though We Fall, We Can Conquer

Oh, satisfy us early with Your mercy, that we may rejoice and be glad all our days! Psalm 90:14, NKJV.

IF GOD'S PEOPLE would recognize His dealings with them and accept His teachings, they would find a straight path for their feet and a light to guide them through darkness and discouragement. David learned wisdom from God's dealings with him and bowed in humility beneath the chastisement of the Most High. The faithful portrayal of his true state by the prophet Nathan made David acquainted with his own sins and aided him to put them away. He accepted counsel meekly and humiliated himself before God. "The law of the Lord," he exclaims, "is perfect, converting the soul."

Repentant sinners have no cause to despair because they are reminded of their transgressions and warned of their danger. These very efforts in their behalf show how much God loves them and desires to save them. They have only to follow His counsel and do His will to inherit eternal life. God sets the sins of His erring people before them, that they may behold them in all their enormity under the light of divine truth. It is then their duty to renounce them forever.

God is as powerful to save from sin today as He was in the times of the patriarchs, of David, and of the prophets and apostles. The multitude of cases recorded in sacred history where God has delivered His people from their own iniquities should make the Christian of this time eager to receive divine instruction and zealous to perfect a character that will bear the close inspection of the judgment.

Bible history stays the fainting heart with the hope of God's mercy. We need not despair when we see that others have struggled through discouragements like our own, have fallen into temptations even as we have done, and yet have recovered their ground and been blessed of God. The words of inspiration comfort and cheer the erring soul.

Although the patriarchs and apostles were subject to human frailties, yet through faith they obtained a good report, fought their battles in the strength of the Lord, and conquered gloriously. Thus may we trust in the virtue of the atoning sacrifice and be overcomers in the name of Jesus. Humanity is humanity the world over from the time of Adam down to the present generation, and the love of God through all ages is without a parallel.—*Testimonies for the Church,* vol. 4, pp. 14, 15.

Move Forward
in Faith and Unity

*Therefore if there is any consolation in Christ, if any comfort of love, if any fellowship
of the Spirit, if any affection and mercy, fulfill my joy by being like-minded,
having the same love, being of one accord, of one mind. Philippians 2:1, 2, NKJV.*

I WELL REMEMBER how, when we were living in the Carroll House [in
Takoma Park, Maryland], near the water tower, the young men working
on the school land would meet together in a large room in this house at
half-past five every morning for family worship. As we worshiped God
together, we knew that the Holy Spirit was among us.

We sought the Lord with the whole heart, and He came very near to
us. We presented the promise "Ask, and it shall be given unto you; seek,
and ye shall find; knock, and it shall be opened unto you." Is not this assurance strong enough? We took this promise with us into the place of prayer,
asking the Lord to lead and direct in the work to be done here. . . .

If there are any of you who have weak faith, remember that it is because you do not work on the affirmative side. It is of no use for us to think
that we can carry forward the glorious work of God without strong, un-
faltering faith. The world is fast becoming as it was in the days of Noah.
Satan is working with intensity of effort, knowing that he has but a short
time. Wickedness prevails to an appalling extent. God's people are but a
handful, compared with the ungodly, and we can gain success only as we
cooperate with the heavenly angels, who will go before all who press forward to do that which God has said should be done. . . .

When I think of all that God has done for us, I say, "Praise God, from
whom all blessings flow." As the work is opened up in the various places,
may we ever remember that we are to draw in even cords. Those who
have educated themselves to stand on the negative side should without
delay repent and be converted. . . . Remember that when you stand on the
negative side, accusing and condemning, you make room for the agencies
of the power of darkness. Precious time has to be spent in waging war
against these agencies, because there were those who refused to stand on
the affirmative side. . . .

"Let nothing be done through strife or vainglory." Satan is behind all
strife and vainglory. Let us get out of his company, and stand with those
who say, "Victory is for us, and we will cling to the arm of infinite
power."—*Review and Herald,* June 15, 1905.

Make Family Worship Interesting

Many, O Lord my God, are Your wonderful works which You have done;
and Your thoughts which are toward us cannot be recounted to You in order; if I would
declare and speak of them, they are more than can be numbered. Psalm 40:5, NKJV.

YOUR CHILDREN SHOULD be educated to be kind, thoughtful of others, gentle, easy to be entreated, and, above everything else, to respect religious things and feel the importance of the claims of God. They should be taught to respect the hour of prayer; they should be required to rise in the morning so as to be present at family worship.—*Testimonies for the Church,* vol. 5, p. 424.

The father, who is the priest of his household, should conduct the morning and evening worship. There is no reason why this should not be the most interesting and enjoyable exercise of the home life, and God is dishonored when it is made dry and irksome. Let the seasons of family worship be short and spirited. Do not let your children or any member of your family dread them because of their tediousness or lack of interest. When a long chapter is read and explained and a long prayer offered, this precious service becomes wearisome, and it is a relief when it is over.

It should be the special object of the heads of the family to make the hour of worship intensely interesting. By a little thought and careful preparation for this season, when we come into the presence of God, family worship can be made pleasant and will be fraught with results that eternity alone will reveal. . . .

Select a portion of Scripture that is interesting and easily understood; a few verses will be sufficient to furnish a lesson which may be studied and practiced through the day. . . . At least a few verses of spirited song may be sung, and the prayer offered should be short and pointed. The one who leads in prayer should not pray about everything, but should express the needs in simple words and praise God with thanksgiving.—*Signs of the Times,* Aug. 7, 1884.

In arousing and strengthening a love for Bible study, much depends on the use of the hour of worship. The hours of morning and evening worship should be the sweetest and most helpful of the day. Let it be understood that into these hours no troubled, unkind thoughts are to intrude; that parents and children assemble to meet with Jesus and to invite into the home the presence of holy angels.

Let the services be brief and full of life, adapted to the occasion, and varied from time to time. Let all join in the Bible reading and learn and often repeat God's law. It will add to the interest of the children if they are sometimes permitted to select the reading.—*Education,* p. 186.

Daily Family Worship Yields Precious Results

Then it shall come to pass, because you listen to these judgments,
and keep and do them, that the Lord your God will keep with you the
covenant and the mercy which He swore to your fathers. Deuteronomy 7:12, NKJV.

FOR SOME REASON many parents dislike to give their children religious instruction, and they leave them to pick up in Sabbath school the knowledge which it is their privilege and duty to impart. Such parents fail to fulfill the responsibility laid upon them, to give their children an all-around education. God commands His people to bring up their children in the nurture and admonition of the Lord. . . .

Parents, let the instruction you give your children be simple, and be sure that it is clearly understood. The lessons that you learn from the Word you are to present to their young minds so plainly that they cannot fail to understand. By simple lessons drawn from the Word of God and their own experience, you may teach them how to conform their lives to the highest standard. Even in childhood and youth they may learn to live thoughtful, earnest lives that will yield a rich harvest of good.

In every Christian home God should be honored by the morning and evening sacrifices of prayer and praise. Children should be taught to respect and reverence the hour of prayer. It is the duty of Christian parents, morning and evening, by earnest prayer and persevering faith, to make a hedge about their children.

In the church at home the children are to learn to pray and to trust in God. Teach them to repeat God's law. Concerning the commandments the Israelites were instructed: "Thou shalt teach them diligently unto thy children, and shalt talk of them when thou sittest in thine house, and when thou walkest by the way, and when thou liest down, and when thou risest up" (Deut. 6:7).

Come in humility, with a heart full of tenderness, and with a sense of the temptations and dangers before yourselves and your children; by faith bind them to the altar, entreating for them the care of the Lord. Train the children to offer their simple words of prayer. Tell them that God delights to have them call upon Him.

Will the Lord of heaven pass by such homes and leave no blessing there? Nay, verily. Ministering angels will guard the children who are thus dedicated to God. They hear the offering of praise and the prayer of faith, and they bear the petitions to Him who ministers in the sanctuary for His people, and offers His merits in their behalf.—*Counsels to Parents, Teachers, and Students,* pp. 109, 110.

Worship Faithfully
Every Morning and Evening

Therefore whoever hears these sayings of Mine, and does them, I will liken him to a wise man who built his house on the rock. Matthew 7:24, NKJV.

LET THE MEMBERS of every family bear in mind that they are closely allied to heaven. The Lord has a special interest in the families of His children here below. Angels offer the smoke of the fragrant incense for the praying saints. Then in every family let prayer ascend to heaven both in the morning and at the cool sunset hour, in our behalf presenting before God the Savior's merits. Morning and evening the heavenly universe take notice of every praying household.—*Child Guidance,* p. 519.

Before leaving the house for labor, all the family should be called together; and the father, or the mother in the father's absence, should plead fervently with God to keep them through the day. Come in humility, with a heart full of tenderness, and with a sense of the temptations and dangers before yourselves and your children; by faith bind them upon the altar, entreating for them the care of the Lord. Ministering angels will guard children who are thus dedicated to God.—*Testimonies for the Church,* vol. 1, pp. 397, 398.

In every family there should be a fixed time for morning and evening worship. How appropriate it is for parents to gather their children about them before the fast is broken, to thank the heavenly Father for His protection during the night, and to ask Him for His help and guidance and watch care during the day! How fitting, also, when evening comes, for parents and children to gather once more before Him and thank Him for the blessings of the day that is past!—*Ibid.,* vol. 7, p. 43.

Family worship should not be governed by circumstances. You are not to pray occasionally and, when you have a large day's work to do, neglect it. In thus doing you lead your children to look upon prayer as of no special consequence. Prayer means very much to the children of God, and thank offerings should come up before God morning and evening.—*Child Guidance,* p. 520.

In our efforts for the comfort and happiness of guests, let us not overlook our obligations to God. The hour of prayer should not be neglected for any consideration. Do not talk and amuse yourselves till all are too weary to enjoy the season of devotion. To do this is to present to God a lame offering. At an early hour of the evening, when we can pray unhurriedly and understandingly, we should present our supplications and raise our voices in happy, grateful praise.—*Messages to Young People,* p. 342.

Parents to Begin
Reformation in the Home

Cause me to hear Your lovingkindness in the morning,
for in You do I trust; cause me to know the way in which I
should walk, for I lift up my soul to You. Psalm 143:8, NKJV.

WHEN [GOD] GAVE Jesus to our world, He included all heaven in that one gift. He did not leave us to retain our defects and deformities of character, or to serve Him as best we could in the corruption of our sinful nature. He has made provision that we may be complete in His Son, not having our own righteousness, but the righteousness of Christ. In Christ the whole storehouse of knowledge and of grace is at our command; for in Him dwells "all the fullness of the Godhead bodily."

Christ has given His life for us; we are His property. "Know ye not," He says, "that your body is the temple of the Holy Ghost which is in you, which ye have of God, and ye are not your own? For ye are bought with a price: therefore glorify God in your body, and in your spirit, which are God's." God's children are to show their love for Him by meeting His requirements, by giving themselves to Him. Then only can He use them in His service, that others, through them, may discern the truth and rejoice in it.

But the people of God are asleep to their present and eternal good. The Lord says to them, "Arise, shine; for thy light is come, and the glory of the Lord is risen upon thee." He desires them to go to work in unity, in faith, and love. He desires that the work of reformation shall begin in the home, with the fathers and mothers, and then the church will realize the Holy Spirit's working. The influence of this work will go through the church like leaven. Fathers and mothers need converting. They have not educated themselves to mold and fashion the characters of their children aright.

As God's ministers, dear parents, you must use the precious remnant of time in doing the work He has left for you. He desires that by wise methods in your home you shall train your children for Him. Learn of Jesus; be doers of His Word. . . .

Children need to have religion made attractive, not repulsive. The hour of family worship should be made the happiest hour of the day. Let the reading of the Scriptures be well chosen and simple; let the children join in singing; and let the prayers be short, and right to the point. . . . Consider . . . that you are in the service of God, that you have access to One who is a present help in every time of need.—*Review and Herald,* Mar. 18, 1902.

Time for Worship to Be Set Apart as Sacred

*I am the living bread which came down from heaven. If anyone
eats of this bread, he will live forever; and the bread that I shall give is
My flesh, which I shall give for the life of the world. John 6:51, NKJV.*

THE INCENSE, ASCENDING with the prayers of Israel, represents the merits and intercession of Christ, His perfect righteousness, which through faith is imputed to His people, and which can alone make the worship of sinful beings acceptable to God. Before the veil of the most holy place was an altar of perpetual intercession, before the holy, an altar of continual atonement. By blood and by incense God was to be approached—symbols pointing to the great Mediator, through whom sinners may approach Jehovah, and through whom alone mercy and salvation can be granted to the repentant, believing soul.

As the priests morning and evening entered the holy place at the time of incense, the daily sacrifice was ready to be offered upon the altar in the court without. This was a time of intense interest to the worshipers who assembled at the tabernacle. Before entering into the presence of God through the ministration of the priest, they were to engage in earnest searching of heart and confession of sin. They united in silent prayer, with their faces toward the holy place. Thus their petitions ascended with the cloud of incense, while faith laid hold upon the merits of the promised Savior prefigured by the atoning sacrifice.

The hours appointed for the morning and the evening sacrifice were regarded as sacred, and they came to be observed as the set time for worship throughout the Jewish nation. And when in later times the Jews were scattered as captives in distant lands, they still at the appointed hour turned their faces toward Jerusalem and offered up their petitions to the God of Israel. In this custom Christians have an example for morning and evening prayer. While God condemns a mere round of ceremonies without the spirit of worship, He looks with great pleasure upon those who love Him, bowing morning and evening to seek pardon for sins committed and to present their requests for needed blessings.—*Patriarchs and Prophets,* pp. 353, 354.

God's People Will Be
Refined by Time of Trouble

O Lord, be gracious to us; we have waited for You. Be their arm every morning, our salvation also in the time of trouble. Isaiah 33:2, NKJV.

JACOB'S HISTORY IS also an assurance that [in the final time of trouble] God will not cast off those who have been deceived and tempted and betrayed into sin, but who have returned unto Him with true repentance. While Satan seeks to destroy this class, God will send His angels to comfort and protect them in the time of peril.

The assaults of Satan are fierce and determined, his delusions are terrible; but the Lord's eye is upon His people, and His ear listens to their cries. Their affliction is great, the flames of the furnace seem about to consume them; but the Refiner will bring them forth as gold tried in the fire. God's love for His children during the period of their severest trial is as strong and tender as in the days of their sunniest prosperity; but it is needful for them to be placed in the furnace of fire; their earthliness must be consumed, that the image of Christ may be perfectly reflected.

The season of distress and anguish before us will require a faith that can endure weariness, delay, and hunger—a faith that will not faint though severely tried. The period of probation is granted to all to prepare for that time. Jacob prevailed because he was persevering and determined. His victory is an evidence of the power of importunate prayer. All who will lay hold of God's promises, as he did, and be as earnest and persevering as he was, will succeed as he succeeded. Those who are unwilling to deny self, to agonize before God, to pray long and earnestly for His blessing, will not obtain it.

Wrestling with God—how few know what it is! How few have ever had their souls drawn out after God with intensity of desire until every power is on the stretch. When waves of despair which no language can express sweep over the suppliant, how few cling with unyielding faith to the promises of God.

Those who exercise but little faith now are in the greatest danger of falling under the power of satanic delusions and the decree to compel the conscience. And even if they endure the test they will be plunged into deeper distress and anguish in the time of trouble, because they have never made it a habit to trust in God. The lessons of faith which they have neglected they will be forced to learn under a terrible pressure of discouragement.—*The Great Controversy*, pp. 621, 622.

Consecrate Your Family to God, and Look to Calvary

Let us know, let us pursue the knowledge of the Lord.
His going forth is established as the morning; He will come to us like
the rain, like the latter and former rain to the earth. Hosea 6:3, NKJV.

YOU SHOULD NEVER separate Christ from your life and family, and close the doors against Him by un-Christlike words and actions. There are those who profess the truth who neglect family prayer. But how can you venture to go to your labor without committing the care of your souls to your heavenly Father? You should show that you trust in Him. You should consecrate your families to God before you leave your homes.

Every prayer that you offer up to God in faith will surely be respected and answered by your heavenly Father. When Abraham was told to go out into a place which he knew not, wherever he pitched his tent he built an altar, and offered up his prayer morning and evening; and the Lord said of Abraham, "I know him, that he will command his children and his household after him, and they shall keep the way of the Lord, to do justice and judgment."

This is the very work that should be done in every family, but it is strangely neglected. We want to live as in the sight of God in this world. It is of the greatest importance that we constantly make preparation here for the future, immortal life. We may have that life that measures with the life of God; if we are faithful, we shall have an immortal inheritance, an eternal substance; we shall see the King in His beauty; we shall behold the matchless charms of our blessed Savior.

We should feel the importance of educating and training our children, that they shall seek and appreciate eternal life. Their will must be brought into subjection to the will of God, and they must seek constantly to repress everything that is evil in their natures. If fathers and mothers want their children to be Christlike in disposition, they must set them the example. Your every act should be one to fit yourself and your children for heaven, and you will have special help in the matter.

The Savior desires your joy to be full; therefore He tells you to abide in Him and He will abide in you. Open the door of your heart, and let in Jesus and the bright rays of His righteousness. He loves us with a love that is inexpressible, and if at any time you begin to fear that you will be lost, that Jesus does not love you, look to Calvary.—*Review and Herald,* Aug. 5, 1890.

The Way Opens When We Advance by Faith

Whoever offers praise glorifies Me; and to him who orders his conduct aright I will show the salvation of God. Psalm 50:23, NKJV.

ALL THE INHABITANTS of heaven unite in praising God. Let us learn the song of the angels now, that we may sing it when we join their shining ranks. Let us say with the psalmist, "While I live will I praise the Lord: I will sing praises unto my God while I have any being" (Ps. 146:2). "Let the people praise thee, O God; let all the people praise thee" (Ps. 67:5).

God in His providence brought the Hebrews into the mountain fastnesses before the sea, that He might manifest His power in their deliverance and signally humble the pride of their oppressors. He might have saved them in any other way, but He chose this method in order to test their faith and strengthen their trust in Him. The people were weary and terrified, yet if they had held back when Moses bade them advance, God would never have opened the path for them.

It was "by faith" that "they passed through the Red Sea as by dry land" (Heb. 11:29). In marching down to the very water, they showed that they believed the word of God as spoken by Moses. They did all that was in their power to do, and then the Mighty One of Israel divided the sea to make a path for their feet.

The great lesson here taught is for all time. Often the Christian life is beset by dangers, and duty seems hard to perform. The imagination pictures impending ruin before and bondage or death behind. Yet the voice of God speaks clearly, "Go forward." We should obey this command, even though our eyes cannot penetrate the darkness, and we feel the cold waves about our feet. The obstacles that hinder our progress will never disappear before a halting, doubting spirit.

Those who defer obedience till every shadow of uncertainty disappears and there remains no risk of failure or defeat will never obey at all. Unbelief whispers, "Let us wait till the obstructions are removed, and we can see our way clearly"; but faith courageously urges an advance, hoping all things, believing all things.—*Patriarchs and Prophets,* pp. 289, 290.

Angels in Heaven
Worship With Us

*And every creature which is in heaven and on the earth . . . I heard
saying: "Blessing and honor and glory and power be to Him who sits
on the throne, and to the Lamb, forever and ever!" Revelation 5:13, NKJV.*

THE CHURCH OF God upon the earth is one with the church of God above. Believers on the earth, and those who have never fallen in heaven, are one church. Every heavenly intelligence is interested in the assemblies of the saints, who on earth meet to worship God in spirit and in truth, and in the beauty of holiness. In the inner court of heaven, they listen to the testimonies of the witnesses for Christ in the outer court on earth. And the praise and thanksgiving that come from the church below are taken up in the heavenly anthem, and praise and rejoicing resound through the heavenly courts because Christ has not died in vain for the fallen sons and daughters of Adam.

While angels drink from the fountainhead, the saints on earth drink from the pure streams flowing from the throne of God, making glad the City of God. Oh, that we could all realize the nearness of heaven to earth! When the earthborn children know it not, they have the angels of light as their companions; for the heavenly messengers are sent forth to minister to those who shall be heirs of salvation.

A silent witness guards every soul that lives, seeking to win and draw it to Christ. The angels never leave the tempted ones a prey to the enemy who would destroy the souls of men and women if permitted to do so. As long as there is hope, until they resist the Holy Spirit to their eternal ruin, they are guarded by heavenly intelligences.

Let us all bear in mind that in every assembly of the saints below are the angels of God, listening to the thanksgiving, the praise, the supplication that is offered by the people of God in testimonies, songs, and prayers. Let them remember that their praises are supplemented by the choir of the angelic host above.—*General Conference Bulletin,* Feb. 15, 1895.

The image of Christ engraved upon the heart is reflected in character, in practical life, day by day, because we represent a personal Savior. The Holy Spirit is promised to all who will ask for it. When you search the Scriptures, the Holy Spirit is by your side, personating Jesus Christ.

If we will open the door to Jesus, He will come in and abide with us. Our strength will always be reinforced by His actual representative, the Holy Spirit.—*Ibid.*

Christ's Blood and Righteousness Purify Our Worship

Now this is the main point of the things we are saying:
We have such a High Priest, who is seated at the right hand of
the throne of the Majesty in the heavens. Hebrews 8:1, NKJV.

CHRIST JESUS IS represented as continually standing at the altar, momentarily offering up the sacrifice for the sins of the world. He is a minister of the true tabernacle which the Lord pitched and not man. The typical shadows of the Jewish tabernacle no longer possess any virtue. A daily and yearly typical atonement is no longer to be made, but the atoning sacrifice through a mediator is essential because of the constant commission of sin. Jesus is officiating in the presence of God, offering up His shed blood, as it had been a lamb slain. Jesus presents the oblation offered for every offense and every shortcoming of the sinner.

Christ, our Mediator, and the Holy Spirit are constantly interceding in humanity's behalf, but the Spirit pleads not for us as does Christ who presents His blood, shed from the foundation of the world; the Spirit works upon our hearts, drawing out prayers and penitence, praise and thanksgiving. The gratitude which flows from our lips is the result of the Spirit striking the chords of the soul in holy memories, awakening the music of the heart.

The religious services, the prayers, the praise, the penitent confession of sin ascend from true believers as incense to the heavenly sanctuary; but passing through the corrupt channels of humanity, they are so defiled that unless purified by blood, they can never be of value with God. They ascend not in spotless purity, and unless the Intercessor who is at God's right hand presents and purifies all by His righteousness, it is not acceptable to God.

All incense from earthly tabernacles must be moist with the cleansing drops of the blood of Christ. He holds before the Father the censer of His own merits, in which there is no taint of earthly corruption. He gathers into this censer the prayers, the praise, and the confessions of His people, and with these He puts His own spotless righteousness. Then, perfumed with the merits of Christ's propitiation, the incense comes up before God wholly and entirely acceptable. Then gracious answers are returned.

Oh, that all may see that everything in obedience, in penitence, in praise and thanksgiving, must be placed upon the glowing fire of the righteousness of Christ. The fragrance of this righteousness ascends like a cloud around the mercy seat.—*The Seventh-day Adventist Bible Commentary,* Ellen G. White Comments, vol. 6, pp. 1077, 1078.

Talk of Jesus, and Reflect the Joy of Being a Christian

Blessed be the God and Father of our Lord Jesus Christ, . . . who comforts us in all our tribulation, that we may be able to comfort those who are in any trouble, with the comfort with which we ourselves are comforted by God. 2 Corinthians 1:3, 4, NKJV.

IF OUR PEOPLE do not enjoy much ministerial labor, it is all the more important that they place themselves in a right relation to God, so that they can receive of His blessing themselves, and become channels of light to others. Much more is included in the term "missionary work" than is commonly supposed. Every true follower of Christ is a missionary, and there is almost an endless variety of ways in which to work.

But there is one thing which is frequently overlooked and neglected. It is the work of making the prayer and social meetings as interesting as they should be. If all would do their duty with fidelity, they would be so filled with peace, faith, and courage, and would have such an experience to relate when they came to the meetings, that others would be refreshed by their clear, strong testimony for God.

Our prayer and social meetings are not what they should be—seasons of special help and encouragement to one another. Each one has a duty to do to make these gatherings as interesting and profitable as possible. This can best be done by having a fresh experience daily in the things of God, and by not hesitating to speak of His love in the assemblies of His saints.

If you do not allow darkness and unbelief to enter your hearts, they will not be manifest in your meetings. Do not gratify the enemy by dwelling upon the dark side of your experience, but trust Jesus more fully for help to resist temptation. If we thought and talked more of Jesus and less of ourselves, we should have much more of His presence in our meetings.

When we make our Christian experience appear to unbelievers, or to one another, as one that is joyless, filled with trial, doubt, and perplexity, we dishonor God; we do not correctly represent Jesus or the Christian faith. We have a friend in Jesus, who has given us the most marked evidence of His love, and who is able and willing to give life and salvation to all who come unto Him. . . .

It is not necessary for us to be ever stumbling and repenting and mourning and writing bitter things against ourselves. It is our privilege to believe the promises of the Word of God, and accept the blessings that Jesus loves to bestow, that our joy may be full.—*Review and Herald,* July 20, 1886.

Jesus in the Heart
Makes the Life Fragrant

*My voice You shall hear in the morning, O Lord; in the morning
I will direct it to You, and I will look up. Psalm 5:3, NKJV.*

CHRISTIAN READER, let the great purpose that constrained Paul to press forward in the face of hardship and difficulty lead you to consecrate yourself wholly to God's service. Whatever your hands find to do, do it with your might. Let your daily prayer be "Lord, help me to do my best. Teach me how to do better work. Help me to bring into my service the loving ministry of the Savior."

The responsibility of each human agent is measured by the gifts he or she holds in trust. All are to be workers; but upon the worker who has had the greatest opportunities, the greatest clearness of mind in understanding the Scriptures, rests the highest responsibility. All receivers should hold themselves accountable to God, and use their talents for God's glory.

Success in the work of God is not the result of chance, of accident, or of destiny; it is the outworking of God's providence, and the award of faith and discretion, of virtue and persevering labor. It is the practice of the truth that brings success and moral power. The bright rays of the Sun of Righteousness are to be welcomed as the light of the mind; the principles of the character of Christ are to be made the principles of the human character. . . .

"God so loved the world, that he gave his only begotten Son, that whosoever believeth in him should not perish, but have everlasting life." This is the love that is the fulfilling of the law. Every person whose heart is filled with compassion for fallen humanity, who loves to a purpose, will reveal that love by the performance of Christlike deeds. True Christianity diffuses love through the whole being. It touches every vital part—the brain, the heart, the helping hands, the feet—enabling us to stand firmly where God requires us to stand, lest the lame be turned out of the way. The contemplation of Him who loved us and gave Himself for us will make the life fragrant and give power to perfect a Christian experience.

We can, *we can,* reveal the likeness of our divine Lord. We can know the science of spiritual life. We can glorify God in our bodies and in our spirits, which are His. Christ has shown us what we may accomplish through cooperation with Him. "Abide in me," He says, "and I in you."—*Review and Herald,* Apr. 4, 1912.

Family Worship Can
Help Create Harmony

Who can endure the day of His coming? And who can stand when He appears?
For He is like a refiner's fire and like fullers' soap. Malachi 3:2, NKJV.

WE ARE RAPIDLY nearing the close of this earth's history. The end is very near, much nearer than many suppose, and I feel burdened to urge upon our people the necessity of seeking the Lord earnestly. Many are asleep, and what can be said to arouse them from their carnal slumber? The Lord would have His church purified before His judgments shall fall more signally upon the world. . . .

Christ will remove every pretentious cloak. No mingling of the true with the spurious can deceive Him. "He is like a refiner's fire," separating the precious from the vile, the dross from the gold.

Like the Levites, God's chosen people are set apart by Him for His special work. Every true Christian bears priestly credentials. All are honored with the sacred responsibility of representing to the world the character of their heavenly Father. They are to heed well the words "Be ye therefore perfect, even as your Father which is in heaven is perfect." . . .

I am instructed to urge upon our people most earnestly the necessity of religion in the home. Among the members of the household there is ever to be a kind, thoughtful consideration. Morning and evening let all hearts be united in reverent worship. At the season of evening worship, let every member of the family search well his own heart. Let every wrong that has been committed be made right. If, during the day, one has wronged another, or spoken unkindly, let the transgressor seek pardon of the one injured. Often grievances are cherished in the mind, and misunderstandings and heartaches are created that need not be. If the one who is suspected of wrong be given an opportunity, he or she might be able to make explanations that would bring relief to other members of the family.

"Confess your faults one to another, and pray one for another," that ye may be healed of all spiritual infirmities, that sinful dispositions may be changed. Make diligent work for eternity. Pray most earnestly to the Lord, and hold fast to the faith. Trust not in the arm of flesh, but trust implicitly in the Lord's guidance. Let each one now say, "As for me, I will come out, and be separate from the world. I will serve the Lord with full purpose of heart."—*Review and Herald,* Nov. 8, 1906.

Victory Is Assured for All Who Obey Christ's Orders

These things I have spoken to you, that in Me you may have peace. In the world you will have tribulation; but be of good cheer, I have overcome the world. John 16:33, NKJV.

CHRIST CAME TO our world as the surety for humanity, preparing the way for all to gain the victory by giving them moral power. It is not His will that any shall be placed at a disadvantage. He would not have those who are striving to overcome intimidated and discouraged by the crafty assaults of the serpent. "Be of good cheer," He says, "I have overcome the world."

With such a General to lead us on to victory, we may indeed have joy and courage. He came as our champion. He takes cognizance of the battle that all who are at enmity with Satan must fight. He lays before His followers a plan of the battle, pointing out its peculiarities and severity, and warning them not to join His army without first counting the cost. He tells them that the vast confederacy of evil is arrayed against them, and shows them that they are fighting for an invisible world, and that His army is not composed merely of human agencies. His soldiers are coworkers with heavenly intelligences, and One higher than angels is in the ranks; for the Holy Spirit, Christ's representative, is there.

Then Christ summons every decided follower, every true soldier, to fight for Him, assuring them that there is deliverance for all who will obey His orders. If Christ's soldiers look faithfully to their Captain for their orders, success will attend their warfare against the enemy. No matter how they may be beset, in the end they will be triumphant.

Their infirmities may be many, their sins great, their ignorance seemingly insurmountable; but if they realize their weakness, and look to Christ for aid, He will be their efficiency. He is ever ready to enlighten their dullness and overcome their sinfulness. If they avail themselves of His power, their characters will be transformed; they will be surrounded with an atmosphere of light and holiness. Through His merits and imparted power they will be "more than conquerors." Supernatural help will be given them, enabling them in their weakness to do the deeds of omnipotence.

Those who fight for Christ are fighting in the sight of the heavenly universe, and they should be soldiers, not cowards. . . . By faith they are to look calmly upon every foe, exclaiming: "We fight the good fight of faith, under the command of an omnipotent Power. Because He lives, we shall live also."—*Signs of the Times,* May 27, 1897.

In Every Situation
Jesus Gives Fresh Blessings

Why are you cast down, O my soul? And why are
you disquieted within me? Hope in God; for I shall yet praise
Him, the help of my countenance and my God. Psalm 42:11, NKJV.

WE HAVE LEARNED in the midst of dark providences that it was not wise to have a will or way of our own, and to cast not reflection and surmises on the divine faithfulness. I feel that we are those who can understand and sympathize with each other. We are bound together by the grace of Jesus Christ and in the bonds of Christian sympathies made sacred by afflictions. . . .

Afflictions are oft mercies in disguise. We know not what we might have been without them. When God in His mysterious providence overthrows all our cherished plans, and we may receive sorrow in the place of joy, we will bow in submission and say, "Thy will, O God, be done." We must and we will ever cherish a calm, religious trust in One who loves us, who gave His life for us. "The Lord will command his lovingkindness in the daytime, and in the night his song shall be with me, and my prayer unto the God of my life. I will say unto God my rock, Why hast thou forgotten me? why go I mourning because of the oppression of the enemy?" . . .

The Lord looks upon our afflictions. He graciously and discriminately metes them out and apportions them. As a refiner of silver He watches us every moment until the purification is complete. The furnace is to purify and refine, not to destroy and consume. He will cause those who put their trust in Him to sing of mercies in the midst of judgments. He is ever watching to impart, when most needed, new and fresh blessings, strength in the hour of weakness, succor in the hour of danger, friends in the hour of loneliness, sympathy, human and divine, in the hour of sorrow.

We are homeward bound. He that loveth us so much as to die for us hath builded for us a city. The New Jerusalem is our place of rest. There will be no sadness in the City of God. No wail of sadness. No dirge of crushed hopes and buried affection shall ever more be heard.—*Daughters of God*, pp. 223, 224.

In Love and Mercy Jesus Pleads With Us and for Us

Through the Lord's mercies we are not consumed, because His compassions fail not. They are new every morning; great is Your faithfulness. Lamentations 3:22, 23, NKJV.

"BE YE THEREFORE merciful, as your Father also is merciful." The Lord honors His human agents by taking them into partnership with Himself. The heart of Christ is full of forgiving mercy and truth. He is afflicted in all the afflictions of His people. We are to be compassionate, and find joy in coming with a kindly interest to bind up the wounds of those who have been pursued and left half dead by the ruthless hand of the destroyer. We are to be ready to heal the bruises that sin has made.

Those who do this are Christ's ministers, and the world has a living testimony of the love of God before them in His representatives. God is revealed before the world in those who practice the works of Christ, and through His messengers He is known as a God of mercy, goodness, and forgiveness. "He that spared not his own Son, but delivered him up for us all, how shall he not with him also freely give us all things?"

God in Christ is ours, and His bounties of love and mercy are inexhaustible. He desires that everyone shall be benefited by the rich provisions that He has made for those who love Him; He invites us all to share with Him in His glory. The bliss of heaven has been provided for all who love God supremely and their fellow mortals as themselves.

Men and women would no longer be the slaves of sin if they would but turn from Satan's alluring, delusive attractions, and look to Jesus long enough to see and understand His love. New habits will be formed, and powerful propensities for evil will be held in check. Our Leader is a conqueror, and He guides us on to certain victory.

Our Advocate, Jesus, is pleading before His Father's throne in our behalf, and He is also pleading with the sinner, saying, "Turn ye, for why will ye die?" Has not God done everything possible through Christ to win us from satanic deception? . . . Is He not a risen Savior, ever living to make intercession for us? Is He not ever following up His great work of atonement by the work of the Holy Spirit on every heart? The bow of mercy still arches the throne of God, testifying to the fact that every soul who believes in Christ as a personal Savior shall have everlasting life. Mercy and justice are blended in God's dealing with His heritage.—*Signs of the Times,* Sept. 19, 1895.

Diffuse the Light
Throughout the Dark World

As I was passing through and considering the objects of your worship, I even found an altar with this inscription: TO THE UNKNOWN GOD. Therefore, the One whom you worship without knowing, Him I proclaim to you. Acts 17:23, NKJV.

JESUS TAUGHT HIS followers that they were debtors both to the Jews and the Greeks, to the wise and the unwise, and gave them to understand that race distinction, caste, and lines of division made by human beings were not approved of Heaven, and were to have no influence in the work of disseminating the gospel. The disciples of Christ were not to make distinctions between their neighbors and their enemies, but they were to regard every person as a neighbor who needed help, and they were to look upon the world as their field of labor, seeking to save the lost.

Jesus has given to both men and women their work, taking them from the narrow circle which their selfishness has prescribed, annihilating territorial lines, and all artificial distinctions of society. He marks off no limited boundary for missionary zeal, but bids His followers extend their labors to the uttermost parts of the earth. . . .

The field of labor presents one vast community of human beings who are in the darkness of error, who are filled with longing, who are praying to One they know not. They need to hear the voice of those who are laborers together with God, saying to them, as Paul said to the Athenians, "Whom therefore ye ignorantly worship, him declare I unto you."

The members of the church of Christ are to be faithful workers in the great harvest field. They are to be diligently working and earnestly praying, making progress, and diffusing light amid the moral darkness of the world; for are not the angels of heaven imparting to them divine inspiration? They are never to think of, and much less to speak of, failure in their work. . . . They are to be filled with hope, knowing that they do not rely upon human ability or upon finite resources, but upon the promised divine aid, the ministry of heavenly agencies who are pledged to open the way before them. . . .

Angels of God will break the way before us, preparing hearts for the gospel message, and the promised power will accompany the laborer, and "the glory of the Lord shall be thy rereward."—*Review and Herald,* Oct. 30, 1894.

God Alone Is
to Be Worshiped

You shall destroy their altars, and break down their sacred pillars,
and cut down their wooden images, and burn their carved images with fire.
For you are a holy people to the Lord your God. Deuteronomy 7:5, 6, NKJV.

GOD WOULD HAVE His people understand that He alone should be the object of their worship; and when they should overcome the idolatrous nations around them, they should not preserve any of the images of their worship, but utterly destroy them. Many of these heathen deities were very costly, and of beautiful workmanship, which might tempt those who had witnessed idol worship, so common in Egypt, to even regard these senseless objects with some degree of reverence. The Lord would have His people know that it was because of the idolatry of these nations, which had led them to every degree of wickedness, that He would use the Israelites as His instruments to punish them, and destroy their gods. . . .

"I will set thy bounds from the Red Sea even unto the sea of the Philistines, and from the desert unto the river: for I will deliver the inhabitants of the land into your hand; and thou shalt drive them out before thee." . . .

These promises of God to His people were on condition of their obedience. If they would serve the Lord fully, He would do great things for them. After Moses had received the judgments from the Lord, and had written them for the people, also the promises, on condition of obedience, the Lord said unto him, "Come up unto the Lord, thou, and Aaron, Nadab, and Abihu, and seventy of the elders of Israel, and worship ye afar off. And Moses alone shall come near the Lord: but they shall not come nigh; neither shall the people go up with him. And Moses came and told the people all the words of the Lord, and all the judgments: and all the people answered with one voice, and said, All the words which the Lord hath said will we do."

Moses had written—not the ten commandments, but the judgments which God would have them observe, and the promises, on conditions that they would obey Him. He read this to the people, and they pledged themselves to obey all the words which the Lord had said. Moses then wrote their solemn pledge in a book, and offered sacrifice unto God for the people. "And he took the book of the covenant, and read in the audience of the people, and they said, All that the Lord hath said will we do, and be obedient."—*Spiritual Gifts*, vol. 3, pp. 269, 270.

341

Christ's Self-sacrificing Life Is Our Lesson Book

It is good to give thanks to the Lord, and to sing praises to Your name, O Most High; to declare Your lovingkindness in the morning, and Your faithfulness every night. Psalm 92:1, 2, NKJV.

PRACTICAL CHRISTIANITY means laboring together with God every day; working for Christ, not now and then, but continuously. A neglect to reveal practical righteousness in our lives is a denial of our faith and of the power of God. God is seeking for a sanctified people, a people set apart for His service, a people who will heed and accept the invitation "Take my yoke upon you, and learn of me."

How earnestly Christ prosecuted the work of our salvation! What devotion His life revealed as He sought to give value to fallen humanity by imputing to every repenting, believing sinner the merits of His spotless righteousness! How untiringly He worked! In the temple and the synagogue, in the streets of the cities, in the marketplace, in the workshop, by the seaside, among the hills, He preached the gospel and healed the sick. He gave all there was of Himself, that He might work out the plan of redeeming grace.

Christ was under no obligation to make this great sacrifice. Voluntarily He pledged Himself to bear the punishment due to the transgressor of His law. His love was His only obligation, and without a murmur He endured every pang and welcomed every indignity that was part of the plan of salvation. The life of Christ was one of unselfish service, and His life is our lesson book. The work that He began we are to carry forward.

With His life of toil and sacrifice before them, can those who profess His name hesitate to deny self, to lift the cross and follow Him? He humbled Himself to the lowest depths that we might be lifted to the heights of purity and holiness and completeness. He became poor that He might pour into our poverty-stricken souls the fullness of His riches. He endured the cross of shame that He might give us peace and rest and joy, and make us partakers of the glories of His throne.

Should we not appreciate the privilege of working for Him, and be eager to practice self-denial and self-sacrifice for His sake? Should we not give back to God all that He has redeemed, the affections He has purified, and the body that He has purchased, to be kept unto sanctification and holiness?—*Review and Herald,* Apr. 4, 1912.

Memorize the Scriptures,
Preparing for the Future

You will be hated by all because of my name. But the one
who endures to the end will be saved. Mark 13:13, NRSV.

THE SERVANTS OF Christ were to prepare no set speech to present when brought to trial. Their preparation was to be made day by day in treasuring up the precious truths of God's Word, and through prayer strengthening their faith. When they were brought into trial, the Holy Spirit would bring to their remembrance the very truths that would be needed.

A daily, earnest striving to know God, and Jesus Christ, whom He has sent, would bring power and efficiency to the soul. The knowledge obtained by diligent searching of the Scriptures would be flashed into the memory at the right time. But if any had neglected to acquaint themselves with the words of Christ, if they had never tested the power of His grace in trial, they could not expect that the Holy Spirit would bring His words to their remembrance. They were to serve God daily with undivided affection, and then trust Him.

So bitter would be the enmity to the gospel that even the tenderest earthly ties would be disregarded. The disciples of Christ would be betrayed to death by the members of their own households. . . . But He bade them not to expose themselves unnecessarily to persecution. He Himself often left one field of labor for another, in order to escape from those who were seeking His life. When He was rejected at Nazareth, and His own townsmen tried to kill Him, He went down to Capernaum, and there the people were astonished at His teaching, "for his word was with power" (Luke 4:32). So His servants were not to be discouraged by persecution, but to seek a place where they could still labor for the salvation of souls.

The servant is not above his master. The Prince of heaven was called Beelzebub, and His disciples will be misrepresented in like manner. But whatever the danger, Christ's followers must avow their principles. They should scorn concealment. They cannot remain uncommitted until assured of safety in confessing the truth. They are set as watchmen, to warn men and women of their peril. The truth received from Christ must be imparted to all, freely and openly.—*The Desire of Ages,* p. 355.

We May Receive God's Unlimited Grace, to Do Good

If you then, being evil, know how to give good gifts to your children, how much more will your Father who is in heaven give good things to those who ask Him! Matthew 7:11, NKJV.

WE ARE ALL under obligation to deny self daily for Christ's sake. Jesus says, "If any man will come after me, let him deny himself, and take up his cross, and follow me"; "whosoever doth not bear his cross, and come after me, cannot be my disciple."

As we call upon God at every step, pleading for divine wisdom as we advance, seeking for light and grace in order that under all and in every circumstance we shall do unto others as we would that they should do unto us were we in their place, we shall feel the necessity of fulfilling the broad and deep requirements of the holy law of God. Thus shall we lose sight of self, and looking unto Jesus, the author and finisher of our faith, we shall lay upon the foundation deeds of mercy, benevolence, compassion, and love, which are compared to gold, silver, and precious stones, which the fires of the last days cannot consume.

The Lord Jesus is our efficiency in all things; His Spirit is to be our inspiration; and as we place ourselves in His hands to be channels of light, our means of doing good will never be exhausted; for the resources of the power of Jesus Christ are to be at our command. We may draw upon His fullness, and receive of that grace which has no limit. The Captain of our salvation at every step would teach us that almighty power is at the demand of living faith. He says, "Without me ye can do nothing"; but again declares that "greater works than these shall [ye] do; because I go unto my Father."

We are to pray without ceasing. In supplicating the throne of grace in the name of Christ, the promise is sure, "Whatsoever ye shall ask the Father in my name, he will give it you. Hitherto have ye asked nothing in my name; ask, and ye shall receive, that your joy may be full." When you make God your trust, when you call upon Him with your whole heart, He will be found of you. "Then shalt thou call, and the Lord shall answer; thou shalt cry, and he shall say, Here I am."—*Review and Herald,* Oct. 30, 1894.

To Feed the Soul,
Commune Constantly With Jesus

O God, You are my God; early will I seek You; my soul thirsts for You; my flesh longs for You in a dry and thirsty land where there is no water. Psalm 63:1, NKJV.

NO HUMAN AGENT can supply that which will satisfy the hunger and thirst of the soul. But Jesus says, "Behold, I stand at the door, and knock: if any man hear my voice, and open the door, I will come in to him, and will sup with him, and he with me" (Rev. 3:20). "I am the bread of life: he that cometh to me shall never hunger; and he that believeth on me shall never thirst" (John 6:35).

As we need food to sustain our physical strength, so do we need Christ, the Bread from heaven, to sustain spiritual life and impart strength to work the works of God. As the body is continually receiving the nourishment that sustains life and vigor, so the soul must be constantly communing with Christ, submitting to Him and depending wholly upon Him.

As the weary traveler seeks the spring in the desert and, finding it, quenches his burning thirst, so will the Christian thirst for and obtain the pure water of life, of which Christ is the fountain.

As we discern the perfection of our Savior's character we shall desire to become wholly transformed and renewed in the image of His purity. The more we know of God, the higher will be our ideal of character and the more earnest our longing to reflect His likeness. A divine element combines with the human when the soul reaches out after God and the longing heart can say, "My soul, wait thou only upon God; for my expectation is from him" (Ps. 62:5).

If you have a sense of need in your soul, if you hunger and thirst after righteousness, this is an evidence that Christ has wrought upon your heart, in order that He may be sought unto to do for you, through the endowment of the Holy Spirit, those things which it is impossible for you to do for yourself. . . .

The words of God are the wellsprings of life. As you seek unto those living springs you will, through the Holy Spirit, be brought into communion with Christ. Familiar truths will present themselves to your mind in a new aspect, texts of Scripture will burst upon you with a new meaning as a flash of light, you will see the relation of other truths to the work of redemption, and you will know that Christ is leading you, a divine Teacher is at your side.—*Thoughts From the Mount of Blessing,* pp. 18-20.

Be Courteous, Lifting Others' Burdens, as Did Jesus

Finally, all of you be of one mind, having compassion for one
another; love as brothers, be tenderhearted, be courteous; not returning
evil for evil or reviling for reviling, but on the contrary blessing, knowing that
you were called to this, that you may inherit a blessing. 1 Peter 3:8, 9, NKJV.

THOSE WHO WORK for Christ are to be pure, upright, and trustworthy, and they are also to be tenderhearted, compassionate, and courteous. There is a charm in the dealings and conversation of those who are truly courteous. Kind words, pleasant looks, a courteous demeanor, are of inestimable value. Uncourteous Christians, by their neglect of others, show that they are not in union with Christ. It is impossible to be in union with Christ and yet be uncourteous.

What Christ was in His life on this earth, that every Christian should be. He is our example, not only in His spotless purity but in His patience, gentleness, and winsomeness of disposition. He was as firm as a rock where truth and duty were concerned, but He was invariably kind and courteous. His life was a perfect illustration of true courtesy. He had ever a kind look and a word of comfort for the needy and oppressed.

His presence brought a purer atmosphere into the home, and His life was as leaven working amid the elements of society. Harmless and undefiled, He walked among the thoughtless, the rude, the uncourteous; amid the unjust publicans, the unrighteous Samaritans, the heathen soldiers, the rough peasants, and the mixed multitude. He spoke a word of sympathy here, and a word there, as He saw people weary, and compelled to bear heavy burdens. He shared their burdens, and repeated to them the lessons He had learned from nature of the love, the kindness, the goodness of God.

He sought to inspire with hope the most rough and unpromising, setting before them the assurance that they might become blameless and harmless, attaining such a character as would make them manifest as children of God. . . .

The love of Christ mellows the heart and smooths all roughness from the disposition. Let us learn from Him how to combine a high sense of purity and integrity with sunniness of temperament. A kind, courteous Christian is the most powerful argument in favor of the gospel that can be produced.—*Review and Herald*, Aug. 20, 1959.

We Are to Grow in
Piety, Purity, and Love

As newborn babes, desire the pure milk of the word, that you may grow thereby,
if indeed you have tasted that the Lord is gracious. 1 Peter 2:2, 3, NKJV.

GOD HAS MADE every provision for the saving of every soul; but if we spurn the gift of everlasting life, purchased at infinite cost for us, the time will come when God will also spurn us from His presence, whether we are rich or poor, high or low, learned or unlearned. The principles of eternal justice will have full control in the great day of God's wrath.

We shall not hear a charge against us on the ground of the outbreaking sins we have committed, but the charge will be made against us for the neglect of good and noble duties enjoined upon us by the God of love. The deficiencies of our characters will be held up to view. It will then be known that all who are so condemned had light and knowledge, were entrusted with their Lord's goods, and were found unfaithful to their trust. It will be seen that they had no appreciation of the heavenly trust, that they did not use their capital in loving service to others, that they did not, by precept and example, cultivate faith and devotion in those with whom they associated. It will be according to the light they have had that they will be judged and punished.

God requires that every human agent shall improve all the means of grace heaven has provided, and become more and more efficient in the work of God. Every provision has been made that the piety, purity, and love of Christ's followers shall ever increase, that their talents may double, and their ability increase in the service of their divine Master.

But though this provision has been made, many who profess to believe in Jesus do not make it manifest by growth that testifies to the sanctifying power of the truth upon life and character. When we first receive Jesus into our hearts, we are as babes in religion; but we are not to remain babes in experience. We are to grow in grace and in the knowledge of our Lord and Savior Jesus Christ; we are to attain to the full measure of the stature of men and women in Him. We are to make advances, to gain new and rich experiences through faith, growing in trust and confidence and love, knowing God and Jesus Christ whom He hath sent.—*Youth's Instructor,* June 8, 1893.

God's Word and Love Will Open Hearts to Jesus

*With my soul I have desired You in the night, yes, by my spirit
within me I will seek You early; for when Your judgments are in the earth,
the inhabitants of the world will learn righteousness. Isaiah 26:9, NKJV.*

IT IS THE Savior's love that constrains the messenger to bear the message to the lost. Oh, how wonderful is the importuning of Christ with sinners! Although His love is beaten back by the refusal of hard, stubborn hearts, He returns to plead with greater force, "Behold, I stand at the door, and knock." His love woos with winning force, until souls are compelled to come in.

Those who come to the supper turn to the blessed Jesus and say, "Thy gentleness hath made me great." He wins them by the word of His love and power; for the Word of God is the rod of His power. He says, "Is not my word like a fire? saith the Lord; and like a hammer that breaketh the rock in pieces?"

When the Word of God is sent home to the human heart by the Holy Spirit, it is mighty to the pulling down of the strongholds of Satan. Finite men and women could do nothing in the great warfare, were it not for the Word of God. They could not plead successfully with human hearts that are as hard as steel, that are bolted and barred lest Jesus should find an entrance there; but the Lord endows men and women with His wisdom, and the weakest one may become as David by faith in God.

The Lord takes those who are devoted to Him, even though they may be uneducated, humble men and women, and sends them forth with His warning message. He stirs their hearts by His Spirit, He gives them spiritual muscle and sinew, and they are enabled to go forth with the Word of God, and to compel human beings to come in. Thus many poor, fainting souls, who are starving for the Bread of Life, are out of weakness made strong, and wax valiant in the fight, and put to flight the armies of the aliens.

"See that ye refuse not him that speaketh." Every time you turn away your ear and refuse to listen, every time you fail to open the door of your heart, you strengthen yourself in unbelief, and make yourself more and more unwilling to listen to the voice of Him that speaketh, and you diminish your chance of responding to the last appeal of mercy. . . . Let not Christ weep over you as He wept over Jerusalem, saying, "How often would I have gathered thy children together, even as a hen gathereth her chickens under her wings, and ye would not! Behold, your house is left unto you desolate."—*Review and Herald,* Sept. 24, 1895.

Special Endowment of Grace and Power Needed Today

The coming of the lawless one is according to the working
of Satan, with all power, signs, and lying wonders, and with all
unrighteous deception among those who perish, because they did not receive the
love of the truth, that they might be saved. 2 Thessalonians 2:9, 10, NKJV.

THE GREAT CONTROVERSY between good and evil will increase in intensity to the very close of time. In all ages the wrath of Satan has been manifested against the church of Christ; and God has bestowed His grace and Spirit upon His people to strengthen them to stand against the power of the evil one. When the apostles of Christ were to bear His gospel to the world and to record it for all future ages, they were especially endowed with the enlightenment of the Spirit.

But as the church approaches its final deliverance, Satan is to work with greater power. He comes down "having great wrath, because he knoweth that he hath but a short time" (Rev. 12:12). . . . For six thousand years that mastermind that once was highest among the angels of God has been wholly bent to the work of deception and ruin. And all the depths of satanic skill and subtlety acquired, all the cruelty developed, during these struggles of the ages, will be brought to bear against God's people in the final conflict.

And in this time of peril the followers of Christ are to bear to the world the warning of the Lord's second advent; and a people are to be prepared to stand before Him at His coming, "without spot, and blameless" (2 Peter 3:14). At this time the special endowment of divine grace and power is not less needful to the church than in apostolic days. . . .

Satan's efforts to misrepresent the character of God, to cause men and women to cherish a false conception of the Creator, and thus to regard Him with fear and hate rather than with love; his endeavors to set aside the divine law, leading the people to think themselves free from its requirements; and his persecution of those who dare to resist his deceptions have been steadfastly pursued in all ages. They may be traced in the history of patriarchs, prophets, and apostles, of martyrs and reformers.—*The Great Controversy,* pp. ix-xi.

When We Thirst for
Righteousness, Jesus Draws Near

As the deer pants for the water brooks, so pants my soul for You,
O God. My soul thirsts for God, for the living God. Psalm 42:1, 2, NKJV.

THE LORD HAS momentous truths to reveal to those who would understand the things of the Spirit. His lessons are for all, and adapted to the
needs of all. While His lessons are clothed in language so simple that a child
might understand them, the truth is so deep that the most learned may well
be charmed, and worship the Author of matchless wisdom. Though the
wisest may find abundant food for thought in His simplest utterance, the
humblest may comprehend His truth, and appropriate His promises to the
need of the soul.

Jesus taught men and women for the purpose of arousing desire to understand the things of God, that they might behold the excellence of the
divine character, and make application for the righteousness of Christ, in
which they might stand accepted before the Lord Jehovah.

Have you a sense of want in your soul? Do you hunger and thirst after
righteousness? Then this is an evidence that Christ has wrought upon your
heart, and created this sense of need in your soul, in order that He may be
sought unto to do for you, through the endowment of the Holy Spirit,
those things which it is impossible for you to do for yourself. . . .

The parables of Christ have been placed on record, and to the honest,
diligent searcher after truth, their meaning will be made plain, their mystery unveiled. Those who will not seek for truth as for hidden treasure
make manifest the fact that they do not sincerely desire to know what is
truth. Christ still says to His true followers, "It is given unto you to know
the mysteries of the kingdom of heaven." "Whosoever hath, to him shall
be given, and he shall have more abundance."

Those who respond to the drawing of Christ will be found inquiring
as to what is truth, that their feet may be directed into the way of righteousness. Christ is drawing all, but not all respond to His drawing. Those
who yield their will to God's will, who are willing to follow where the
Spirit of God may lead, who receive the light and walk therein, will seek
for still more of heavenly enlightenment, and "shall have more abundance."—*Signs of the Times,* Nov. 7, 1892.

Angels Join Us as
We Help Those in Need

*Let him take hold of My strength, that he may make peace with
Me; and he shall make peace with Me. Isaiah 27:5, NKJV.*

THERE ARE MANY who err, and who feel their shame and their folly.
They look upon their mistakes and errors until they are driven almost to
desperation. These souls we are not to neglect. When one has to swim
against the stream, there is all the force of the current driving him or her
back. Let a helping hand then be held out . . . as was the Elder Brother's
hand to the sinking Peter. Speak hopeful words, words that will establish
confidence and awaken love.

Thy brother and sister, sick in spirit, need thee, as thou thyself hast
needed their love. . . . The knowledge of our own weakness should help
us to help others in their bitter need. Never should we pass by one suffering soul without seeking to impart the comfort wherewith we are comforted of God.

It is fellowship with Christ, personal contact with a living Savior, that
enables the mind and heart and soul to triumph over the lower nature. . . .
[The wanderers] need to clasp a hand that is warm, to trust in a heart full of
tenderness. Keep their minds stayed upon the thought of a divine presence
ever beside them, ever looking upon them with pitying love. . . .

As you engage in this work, you have companions unseen by human
eyes. Angels of heaven were beside the Samaritan who cared for the
wounded stranger. Angels from the heavenly courts stand by all who do
God's service in ministering to their fellow beings. And you have the cooperation of Christ Himself. He is the Restorer, and as you work under
His supervision, you will see great results.

Upon your faithfulness in this work not only the well-being of others
but your own eternal destiny depends. Christ is seeking to uplift all who
will be lifted to companionship with Himself, that we may be one with
Him as He is one with the Father. He permits us to come in contact with
suffering and calamity in order to call us out of our selfishness; He seeks to
develop in us the attributes of His character—compassion, tenderness, and
love. By accepting this work of ministry we place ourselves in His school,
to be fitted for the courts of God.—*Christ's Object Lessons*, pp. 387-389.

DECEMBER

❧

Repenting, Then Growing

Jesus, the Chief Shepherd, Knows Each Sheep

I say to you that likewise there will be more joy in heaven over one sinner who repents than over ninety-nine just persons who need no repentance. Luke 15:7, NKJV.

THE MINISTER IS to be a shepherd. Our Redeemer is called the chief Shepherd. The apostle writes, "Now the God of peace, that brought again from the dead our Lord Jesus, that great shepherd of the sheep, through the blood of the everlasting covenant, make you perfect in every good work to do his will, working in you that which is well-pleasing in his sight, through Jesus Christ." However lowly, however elevated we may be, whether we are in the shadow of adversity or in the sunshine of prosperity, we are His sheep, the flock of His pasture, and under the care of the chief Shepherd.

But the chief Shepherd has His undershepherds, whom He has delegated to care for His sheep and lambs. The great Shepherd never loses one from His care, is never indifferent even to the feeblest one of His flock. The beautiful parable that Christ gave of the one lost sheep, of the shepherd that left the ninety and nine to go in search of that which was lost, illustrates the care of the great Shepherd. He did not look carelessly over the sheep of the fold, and say, "I have ninety and nine, and it will cost me too much trouble to go in search of the straying one; let it come back, and I will open the door of the sheepfold and let it in; but I cannot go after it."

No; for no sooner does the sheep go astray than the countenance of the shepherd is filled with grief and anxiety. He counts and recounts the flock, and when he is certain that one sheep is lost, he slumbereth not. He leaves the ninety and nine within the fold; however dark and tempestuous the night, however perilous and unpleasant the way, however long and tedious the search, he does not weary, he does not falter, until the lost is found.

But when it is found, does he act indifferently? Does he call the sheep, and command the straying one to follow him? Does he threaten and beat it, or drive it before him, recounting the bitterness and discomfiture and anxiety that he has had on its account? No; he lays the weary, exhausted, wandering sheep on his shoulder, and with cheerful gratitude that his search has not been in vain, he returns it to the fold. His gratitude finds expression in melodious songs of rejoicing, and heavenly choirs respond to the shepherd's note of joy.

When the lost is found, heaven and earth unite in rejoicing and thanksgiving. . . . Jesus says, "I am the good shepherd, and know my sheep, and am known of mine." Just as the shepherds of earth know their sheep, so does the chief Shepherd know His flock that are scattered throughout the whole world.—*Review and Herald*, Aug. 23, 1892.

True Christians Focus on Christ, Not Self

When He had called the people to Himself, with His disciples
also, He said to them, "Whoever desires to come after Me, let him
deny himself, and take up his cross, and follow Me." Mark 8:34, NKJV.

THE WORD OF God gives the description of a true Christian, which corresponds with the work of the Holy Spirit on the heart and life. The children of God know at once they have the evidence in their own hearts that they are born of God. . . . It means depth and breadth of experience to follow the Lamb whithersoever He goeth. Self-denial and self-sacrifice will always be found in the path that leads through the strait gate to the broad meadows of the Lord's pastures.

To them that believe, Christ is precious. His Spirit moving upon the mind and heart of the believer is in perfect agreement with that which is written in the Word. The Spirit and the Word agree perfectly. Thus the Spirit beareth witness with our spirit that we are born of God.

The ones who find in their heart no resemblance to the great moral standard of righteousness, the Word of God, have no Christ to confess. Their language, their thoughts, are not in harmony with the Spirit of Christ. Their profession of faith is a counterfeit one. Do you ever find cream rising on water? The soul must have the vivifying influences of the breath of life from Christ in order to reveal in the conversation that Christ is formed within, the hope of glory.

One never gathers grapes from thistles. The words of Christians will be in accordance with their enjoyment of Christ. Those who are perpetually talking doubts and demanding additional evidence to banish their cloud of unbelief do not build on the Word. Their faith rests on haphazard circumstances; it is founded in feeling. But feeling, be it ever so pleasing, is not faith. God's Word is the foundation upon which our hopes of heaven must be built.

It is a great misfortune to be a chronic doubter, keeping the eye and thoughts on self. While you are beholding self, while this is the theme of thought and conversation, you cannot expect to be conformed to the image of Christ. Self is not your savior. You have no redeeming qualities in yourself. "I" is a very leaky boat for your faith to embark in. Just as surely as you trust yourself in it, it will founder. The lifeboat, to the lifeboat! This is your only safety. Jesus is the Captain of the lifeboat, and He has never lost a passenger.—*Manuscript Releases*, vol. 21, pp. 23, 24.

Truly Converted People
Aim for Perfection

*Therefore you shall be perfect, just as your Father
in heaven is perfect. Matthew 5:48, NKJV.*

IT MEANS MUCH to be a consistent Christian. It means to walk circumspectly before God, to press toward the mark of the prize of our high calling in Christ. It means to bear much fruit to the glory of Him who gave His Son to die for us. As sons and daughters of God, Christians should strive to reach the high ideal set before them in the gospel. They should be content with nothing less than perfection. . . .

Let us make God's holy Word our study, bringing its holy principles into our lives. Let us walk before God in meekness and humility, daily correcting our faults. Let us not by selfish pride separate the soul from God. Cherish not a feeling of lofty supremacy, thinking yourself better than others. "Let him that thinketh he standeth take heed lest he fall." Peace and rest will come to you as you bring your will into subjection to the will of Christ. Then the love of Christ will rule in the heart, bringing into captivity to the Savior the secret springs of action. The hasty, easily roused temper will be soothed and subdued by the oil of Christ's grace. The sense of sins forgiven will bring that peace that passeth all understanding. There will be an earnest striving to overcome all that is opposed to Christian perfection. Variance will disappear. People who once found fault with those around them will see that far greater faults exist in their own character.

There are those who listen to the truth, and are convinced that they have been living in opposition to Christ. They are condemned, and they repent of their transgressions. Relying upon the merits of Christ, exercising true faith in Him, they receive pardon for sin. As they cease to do evil and learn to do well, they grow in grace and in the knowledge of God. They see that they must sacrifice in order to separate from the world; and after counting the cost, they look upon all as loss if they may but win Christ. They have enlisted in Christ's army. The warfare is before them, and they enter it bravely and cheerfully, fighting against their natural inclinations and selfish desires, bringing the will into subjection to the will of Christ. Daily they seek the Lord for grace to obey Him, and they are strengthened and helped.

This is true conversion. In humble, grateful dependence those who have been given a new heart rely upon the help of Christ. They reveal in their life the fruit of righteousness. They once loved themselves. Worldly pleasure was their delight. Now their idol is dethroned, and God reigns supreme.—*Youth's Instructor,* Sept. 26, 1901.

Converted Sinners
Live a New Life

Then I will sprinkle clean water on you, and you shall be clean;
I will cleanse you from all your filthiness and from all your idols. I will
give you a new heart and put a new spirit within you; I will take the heart of
stone out of your flesh and give you a heart of flesh. Ezekiel 36:25, 26, NKJV.

MANY WHO SPEAK to others of the need of a new heart do not themselves know what is meant by these words. The youth especially stumble over this phrase, "a new heart." They do not know what it means. They look for a special change to take place in their feelings. This they term conversion. Over this error thousands have stumbled to ruin, not understanding the expression "Ye must be born again."

Satan leads people to think that because they have felt a rapture of feeling, they are converted. But their experience does not change. Their actions are the same as before. Their lives show no good fruit. They pray often and long, and are constantly referring to the feelings they had at such and such a time. But they do not live the new life. They are deceived. Their experience goes no deeper than feeling. They build upon the sand, and when adverse winds come, their house is swept away.

Many poor souls are groping in darkness, looking for the feelings which others say they have had in their experience. They overlook the fact that the believers in Christ must work out their own salvation with fear and trembling. The convicted sinners have something to do. They must repent and show true faith.

When Jesus speaks of the new heart, He means the mind, the life, the whole being. To have a change of heart is to withdraw the affections from the world, and fasten them upon Christ. To have a new heart is to have a new mind, new purposes, new motives. What is the sign of a new heart? A changed life. There is a daily, hourly dying to selfishness and pride.

Some make a great mistake by supposing that a high profession will compensate for real service. But a religion which is not practical is not genuine. True conversion makes us strictly honest in our dealings with our fellow beings. It makes us faithful in our everyday work. All sincere followers of Christ will show that the religion of the Bible qualifies them to use their talents in the Master's service. . . .

It is the noble principles which are brought into the work that make it wholly acceptable in the Lord's sight. True service links the lowliest of God's servants on earth with the highest of His servants in the courts above.—*Youth's Instructor,* Sept. 26, 1901.

Repent Today, and Receive Christ's Robe of Righteousness

So I say to you, Ask, and it will be given to you; search, and you will find; knock, and the door will be opened for you. For everyone who asks receives, and everyone who searches finds, and for everyone who knocks, the door will be opened. Luke 11:9, 10, NRSV.

WE ARE TO surrender our hearts to God, that He may renew and sanctify us, and fit us for His heavenly courts. We are not to wait for some special time, but today we are to give ourselves to Him, refusing to be the servants of sin. Do you imagine you can leave off sin a little at a time? Oh, leave the accursed thing at once! Hate the thing that Christ hates, love the thing that Christ loves. Has He not by His death and suffering made provision for your cleansing from sin?

When we begin to realize that we are sinners, when we fall on the Rock and are broken, the everlasting arms are placed about us, and we are brought close to the heart of Jesus. Then we shall be charmed with His loveliness and disgusted with our own righteousness.

We need to come close to the foot of the cross. The more we humble ourselves there, the more exalted will God's love appear. The grace and righteousness of Christ will not avail for those who feel whole, for those who think they are reasonably good, who are contented with their own condition. There is no room for Christ in the heart of those who do not realize their need of divine light and aid.

Jesus says, "Blessed are the poor in spirit: for theirs is the kingdom of heaven." There is fullness of grace in God, and we may have His Spirit and power in large measure. Do not feed on the husks of self-righteousness, but go to the Lord; He has the best robe to put upon you, and His arms are open to receive you. . . .

You are proved of God through His Word. You are not to wait for wonderful emotions before you believe that God has heard you; feeling is not to be your criterion, for emotions are as changeable as the clouds. You must have something solid for the foundation of your faith. The Word of the Lord is a word of infinite power, upon which you may rely; and He has said, "Ask, and ye shall receive." Look to Calvary. Has not Jesus said that He is your Advocate? Has He not said that if you ask anything in His name, you shall receive?

You are to come to God as a repenting sinner, through the name of Jesus, the divine Advocate; to a merciful, forgiving Father, believing that He will do just as He has promised. Let those who desire the blessing of God knock, and wait at the throne of mercy with firm assurance.—*Bible Echo,* Apr. 1, 1893.

Jesus Lovingly Calls, but Many Wait Too Long to Respond

*Nevertheless I have this against you, that you have
left your first love. Remember therefore from where you have fallen;
repent and do the first works, or else I will come to you quickly and remove
your lampstand from its place—unless you repent. Revelation 2:4, 5, NKJV.*

THE REDEEMER OF the world declares that there are greater sins than that for which Sodom and Gomorrah were destroyed. Those who hear the gospel invitation calling sinners to repentance, and heed it not, are more guilty before God than were the dwellers in the vale of Siddim. And still greater sin is theirs who profess to know God and to keep His commandments, yet who deny Christ in their character and their daily life. In the light of the Savior's warning, the fate of Sodom is a solemn admonition, not merely to those who are guilty of outbreaking sin, but to all who are trifling with Heaven-sent light and privileges. . . .

The Savior watches for a response to His offers of love and forgiveness with a more tender compassion than that which moves the heart of an earthly parent to forgive a wayward, suffering son or daughter. He cries after the wanderer, "Return unto me, and I will return unto you" (Mal. 3:7). But if the erring one persistently refuses to heed the voice that calls him or her with pitying, tender love, he or she will at last be left in darkness.

The heart that has long slighted God's mercy becomes hardened in sin and is no longer susceptible to the influence of the grace of God. Fearful will be the doom of that soul of whom the pleading Savior shall finally declare, he "is joined to idols: let him alone" (Hosea 4:17). It will be more tolerable in the day of judgment for the cities of the plain than for those who have known the love of Christ, and yet have turned away to choose the pleasures of a world of sin.

You who are slighting the offers of mercy, think of the long array of figures accumulating against you in the books of heaven; for there is a record kept of the impieties of nations, of families, of individuals. God may bear long while the account goes on, and calls to repentance and offers of pardon may be given; yet a time will come when the account will be full; when the soul's decision has been made; when by a person's own choice one's destiny has been fixed. Then the signal will be given for judgment to be executed.—*Patriarchs and Prophets*, p. 165.

When Sinners Repent,
Heaven Rejoices

As You sent Me into the world, I also have sent them into the world. And for their sakes I sanctify Myself, that they also may be sanctified by the truth. John 17:18, 19, NKJV.

IN THE PARABLE of the lost sheep, Christ teaches that salvation does not come through our seeking after God but through God's seeking after us. "There is none that understandeth, there is none that seeketh after God. They are all gone out of the way" (Rom. 3:11, 12). We do not repent in order that God may love us, but He reveals to us His love in order that we may repent. . . .

The rabbis had a saying that there is rejoicing in heaven when one who has sinned against God is destroyed; but Jesus taught that to God the work of destruction is a strange work. That in which all heaven delights is the restoration of God's own image in the souls whom He has made.

When some who have wandered far in sin seek to return to God, they will encounter criticism and distrust. There are those who will doubt whether their repentance is genuine, or will whisper, "They have no stability; I do not believe that they will hold out."

These persons are doing not the work of God but the work of Satan, who is the accuser of the brethren. Through their criticisms the wicked one hopes to discourage those souls, and to drive them still farther from hope and from God. Let the repenting sinners contemplate the rejoicing in heaven over the return of the one that was lost. Let them rest in the love of God and in no case be disheartened by the scorn and suspicion of the Pharisees.

The rabbis understood Christ's parable as applying to the publicans and sinners; but it has also a wider meaning. By the lost sheep Christ represents not only the individual sinner but the one world that has apostatized and has been ruined by sin. This world is but an atom in the vast dominions over which God presides, yet this little fallen world—the one lost sheep—is more precious in His sight than are the ninety and nine that went not astray from the fold.

Christ, the loved Commander in the heavenly courts, stooped from His high estate, laid aside the glory that He had with the Father, in order to save the one lost world. For this He left the sinless worlds on high, the ninety and nine that loved Him, and came to this earth, to be "wounded for our transgressions" and "bruised for our iniquities" (Isa. 53:5). God gave Himself in His Son that He might have the joy of receiving back the sheep that was lost. . . .

Every soul whom Christ has rescued is called to work in His name for the saving of the lost. This work had been neglected in Israel. Is it not neglected today by those who profess to be Christ's followers?—*Christ's Object Lessons*, pp. 189-191.

Conversion Creates
New Interests and New Loves

Put away your former way of life, your old self,
corrupt and deluded by its lusts. Ephesians 4:22, NRSV.

GOD NOW CALLS upon you to repent, to be zealous in the work. Your eternal happiness will be determined by the course you now pursue. Can you reject the invitations of mercy now offered? Can you choose your own way? Will you cherish pride and vanity, and lose your soul at last? The Word of God plainly tells us that few will be saved, and that the greater number even of those who are called will prove themselves unworthy of everlasting life. They will have no part in heaven, but will have their portion with Satan, and experience the second death.

Men and women may escape this doom if they will. It is true that Satan is the great originator of sin; yet this does not excuse anyone for sinning; for he cannot force any to do evil. He tempts them to it, and makes sin look enticing and pleasant; but he has to leave it to their own wills whether they will do it or not. He does not force people to become intoxicated, neither does he force them to remain away from religious meetings; but he presents temptations in a manner to allure to evil, and human beings are free moral agents to accept or refuse.

Conversion is a work that most do not appreciate. It is not a small matter to transform an earthly, sin-loving mind and bring it to understand the unspeakable love of Christ, the charms of His grace, and the excellency of God, so that souls shall be imbued with divine love and captivated with the heavenly mysteries. When they understand these things, their former life appears disgusting and hateful. They hate sin, and, breaking their heart before God, they embrace Christ as the life and joy of the soul. They renounce their former pleasures. They have a new mind, new affections, new interest, new will; their sorrows, and desires, and love are all new. The lust of the flesh, the lust of the eye, and the pride of life, which have heretofore been preferred before Christ, are now turned from, and Christ is the charm of the life, the crown of rejoicing.

Heaven, which once possessed no charms, is now viewed in its riches and glory; and they contemplate it as their future home, where they shall see, love, and praise the One who hath redeemed them by His precious blood.—*Testimonies for the Church*, vol. 2, pp. 293, 294.

Repentant Souls Hate
Sin and Love Righteousness

Now when they heard this, they were cut to the heart, and said to Peter and the rest of the apostles, "Men and brethren, what shall we do?" Then Peter said to them, "Repent, and let every one of you be baptized in the name of Jesus Christ for the remission of sins; and you shall receive the gift of the Holy Spirit." Acts 2:37, 38, NKJV.

HOW SHALL A person be just with God? How shall the sinner be made righteous? It is only through Christ that we can be brought into harmony with God, with holiness; but how are we to come to Christ? Many are asking the same question as did the multitude on the day of Pentecost, when, convicted of sin, they cried out, "What shall we do?" The first word of Peter's answer was "Repent" (Acts 2:37, 38). At another time, shortly after, he said, "Repent . . . , and be converted, that your sins may be blotted out" (Acts 3:19).

Repentance includes sorrow for sin and a turning away from it. We shall not renounce sin unless we see its sinfulness; until we turn away from it in heart there will be no real change in the life.

There are many who fail to understand the true nature of repentance. Multitudes sorrow that they have sinned and even make an outward reformation because they fear that their wrongdoing will bring suffering upon themselves. But this is not repentance in the Bible sense. They lament the suffering rather than the sin. Such was the grief of Esau when he saw that the birthright was lost to him forever. Balaam, terrified by the angel standing in his pathway with drawn sword, acknowledged his guilt lest he should lose his life; but there was no genuine repentance for sin, no conversion of purpose, no abhorrence of evil.

Judas Iscariot, after betraying his Lord, exclaimed, "I have sinned in that I have betrayed the innocent blood" (Matt. 27:4). The confession was forced from his guilty soul by an awful sense of condemnation and a fearful looking for of judgment. The consequences that were to result to him filled him with terror, but there was no deep, heartbreaking grief in his soul that he had betrayed the spotless Son of God and denied the Holy One of Israel. . . . These all lamented the results of sin, but did not sorrow for the sin itself.

But when the heart yields to the influence of the Spirit of God, the conscience will be quickened, and the sinner will discern something of the depth and sacredness of God's holy law, the foundation of His government in heaven and on earth. . . . [The sinner] sees the love of God, the beauty of holiness, the joy of purity; [and] longs to be cleansed and to be restored to communion with Heaven.—*Steps to Christ, pp. 23, 24.*

Humanity, Allied With Divinity, Can Keep the Law

Then Jesus came from Galilee to John at the Jordan to be baptized by him. And John tried to prevent Him, saying, "I need to be baptized by You, and are You coming to me?" But Jesus answered and said to him, "Permit it to be so now, for thus it is fitting for us to fulfill all righteousness." Then he allowed Him. Matthew 3:13-15, NKJV.

IN FULFILLING "all righteousness," Christ did not bring all righteousness to an end. He fulfilled all the requirements of God in repentance, faith, and baptism, the steps in grace in genuine conversion. In His humanity Christ filled up the measure of the law's requirements. He was the head of humanity, its substitute and surety. Human beings, by uniting their weakness to the divine nature of Christ, may become partakers of His character.

Christ came to give an example of the perfect conformity to the law of God required of Adam, the first man, down to the last person that shall live on the earth. He declares that His mission is not to destroy the law, but to fulfill it in perfect and entire obedience.

In this way He magnified the law and made it honorable. In His life He revealed its spiritual nature. He revealed to heavenly beings, to worlds unfallen, to a disobedient, unthankful, unholy world, that He fulfilled the far-reaching principles of the law. He came to demonstrate the fact that humanity, allied by living faith to divinity, can keep all God's commandments.

The typical offerings pointed to Christ, and when the perfect sacrifice was made the sacrificial offerings were no longer acceptable to God. Type met antitype in the death of the only begotten Son of God. He came to make plain the immutable character of the law, to declare that disobedience and transgression could never be rewarded by God with eternal life. He came as a man to humanity, that humanity might touch humanity.

But in no case did He come to lessen the obligations of mortals to be perfectly obedient. He did not destroy the validity of the Old Testament Scriptures. He fulfilled that which was predicted by God Himself. He did not come to set human beings free from the law: He came to open a way by which they might obey that law and teach others to do the same.—*Manuscript Releases,* vol. 10, pp. 292, 293.

Conscientious Persons Must Guard Against Being Deceived

Watch and pray, lest you enter into temptation. The spirit indeed is willing, but the flesh is weak. Mark 14:38, NKJV.

THOSE PROFESSING TO have new light, claiming to be reformers, will have great influence over a certain class who are convinced of the heresies that exist in the present age and who are not satisfied with the spiritual condition of the churches. With true, honest hearts, these desire to see a change for the better, a coming up to a higher standard. If the faithful servants of Christ would present the truth, pure and unadulterated, to this class, they would accept it, and purify themselves by obeying it. But Satan, ever vigilant, sets upon the track of these inquiring souls. Someone making high profession as a reformer comes to them, as Satan came to Christ disguised as an angel of light, and draws them still further from the path of right.

The unhappiness and degradation that follow in the train of licentiousness cannot be estimated. The world is defiled under its inhabitants. They have nearly filled up the measure of their iniquity; but that which will bring the heaviest retribution is the practice of iniquity under the cloak of godliness. The Redeemer of the world never spurned true repentance, however great the guilt; but He hurls burning denunciations against Pharisees and hypocrites. There is more hope for the open sinner than for this class. . . .

This man [a pseudoreformer] and those deceived by him love not the truth but have pleasure in unrighteousness. And what stronger delusion could come upon them than that there is nothing displeasing to God in licentiousness and adultery? The Bible contains many warnings against these sins. Paul writes to Titus of those who "profess that they know God; but in works they deny him, being abominable, and disobedient, and unto every good work reprobate." . . .

In this age of corruption when our adversary the devil, as a roaring lion, walketh about seeking whom he may devour, I see the necessity of lifting my voice in warning. "Watch ye and pray, lest ye enter into temptation." There are many who possess brilliant talents who wickedly devote them to the service of Satan. . . . Many of them cherish impure thoughts, unholy imaginations, unsanctified desires, and base passions. God hates the fruit borne upon such a tree. Angels, pure and holy, look upon the course of such with abhorrence, while Satan exults.

Oh, that men and women would consider what is to be gained by transgressing God's law! Under any and every circumstance, transgression is a dishonor to God and a curse to humanity. We must regard it thus, however fair its guise, and by whomsoever committed.—*Testimonies for the Church,* vol. 5, pp. 144-146.

True Repentance Involves Remorse for Sin and Forsaking It

For godly sorrow produces repentance leading to salvation, not to be regretted; but the sorrow of the world produces death. 2 Corinthians 7:10, NKJV.

THE LOVE OF God will never lead to the belittling of sin; it will never cover or excuse an unconfessed wrong. Achan learned too late that God's law, like its Author, is unchanging. It has to do with all our acts and thoughts and feelings. It follows us, and reaches every secret spring of action. By indulgence in sin, men and women are led to lightly regard the law of God. Many conceal their transgressions from other people, and flatter themselves that God will not be strict to mark iniquity.

But His law is the great standard of right, and with it every act of life must be compared in that day when God shall bring every work into judgment, with every secret thing, whether it be good or evil. Purity of heart will lead to purity of life. All excuses for sin are vain. Who can plead for sinners when God testifies against them?—*Signs of the Times,* Apr. 21, 1881.

There are many professed Christians whose confessions of sin are similar to that of Achan. They will, in a general way, acknowledge their unworthiness, but they refuse to confess the sins whose guilt rests upon their conscience, and which have brought the frown of God upon His people. . . .

Genuine repentance springs from a sense of the offensive character of sin. These general confessions are not the fruit of true humiliation of soul before God. They leave sinners with a self-complacent spirit to go on as before, until the conscience becomes hardened, and warnings that once aroused them produce hardly a feeling of danger, and after a time their sinful course appears right. All too late their sins will find them out, in that day when they shall not be purged with sacrifice nor offering forever. There is a vast difference between admitting facts after they are proved, and confessing sins known only to ourselves and God.—*Signs of the Times,* May 5, 1881.

Achan, the guilty party, did not feel the burden. He took it very coolly. We find nothing in the account to signify that he felt distressed. There is no evidence that he felt remorse, or reasoned from cause to effect, saying. "It is my sin that has brought the displeasure of the Lord upon the people." . . . He had no idea of making his wrong right by confession of sin and humiliation of soul.—*The Seventh-day Adventist Bible Commentary,* Ellen G. White Comments, vol. 2, p. 997.

The confession of Achan, although too late to be available in bringing to him any saving virtue, yet vindicated the character of God in His manner of dealing with him, and closed the door to the temptation that so continually beset the children of Israel, to charge upon the servants of God the work that God Himself had ordered to be done.—*Ibid.*

By Grace You Can
Reach Christ's Ideal

For thus says the Lord God, the Holy One of Israel: "In returning and rest you shall be saved; In quietness and confidence shall be your strength." Isaiah 30:15, NKJV.

THE LORD WILL recognize every effort you make to reach His ideal for you. When you make a failure, when you are betrayed into sin, do not feel that you cannot pray, that you are not worthy to come before the Lord. "My little children, these things write I unto you, that ye sin not. And if any man sin, we have an advocate with the Father, Jesus Christ the righteous." With outstretched arms He waits to welcome the prodigal. Go to Him, and tell Him about your mistakes and failures. Ask Him to strengthen you for fresh endeavor. He will never disappoint you, never abuse your confidence.

Trial will come to you. Thus the Lord polishes the roughness from your character. Do not murmur. You make the trial harder by repining. Honor God by cheerful submission. Patiently endure the pressure. Even though a wrong is done you, keep the love of God in the heart. . . .

Christ knows the strength of your temptations and the strength of your power to resist. His hand is always stretched out in pitying tenderness to every suffering child. To the tempted, discouraged one He says, Child for whom I suffered and died, cannot you trust Me? "As thy days, so shall thy strength be." . . .

Words cannot describe the peace and joy possessed by those who take God at His word. Trials do not disturb them, slights do not vex them. Self is crucified. Day by day their duties may become more taxing, their temptations stronger, their trials more severe; but they do not falter; for they receive strength equal to their need.—*Youth's Instructor,* June 26, 1902.

Christ has given us no assurance that to attain perfection of character is an easy matter. A noble all-around character is not inherited. It does not come to us by accident. A noble character is earned by individual effort through the merits and grace of Christ. God gives the talents, the powers of the mind; we form the character. It is formed by hard, stern battles with self. Conflict after conflict must be waged against hereditary tendencies. We shall have to criticize ourselves closely, and allow not one unfavorable trait to remain uncorrected.

Let no one say, I cannot remedy my defects of character. If you come to this decision, you will certainly fail of obtaining everlasting life. The impossibility lies in your own will. If you will not, then you cannot overcome. The real difficulty arises from the corruption of an unsanctified heart, and an unwillingness to submit to the control of God.—*Christ's Object Lessons,* p. 331.

God's People Are Polished Stones in His Spiritual Temple

Therefore the Lord will wait, that He may be gracious to you; and therefore He will be exalted, that He may have mercy on you. For the Lord is a God of justice; blessed are all those who wait for Him. Isaiah 30:18, NKJV.

THE GOSPEL IS designed for all, and it will bring together in church capacity men and women who are different in training, in character, and in disposition. Among these will be some who are naturally slack, who feel that order is pride, and that it is not necessary to be so particular. God will not come down to their low standard; He has given them probation, and the necessary directions in His Word, and He requires them to be transformed, to perfect holy characters. Everyone who is converted from sin to righteousness, from error to truth, will exemplify in words and acts the sanctifying power of the truth.

The people of God have a high and holy calling. They are Christ's representatives. Paul addresses the church in Corinth as those who are "sanctified in Christ Jesus, called to be saints." . . . Says Peter, "Ye are a chosen generation, a royal priesthood, an holy nation, a peculiar people; that ye should shew forth the praises of him who hath called you out of darkness into his marvellous light."

These passages are calculated to impress the mind with the sacred, exalted character of God's work, and with the high and holy position His people are to occupy. Could these things be said of those who do not seek to be refined by the truth?

The Jewish Temple was built of hewn stones quarried out of the mountains; and every stone was fitted for its place in the Temple, hewed, polished, and tested, before it was brought to Jerusalem. And when all were brought to the ground, the building went together without the sound of an ax or hammer.

This building represents God's spiritual temple, which is composed of material gathered out of every nation and tongue and people, of all grades, high and low, rich and poor, learned and ignorant. These are not dead substances, to be fitted by hammer and chisel. They are living stones quarried out from the world by the truth; and the great Master Builder, the Lord of the Temple, is now hewing and polishing them, and fitting them for their respective places in the spiritual temple. When completed, this temple will be perfect in all its parts, the admiration of angels and of men and women; for its builder and maker is God. Truly, those who are to compose this glorious building are "called to be saints."—*Review and Herald,* May 6, 1884.

Advance the Kingdom by Leading Sinners to Repentance

All these things my hand has made, and so all these things are mine, says the Lord. But this is the one to whom I will look, to the humble and contrite in spirit, who trembles at my word. Isaiah 66:2, NRSV.

IN HIS WORD God has shown us the only way in which this work should be done. We are to do earnest, faithful work, laboring for souls as they that must give an account. "Repent, repent" was the message rung out by John in the wilderness. . . .

Christ's message to the people was "Except ye repent, ye shall all likewise perish." And the apostles were commanded to preach everywhere that sinners should repent. The Lord would have His servants preach today the old gospel doctrine, sorrow for sin, repentance, and confession. We want old-fashioned sermons, old-fashioned customs, old-fashioned fathers and mothers in Israel, who have the tenderness of Christ.

Sinners must be labored for perseveringly, earnestly, wisely, until they shall see that they are transgressors of God's law, and shall exercise repentance toward God and faith toward the Lord Jesus Christ. When they are conscious of their helpless condition, and feel their need of a Savior, they may come with faith and hope to "the Lamb of God, which taketh away the sin of the world." Christ will accept the soul who comes to Him in true repentance. A broken and a contrite heart He will not despise.

The battle cry is sounding along the line. Let every soldier of the cross push to the front, not in self-sufficiency, but in meekness and lowliness of heart. Your work, my work, will not cease with this life. For a little while we may rest in the grave; but when the call comes, we shall take up our work in the kingdom of God to advance the glory of Christ. This holy work must be begun upon earth. We are not to study our own pleasure or convenience. Our question must be What can I do to lead others to Christ? How can I make known to others the love of God which passeth knowledge?—*Signs of the Times,* Dec. 27, 1899.

Look to Jesus, and He Will Give You Victory

And the Lord said, "Who then is that faithful and wise
steward, whom his master will make ruler over his household, to
give them their portion of food in due season? Blessed is that servant whom
his master will find so doing when he comes." Luke 12:42, 43, NKJV.

I HOPE THAT none will obtain the idea that they are earning the favor of God by confession of sins or that there is special virtue in confessing to human beings. There must be in the experience that faith that works by love and purifies the soul. The love of Christ will subdue the carnal propensities. The truth not only bears within itself the evidence of its heavenly origin, but proves that by the grace of God's Spirit it is effectual in the purification of the soul. The Lord would have us come to Him daily with all our troubles and confessions of sin, and He can give us rest in wearing His yoke and bearing His burden. His Holy Spirit, with its gracious influences, will fill the soul, and every thought will be brought into subjection to the obedience of Christ.

Now I am fearful that by some error on your part the blessing of God which has come to you . . . will be turned into a curse; that some false idea will obtain, so that you will be in a worse condition in a few months than you were before this work of revival. If you do not keep your souls guarded you will appear in the worst possible light to unbelievers. God would not be glorified with this fitful kind of service. Be careful not to carry matters to extremes and bring lasting reproach upon the precious cause of God. The failure that many make is that after they have been blessed of God they do not, in the humility of Christ, seek to be a blessing to others. Now that words of eternal life have been sown in your hearts, I entreat you to walk humbly with God, do the works of Christ, and bring forth much fruit unto righteousness. I do hope and pray that you will act like sons and daughters of the Most High and not become extremists or do anything that shall grieve the Spirit of God.

Do not look to human beings nor hang your hopes upon them, feeling that they are infallible; but look to Jesus constantly. Say nothing that would cast a reproach upon our faith. Confess your secret sins alone before your God. Acknowledge your heart wanderings to Him who knows perfectly how to treat your case. If you have wronged your neighbor, acknowledge . . . your sin and show fruit of the same by making restitution. Then claim the blessing. Come to God just as you are, and let Him heal all your infirmities. Press your case to the throne of grace; let the work be thorough. Be sincere in dealing with God and your own soul. If you come to Him with a heart truly contrite, He will give you the victory.— *Testimonies for the Church,* vol. 5, pp. 648, 649.

Lift Up the Standard as the Great Controversy Intensifies

For we can do nothing against the truth, but for the truth.
For we are glad when we are weak and you are strong. And this also
we pray, that you may be made complete. 2 Corinthians 13:8, 9, NKJV.

GOD HAS APPOINTED apostles, pastors, evangelists, and teachers, for the perfecting of the saints, for the work of the ministry, for the edifying of the body of Christ, till we all come to the unity of the faith. God declares to His people, "Ye are God's husbandry, ye are God's building." There must be a continual advancement. Step by step His followers must make straight paths for their feet, lest that which is lame be turned out of the way.

Those who would labor for God must work intelligently to replenish the deficiencies in themselves and glorify the Lord God of Israel by standing in the light, working in the light of the Sun of Righteousness. Thus they will carry the church forward and upward and heavenward, making its separation from the world more and more distinct.

As they assimilate their character to the divine Pattern, men and women will not guard their own personal dignity. With jealous, sleepless, loving, devoted interest, they will guard the sacred interest of the church from the evil which threatens to dim and cloud the glory that God intends shall shine forth through it. They will see that Satan's devices have no place or countenance in it by encouraging faultfinding, gossiping, evilspeaking, and accusing of the members; for those things would weaken and overthrow it.

There never will be a time in the history of the church when God's workers can fold their hands and be at ease, saying, "All is peace and safety." Then it is that sudden destruction cometh. Everything may move forward amid apparent prosperity; but Satan is wide awake, and is studying and counseling with his evil angels another mode of attack where he can be successful. The contest will wax more and more fierce on the part of Satan; for he is moved by a power from beneath.

As the work of God's people moves forward with sanctified, resistless energy, planting the standard of Christ's righteousness in the church, moved by a power from the throne of God, the great controversy will wax stronger and stronger, and will become more and more determined. Mind will be arrayed against mind, plans against plans, principles of heavenly origin against principles of Satan. Truth in its varied phases will be in conflict with error in its ever-varying, increasing forms, and which, if possible, will deceive the very elect.—*Testimonies to Ministers,* pp. 406, 407.

Bible Sanctification Involves Humility and Constant Growth

For though I might desire to boast, I will not be a fool; for I
will speak the truth. But I refrain, lest anyone should think of me
above what he sees me to be or hears from me. 2 Corinthians 12:6, NKJV.

THE FOLLOWERS OF Christ are to become like Him—by the grace of God to form characters in harmony with the principles of His holy law. This is Bible sanctification.

This work can be accomplished only through faith in Christ, by the power of the indwelling Spirit of God. . . . The Christian will feel the promptings of sin, but will maintain a constant warfare against it. Here is where Christ's help is needed. Human weakness becomes united to divine strength, and faith exclaims: "Thanks be to God, which giveth us the victory through our Lord Jesus Christ" (1 Cor. 15:57).

The Scriptures plainly show that the work of sanctification is progressive. When in conversion the sinner finds peace with God through the blood of the atonement, the Christian life has but just begun. Now he or she is to "go on unto perfection;" to grow up "unto the measure of the stature of the fulness of Christ." . . . Peter sets before us the steps by which Bible sanctification is to be attained: "Giving all diligence, add to your faith virtue; and to virtue knowledge; and to knowledge temperance; and to temperance patience; and to patience godliness; and to godliness brotherly kindness; and to brotherly kindness charity. . . . If ye do these things, ye shall never fall" (2 Peter 1:5-10).

Those who experience the sanctification of the Bible will manifest a spirit of humility. Like Moses, they have had a view of the awful majesty of holiness, and they see their own unworthiness in contrast with the purity and exalted perfection of the Infinite One. The prophet Daniel was an example of true sanctification. His long life was filled up with noble service for his Master. He was a man "greatly beloved" (Dan. 10:11) of Heaven. Yet instead of claiming to be pure and holy, this honored prophet identified himself with the really sinful of Israel as he pleaded before God in behalf of his people. . . . When at a later time the Son of God appeared, to give him instruction, Daniel says: "My comeliness was turned in me into corruption, and I retained no strength" (verse 8). . . .

There can be no self-exaltation, no boastful claim to freedom from sin, on the part of those who walk in the shadow of Calvary's cross. They feel that it was their sin which caused the agony that broke the heart of the Son of God, and this thought will lead them to self-abasement. Those who live nearest to Jesus discern most clearly the frailty and sinfulness of humanity, and their only hope is in the merit of a crucified and risen Savior.—*The Great Controversy*, pp. 469-471.

Repentance to Be Followed by Change of Character

"Therefore I will judge you, O house of Israel, every one according to his ways," says the Lord God. "Repent, and turn from all your transgressions, so that iniquity will not be your ruin." Ezekiel 18:30, NKJV.

THE LEARNED NICODEMUS had read these pointed prophecies [e.g., Psalm 51:10-13; Ezekiel 36:26, 27] with a clouded mind, but now he began to comprehend their true meaning, and to understand that even a man as just and honorable as himself must experience a new birth through Jesus Christ, as the only condition upon which he could be saved and secure an entrance into the kingdom of God. Jesus spoke positively that unless a person is born again he or she cannot discern the kingdom which Christ came upon earth to set up. Rigid precision in obeying the law would entitle no one to enter the kingdom of heaven.

There must be a new birth, a new mind through the operation of the Spirit of God, which purifies the life and ennobles the character. This connection with God fits mortals for the glorious kingdom of heaven. No human invention can ever find a remedy for the sinning soul. Only by repentance and humiliation, a submission to the divine requirements, can the work of grace be performed. Iniquity is so offensive in the sight of God, whom the sinner has so long insulted and wronged, that a repentance commensurate with the character of the sins committed often produces an agony of spirit hard to bear.

Nothing less than a practical acceptance and application of divine truth opens the kingdom of God to human beings. Only a pure and lowly heart, obedient and loving, firm in the faith and service of the Most High, can enter there. Jesus also declares that as "Moses lifted up the serpent in the wilderness, even so must the Son of Man be lifted up, that whosoever believeth in him should not perish, but have eternal life."

The serpent in the wilderness was lifted up on a pole before the people, that all who had been stung unto death by the fiery serpent might look upon this brazen serpent, a symbol of Christ, and be instantly healed. But they must look in faith, or it would be of no avail. Just so must people today look upon the Son of man as their Savior unto eternal life. The human race had separated itself from God by sin. Christ brought His divinity to earth, veiled by humanity, in order to rescue the race from its lost condition. Human nature is vile, and the character must be changed before it can harmonize with the pure and holy in God's immortal kingdom. This transformation is the new birth.—*Signs of the Times,* Nov. 15, 1883.

Both Repentance and Forgiveness Are Gifts From Christ

Him God has exalted to His right hand to be Prince and Savior,
to give repentance to Israel and forgiveness of sins. Acts 5:31, NKJV.

THERE ARE MANY who have erroneous ideas in regard to the nature of repentance. They think that they cannot come to Christ unless they first repent, and that repentance prepares them for the forgiveness of their sins. It is true that repentance does precede the forgiveness of sins; for it is only the broken and contrite heart that will feel the need of a Savior.

But must sinners wait until they have repented before they can come to Jesus? Is repentance to be made an obstacle between the sinner and the Savior? Jesus has said, "And I, if I be lifted up from the earth, will draw all men unto me." Christ is constantly drawing people to Himself, while Satan is as diligently seeking by every imaginable device to draw them away from their Redeemer. Christ must be revealed to sinners as the Savior dying for the sins of the world; and as they behold the Lamb of God on the cross of Calvary, the mysteries of redemption begin to unfold to the mind, and the goodness of God leads to repentance.

Although the plan of salvation calls for the deepest study of the philosopher, it is not too deep for the comprehension of a child. In dying for sinners, Christ manifested a love that is incomprehensible; and in beholding this love the heart is impressed, the conscience is aroused, and the soul is led to inquire, "What is sin, that it should require such a sacrifice for the redemption of its victim?" . . . The apostle Paul gave instruction in regard to the plan of salvation. He declares, "I kept back nothing that was profitable unto you, but have shewed you, and have taught you publicly, and from house to house, testifying both to the Jews, and also to the Greeks, repentance toward God, and faith toward our Lord Jesus Christ." John, speaking of the Savior, says, "Ye know that he was manifested to take away our sins; and in him is no sin." . . .

Sinners must come to Christ because they see Him as their Savior, their only helper, that they may be enabled to repent; for if they could repent without coming to Christ, they could also be saved without Christ. It is the virtue that goes forth from Christ that leads to genuine repentance. . . . Repentance is as much the gift of Christ as is forgiveness, and it cannot be found in the heart where Jesus has not been at work. We can no more repent without the Spirit of Christ to awaken the conscience than we can be pardoned without Christ. Christ draws the sinner by the exhibition of His love upon the cross, and this softens the heart, impresses the mind, and inspires contrition and repentance in the soul.—*Review and Herald*, Apr. 1, 1890.

God Calls for Repentance
and Holy Living

For I have known him, in order that he may command his children and his household after him, that they keep the way of the Lord, to do righteousness and justice, that the Lord may bring to Abraham what He has spoken to him. Genesis 18:19, NKJV.

GOD'S PLAN FOR our salvation is perfect in every particular. If we will faithfully perform our allotted part, all will be well with us. It is our apostasy that causes discord, and brings wretchedness and ruin. God never uses His power to oppress the creatures of His hand. He never requires more than they are able to perform; never punishes His disobedient children more than is necessary to bring them to repentance; or to deter others from following their example. Rebellion against God is inexcusable.

The judgments of God quickly following upon transgression, His counsels and reproofs, the manifestations of His love and mercy, and the oft-repeated exhibitions of His power—all were a part of God's plan to preserve His people from sin, to make them pure and holy, that He might be their strength and shield and their exceeding great reward. But the persistent transgressions of the Israelites, their readiness to depart from God, and their forgetfulness of His mercies, showed that many had chosen to be servants of sin, rather than children of the Most High.

God had created them, Christ had redeemed them. From the house of bondage their cry of anguish went up to the throne of God, and He put forth His arm to rescue them, for their sake, bringing desolation upon the whole land of Egypt. He had granted them high honors. He had made them His peculiar people, and had showered upon them unnumbered blessings. If they would obey Him, He would make them a mighty nation—a praise and excellence in all the earth. God designed to magnify His name through His chosen people, by showing the vast difference existing between the righteous and the wicked, the servants of God and the worshipers of idols.

Joshua sought to show his people the inconsistency of their course of backsliding. He wished them to feel that the time had come to make a decided change, to put away every vestige of idolatry, and to turn to the Lord with full purpose of heart. He endeavored to impress upon their minds the fact that open apostasy would not be more offensive to God than hypocrisy, and a lifeless form of worship.

If the favor of God was worth anything, it was worth everything. Thus Joshua had decided; and after weighing the whole matter, he had determined to serve Him with full purpose of heart. And more than this, he would endeavor to induce his family to pursue the same course.—*Signs of the Times,* May 19, 1881.

God Waits to Receive All Who Repent

Then I will give them one heart, and I will put a new spirit within them, and take the stony heart out of their flesh, and give them a heart of flesh, that they may walk in My statutes and keep My judgments and do them; and they shall be My people, and I will be their God. Ezekiel 11:19, 20, NKJV.

THE LORD HAS plainly revealed His will concerning the salvation of the sinner. And the attitude which many assume in expressing doubts and unbelief as to whether the Lord will save them is a reflection upon the character of God. Those who complain of His severity are virtually saying: "The way of the Lord is not equal." But He distinctly throws back the imputation upon the sinner: "Are not your ways unequal? Can I pardon your transgressions when you do not repent and turn from your sins?" . . .

The Lord will receive sinners when they repent and forsake their sins so that God can work with their efforts in seeking perfection of character. . . . The whole purpose in giving His Son for the sins of the world is that people may be saved, not in transgression and unrighteousness, but in forsaking sin, washing their robes of character, and making them white in the blood of the Lamb. He proposes to remove from sinners the offensive thing that He hates, but they must cooperate with God in the work. Sin must be given up, hated, and the righteousness of Christ must be accepted by faith. Thus will the divine cooperate with the human.

We should beware that we do not give place to doubt and unbelief, and in our attitude of despair complain of God and misrepresent Him to the world. This is placing ourselves on Satan's side of the question. "Poor souls," he says, "I pity you, mourning under sin; but God has no pity. You long for some ray of hope; but God leaves you to perish, and finds satisfaction in your misery."

This is a terrible deception. Do not give ear to the tempter, but say: "Jesus has died that I might live. He loves me, and wills not that I should perish. I have a compassionate heavenly Father; and although I have abused His love, though the blessings He has graciously given me have been squandered, I will arise, and go to my Father, and say: 'I have sinned . . . , and am no more worthy to be called thy son: make me as one of thy hired servants.'"

The parable tells you how the wanderer will be received. . . . Thus the Bible represents God's willingness to receive the repentant, returning sinner.—*Testimonies for the Church,* vol. 5, pp. 631, 632.

Jesus' Love Draws
Sinners to Repentance

Now is the judgment of this world; now the ruler of this world will be cast out. And I, if I am lifted up from the earth, will draw all peoples to Myself. John 12:31, 32, NKJV.

CHRIST CAME TO manifest the love of God to the world to draw the hearts of all to Himself. . . . The first step toward salvation is to respond to the drawing of the love of Christ. God sends message after message to people, entreating them to repentance, that He may forgive, and write pardon against their names. Shall there be no repentance? Shall His appeals be unheeded? Shall His overtures of mercy be ignored, and His love utterly rejected?

Oh, then sinners will cut themselves off from the medium through which they may gain life eternal; for God only pardons the penitent. By the manifestation of His love, by the entreating of His Spirit, He woos them to repentance; for repentance is the gift of God, and whom He pardons He first makes penitent. The sweetest joy comes through sincere repentance toward God for the transgression of His law, and through faith in Christ as the sinner's Redeemer and Advocate.

It is that all may understand the joy of forgiveness, the peace of God, that Christ draws them through the manifestation of His love. If they respond to His drawing, yielding their hearts to His grace, He will lead them on step by step, to a full knowledge of Himself; and this is life eternal.

Christ came to reveal to the sinner the justice and love of God, that He might give repentance to Israel, and remission of sins. When sinners behold Jesus lifted up upon the cross, suffering the guilt of the transgressor, bearing the penalty of sin; when they behold God's abhorrence of evil in the fearful manifestation of the death of the cross, and His love for fallen humanity, they are led to repentance toward God because of their transgression of the law which is holy, and just, and good. They exercise faith in Christ, because the divine Savior has become their Substitute, Surety, and Advocate, the one in whom their very life is centered. To repenting sinners God can show His mercy and truth, and bestow upon them His forgiveness and love. . . .

By the suffering and death of Christ is proved His boundless love to human beings. He is willing and able to save to the uttermost all that come to God by Him.—*Signs of the Times,* Sept. 12, 1911.

Good Works
to Follow Revival

If we confess our sins, He is faithful and just to forgive us our
sins and to cleanse us from all unrighteousness. 1 John 1:9, NKJV.

THE SOUL THAT lives by faith in Christ desires no other nor greater good than to know and to do the will of God. It is God's will that faith in Christ shall be made perfect by works; He connects the salvation and eternal life of those who believe with these works, and through them provides for the light of truth to go to all countries and peoples. This is the fruit of the working of God's Spirit.

The truth has taken hold of hearts. It is not a fitful impulse, but a true turning unto the Lord, and the perverse will of human beings is brought into subjection to the will of God. To rob God in tithes and offerings is a violation of the plain injunction of Jehovah and works the deepest injury to those who do it; for it deprives them of the blessing of God, which is promised to those who deal honestly with Him. . . .

If Satan cannot keep souls bound in the ice of indifference, he will try to push them into the fire of fanaticism. When the Spirit of the Lord comes among His people, the enemy seizes the opportunity to work also, seeking to mold the work of God through the peculiar, unsanctified traits of different ones who are connected with that work. Thus there is always danger that unwise moves will be made. Many carry on a work of their own devising, a work which God has not prompted. . . .

If the enemy can push individuals to extremes, he is well pleased. He can thus do greater harm than if there had been no religious awakening. We know that there has never yet been a religious effort made in which Satan has not tried his best to intrude himself, and in these last days he will do this as never before. He sees that his time is short, and he will work with all deceivableness of unrighteousness to mingle errors and incorrect views with the work of God and push men and women into false positions. . . .

Hearts that are under the influence of the Spirit of God will be in sweet harmony with His will. I have been shown that when the Lord works by His Holy Spirit, there will be nothing in its operations which will degrade the Lord's people before the world, but it will exalt them. The religion of Christ does not make those who profess it coarse and rough. The subjects of grace are not unteachable, but ever willing to learn of Jesus and to counsel with one another.—*Testimonies for the Church,* vol. 5, pp. 644-647.

Jesus Pays the Debt
of Repentant Sinners

Or do you despise the riches of His goodness, forbearance, and longsuffering,
not knowing that the goodness of God leads you to repentance? Romans 2:4, NKJV.

AMONG THE DISCIPLES who ministered to Paul at Rome was Onesimus, a fugitive slave from the city of Colosse. He belonged to a Christian named Philemon, a member of the Colossian church. But he had robbed his master and fled to Rome. . . . In the kindness of his heart, the apostle sought to relieve the poverty and distress of the wretched fugitive, and then endeavored to shed the light of truth into his darkened mind. Onesimus listened attentively to the words of life which he had once despised, and was converted to the faith of Christ. He now confessed his sin against his master, and gratefully accepted the counsel of the apostle.

He had endeared himself to Paul by his piety, meekness, and sincerity, no less than by his tender care for the apostle's comfort and his zeal to promote the work of the gospel. Paul saw in him traits of character that would render him a useful helper in missionary labor, and he would gladly have kept him at Rome. But he would not do this without the full consent of Philemon.

He therefore decided that Onesimus should at once return to his master. . . . It was a severe test for this servant to thus deliver himself up to the master he had wronged; but he had been truly converted, and, painful as it was, he did not shrink from this duty. Paul made Onesimus the bearer of a letter to Philemon, in which he with great delicacy and kindness pleaded the cause of the repentant slave, and intimated his own wishes concerning him. . . .

He requests Philemon to receive him as his own child. He says that it was his desire to retain Onesimus, that he might act the same part in ministering to him in his bonds as Philemon would have done. But he did not desire his services unless Philemon should voluntarily set him free; for it might be in the providence of God that Onesimus had left his master for a season in so improper a manner, that, being converted, he might on his return be forgiven and received with such affection that he would choose to dwell with him ever after, "not now as a servant, but above a servant, a brother beloved." . . .

How fitting an illustration of the love of Christ toward repenting sinners! As the servant who had defrauded his master had nothing with which to make restitution, so sinners who have robbed God of years of service have no means of canceling their debt; Jesus interposes between them and the just wrath of God, and says, I will pay the debt. Let them be spared the punishment of their guilt. I will suffer in their stead.—*Sketches From the Life of Paul,* pp. 284-287.

God's People to Reflect His Glory

The Spirit of the Lord God is upon Me, because the Lord has anointed Me to preach good tidings to the poor; He has sent Me to heal the brokenhearted, to proclaim liberty to the captives, and the opening of the prison to those who are bound. Isaiah 61:1, NKJV.

THE LORD IS not pleased to have His people a band of mourners. He wants them to repent of their sins, that they may enjoy the liberty of the children of God. Then they will be filled with the praises of God, and will be a blessing to others. The Lord Jesus was anointed also "to appoint unto them that mourn in Zion, to give unto them beauty for ashes, the oil of joy for mourning, the garments of praise for the spirit of heaviness; that they might be called trees of righteousness, the planting of the Lord, that He might be glorified." . . .

Oh, that this might be the purpose of our lives! Then we should have regard even to the expression of our countenance, to our words, and even to the tone of our voice when we speak. All our business transactions would be wrought in faith and integrity. Then would the world be convinced that there is a people that are loyal to the God of heaven. . . .

God calls for all to come into harmony with Himself. He will receive them if they will put away their evil actions. By a union with the divine nature of Christ, they may escape the corrupting influences of this world. It is time for every one of us to decide whose side we are on. The agencies of Satan will work with every mind that will allow itself to be worked by him. But there are also heavenly agencies waiting to communicate the bright rays of the glory of God to all that are willing to receive Him. It is truth that we want, precious truth in all its loveliness. Truth will bring liberty and gladness.—*The Seventh-day Adventist Bible Commentary,* Ellen G. White Comments, vol. 4, pp. 1153, 1154.

Everyone to
Work for the Lost •

And we have known and believed the love that God has for us. God is love,
and he who abides in love abides in God, and God in him. 1 John 4:16, NKJV.

"IF WE LOVE one another, God dwelleth in us, and his love is perfected in us"; and that love cannot be restrained. . . . Only by becoming partakers of the divine nature can the law of God be fulfilled by men and women. Only those who love God with all their heart, soul, mind, and strength, and their neighbor as themselves, can give glory to God in the highest, and peace on earth, good will to men. This was the work of Christ; and when His work is appreciated and represented by His followers, the great result will be achieved in the "joy that was set before him" in the saving of the souls for whom He gave His life.

The Lord has been laboring constantly from age to age to awaken in the souls of human beings a sense of their divine kinship, and thus to establish an order and divine harmony proportionate to the great and eternal deliverance He has wrought out for everyone who will receive Him. The Lord calls upon all who profess to believe in Him to be coworkers with Him, to use every God-given ability, opportunity, and privilege to lead perishing souls within the sphere of their influence to Jesus Christ.

Here is the only hope for transformation of character; this will give peace and joy in believing, and fit them for the society of the heavenly angels in the kingdom of God. Oh, how earnest, persevering, and untiring should be the efforts of every sin-pardoned soul to seek to bring other souls to Jesus Christ, that their neighbors shall become joint-heirs with Jesus!

Whoever is your neighbor is to be sought for, labored for. Are they ignorant? Let your communication, your association, make them more intelligent. The outcast, the youth, full of defects in character, are the very ones God enjoins upon us to help. "I came not to call the righteous," said Christ, "but sinners to repentance." . . .

Those who will be humble enough to learn, the very nobility of the world will consider it an honor to go to heaven in their company, and angels of God will cooperate with such as are workers together with God. We need to hunger and thirst after righteousness, that we may have Christ in us as a well of water, springing up into everlasting life.—*Special Instruction Relating to the Review and Herald Office and the Work in Battle Creek*, pp. 4-6.

Repentance Essential
During Day of Atonement

Then I heard a loud voice saying in heaven, "Now salvation,
and strength, and the kingdom of our God, and the power of His
Christ have come, for the accuser of our brethren, who accused them before
our God day and night, has been cast down." Revelation 12:10, NKJV.

GOD IS LEADING His people out from the abominations of the world, that they may keep His law; and because of this, the rage of "the accuser of our brethren" knows no bounds. "The devil is come down unto you, having great wrath, because he knoweth that he hath but a short time."

The antitypical land of promise is just before us, and Satan is determined to destroy the people of God, and cut them off from their inheritance. The admonition "Watch ye and pray, lest ye enter into temptation" was never more needed than now. We are now living in the great day of atonement. In the typical service, while the high priest was making the atonement for Israel, all were required to afflict their souls by repentance of sin and humiliation before the Lord, lest they be cut off from among the people.

In like manner, all who would have their names retained in the book of life should now, in the few remaining days of their probation, afflict their souls before God by sorrow for sin, and true repentance. There must be deep, faithful searching of heart. The light, frivolous spirit indulged by so many of professed Christians must be put away. There is earnest warfare before all who would subdue the evil tendencies that strive for the mastery.

The work of preparation is an individual work. We are not saved in groups. The purity and devotion of one will not offset the want of these qualities in another. Though all nations are to pass in judgment before God, yet He will examine the case of each individual with as close and searching scrutiny as if there were not another being upon the earth. Everyone must be tested, and found without spot or wrinkle or any such thing.

Solemn are the scenes connected with the closing work of the atonement. Momentous are the interests involved therein. The judgment is now passing in the sanctuary above. . . . Soon—none know how soon—it will pass to the cases of the living. . . .When the work of the investigative judgment closes, the destiny of all will have been decided for life or death. Probation is ended a short time before the appearing of the Lord in the clouds of heaven. Christ in the Revelation, looking forward to that time, declares: . . . "Behold, I come quickly; and my reward is with me, to give every man according as his work shall be."—*Gospel Herald*, August 1910.

God's Law Leads
to True Repentance

Perhaps everyone will listen and turn from his evil way,
that I may relent concerning the calamity which I purpose to bring
on them because of the evil of their doings. Jeremiah 26:3, NKJV.

[THE APOSTLE PAUL writes that] "I had not known sin, but by the law: for I had not known lust, except the law had said, Thou shalt not covet." . . . The law which promised life to the obedient pronounced death upon the transgressor. "Wherefore," he says, "the law is holy, and the commandment holy, and just, and good."

How wide the contrast between these words of Paul and those that come from many of the pulpits of today. The people are taught that obedience to God's law is not necessary to salvation; that they have only to believe in Jesus, and they are safe. Without the law, human beings have no conviction of sin, and feel no need of repentance. Not seeing their lost condition as violators of God's law, they do not feel their need of the atoning blood of Christ as their only hope of salvation.

The law of God is an agent in every genuine conversion. There can be no true repentance without conviction of sin. The Scriptures declare that "sin is the transgression of the law," and that "by the law is the knowledge of sin."

In order to see their guilt, sinners must test their character by God's great standard of righteousness. To discover their defects, they must look into the mirror of the divine statutes. But while the law reveals their sins, it provides no remedy. The gospel of Christ alone can offer pardon. In order to stand forgiven, sinners must exercise repentance toward God, whose law has been transgressed, and faith in Christ, their atoning sacrifice.

Without true repentance, there can be no true conversion. Many are deceived here, and too often their entire experience proves to be a deception. This is why so many who are joined to the church have never been joined to Christ.

"The carnal mind is enmity against God; for it is not subject to the law of God, neither indeed can be." In the new birth, the heart is renewed by divine grace, and brought into harmony with God as it is brought into subjection to His law. When this mighty change has taken place, the sinner has passed from death unto life, from sin unto holiness, from transgression and rebellion to obedience and loyalty. The old life of alienation from God has ended; the new life of reconciliation, of faith and love, has begun. Then will "the righteousness of the law" "be fulfilled in us, who walk not after the flesh, but after the Spirit."—*The Spirit of Prophecy,* vol. 4, pp. 297, 298.

Christ's Robe of Righteousness Is for the Repentant

*Now therefore, amend your ways and your doings, and obey
the voice of the Lord your God; then the Lord will relent concerning
the doom that He has pronounced against you. Jeremiah 26:13, NKJV.*

ALTHOUGH AS SINNERS we are under the condemnation of the law, yet Christ, by His obedience rendered to the law, claims for the repentant soul the merit of His own righteousness. In order to obtain the righteousness of Christ, it is necessary for the sinner to know what that repentance is which works a radical change of mind and spirit and action. The work of transformation must begin in the heart, and manifest its power through every faculty of the being; but human beings are not capable of originating such a repentance as this, and can experience it alone through Christ, who ascended up on high, led captivity captive, and gave gifts unto humanity.

Who is desirous of becoming truly repentant? What must they do? They must come to Jesus, just as they are, without delay. They must believe that the word of Christ is true, and, believing the promise, ask, that they may receive. When sincere desire prompts people to pray, they will not pray in vain. The Lord will fulfill His word, and will give the Holy Spirit to lead to repentance toward God and faith toward our Lord Jesus Christ. They will pray and watch, and put away their sins, making manifest their sincerity by the vigor of their endeavor to obey the commandments of God. With prayer they will mingle faith, and not only believe in but obey the precepts of the law. They will announce themselves as on Christ's side of the question. They will renounce all habits and associations that tend to draw the heart from God.

All sinners who would become children of God must receive the truth that repentance and forgiveness are to be obtained through nothing less than the atonement of Christ. Assured of this, they must put forth an effort in harmony with the work done for them, and with unwearied entreaty they must supplicate the throne of grace, that the renovating power of God may come into their souls.

Christ pardons none but the penitent, but whom He pardons He first makes penitent. The provision made is complete, and the eternal righteousness of Christ is placed to the account of every believing soul. The costly, spotless robe, woven in the loom of heaven, has been provided for the repenting, believing sinner, and everyone may say: "I will greatly rejoice in the Lord, my soul shall be joyful in my God; for he hath clothed me with the garments of salvation, he hath covered me with the robe of righteousness" (Isa. 61:10).—*Selected Messages,* book 1, pp. 393, 394.

All Who Repent Will
Be Forgiven and Accepted

*Ho! Everyone who thirsts, come to the waters; and you
who have no money, come, buy and eat. Yes, come, buy wine
and milk without money and without price. Isaiah 55:1, NKJV.*

THOUGH DAVID HAD fallen, the Lord lifted him up. He was now more fully in harmony with God and in sympathy with his fellow men than before he fell. In the joy of his release he sang: "I acknowledged my sin unto thee, and mine iniquity have I not hid. I said, I will confess my transgressions unto the Lord; and thou forgavest the iniquity of my sin. . . . Thou art my hiding place; thou shalt preserve me from trouble; thou shalt compass me about with songs of deliverance" (Ps. 32:5-7).

Many have murmured at what they called God's injustice in sparing David, whose guilt was so great, after having rejected Saul for what appear to them to be far less flagrant sins. But David humbled himself and confessed his sin, while Saul despised reproof and hardened his heart in impenitence.

This passage in David's history is full of significance to the repenting sinner. It is one of the most forcible illustrations given us of the struggles and temptations of humanity, and of genuine repentance toward God and faith in our Lord Jesus Christ. Through all the ages it has proved a source of encouragement to souls that, having fallen into sin, were struggling under the burden of their guilt. Thousands of the children of God, who have been betrayed into sin, when ready to give up to despair have remembered how David's sincere repentance and confession were accepted by God, notwithstanding he suffered for his transgression; and they also have taken courage to repent and try again to walk in the way of God's commandments.

Whoever under the reproof of God will humble the soul with confession and repentance, as did David, may be sure that there is hope for him or her. Whoever will in faith accept God's promises will find pardon. The Lord will never cast away one truly repentant soul. He has given this promise: "Let him take hold of my strength, that he may make peace with me; and he shall make peace with me" (Isa. 27:5). "Let the wicked forsake his way, and the unrighteous man his thoughts: and let him return unto the Lord, and he will have mercy upon him; and to our God, for he will *abundantly* pardon" (Isa. 55:7).—*Patriarchs and Prophets*, p. 726.